Teaching Children with Learning and Behavior Problems

Third Edition

Donald D. Hammill   ·   **Nettie R. Bartel**

ALLYN AND BACON, INC.
Boston   London   Sydney   Toronto

Library of Congress Cataloging in Publication Data

Hammill, Donald D., 1934–
    Teaching children with learning and behavior problems.

    Bibliography: p. 437
    Includes index.
    1. Learning disabilities.   2. Problem children—
Education.   I. Bartel, Nettie R.   II. Title.
LC4704.H35   1982   371.9   81–14908
ISBN 0–205–07678–5   AACR2
ISBN 0–205–07694–7 (pbk.)

Printed in the United States of America.
10 9 8 7 6 5 4 3 2 1   86 85 84 83 82

CONTENTS

PREFACE

All teachers, whether they teach regular or exceptional children, frequently encounter youngsters at the preschool or elementary levels who are not responsive to instruction or who are disruptive in class. These children may evidence problems in reading, arithmetic, language, or writing or in social adjustment or motivation. Most of these pupils are probably the victims of poor teaching, insufficient background experience, and/or inadequate motivation. No children are immune to the debilitating effects of these three factors; bright or retarded, sound or crippled, stable or difficult children can be affected at one time or another.

Over the years the schools have evolved numerous alternatives for handling below-average learners. Psychological services, special education classes, and remedial programs have been provided. However, with this proliferation of specialized educational services, teachers have become increasingly dependent upon noninstructional personnel to assist them in teaching children with school-related problems. Thus educational assessment has become the responsibility of the school psychologist; slow learners are shunted off to the "retarded" class; poor readers are referred to the remedial reading specialist; speech articulation cases are sent to the speech therapist; and troublesome children eventually are placed in classes for the "emotionally disturbed." The great majority of difficult pupils, however, remain in the regular class under the supervision of the teacher, who is expected to meet their individual needs.

It is quite clear today that many children presently enrolled in special education classes will be integrated into regular classes within the next few years. The trend of isolating problem children, which has been so prevalent during the past few decades, is being reversed as educators recognize that special class placements bring few benefits to mildly handicapped children. Educators and others find the special-class solution philosophically objectionable in the 1980s. These children are not likely to be returned to the educational mainstream without some provisions made on their behalf. These provisions will likely take the forms of resource rooms, consultants, tutors, and itinerant programs.

Teachers are currently responsible for the achievement of many children who are difficult to teach. In the future they will probably be responsible for more, not fewer, of these children. However, many teachers lack the necessary information that would enable them to cope with these children. Many elementary and early childhood education teacher-training programs fail to sufficiently familiarize their students with basic assessment procedures, diagnostic and prescriptive teacher techniques, and remedial materials and methods. Yet knowledge of a wide variety of remedial and developmental instructional approaches and activities is necessary to accommodate the disparate educational needs of nonachieving pupils.

With these ideas in mind, we have written this book for teachers. Our intention was (1) to succinctly review the roles and duties of teachers in the management of children with school-related problems; (2) to provide teachers with a series of discussions which focus upon these school-related difficulties (for example, reading, spelling, arithmetic, language, perception, handwriting, and behavior); (3) to provide in each of these discussions basic information regarding appropriate assessment techniques and instructional methods; and finally (4) to provide teachers with a list of specific materials, sources, and teacher evaluations of their merit.

It was not our intention to present and discuss all the possible evaluation devices and instructional methods that are available to teachers today. This would have been a monumental effort, and one which we had neither the energy nor the experience to undertake. Instead, we have shared with the reader those exceptional approaches and ideas with which we have had some direct personal experience. We have also included several new programs which appear to be promising, although we have not used them.

We are not necessarily endorsing the materials or methods described here; rather, we have tried to provide information on representative techniques to enable teachers to choose appropriate materials for their pupils. Teachers are urged to evaluate the effectiveness of their selections in their own classrooms, as research on the efficacy of most programs is nonexistent.

D. D. H.

N. R. B.

1

MEETING THE SPECIAL NEEDS OF CHILDREN

Donald D. Hammill   Nettie R. Bartel

Most experienced teachers are able to recognize children and adolescents who seem bright but who fail to make expected gains in a particular skill after repeated exposure to training. If the skill is reading, the teacher may notice that the child reads aloud quite well but has great difficulty with comprehension during silent reading. Another child may become confused when directions are given orally but exhibits comparative superiority in reading and writing. A third youngster may have adequate listening and speech skills but manifest problems when he or she engages in math activities.

Some pupils evidence discrepancies of varying degrees between their estimated intellectual ability and their actual performance; others show marked divergence between the skills in which they excel and those in which they are inadequate or marginal; and others are merely slow in acquiring necessary school behaviors. To a large extent, these problems involve the understanding or the use of spoken or written language and are manifested in difficulty with reading, thinking, talking, listening, writing, spelling, or arithmetic. They may also include behavior problems. The problems range from mild to intense and are occasionally associated with blindness, deafness, psychosis, and/or severe mental defect. For the most part, however, the difficulties are found in mild to moderate degree in individuals who are otherwise "normal."

In the past, school personnel have been quick to confuse a child's school problem with a diagnostic label. Children who performed inadequately in the classroom tended to be labeled "retarded," "disturbed," "learning disabled," or "deprived," when their problems in fact were reading, writing, or mathematics. While it is recognized that children exist for whom these labels are

1

appropriate, teachers should be cautioned that labels have been applied to children in a rather indiscriminate fashion and that an uncounted number of pupils have been misdiagnosed and misplaced. Such terms have little utility for the classroom teacher who must devise instructional techniques that are effective for individual children, especially children with mild to moderate problems.

In practice, an educational program must be prepared by a teacher in response to an individual child's educational needs and behaviors, not in response to a diagnostic label or definition the child may or may not satisfy. The nature of the program that is prepared will reflect in large part the teacher's (and the school's) philosophy and attitudes regarding a number of educational matters. We direct the remainder of this chapter to a delineation of these factors and to a discussion of the issues that relate to them.

We have found it helpful to organize our thinking about these educationally important factors in terms of an instructional model, which is presented in Figure 1–1. While in practice the elements of the model are quite interrelated, for discussion purposes we have separated them arbitrarily into three basic parts: (1) the assumptions that influence instruction, (2) the components that are involved in instruction, and (3) the cycle that is used to implement instructional programs.

ASSUMPTIONS INFLUENCING INSTRUCTION

The program that the teacher elects for each child will necessarily reflect his or her assumptions and beliefs about the purpose of education, the nature of learning, and the role of the child, the teacher, and even of society in the schooling process. These assumptions are rarely made explicit as far as teachers are concerned; yet they govern almost all the decisions that a teacher makes. These assumptions include the answers (implicit or explicit) to such questions as: What are the schools for? What is this particular child supposed to get out of school? How is this child supposed to fit into society ultimately? What is the nature of the world and of the role of the child and the teacher within it? Let us briefly turn to this last question first.

A perusal of the many approaches to educating the child with learning and behavioral problems presented in this book will quickly lead the reader to the conclusion that the last question posed in the previous paragraph has not been answered. The various approaches are quite obviously based on differing, even inconsistent, assumptions about the nature of the world and of the child and

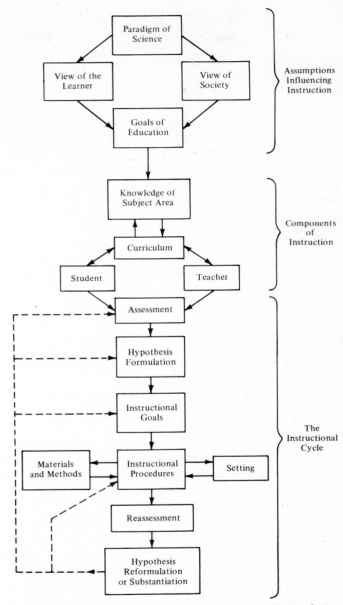

Figure 1–1. Instructional Sequence Model

Adapted from N. R. Bartel, D. N. Bryen, and H. W. Bartel, Approaches for alternative programming. In E. L. Meyen, G. A. Vergason, and R. J. Whelan (eds.), *Alternatives for Teaching Exceptional Children*, (Denver, Colo.: Love, 1975).

the teacher within it. For example, among the approaches reviewed, one will see evidence of a world view that is highly mechanistic and predictable. For such a perspective, the machine is the most appropriate metaphor. Here the child is seen as a relatively passive component in a setting which is arranged so that events (instructional happenings) impinge on him or her in such a way that fully predictable outcomes will come about. The teacher serves as the master technician who engineers the learning environment in such a way that the most desirable results will occur. The act of learning, then, is something that happens to the child as a result of the application of predetermined forces. It follows that the ideal curriculum for such a viewpoint is "teacher-proof." That is, the program is packaged in such a way pedagogically and substantively that the teacher cannot interfere with the learning process. Similarly, the program is designed so that the probabilities are great that the child will emit the desired responses, and only the desired responses.

The contrasting position is that the essence of the world is not static and controllable, but on the contrary is in continuous transition from one state to another by means of progressive differentiation. This leads one to think of students, even students with learning and behavioral problems, as active individuals who not only make predetermined "correct" responses, but who also interact with, and change, their learning environment. Thus, learning is not merely the quantitative accumulation of objective facts but is an active cognitive construction and transformation of reality.

That these issues have not been resolved in the education of children with learning problems is evident in the competing curricula. On the one hand, one sees a widespread use of programmed materials, which promise precision, ease of measurement, and ready accountability. Clearly, the implicit assumption is that the curriculum developer has access to society's knowledge store and has arranged this knowledge in appropriate bits and sequences to which the learner needs only to be exposed following prescribed procedures. The behavior of both the teacher and the child is predictable. Seen from this orientation, the effective teacher is one who is able to move the child quickly through the prescribed components of the curriculum with minimal obtrusion stemming from teacher or child idiosyncracies.

On the other hand, the alternative world view is noted for its openendedness and unpredictability. Here curriculum designers and implementers frequently follow some variation of the Piagetian notion of assimilation and accommodation. That is, they acknowledge that the learner is shaped repeatedly by the realities of the world and that he or she returns the favor by continuously moving to reshape those world realities. To them, education is not getting children to make predictable responses, but is seeing to it that they are progressively being changed by and changing their environment. Clearly, these underlying assumptions have major implications for the choices that a teacher makes in instructional planning and implementation.

COMPONENTS OF INSTRUCTION

The choices that the teacher must make are further complicated by additional decisions that must be made concerning the components of instruction. As can be seen in Figure 1–1, the teacher's job is to bring the child and the learning task into some kind of proximity with each other. However, even this seemingly simple responsibility turns out to be complicated.

It has long been taken for granted in educational circles that pupils and curricular materials cannot be randomly matched to each other. That is, if one is teaching social studies to a group of second graders, one cannot simply walk down to the school library and pull any text from the social studies section of the shelves and assume that it will meet the learners' needs. There is general agreement that the teacher should consider such factors as the age of the children, their overall developmental level, and their interests in selecting materials. Conversely, just because a teacher is fond of a particular reading series or spelling book does not mean that is can be used effectively with the group of children being instructed.

This brings us to a most interesting question and one that will surface repeatedly throughout this book. Just what are the child's characteristics that a teacher should take onto account in selecting instructional materials? Conversely, just what are the curricular characteristics that a teacher must reckon with in determining their potential effectiveness with children? A perusal of the educational research literature quickly leads one to conclude that each of an almost infinite array of characteristics—ranging from whether or not the child went through a creeping stage to whether the child's father lives in the home—has been thought by someone to be a significant child variable that should be taken into account by the teacher. By no means does everyone agree on what to look for. Obviously, if the teacher is ever going to have any time to do any teaching, he or she must select from an almost endless range of pupil behaviors those that have sufficient implications for instruction to be worth noting and reporting.

A similar situation pertains as far as variability among curricula approaches is concerned. Thus, to use an example from beginning reading, serious claims have been made that picture words, words using a unique alphabet, or words printed in different colors, to name a few, should be considered by the classroom teacher for teaching reading to certain children. Is the teacher to assume that letter-color aptitude, for example, is a significant child characteristic that should be measured and related to the use of color in the curriculum?

When one considers the possible permutations in the infinite range of potential child characteristics that could be measured and matched to an almost infinite range of curriculum characteristics, the problem becomes staggering indeed. This book represents an effort to reduce the teacher's task to more manageable proportions. First of all, we have tried to indicate the most promising aspects of the child's functioning to consider in instructional planning. We have drawn heavily from developmental psychology, particularly the work of Piaget, Bruner, and Gagné.

On the curriculum side, some observations are also in order. We note that curricula may be said to spread themselves on a continuum ranging from (1) the wholistic, open-ended approaches that rely heavily on the child's ability to learn inductively and incidentally to (2), at the other end of the continuum, approaches that are narrow in focus—specific and prescribed. We recognized that as one would expect from the brief discussion above on variations in world view, this question, being a derivative of the larger question noted above, is also unresolved.

It is probably fair to say that many of the newer approaches that have been found to be most successful with children who have learning and behavioral problems are found at the prescriptive end of the scale, and the reader will find such approaches heavily represented in the chapters of this book. One could probably make a case that the boys and girls for whom this book is written are precisely those for whom the more widely used unstructured wholistic educational approaches have been unsuccessful. That is, they are the youngsters who have failed to learn intuitively, inductively, and incidentally. The generalizations, concepts, cognitive structures, and facts that other children seem to pick up without any specific instruction have, for some reason, not been acquired by these children. It is for that reason that we have included throughout the book so many references to prescriptive teaching approaches. In doing so, however, we caution the reader that to date no instructional system or program has been devised that can anticipate all the learning possibilities that occur in the classroom. No program can preplan every possible utterance or action of the teacher or pupil.

Even while using one of the many structured approaches described in the subsequent pages, we urge teachers to look for those unique teaching/learning interactions which cannot be fully planned in advance. Furthermore, we caution teachers against making the presumption that the only significant learning is that which the teacher has decided on ahead of time and against the further presumption that everything that is important can be reduced to a paper-and-pencil test or lesson. The highly structured approaches have been at their best in teasing out the subelements of such complicated tasks as decoding words and sentences and arithmetic computation. They have been much less successful in helping teachers develop ways of teaching and measuring reading comprehension and arithmetic understanding. The problem that faces the classroom teacher, however, is that she or he cannot sit still, letting time go by, while the theoreticians and the experts decide whether, for example, the reading act is a unitary phenomenon or whether it can be validly broken into subelements.

The seeming inability of many children to master content that is presented in the traditional way has led to numerous efforts at presenting the content in a different format or medium or in the same content but in different-sized chunks. This breaking down of a body of content into its component parts or steps has become known as "task analysis," "learning hierarchies," or the "diagnostic approach." In each instance, the specific step presented to the child is based on what he or she has previously mastered and is "tailored" in such a way that the child has a high likelihood of mastering the task. Although the specifics of the procedures recommended by the various proponents of task analysis vary, several general commonalities characterize the approach. All advocates of task analysis recommend the differentiation of tasks into micro units or subordinate subskills or lower-level topics that the learner can master one step at a time. Only when the child has demonstrated success on one task is the next task in the hierarchy presented. The teacher does not have to undertake a complete task analysis for every bit of classroom instruction. Most curricular guides, if well organized and well differentiated, can be used as rough task analytic outlines. In fact, a good scope-and-sequence chart can serve many of the functions of a task analysis.

Having reviewed in some detail the assumptions influencing instruction and the components of instruction, we turn next to a consideration of the sequential nature of the instructional process itself.

THE INSTRUCTIONAL CYCLE (THE INDIVIDUALIZED EDUCATIONAL PLAN)

The various stages of the instructional cycle coincide to a great extent with what has become known as the Individualized Educational Plan (IEP). The IEP is a requirement of the federal law, Education of All Handicapped Children Act (P.L. 94–142), which mandates that every handicapped child must have an individually planned and implemented educational program. While, legally speaking, the IEP is required only for handicapped children, we assert that it is equally appropriate for every child, handicapped or not, who has been singled put to recieve special instruction or services. The elements of the IEP include: the assessment of the child, the formulation of long-range goals and short-term objectives, a description of the proposed educational intervention with specification of type and duration of each aspect of instruction, and an evaluation of the effort. These elements are closely related to the steps specified in the instructional cycle of our model (Figure 1–1). Because the IEP will be required of all handicapped children, no matter what their educational setting, and because the IEP concept is implicit in subsequent chapters of this book, we offer the following as a general overview, which is adaptable to each of the subsequent chapter contents. Specific and abundant procedures for generating IEPs are available in the book *Methods for Educating the Handicapped: An Individualized Education Program Approach* (Larsen and Poplin, 1980). Topics covered include referral/screening, goal setting, programmatic evaluation, and parent/teacher meetings; useful case histories are also provided.

ASSESSMENT

Before an instructional plan can be developed, the teacher must have a picture of the child's overall functioning and specific abilities and problem areas. In general, the teacher will find that norm-referenced standardized tests, readily available from commercial publishers, are quite helpful in establishing a summary statement of the child's status; for more specific, directly instructionally relevant information, more informal techniques will be most helpful. Because of the more important differences in the functions of norm-referenced and informal assessment, we present separate descriptions in the following section.

Norm-Referenced Assessment

The norm-referenced evaluation, a part of the total diagnostic effort, (1) is characterized by the use of standardized tests, (2) often requires some degree of training for proper administration, and (3) may be undertaken in the classroom by the teacher or in settings other than the classroom by personnel employed for the expressed purpose of testing children. The information acquired is of a decidedly quantitative nature and tends to compare a specific child's performance with national or regional normative data. The results, therefore, are often reported in terms of quotients, scaled scores, grade equivalents, or percentiles. In general, such evaluation attempts to assess many areas of mental function, including intelligence, language development, academic achievement, speech development, perceptual–motor skills, and social and emotional development.

The number of standardized testing instruments which the teacher may select are almost limitless. A comprehensive resource is Buros (1978), *The Eighth Mental Measurements Yearbook,* in which most of the commonly used tests are reviewed. If the teacher needs a quick critical evaluation of an instrument, he or she should consult Hoepfner, Strickland, Stangel, Jansen, and Patalino (1970). In their book, *Elementary School Test Evaluations,* tests relating to language arts, social studies, social skills, perception, mathematics, intelligence, and perception, among other abilities, are rated "poor," "fair," or "good." On such factors as test validity, format, norm adequacy, and administration time.

Regrettably, not all of the available tests have been carefully constructed, so the teacher must choose among them with care. It is essential that the teacher have a clear idea of what to measure and be able to specify it precisely. It is not enough to express an interest in obtaining a test of reading. Instead, the teacher must specify the kind of reading to be measured—silent, oral, word-call, word-recognition, or comprehension.

Once the type of reading skill to be tested has been decided upon, the teacher must review the tests that are applicable. The major concern now shifts to reliability. If the teacher intends to utilize the test information for diagnosing problems in individual pupils, the test employed must have a sufficiently high reliability coefficient; it must exceed .80 (Anastasi, 1976), although some authorities prefer .90 or better (Guilford and Fruchter, 1978). Tests whose reliabilities do not reach this level are of dubious diagnostic value to the teacher. If, however, the teacher is involved in conducting research, where the performance of groups rather than of individuals is of primary interest, tests of lower reliability are suitable. For teachers who would like to know more about the concepts of reliability and validity and their role in the classroom, the books by Anastasi (1976), Wallace and Larsen (1978), Salvia and Ysseldyke (1981), and McLoughlin and Lewis (1981), or any other introductory measurement textbook are recommended.

The advantages of norm-referenced tests lie in their objectivity. They are standardized; their reliabilities and validities are known; and they have national reputations. Their grade-equivalent figure or percentile score provides a capsule description of the child's overall skills, providing useful information if the child has just been assigned to a new classroom, if the teacher is attempting to summarize the child's achievement or note the year-to-year overall growth, or if the teacher is trying to decide whether the child is in need of more intensive and detailed informal evaluation.

The disadvantages of most standardized tests should, however, be kept firmly in mind. The results of a sound-blending test may enable the teacher to identify particular children with problems in that area, but they do not indicate the specific blends in need of development. Problem children vary widely in day-to-day performance; tests administered on any given day can reflect pupil fatigue, attitude, or temperament, rather than specific skill in a subject.

Many tests and scales described in this book are not recommended for teacher use. Usually, the reason is the test's low reliability or lack of demonstrated school value. They are included because, whether good or inadequate, these tests are employed extensively in schools, and therefore discussion of them is necessary to point out their shortcomings and specify possible situations in which they might be used.

Informal Assessment

The informal evaluation should be undertaken by an educationally oriented person, usually an educational diagnostician or a teacher. Informal evauation is used to detect areas of weakness and strength; to verify, probe, or discard the conclusions and recommendations based on the formal evaluation; to deduce the child's particular instructional or behavioral needs; and to formulate a remedial program. This is accomplished through an ongoing process of teaching the child and analyzing his or her responses to various instructional tasks. For example, the teacher may wish to determine if John knows his colors. To our knowledge, there are no norm-referenced tests that yield this information; therefore, the teacher must discover John's competency by probing for answers to the following questions.

1. Can John match the basic colors (place red chips together, blue chips together, and so forth)? If not, what colors does he have difficulty in matching?
2. If asked to point to the red chip, then to the blue chip, and so forth, can John select the correct chip from among others of different colors?
3. If the teacher points to the red chip, then to the blue chip, and so forth and says "What color is this?" does John answer correctly?

These three questions all relate to the general question of whether or not the child can recognize colors, but they also provide different kinds of information about the level of his knowledge, the particular colors he does not know, and how to begin to teach him. First he learns to discriminate among the colors, then he learns the labels (receptive language), and finally he uses the labels in speech (expressive language).

The testing process just described is called analytic, diagnostic, or prescriptive teaching. For the teacher, it is by far the most profitable assessment procedure, but it too has hazards that should be pointed out. First, the method is only as good as the competency of the teacher; second, the teacher's experience often is a poor substitute for normative data; and third, the reliability of the teacher as an observer is always unknown. However, the effectiveness of a teacher is invariably dependent on his or her capacity to provide individualization of instruction for the pupils (i.e., individual planning, not necessarily tutoring on a one-to-one basis). To individualize instruction the teacher must engage in diagnostic teaching.

A carefully conceived description of how instructional decisions based on diagnostic information are actually made has recently been offered by Drew, Freston, and Logan (1972). Speaking from a perspective of what they call "a combined evaluative approach," Drew et al. portray the teacher's role as heavily oriented toward criterion-referenced evaluation. Criterion-referenced evaluation implies that the teacher will assess a youngster's skills primarily in terms of the actual operations the child can or cannot perform, rather than in terms of how the child stands relative to some norm or relative standard (such as that utilized in formal assessment). For example, the child is described as having mastered the sounds of all the vowels and consonants, including blends, except for "str," "thr," and "scr," instead of being designated as one who reads orally at a grade equivalent of 2.2. The most enthusiastic supporters of criterion-referenced evaluation are teachers; this is not surprising in view of the fact that this approach yields information that is very directly usable by the teacher in planning remediation activities. Knowing that a child has not yet mastered the blends "str," "thr," and "scr" is more helpful for making day-to-day instructional decisions than knowing that the child reads at a grade equivalent of 2.2.

SETTING LONG-RANGE GOALS AND SHORT-TERM OBJECTIVES

Once the teacher has completed the analysis of a child's performance and has identified those areas of functioning that need strengthening, goals and objectives for that child can be developed. As noted previously, the specific goals that are established will be heavily affected by the teacher's assumptions concerning the nature of the child and by his or her beliefs about the overall goals of education. Thus, the teacher who states in the IEP that a long-range goal is for the child to become familiar with certain classic English poems is manifesting a belief that the job of the schools is to transmit culture. Similarly, the teacher who states that a long-range goal is for the child to attain a fifth-grade reading comprehension level is expressing a belief that a purpose of education is to help the child develop functional adult competencies. A third type of goal might be even more open-ended, in that the child may be expected to become a more creative citizen or in some way to positively affect his or her environment.

Short-range objectives are also required in the IEP and should be derivatives of the long-range goals. Objectives serve an important communication function in that, if well expressed, they convey a picture of the behaviors the child will perform after instruction is completed. Several additional criteria characterize well-written objectives. For example, the desired behavior should be stated in terms that are objective and measurable; furthermore, the conditions under which the student is supposed to perform should be described. Additional information about objectives that relate to the various areas of pupil performance are addressed in the chapters that follow.

INSTRUCTIONAL MATERIALS, PROCEDURES, AND SETTINGS

Once the objectives have been specified, the teacher is faced with the task of selecting appropriate instructional materials and methods. In addition, an educational setting that enhances the child's likelihood of meeting the objectives must be selected. These two considerations are addressed next.

Materials and Procedures

The selection and implementation of the most effective materials for a given child is based directly on the observed abilities and problems that the child manifests. For example, in the arithmetic area, a child's initial profile might appear as shown in Figure 1–2. The child's profile in this graph would be

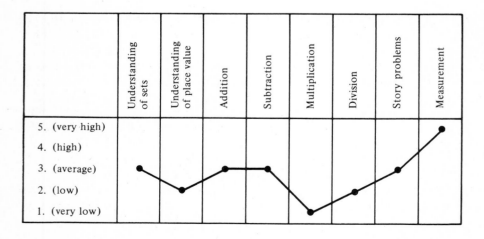

Figure 1– 2. Graph of Arithmetic Ability

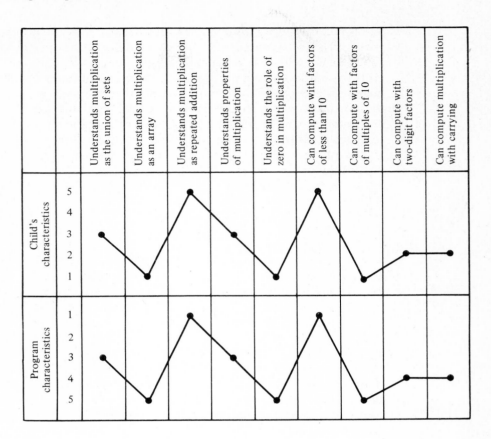

Figure 1–3. Graph of Multiplication Ability

interpreted to indicate that the child is having a great deal of difficulty in multiplication (he or she has not yet been exposed to division), and a further weakness is apparent in his or her understanding of place value.

The next task for the teacher is to further explore the child's trouble in multiplication and place value. To consider the multiplication example only, the teacher might probe as reflected in Figure 1–3.

In the second level of this graph, immediately below the child's characteristics, the profile of a multiplication program is sketched that should be maximally effective with the child. Note, for example, that the program is very strong in presenting multiplication as an array of rows and columns (precisely where the child is weakest), pays little attention to multiplication as repeated addition (which the child has already mastered), and emphasizes the role of zero and multiplying by multiples of ten (both areas where the child is very weak).

It is not expected that the teacher will find ready-made programs for every profile of abilities and disabilities that might be discovered in the classroom. The teacher will have to adapt, modify, and improvise. Sometimes the two profiles—child characteristics and program characterısteristics—will not fit well. In that case, it is still important for the teacher to sketch the interface, so that he or she will be cognizant of potential problems and be able to anticipate program failures. There will be cases in which the teacher is at a loss as to how to plan a program that fits a particular child's needs. In those cases, the teacher should plot the child's profile in the area of difficulty and consult with the nearest regional Instructional Materials Center and possibly acquire the appropriate materials there. A perusal of the many approaches suggested in the subsequent chapters of this book for arithmetic, reading, language, spelling, and writing should also provide ideas for the teacher who is faced with the difficult but crucial task of matching child variables to program variables.

It is not suggested that every time a teacher wants to make an instructional decision he or she go through the lengthy, time-consuming procedures spelled out here. It would be impossible for the teacher to have any time left to teach if that were the case. However, we are aware that in every classroom there are certain children who have particular difficulty in given subject areas. With these children, previous efforts at remediation usually have yielded little improvement. Ultimately, the time spent in detailed diagnosis and planning is time well spent for these children, and the pinpointing of areas of difficulty is well worth the extra effort involved. To some extent the selection of instructional materials reflects an individual teacher's subjective preferences in style, format, and response mode. However, an awareness of certain guidelines can facilitate intelligent curricular decision making. These guidelines have to do with three basic aspects involving material selection: design, method, and practicality.

Design.   Curriculum design is concerned with the overall organization of the school experiences of a child. Specific questions that might be posed as questions of design are:

1. Is the material organized into subject areas such as reading, arithmetic, and social studies, or is it organized in terms of "experiences" or "units" that cut across traditional subjects? Which approach makes the most sense for the child under consideration?

2. If organized in terms of subject areas, is the material ordered in hierarchical, sequential steps? Are there sequences related to known facts in child development (e.g., the Piagetian stages of cognitive development)? Is the order of sequences logically related to such order as exists within the subject area itself—that is, in arithmetic, multiplication should be

taught before division because multiplication skills are required in the operations of division? Ideally, instructional materials should incorporate both what is known about child development and what is known about the structure of the discipline itself.

3. What criterion is required for the student to proceed from one step to the next? Is mastery of a preceding task a prerequisite to going on to a subsequent task? Is some kind of prerequisite external "readiness score" required before entry into the program or before going on to new units? If so, do these readiness scores bear a manifest relationship to the material they are supposed to make the child ready for? In general, the closer the readiness task is to the actual required skill, the more effective its prediction. For example, ability to walk a balance beam has much less "face validity" as a reading readiness predictor than, say, being able to distinguish "d" from "b."

4. A further consideration underlying the design of materials has to do with its rationale. Is there implicit evidence that sound teaching and/or learning principles were involved? For example, have the authors and producers accounted for motivational factors? Is there any utilization of reinforcement (tangible rewards, social approval, or immediate feedback to the child)? Are basic skills incorporated as a basis for further learning? Is there any research evidence on soundness of the rationale (i.e., are there basic or applied studies supporting the approach)?

A well-designed program has clearly defined objectives for each program component. In any given lesson, the teacher should be able to state unequivocally what the purpose of the lesson is. How clear are the objectives for the materials under consideration? Are the objectives precise enough for the teacher to ascertain whether they have been reached or not? Are the objectives compatible with the learning experiences of the child in other subject areas (e.g., do they permit coordination between social studies and reading)?

Method.   Questions of method are variations of the question, what do the teacher and the pupils have to do to successfully use the materials? One set of these questions concerns the "who" of the instructional process. Can the children be instructed as one large group? If not, are provisions made for occupying the other members of the class productively? Can the material be adapted for either a tutoring, small-group, or large group situation? Must the teacher be actively involved in all phases of the instruction, or can the youngsters work on their own some or all of the time? To use the materials, what does the teacher have to do or say? Are the instructions too complicated? Is it physically possible for the teacher to do what is required (e.g., position figures on the flannelboard while reading verbatim instructions, and at the same time walk up and down the aisles to check each child's response)? Is there a balance between teacher-doing and pupil-doing, and between teacher-talk and pupil-talk? Are a variety of responses elicited from the pupils (e.g., oral and written responses, manipulation, painting, demonstrating)? Are several sensory modalities, either simply or in combination, involved? Is there undue penalty for a child who is deficient in one response (e.g., the child who cannot use his or her hands or has difficulty in oral expression)? Are the required responses related to the desired learning? For example, if the desired outcome is silent reading comprehension, is the child required to read silently and tested on mastery, or is the child required to "word-call" orally?

Is the material sufficiently flexible to make possible adaptions that facilitate learning? For example, can the child who has a sight problem still learn through listening and touch? Is there a way that children can serve as each other's tutors, to relieve pressure on the teacher? Can the material readily be broken into smaller steps, or supplemented with other materials, for those children who have difficulty?

Can the material be individualized, both in terms of rate presentation and in terms of intensity? That is, can the rapid learner move through the material quickly, and the slow learner more deliberately? Are there provisions for the child who is making virtually no incorrect responses to skip unnecessary examples or pages? Conversely, does the material incorporate an opportunity for the child who is making many errors to relearn the material, perhaps through a different format or presentation?

Is the material flexible to allow switching to another approach if that should appear desirable? Some programs are so unique that switching to another is impractical because of the material's limited ability to generalize to other areas. For example, if a teacher decided to use a reading program with a unique orthography, he or she must be aware of the fact that this is a long-term decision, and difficult to change. One cannot switch orthographies every few months without seriously hampering a child's growth in reading. Similarly, certain programmed programs in reading and arithmetic are so unique that there are really no alternatives to which the child may reasonably be switched if it becomes necessary to do so for reasons such as program failure.

Practicality. Finally, there are some practical considerations that need to be taken into account in instructional material selection. First, how attractive is the material? Would a youngster want to use it because of its appeal, effective use of color, format, motivational devices, attractive visual arrangement, uniqueness, or variation in presentation? Are the materials practical and durable? Is the price reasonable? Are there any hazardous elements present? Can the material be used independently, or does it require close supervision? Is the quality of drawings or photographs adequate? Can the materials be brought out, used, and reassembled for storage in a reasonable length of time? Are the materials reusable, or must new kits, sets, or workbooks be purchased for each additional student? Is use of materials or the grading of the students' responses unnecessarily boring or laborious for the teacher?

The teacher will quickly find that no one program, no matter how excellent, will work with all children, and some programs will not work with any children. For this reason, a teacher needs to have access to many approaches, involving a variety of different formats, strategies, and modalities. Based on knowledge of the needs of a particular child, the teacher can make intelligent decisions regarding the how, what, and when of instruction. This knowledge is particularly imperative, since few products have been widely tested before they are offered to the public. The materials are beautifully packaged, widely advertised, and sold in large quantities, usually long before there is evidence to support their value. Efficacy research follows the availability of commercial materials by three to five years, if ever. Therefore, teachers almost always are required to use invalidated programs. There exists no "consumer's report" for teachers, no book that can be consulted to point out shortcomings, limitations, or strengths of the various materials. It is strictly a "buyer, beware" market.

However, many of the teaching methods commonly used in the schools have existed for years and a body of research has accumulated about many of them. The teacher, therefore, is well advised to undertake a library investigation of the particular method he or she wants to implement to see what success others have had with the program. *Educational Index, Dissertation Abstracts, Mental Retardation Abstracts,* and *Special Education Abstracts* are profitable initial sources of information. Many companies have assembled data on their programs and will provide it upon request; of course, do not expect to find anything critical from this source.

Although research on a particular method may not exist, use of that method should not necessarily be avoided. The teacher could use it on an experimental basis. For example, the teacher can test pupils in arithmetic, implement the unvalidated program for several months, and then retest the pupils to see if the program was indeed profitable. If the pupil performance could be compared to that of a control group, the results of the study would be made considerably more creditable.

Because of our recognition of the importance of this topic to good educational practice, we have devoted a major part of each of the following chapters to descriptions of widely used programs, methods, and materials. Where information is available regarding the effectiveness of the approaches that are described, it too is presented. In addition, an entire chapter dealing specifically with selecting and analyzing methods has been included in the book.

The Educational Setting

It should be stressed again that this book does not purport to deal with the management difficulties of profoundly retarded, psychotic, autistic, aphasic, dyslexic, or severely sensory-impaired children, although the techniques presented can be adapted to ameliorate the children's school-related problems. For these children, the instructional setting is likely to continue to be the special class or the large or small residential facility. Actually, the number of children for whom such placements are appropriate is quite small. The overwhelming majority of children who evidence problems are in need of remedial education designed to enable them to function in the regular class as soon as possible. There are several models that can be employed in the schools to provide pupils with needed services.

The Regular Classroom.   Most children who develop difficulties in school can be successfully managed by their regular teacher; their problems tend to be of a mild and easily corrected variety. The regular classroom is by for the most desirable setting for children to receive remedial help, and the classroom teacher is usually the best person to direct the remedial lessons. In this way, the child remains with peers and does not have to suffer the indignity of leaving the room to obtain corrective help elsewhere. However, often the teacher–pupil ratio is too high, the teacher lacks the experience, or the pupil's problem is too obdurate to be ameliorated in the regular classroom setting. Alternatives must then be sought.

The Special Class.   The most frequently employed alternative for dealing with children with behavioral and/or educational problems has been the self-contained special class. Many arguments set forth in defense of this placement are apparently reasonable. It is often argued that children placed in these classes receive the benefits of specially trained teachers, special materials and methods, smaller classes, and individualized instruction. In fact, this is rarely the case. Until recently, untrained teachers were the rule rather than the exception; although the class enrollments were smaller than regular classes, there did not seem to be any more individualization of instruction; and the teachers seemed to use much the same approach toward classroom management and selection of materials that was used in the regular class.

Research indicates that children placed in special classes achieve in schoolwork no better than, and often not as well as, similar children left in the regular class. Findings regarding the effects of such placements in self-concept and adjustment are equivocal at the present time.

Special classes exist in assorted types and are restricted to children diagnosed as having a specific condition, such as mental retardation, emotional disturbance, or learning disability. For the most part, children placed in these settings are more similar to typical children than thay are different from them. Although they may be poor readers or difficult to cope with, there is little justification for subjecting them to such a drastic measure as isolation from the regular class.

Because of the added stigma that inherently goes with placement in a self-contained class, the segregation of the child from peers, and the doubtful benefits to be derived, this alternative should be used with considerable caution and viewed as a last resort. For readers who are interested in additional references concerning the use of the special class for handling children with learning or behavior problems, the work of Dunn (1968), Christopolos and Renz (1969), and Iano (1972) is strongly recommended.

The Special School.   The special school for children with various learning problems is the natural extension of the self-contained class. Here the child not only is segregated from peers but also is removed from the regular school premises completely. The child may attend the special school and return home after classes or may be in residence at the school. The advantage of such a placement is the child's immersion in a total remedial program. In addition to the expense involved, the pro and con arguments are basically the same as those advanced regarding the special class. This placement should be viewed as a last possible alternative for children who cannot be accommodated to any other setting.

The Resource Room.   The resource room is a promising alternative to self-contained facilities. This model permits the pupil to receive instruction individually or in groups in a special room outfitted for that purpose. The emphasis is on teaching specific skills that the pupil needs. At the end of the lesson, the child returns to the regular classroom and continues his or her education there. In this way, the child is based in the regular class with peers and leaves only for periods of time during the school day. There are several variations of the resource room model that deserve some mention.

1. *The categorical resource room.* These rooms are operated in the same way as the resource rooms; however, to qualify for placement the pupil must satisfy a designated special education category or definition, such as retarded, disturbed, or learning disabled. Readers who are interested in implementing this variation of the resource room model are referred to the work of Glavin, Quay, Annesley, and Werry (1971), who successfully used the resource rooms with emotionally disturbed children; Sabatino (1971) with learning disabled children; and Barksdale and Atkinson (1971) with mentally retarded children.

2. *The noncategorical resource room.* This variation is highly recommended. Children who are referred to the resource room are not labeled by category, and programs are designed for them on a basis of instructional, emotional, and behavioral need. Even "gifted" youngsters can be accommodated. In addition to the fact that the children involved remain in the regular classroom for most of the day, there are distinct advantages to this alternative. They include: (a) handicapped children do not have to be bused to the nearest school where there is an appropriate categorical class; (b) the number of children who can be seen daily is at least two-and-a-half times the number seen in the self-contained class; (c) the room serves all children in the school and is not limited to special-education-type children; and (d) the close communication between resource room and regular teacher allows for cooperative handling of the child and his or her problem. Readers interested in the dynamics of setting up a noncategorical resource room are referred to *The Resource Room: Rationale and Implementation* (Hammill and Wiederholt, 1972a).

3. *The itinerant program.* The problems handled by this program may be either disability based or noncategorical. The program is constructed around mobile resource rooms and the teacher is not "housed" in any one school. Its advantage lies in its mobility, but it has serious limitations. They include: (a) since the teacher is not attached to a particular school, it is difficult for him or her to become fully accepted in any of the schools in which he or she operates; (b) much teacher time is spent in transit; and (c) transportation of materials is a chronic problem.

Readers who desire a comprehensive account of the operation of resource programs are referred to *The Resource Teacher: A Guide to Effective Practices* by Wiederholt, Hammill, and Brown (1983). In this volume, the authors have described in detail the types of resource programs that can be implemented in the schools; have defined the role of the resource teacher relative to assessment, instruction, and consultation; and have outlined the procedures to be followed in setting up a program. In addition, they have reviewed the kinds of teacher activities that help children improve in reading, math, spoken language, spelling, handwriting, written expression, and behavior.

REASSESSMENT AND HYPOTHESIS REFORMULATION

In the instruction model (Figure 1–1), the last stage pertains to the evaluation of pupil progress and its use in reformulating educational goals and objectives and/or in revising instructional procedures. This activity is also an important part of the IEP. The program evaluation should be continual, occurring periodi- cally throughout the year, and the findings should be incorporated im- mediately into instructional action by accelerating, attenuating, modifying, or even discontinuing the child's program. It should be clear to teachers and parents alike that maximum accountability can be derived only from an evalu- ation plan that provides ongoing feedback. It is not in the interests of the child to be evaluated only at the end of the year, when it is too late to do anything about it if objectives have not been met.

Naturally, the evaluation plan should be developed in such a way that it permits the answering of the question: Were the long-term goals and short- term objectives for this child actually achieved? Because at the present time there exists no comprehensive test package that adequately tests children in all areas of functioning, the plan will have to have several dimensions, including the use of both norm-referenced and informal assessment techniques. Also, direct observation of the child's performance may be used. If the objectives are precisely stated in such terms as "The child will be able to correctly read aloud the first ten words of the Dolch Sight List with 90 percent accuracy in three minutes," the objective itself becomes the evaluation plan. There should be little question as to whether or not the child has achieved this particular objective; it can be easily established by direct observation.

It should be clear that the various elements of our instructional model, and of the IEP as well, are interrelated and dependent of each other for consistency and for effectiveness. This is the case because each aspect of the teaching– learning process directly affects, and is affected by, every other aspect. The cyclical, interrelated nature of the elements is implicit in the model.

2

TEACHING CHILDREN WITH READING PROBLEMS

Nettie R. Bartel   John E. Boyd   Susan Tobia

"Why Johnny can't read" is a problem that has concerned teachers, parents, and the general public for many years. In spite of determined efforts on the part of individual teachers, local school districts, state departments of education, and the federal government, the problem of teaching children to read is still very much with us.

One reason that so many different people want to ensure that children learn to read is that reading is involved in every school subject, especially those in the upper grades. It becomes increasingly difficult for students to be successful in any subject area if their reading problems are not remedied.

Furthermore, inadequate reading skill can eventually interfere significantly with an individual's capacity for economic independence and with his or her general knowledge of the world. While much information is communicated nowadays through television, print remains the medium through which most persons seek and find jobs, read maps and other documents, and engage in certain recreational activities. For most people, printed materials provide the only access to information that is available around-the-clock to the user.

Recent writers (e.g., Bartel, in press, Salamon, 1979) point out an additional imperative for reading instruction. Research is beginning to show that it is impossible to convey identical information in nonprint material as compared with print. Furthermore, inherent in the print medium itself is the capacity to develop in the reader certain cognitive skills. By virtue of the differences in the symbol systems used in print and in, say, videotape, different styles of learning are developed. This is not to say that children cannot learn from nonprint sources—they can and do. But the cognitive skills developed by continued exposure to print are qualitatively more complex than those fostered by nonprint instructional materials. This, in turn, will affect the child's later learning capabilities. It is, therefore, with a new urgency that the topic of teaching reading is approached.

Almost every classroom teacher has encountered children who cannot or do not read. Some of these children appear limited in ability; others appear confused, reluctant, or resistant. Regardless of the nature of the problem, we take the position that virtually every child can learn to read if the difficulty is carefully diagnosed and an intervention is planned that is based on a firm understanding of what the reading act entails. It is to help teachers design and implement these needed procedures that the six sections of this chapter were prepared.

The first section deals with the nature of reading; some of the common reading problems that are found in the classroom are described in the second part. The third section deals with specific assessment strategies that can be used to determine the appropriate instructional level of individuals, as well as specific areas of weakness in reading. The fourth section covers how to teach a child with a reading problem. The next section deals with procedures that can be used with most of the major approaches to the teaching of reading. The final section describes some materials that can be used in the ongoing reading program and offers specific examples of methods to overcome reading weaknesses.

The information presented in this chapter should be regarded as a starting point. The teacher should take this initial information and, using his or her experiences, resources, and knowledge, continue to develop and refine materials that will best suit the teaching situation. The teacher must be aware that unanticipated needs will arise that must be met. By careful planning and organization, the teacher can build a file of materials, both commercial and teacher-made, that will be readily available for use when the need arises. Just as children grow in their development of reading skill, teachers must grow in their acquisition of the skills in teaching reading and in their knowledge of the subject.

THE NATURE OF READING

The individual who would attempt to improve reading skills in children must first understand what reading is. Such an understanding is not easily acquired, for "the process of learning to read is not very well understood. Researchers do not yet know enough about the developed skills of the fluent reader, the end product of the instructional process, let alone the process of acquiring these skills" (F. Smith, 1971, p. vii). Dechant (1964) stated that "there are as many definitions or descriptions of reading as there are reading experts" (p. 15). To some authors reading is responding orally to printed symbols (i.e., word-calling). This definition does not acknowledge that obtaining meaning is part of the reading process. Other definitions include both the ability to correctly pronounce the words and to gain the meaning that is being conveyed. For the purpose of this chapter, reading is regarded as the meaningful interpretation of printed symbols in light of the reader's own background of experience and, as such, is regarded as an ability to attach meanings to words, phrases, sentences, and longer selections.

K. Goodman (1976) has described reading as a "psycholinguistic guessing game." What Goodman has in mind is that in the reading act, the reader makes successive sets of hypotheses and uses semantic, syntactic, and graphic cues to confirm or disconfirm these hypotheses or guesses. For example, let us suppose that a second-grader, Tommy, is confronted with the following paragraph to read:

Little Fox and His Friends

Once there was a little fox who didn't like the dark. One morning, before the sun came up, Little Fox woke up all alone. His mother had gone hunting in the forest.

Simply by reading, or by being told what the story is about, the child can develop some expectancies about the content. He can, for example, expect to read about other animals. He can expect that the story will have words that refer to life in the forest. Particularly, if the teacher introduces the story carefully, if a Directed Reading Activity format (to be discussed later in the chapter) is used, the child will have some questions, expectancies, or hypotheses cued for him.

However, the child has other information available to him. By second grade, he has had a lot of experience with his language (presumably English). This experience can help him as he begins to read the paragraph. If he has been exposed to stories such as fairy tales, he will know that the word right after the first word "Once" will probably be "upon" (for "Once upon a time . . .") or "there" (for "Once there was . . ."). Now, although the word "there" in isolation is frequently difficult for second-graders, the cognitively and linguistically active child can be enormously helped in the reading task by, in this case, his prior knowledge of the way stories often begin and by his knowledge of the syntax of the English language.

The next word that may give the child difficulty is "didn't." The main cues that the child can use here are syntactic and visual. By the second grade, the child's knowledge of English is such that he knows when he hears a sentence such as "Once there was a fox who . . ." that the next word will tell something about what the fox did or did not do. This knowledge, coupled with the child's understanding of the acoustic sound of /d/, the initial letter, may provide enough information for him to "guess" or "hypotheisze" the correct word. If he guesses correctly, without too long a hesitation to break his train of thought, the next word, "like," will probably be easy for him. If he had to pause to ponder over "didn't," "like" will be more difficult, because he does not have the string of words "Once there was a little fox who didn't . . ." to help him figure out "like." We could continue our hypothetical analysis, showing how a wrong guess slows the child down and interferes with the cues of meaning and syntax.

According to Goodman, the best readers are those who can "guess" correctly most of the time, with a minimum use of cues. F. Smith (1971) has shown the significance of interaction and balance among the various types of cues—context, syntax, and visual. Smith makes the point that there are a very large number of cues potentially available to the reader—if he or she had to use all of them, the reading act would be very slow indeed. However, since the cues are so redundant, the good reader selects and uses only a few. The effective use of context cues or of syntactic cues takes some of the interpretative load off the graphic cues so that even if the beginning reader is not completely sure of all the distinctive features of a given letter or word, he or she needs only a little extra help to figure out the word. If the reader is uncertain, however, on each of the areas that could potentially help—context or semantics, syntax, and graphic—he or she will slow down in the reading; and because of normal memory limitations, semantic and syntactic cues will fade rapidly. While it is true that semantic and syntactic information can help with the visual, it is also true that unless some visual cues are interpretable by the child, the child quickly loses the semantic and syntactical help. (For a further discussion of this issue, the reader is referred to Blanchard and McNinch, 1980; Fleischer, Jenkins, and Pany, 1980; Perfetti and Hogaboam, 1975; and Schwartz, 1980).

It does not take a great deal of imagination to see the potential reading problems that would be encountered by a child who was unfamiliar with the distinguishing features of the letters of the alphabet and who also was unsure of the content that he or she was supposed to read. When this situation is compounded with unfamiliarity with standard English syntax, as is the case with many children growing up in the inner cities of our nation, it is not difficult to see why so many children have reading problems. Such children are indeed triply handicapped, in that they cannot "trade" one type of information—semantic, syntactic, or graphic—for another the way proficient readers do. It is ironic, indeed, that the process that will ultimately make it possible for the child to gain a knowledge of the world—reading—is in its initial stages itself heavily dependent on such knowledge (Schwartz, 1980).

Teachers who are not sure about the need to provide additional informational "prompting" for beginning readers are urged to consider their own reading behavior when confronted with reading material that is unfamiliar and perhaps highly technical. In such a situation, all of us slow down in rate; we go back over the material; we skip over words, hoping we can make some sense out of them on the basis of the rest of the passage. One way or the other we try to narrow down what the author is saying, to answer the questions in our minds. As Smith (1971) put it: "All information acquisition in reading, from the identification of individual letters or words to the comprehension of entire passages, can be regarded as the reduction of uncertainty" (p. 12).

Given that the child uses any information available to help develop hypotheses about his or her reading, how does the child, in fact, attempt to identify unknown words for which he or she has no syntactic or semantic cues? No one knows for sure what happens in the mind of a child who attempts to identify such a word. However, a number of explanations have been proposed. The most widely known of these are those developed by Gibson (1965, 1970), Venezky and Calfee (1970), and F. Smith (1971). All these persons suggest that the child does not apply a set of decoding rules to identify unknown words. For anything except the shortest words, such a procedure would be too time-consuming for an efficient reader. Rather, they suggest that readers mediate the identification of unfamiliar words by comparing the unknown word to known words or word parts. They do not agree on the form that such words or word parts (stored in the memory) take. There is general agreement that when a child is confronted with a new word, he or she searches through his or her memory store and compares the unknown to the known. The unknown word that cannot be recognized as a whole is segmented in some way. These word segments, or word wholes, are compared with the reader's memory of known words or word segments. Next, a recombining process takes place, resulting in a word for which the reader has an acoustic or semantic category. Some kind of transfer takes place in comparing the unknown to the known.

Gibson and Smith also believe that readers generate their own rules by comparing and contrasting features, and receiving feedback as to the correctness of the responses. This feedback may be generated by the self, as in the case in which a reader "tries out" a word to see if it fits into an acoustic or semantic category (Cunningham, 1975–1976). Samuels, Begy, and Chen (1975–1976) found that good readers are better able to generate a target word given context and fragments, such as the first letter of the target word. They also found that readers who read at, rather than below, grade level were able to recognize words more quickly, even though all subjects had been pretested, and all could read all the words.

These findings led Samuels et al. to interpret their results as supportive of a "hypothesis/test" theory of word identification. Similar to F. Smith (1971), Samuels et al.'s model reflects a cognitive view of word processing which holds that the identification of words is an active, constructive act in which the output is greater than, and different from, the input. That is, the reader does not merely "transcribe" the written word into spoken form, but brings something quite apart from the printed page to the word identification act. That "something" is his or her own knowledge, ideas, experiences, and hypotheses. A good reader uses semantic, syntactic, and visual cues to recognize words and sentences and to get the "sense" of the passage. Word identification is constructive and integrative, with the reader melding together bits of visual, syntactic, and context information to derive meaning. In the fluent reader, the process is enormously efficient; the reader uses just enough visual cues to "fill in," that is, to confirm or disconfirm the ideas that he or she is developing about the passage.

While a number of individuals have attempted to schematically portray the act of reading and its relationship to cognitive structure and to language processes (e.g., Carroll, 1978; Ruddell, 1976; K. Goodman, 1976; Rumelhart, 1977; Williams, 1977), such efforts have not accounted for all the variables involved in reading. Doehring and Aulls (1979) suggest that cognitive and language skills, motivation and cultural backgrounds, level of reading skill acquisition, reading strategy, the influence of instruction, and the properties of the text should all be considered. It may be the case, as they suggest, that different variables are operative during the successive stages of learning to read, as indicated in Table 2–1. In addition to these variables, recent research

Table 2–1. Variables that Interact During Reading Acquisition

Stage of Acquisition	Variables
Pre-Reading	Language Skills
	Cognitive Skills
	Cultural Variables
Stage 1	Text (including language structure)
Beginning Reading	Reading Skills
	Language Skills
Stage 2	Cognitive Skills
Transitional Reading	Instruction
	Motivation
	Cultural Variables
Stage 3	Text
Proficient Reading	Reading Skills
	Cognitive Skills
	Motivation
	Cultural Variables

Source: Reprinted with permission of National Reading Conference, Inc. from Doehring, D.G. and Aulls, M.W. The interactive nature of reading acquisition. *Journal of Reading Behavior,* 1979, 11, 27–40.

(e.g., Mosenthal and Na, 1980) suggests that classroom environment is a factor that affects children's reading behavior.

There are today virtually no reading authorities who seriously contend that the reading act is passive, rather than active (Williams, 1973). There is apparent consistency in the position that reading is a complex cognitive skill, the goal of which is obtaining information. However, if one examines textbooks on the teaching of reading, one finds that there is much more space devoted to topics auch as "phoneme–grapheme correspondence" than to consideration of the teaching of complex information processing and comprehension skills. The methodology of teaching reading has simply not kept up with the changing viewpoint concerning the cognitive, constructive aspects of the reading act. This chapter is evidence of that very point. Currently, there are many more ways available to the teacher who wishes to assess a child's word-attack skills than there are to the teacher who is interested in measuring a child's comprehension skills in anything other than the grossest fashion. The typical scope-and-sequence chart accompanying many reading series invariably shows much greater differentiation of the "decoding" skills as opposed to the "understanding" skills. The scope-and-sequence chart shown as Table 2–5, which is adapted from a well-known text on reading and learning disabilities (Kaluger and Kolson, 1969), exemplifies this point very well. While there are several taxonomies of comprehension skills available (an excellent one is presented in the next section), there are few published accounts on how to translate these aspects of comprehension into teaching procedures.

The simple view of the reading process that was fashionable in some circles in the 1960s and that underlies a number of reading programs has a good deal of initial appeal. Teaching only observable, easily measured reading skills makes it easy to specify precisely what the child can and cannot do. Objectives can be clearly stated, and it can be determined whether they have or have not been met. Such a clearly defined, observable, and easily measured set of skills is clearly appealing to the teacher of a child who has a reading problem. Unfortunately, there is much more to the reading act than learning to say "cat" when presented with the letters c-a-t. Accordingly, it is to comprehension that we turn next.

In recent years, published materials have expanded to include many different aspects of comprehension. This represents a welcome shift from the previous lack of attention to teaching comprehension skills (Durkin, 1978–79; Stein and Glenn, 1978). Most of the new materials regard comprehension as a set of differentiated skills.

There are at least three broad areas of comprehension:

1. Literal—understanding the primary, direct, (literal) meaning of words, sentences, or passages.

2. Inferential—understanding the deeper meanings that are not literally stated in the passage.
3. Critical—passing judgment on the quality, worth, accuracy, and truth of the passage.

Barrett has differentiated comprehension skills even further in *Taxonomy of Cognitive and Affective Dimensions of Reading Comprehension* (see Clymer, 1968). The basic, paraphrased outline of the taxonomy follows.

1.0. *Literal comprehension.* Literal comprehension focuses on ideas and information that are explicitly stated in the selection.
    1.1. *Recognition* requires the student to locate or identify ideas or information explicitly stated in the reading selection.
        1.11. Recognition of details
        1.12. Recognition of main ideas
        1.13. Recognition of a sequence
        1.14. Recognition of comparisons
        1.15. Recognition of cause-and-effect relationship
        1.16. Recognition of character traits
    1.2. *Recall of details.* Recall requires the student to produce from memory ideas and information explicitly stated in the reading selection.
        1.21. Recall of details
        1.22. Recall of main ideas
        1.23. Recall of a sequence
        1.24. Recall of comparisons
        1.25. Recall of cause-and-effect relationship
        1.26. Recall of character traits
2.0. *Reorganization.* Reorganization requires the student to analyze, synthesize, and/or organize ideas or information explicitly stated in the selection.
    2.1. Classifying
    2.2. Outlining
    2.3. Summarizing
    2.4. Synthesizing
3.0. *Inferential comprehension.* Inferential comprehension is demonstrated by the student when he uses the ideas and information explicitly stated in the selection, his intuition, and his personal experiences as a basis for conjectures and hypotheses.
    3.1. Inferring supporting details
    3.2. Inferring main ideas
    3.3. Inferring sequence

        3.4. Inferring comparisons
        3.5. Inferring cause-and-effect relationships
        3.6. Inferring character traits
        3.7. Predicting outcomes
        3.8. Interpreting figurative language

  4.0. *Evaluation.* The purposes for reading and teacher's questions, in this instance, require responses by the student that indicate that he has made an evaluative judgment by comparing ideas presented in the selection with external criteria provided by the teacher or other sources or with internal criteria provided by the student himself.

        4.1. Judgment of reality or fantasy
        4.2. Judgment of fact or opinion
        4.3. Judgment of adequacy and validity
        4.4. Judgment of appropriateness
        4.5. Judgment of worth, desirability, and acceptability

  5.0. *Appreciation.* Appreciation involves all the previously cited cognitive dimensions of reading, for it deals with the psychological and aesthetic impact of the selection on the reader.

        5.1. Emotional response to the content
        5.2. Identification with characters or incidents
        5.3. Reaction to the author's use of language
        5.4. Imagery

This taxonomy gives some idea of the complexity of "reading comprehension." Because of the integral nature of comprehension in the reading act, a subsequent section of this chapter will deal specifically with how to teach it more effectively. Before reading instruction can take place, however, the teacher needs to know the nature of reading difficulty that a given child may have. Accordingly, we next look at types of reading problems.

TYPES OF READING PROBLEMS

Ideally, children should be reading at a level commensurate with their mental age, *not* chronological age or grade placement. Unfortunately, there are many children who for one reason or another do not read at their mental age level. Children with reading problems are often labeled with terms such as "corrective," "retarded," or "remedial." Sometimes more complicated and threatening labels are attached—"strephosymbolic," "dyslexic," "brain injured," and so on. The list could go on *ad nauseum.* However, it does the teacher little good to become acquainted with medical or psychological terminology, since the terminology alone is of no assistance in helping the child with a reading problem. In fact, most of the reading problems found in a classroom are not those of a highly clinical nature; rather, they have a relatively obvious cause.

The types of reading problems that a teacher identifies will be related to the view that the teacher holds about the nature of reading. If the teacher believes that reading consists of saying the word "look" in response to seeing the letters "l-o-o-k," and nothing more, he or she will not identify as a problem the fact that the child may not understand what it means to "look."

Our view of the nature of reading (stated earlier) leads us to identify the following types of reading problems listed in Table 2–2. Naturally, not every poor reader will exhibit *all* of the problems.

Occasionally, the terms "developmental," "corrective," and "remedial" are used in connection with poor readers. It should be pointed out that these words have no precise (i.e., not generally accepted) meaning among professionals working in the field. For example, "developmental" may refer to a class (or to a child) in which the students are taught using regular class methods; sometimes the use of the term is limited to pupils who are performing at a level

Table 2– 2. Comparison Between Good and Poor Readers

What the Good Reader Does	*What the Poor Reader May Do*
Notes the distinctive features in letters and words	Fails to notice distinctions between b and d; or was and saw; or m and n; or the configuration of other letters and words; or focuses only on certain characteristics, e.g., beginnings of words
Predicts the endings of words (e.g., "righ?"), phrases (e.g., "once upon a _____"), or sentences (e.g., "the fire _____ed") with feasible hypothesis	Cannot predict reasonable or possible endings of words, phrases or sentences
Expects what he reads to make sense in terms of his own background	Fails to relate reading content to his own background
Reads to identify meaning rather than to identify letters or words	Reads to identify individual letters or individual words, or reads because he has to
Shifts speed and approach to the type and purpose of reading	Approaches all reading tasks the same way
Formulates hypotheses or expectations about the way the passage will develop an idea	Cannot/does not develop expectations or predictions concerning the direction or main idea of a passage
Takes advantage of the graphic, syntactic, and semantic cues in a passage to speed reading and improve comprehension	Becomes bogged down in attempting to decipher the passage on a letter-by-letter or word-by-word basis

Sources: Portions of this table are adapted from Cooper, C. R. and Petrosky, A. R. A psycholinguistic view of the fluent reading process. *Journal of Reading, 1976, 20,* 184–207.

commensurate with their ability; sometimes it is used also with pupils who are working far behind their expectancy but where regular class methods are being used. A "corrective" class may be one in which the children are functioning below expectancy but do not appear to have any associated learning problems (brain damage, specific learning disabilities, etc.); "corrective" may also refer to any student who is one to two years behind expectancy regardless of the presence or absence of any associated learning problems. To some professionals, "remedial" students have associated learning problems; to others, the term is applied to all pupils who are more than two years behind expectancy in reading. Because of this confusion, we rarely use any of these terms; but if these terms are used in schools for any purpose, we do recommend that teachers become familiar with their local definitions.

Some children may experience temporary lags in reading development due to external causes and a few may have serious word-learning problems. A child may fall behind in reading due to an extended absence from school, a temporary failure in vision (which can be corrected by appropriately prescribed glasses), a temporary failure in hearing (for example, a tonsillectomy sometimes causes a temporary loss of hearing), a constant change in schools, a radical change in the reading program (from a basal approach to an augmental alphabet approach such as i/t/a), or poor teaching. In such cases, nothing is wrong with the child's central nervous system; the child is not mentally retarded, nor is he or she emotionally disturbed. If appropriate steps are taken through the careful assessment of the child's needs and proper instruction is provided, the difficulty can usually be overcome by using appropriate materials designed for the child's instructional level. Most of these problems can be handled in the ongoing classroom situation.

A few children evidence severe reading problems and experience great difficulty in attaching meaning to word or wordlike symbols when taught by the usual visual–auditory techniques. Often these children need specialized word-learning techniques similar to those presented in the Examples of Specific Remedial Techniques in Reading section of this chapter.

ASSESSING READING PROBLEMS

In order to effectively teach a child with reading problems, a teacher needs to learn more about the child's strengths and weaknesses in reading. First of all, the teacher needs to obtain a general picture of the child's overall level of reading performance. Then, additional assessment must be done to explore the precise nature of the child's difficulties. A number of techniques for obtaining this information have been developed and are available for classroom use. This section will describe the various assessment steps that can be taken by teachers to get a precise picture of the level and nature of a child's reading performance.

A discussion of assessment must be introduced with a word of caution. Overtesting can be as undesirable as no testing at all. A full clinical evaluation of a child's reading problems may take as long as two days to complete. Yet very few children need this kind of detailed work. A few teachers who have been exposed to some formal training in the evaluation of reading, as in a graduate course, may become overzealous and feel that every child needs to be given an Informal Reading Inventory (see pp. 35–36), an interest inventory, an attitude scale, an associative learning test, a test of memory span, and so on. Actually, all this testing can consume too many hours that could better be devoted to instruction. A good rule to follow is to test minimally to find out where to initiate instruction and to identify areas of strength and weakness. Then, through diagnostic teaching, the teacher can continue to uncover the student's needs and to meet them with appropriate instruction as they arise.

ESTABLISHING READING LEVEL

Teachers often need to estimate quickly the reading level of a particular child or class of children. Three popular ways of doing this involve the use of survey tests, oral reading, or Informal Reading Inventories.

Standardized Survey Tests

There are a number of ways to determine the appropriate instructional level for each child. Naturally, some kind of assessment process must be employed. This process can range from teacher judgment to complete reliance on standardized tests; neither of these alone can be regarded as adequate. Standardized tests can be used to estimate the range of reading abilities within a specific group. Generally, only two subtests, vocabulary (word meaning) and comprehension (factual understanding), are included on these tests. Some of the most common of these survey tests are the Reading sections of the Metropolitan Achievement Tests, the Sequential Tests of Educational Achievement, the Stanford Achievement Tests, Wide-Range Achievement Test, and the California Achievement Tests. These tests provide an overall grade level in reading performance, as well as a rough estimate on whether the difficulties are mostly in word-attack skills or in comprehension. But such tests alone provide insufficient information on where to begin instructing a child in reading. In fact, sometimes decisions regarding the reading level of children cannot wait for the administration of a standardized test. In some cases, especially when new children come into a classroom, a teacher needs to quickly establish a child's reading level.

Informal Oral Reading

Although today "round robin" reading is generally condemned as a teaching method, the procedure does enable the teacher to quickly identify those children who need immediate attention. Each child is asked to read a short passage from a book to determine whether he or she can pronounce the words successfully. If the child has trouble with more than five running words out of every hundred, reads in a word-by-word manner, reads too slowly, or exhibits other difficulties, it is likely that the material is too difficult.

The oral reading should be carried out in a nonthreatening manner and the teacher should note the more severe cases of reading failure without drawing embarrassing attention to the child. The teacher can accomplish this in a small-group situation by prefacing the lesson by saying, "This is a new reading book; this morning I want to find out if it is the right book for this group." If this approach is not deemed advisable, then the teacher can call on each child to read on an individual basis while the rest of the group is engaged in some other activity. In cases where this approach does not give enough information to establish a child's reading level, an Informal Reading Inventory may be administered.

Informal Reading Inventory

A complete, informal reading inventory (IRI) is usually regarded as a clinical instrument used by reading specialists, although on occasion a teacher may want to use it. Readers who desire a detailed description of these procedures are referred to the discussion of informal inventories by Johnson and Kress (1969). Although informal reading inventories are too time-consuming for classroom administration, they can provide precise and valuable information about a child's reading difficulty. In the event that a teacher desires a detailed evaluation, he or she should probably request that an informal reading inventory be administered by the reading specialist. Botel (1966), Silvaroli (1973), and Sucher and Allred (1971) have developed informal reading inventories that are available commercially.

Initially a child is given a word-recognition test beginning at the pre-primer level. The child is given tests until he or she misses 50 percent of the words on the flash presentation on two successive levels. Starting with the last level at which the child received 100 percent on the flash presentation in the word-recognition test, the child reads two selections (one oral and one silent) at each level and answers questions concerning each selection. When he or she

Table 2–3.   Criteria for Various Levels

Level	Word Recognition in Context (percent)	Comprehension (percent)	Observable Behavior
Independent	99	90	No signs of frustration or tension
Instructional	95	75	No signs of frustration or tension
Frustration	Below 90	Below 50	Signs of frustration and/or tension
Hearing capacity		75	

falls below 90 percent in word recognition, below 50 percent in comprehension (average of oral and silent selection), or is qualitatively frustrated, the child stops reading. Then the examiner reads aloud one selection at each level until the child is unable to answer 50 percent of the questions asked about the material. Levels for word recognition in context and comprehension are computed for each level using the generally accepted criteria as shown by Table 2–3.

MEASURING ATTITUDES TOWARD READING

If an examination of the checklist for a given child shows that the child's attitude toward reading is not a positive one, the teacher may want to explore this question further. Several instruments for measuring attitudes toward reading are available, among them a student self-report inventory (Estes, Estes, Richards, and Roettger, 1981), a paired-activities attitude scale (Gurney, 1966), and an observational checklist (Powell, 1972). Tests of attitudes toward reading should be used in conjunction with other indicators of attitude toward school in general. Paper-and-pencil tests alone sometimes reveal more about what the child thinks the teacher wants him or her to say than the "true" attitude toward reading (Vaughn, 1980).

ANALYSIS OF READING SKILLS

A number of strategies are available to the teacher who wishes to probe a child's word-attack performance. We describe three of these strategies in this section. A fourth approach, analysis of oral reading miscues, is treated separately in a subsequent section because of its special relationship to reading comprehension.

Standardized Diagnostic Reading Tests

A number of commercially prepared diagnostic reading tests are available. All of them assist a teacher in the diagnosis of difficulties in word-attack; several also assess comprehension problems. The best known of these tests are summarized in Table 2–4.

Table 2– 4.   Diagnostic Reading Tests

Test and Publisher	Grade Levels	What the Test Measures
Botel Reading Inventory (Follett)	1–12	Word opposites, word recognition, phonics
Diagnostic Reading Scale (California Testing Service)	1–8 Retarded Readers 9–12	Word recognition, phonics, reading comprehension
Doren Diagnostic Test of Word Recognition Skills (American Guidance)	1–9	Letter and word recognition, beginning and ending sounds, speech vowels and consonants, blending, rhyming, sight words, spelling
Durrell Analysis of Reading Difficulty (Harcourt, Brace, Jovanovich)	Nonreaders to grade 6	Word and letter recognition, blending and sounding, spelling, listening and recall
Gates-McKillop Reading Diagnostic Test (Teachers College Press)	1–8	Oral reading, word and phrase perception, syllabication, letter names and sounds, blending
Gilmore Oral Reading Test (Harcourt, Brace, Jovanovich)	1–8	Comprehension rate and accuracy
Gray Oral Reading Test (Bobbs-Merrill)	1–Adult	Oral reading rate and accuracy, comprehension
Peabody Individual Achievement Test–Reading portion (American Guidance)	K–12+	Reading recognition and comprehension, letter names and sounds, letter and word discrimination
Stanford Diagnostic Reading Test (Harcourt, Brace, Jovanovich)	1–Adult	Vocabulary, auditory discrimination, phonics syllabication, comprehension
Test of Early Reading Ability (Pro-Ed)	Pre–2	Alphabet knowledge; comprehension; conventions of print
Test of Reading Comprehension (Pro-Ed)	2–12	Vocabulary; paragraph comprehension; syntactic reading. Supplemental tests to measure the "language of school" and vocabularies of science, social studies, and mathematics

Word-Recognition Tests

In general, word-recognition tests serve three purposes. First, they serve as an indication of a child's sight vocabulary; second, they give clues to the word-attack skills that the child uses to work out unfamiliar words; and third, they give some indication of where to initiate reading instruction with the child. The words for sample lists below have been taken from basal reader glossaries, the Durrell List, the Thorndike List, and other word lists. Word-recognition tests are easily constructed and administered. It must be remembered that they only measure a child's sight vocabulary and word-attack skills. This kind of test does not measure meaning or comprehension. Therefore, word-recognition tests, if used alone, may place the child above his or her true instructional level. This is because many children can "read" a passage glibly and then not be able to recall the most obvious literal information included in the text. "Oh, I read it; I didn't know that I was supposed to remember anything," has been said by more than one student to a puzzled teacher who cannot understand how a child can word-call so well but not understand or retain any of the author's thoughts expressed in the passage.

A number of commercially prepared word-recognition lists are available. Some of these are arranged by difficulty level by grade (e.g., LaPray and Ross, 1969); others are compilations of words most typically found in basal readers (e.g., D. Johnson, 1971). Teachers may also develop their own lists of words from the reading materials that they are using. Usually twenty to twenty-five words from the word lists or glossaries found in most basal readers are used. The words can be chosen at random or by dividing the total number of words by 20 or 25 and taking every nth word; for example, if there are 375 words in the word list, divide 375 by 25. Since the answer is 15, take every 15th word from the list. This can later be refined to measure a number of phonic skills. (Do not overload the list with compound words, words of two syllables, or have a large group of words at any one level that follows the same phonic or structural pattern.)

The words can be printed on oaktag in individual lists. The lists can be presented in a number of ways. They can be read orally from the list by the student. The words can be flashed by using two 3- by 5-inch index cards, or a slot can be cut in an index card wide enough to show one word at a time. The flash technique quickly exposes each word, but requires some practice on the part of the person presenting it. To flash a word, the teacher holds the two index cards together immediately above the first word on the list. The lower card is moved down to expose the word and the upper card is moved down to close the opening between them. The complete series of motions is carried out quickly with about a one-second exposure, and the child sees the word only briefly. If the child responds correctly on the flash presentation, the examiner goes on to the next word. If, however, the child gives an incorrect response, the process is repeated untimed, and the word is reexposed. No cues are given, but the child has an opportunity to reexamine the word and apply whatever analysis skills he or she has learned to help deduce the word. By carefully recording the child's responses in this untimed presentation, the teacher can get some idea of the child's word-attack skills as a basis for further instruction. Betts (1956) recommends that a child should achieve a flash score of approximately 95 percent at a given reading level before continuing to the next level.

Figure 2–1 provides an example of a teacher-constructed word-recognition test for a third-grade student. In this case, the word-recognition test shows that the student, when given sufficient time, does have the ability to do some word analysis. However, it is apparent that the child will need additional work with the "r" blends (stranger, branches), the digraph "ch" (branches, which), and suffixes in general.

It can be seen that by carefully recording the student's responses, the teacher can assess weaknesses in word-attack skills. Of course, *every* error should not be treated as a significant problem. However, when the child has been administered several levels, patterns usually emerge. For example, if a child in fifth or sixth grade misses many words at the preprimer levels, he or she probably has not established a basic sight vocabulary. At levels beyond this, the child may miss initial consonants, final consonants, endings, or make other errors. A list of some of the common word-attack errors follows.

Problem	*Example*	
	Text Says . . .	Child Reads . . .
1. Omission of letters in a word	grown	gown
	furniture	funiture
2. Insertion of letters into a word	sight	slight
	chimney	chimaney
3. Substitution of consonants in a word (initial, medial, final)	nice	mice
	fright	flight
	lad	lab
4. Substitution of medial vowels	hat	hot
	dog	dug
5. Reversal of letters in a word	saw	was
	there	three
6. Addition of endings	sheep	sheeps
	gave	gaved
7. Omission of endings	friends	friend
	bark	bar
8. Syllable omission	visiting	visting
	trying	trine

Stimulus Word (Third Grade Level)	Flash	Untimed
1. another	* / **	
2. places	✓	
3. helpful		
4. thousand		
5. wishes	✓	✓
6. supper	super ***	
7. November		
8. stranger	✓	✓
9. branches	✓	✓
10. between		
11. decided		
12. quickly	✓	✓
13. haunted	✓	✓
14. mystery		
15. which	✓	✓
16. understand		
17. picture		
18. first	✓	fr...
19. clothes		
20. Monday		

   * denotes correct response
  ** denotes no response
*** denotes incorrect attempt

Name of Child _Betsy Fisher_   Date _1/10/82_   Class _3_

Figure 2–1. Word Recognition—Flash/Untimed

Scope-and Sequence Charts

If an individual teacher wants additional information for in-depth probing, or if commercially prepared tests are not available or appropriate for the word-attack skills in question, the teacher may prepare a test. A good scope-and-sequence chart outlining the major skill areas in the recommended order of presentation may be used as the framework for building the test. Typically, teachers find that word-attack tests are most informative if they are individually tailored for a specific child's difficulties. For example, if a commercially prepared word-attack test indicates that a child is having trouble with initial consonant blends, the teacher should consult a scope-and-sequence chart to establish whether the child is at about the place in the program where the blends are usually taught. On the chart we have provided (Table 2–5), the initial blends *st, pl, bl, br, tr, dr, gr,* and *fr* appear as skills to be taught near the end of first grade. The blends *cr, sn, sl, pr,* and *cl* are not taught until the beginning of the second grade; the blends *thr, gl, squ, apr,* and *str* are typically taught in the latter half of second grade. So, depending on where the child is in the program, the teacher will construct a test with the appropriate items. The skill should be tested in a variety of ways—including the ability to discriminate one blend from another, such as between the spoken words /brown/ and /frown/. The child might be presented with pictures of such items as "clown" and "crown" and be asked to point to the one for which the teacher says the name. Or the child can be asked to circle all the pictures on a page that start with "pl." Other ideas for format can be found in workbook pages and in the Suggested Exercises sections of a good basal reading series. Note that the activities for testing the child are very similar to the activities for teaching him or her. In fact, the teacher should think of each day's instruction as a test/teach/test sequence, with each element of instruction being based specifically on the prior "test" results. This cyclical test/teach/test paradigm is especially adaptable to instruction in word-attack skills.

One word of caution is in order in using the scope-and-sequence chart we have provided, or any chart found in a basal series. At the present time, the sequencing of these skills (i.e., which skills should be taught in first grade, which in second, and so on) are based on the judgment of "experts" and on tradition. Such sequences or hierarchies of skills have not yet been validated (Bourque, 1980). Hence, the teacher cannot be *certain* that Skill A must be mastered before Skill B is introduced or even that the mastery of Skill A will facilitate the learning of Skill B. For this reason, the teacher should use discretion in making decisions for a particular child.

Table 2–5. Typical Scope-and Sequence of Reading Skills Usually Taught at the Elementary Level

	Word-Study Skills	*Comprehension Skills*
Preprimer Stage	A. Word meaning and concept building B. Picture clues C. Visual discrimination 　1. Left-to-right progression 　2. Word configuration 　3. Capital and lowercase letter forms D. Auditory perception 　1. Initial consonants—*b, c, d, f, g, h, l, m, p, r, s, t, w* 　2. Rhyming elements E. Structural analysis—ex. plural nouns: adding *s*	A. Associating text and pictures B. Following oral directions C. Main idea D. Details E. Sequence F. Drawing conclusions G. Seeing relationships
Primer Stage	Review, reteach, or teach all skills that child has not mastered Expand vocabulary A. Context clues B. Phonetic analysis 　1. Initial consonants 　2. Rhymes 　3. Learning letter names—*n, l, p, d, g, r, c* C. Structural analysis	A. All those at preprimer level B. Forming judgments C. Making inferences D. Classifying
First Reader	A. All previous skills B. Phonetic analysis 　1. Final analysis—*n, d, k, m, t, p* 　2. Initial blends—*st, pl, bl, br, tr, dr, gr, fr* C. Structural analysis 　1. Verb forms 　　a. Adding *ed* 　　b. Adding *ing* 　2. Compound words	A. All previously taught skills B. Recalling story facts C. Predicting outcome D. Following printed directions

First Grade (spans all three stages above)

Table 2–5. *Continued*

	Word-Study Skills	Comprehension Skills

Second Grade — Book One	A. Review and practice all first-grade skills
	B. Phonetic analysis
	  1. Rhyming words visually
	  2. Consonants
	    a. Initial—*j*
	    b. Final—*x, r, l*
	    c. Blends—*cr, sn, sl, pr, cl*
	    d. Digraphs—*ai, oa*
	C. Structural analysis
	  1. Plural of nouns—adding *s* and *es*
	  2. Variant forms of verbs
	    a. Adding *es, ing*
	    b. Doubling consonants before adding *ing* or *ed*
		A. All previously taught skills
		B. Making generalizations
		C. Seeing relationships
		D. Interpreting pictures

Second Grade — Book Two	A. All previously taught skills
	B. Recognize words in alphabetical order
	C. Phonetic analysis
	  1. Consonant blends—*thr, gl, squ, apr, str*
	  2. Phonograms—auditory and visual concepts, of *ar, er, ir, ow, ick, ew, own, uck, ed, ex, ouse, ark, oat, ound*
	  3. Vowel differences
	    a. Vowels lengthened by final *e*
	    b. Long and short sounds of *y*
	    c. Digraphs—*ee, ea*
	    d. Diphthongs—different sounds of *ow*
	D. Structural analysis
	  1. Contractions—*it's, I'm, I'll, that's, let's, don't, didn't, isn't*
	  2. Variant forms of verbs—dropping *e* before adding *ing*
	  3. Plural forms of nouns—changing *y* to *ies*
		A. Practice and use of all previously taught skills
		B. Making inferences
		C. Seeing cause-and-effect relationships

Table 2–5. *Continued*

	Word-Study Skills	*Comprehension Skills*

Third Grade — **Book One**	A. All previously learned skills
	B. Word meaning
	  1. Opposites
	  2. Adding *ore, est* to change form and meaning of words
	  3. Words with multiple meanings
	C. Phonetic analysis
	  1. Consonants
	    a. Hard and soft sounds—*c, g*
	    b. Recognizing consonants
	    c. Digraphs
	      (1) *ck*
	      (2) Vowels
	        (a) Silent vowels
	        (b) Digraphs—*ai, ea, ou, ee, ay, ui*
	    d. Structural analysis
	      (1) Contractions—*who's, we're, you're, aren't, that's, I'm, couldn't*
	      (2) Possessive words
	      (3) Suffixes—*en, est, ly*
	      (4) Variant forms of verbs
	        (a) Changing final *y* to *i* before adding *ed*
	        (b) Dropping *e* before adding *ing*
	    e. Alphabetizing—first letter
	    f. Syllabication—up to three-syllable words
		A. All skills previously learned
		B. Detecting mood of situation
		C. Relating story facts to own experiences
		D. Reading pictorial maps
		E. Skimming

	A. All previously learned skills
	B. Word meaning
	  1. Homonyms
	    a. *dew, do*
	    b. *sea, see*
	    c. *whole, hole*
	    d. *made, maid*
	    e. *blew, blue*
	    f. *ewe, you*
	    g. *forth, fourth*
	    h. *thrown, throne*
		A. All previously learned skills
		B. Problem solving

Word-Study Skills	Comprehension Skills

Table 2–5. *Continued*

Book Two

    2. Synonyms
       a. *throw, pitch*
       b. *quiet, still*
       c. *speak, say*
       d. *lift, raise*
       e. *tug, pull*
       f. *large, big*
       g. *swiftly, fast*
       h. *believe, think*
       i. *smart, clever*
       j. *come, arrive*
       k. *daybreak, dawn*
       l. *fastened, tied*

C. Phonetic analysis
    1. Consonants—hard and soft sounds of *g, c*
       a. *c* usually has a soft sound when it comes before *e* or *i*
       b. *g* usually has a soft sound when it comes before *e* or *i*
    2. Vowels
       a. Diphthongs—*ou, ow, or, oy, aw, au*
       b. Sounds of vowels followed by *r*

D. Structural analysis
    1. Plurals—change *f* to *v* when adding *es*
    2. Contractions—*doesn't, you'll, they're*
    3. Suffixes
       a. Recognizing as syllables
       b. Adding *ly* and *ily*
       c. Positive comparative and superlative forms of adjectives
    4. Prefixes—*un* changes meaning of words to the opposite

E. Alphabetizing—using second letter

F. Syllabication
    1. Between double consonants
    2. Prefixes and suffixes as syllables

G. Accent—finding syllables said more heavily

Table 2-5. *Continued*

Word-Study Skills	*Comprehension Skills*

Fourth Grade

Word meaning:
A. Antonyms
B. Synonyms
C. Homonyms
D. Figures of speech
E. Sensory appeals in words

Word analysis:
A. Phonetic analysis
  1. Consonants
    a. Silent
    b. Two sounds of *s*
    c. Hard and soft sounds of *c* and *g*
    d. Diacritical marks
      (1) Long sound of vowels
      (2) Short sounds of vowels
      (3) *a* as in *care*
      (4) *a* as in *bars*
      (5) *u* as in *burn*
      (6) *a* as in *ask*
      (7) *e* as in *wet*
      (8) *e* as in *letter*
      (9) *oo* as in *moon*
      (10) *oo* as in *foot*
    e. Applying vowel principles
      (1) Vowel in the middle of a word or syllable is usually *short*
      (2) Vowel coming at the end of a one-syllable word is usually *long*
      (3) When a one-syllable word ends in *e,* the medial vowel in that word is usually *long*

1. All previously learned skills
2. Reading for comprehension
3. Finding the main ideas
4. Finding details
5. Organizing and summarizing
6. Recalling story facts
7. Recognizing sequence
8. Reading for information
9. Creative reading
  a. Classifying
  b. Detecting the mood of a situation
  c. Drawing conclusions
  d. Forming judgments
  e. Making inferences
  f. Predicting outcomes
  g. Seeing cause-and-effect relationships
  h. Problem solving
10. Following printed directions
11. Skimming

Table 2–5. *Continued*

Word-Study Skills	*Comprehension Skills*

(4) When two vowels come together, the first vowel is usually *long* and the second vowel is *silent*

B. Structural analysis
 1. Hyphenated words—*good-by, thirty-one, rain-maker*
 2. Finding root words in word variants
 3. Prefixes—*dis, re, un, im*
 4. Suffixes—*ly, ness, ment, ful, ish, less*
 5. Syllabication
  a. When a vowel is followed by one consonant, that consonant usually begins the next syllable
  b. When a vowel sound in a word is followed by two consonants, this word is usually divided between the two consonants
  c. Prefixes and suffixes are usually syllables
  d. Compound words are usually divided between the word parts
  e. In two-syllable words ending in *le* preceded by a consonant, the consonant joins the *le* and begins the final syllable
 6. Accent

Table 2–5. *Continued*

	Word-Study Skills	Comprehension and Study Skills	Locating and Using Information (Study Skills)

Fifth Grade	1. Antonyms—review and give practice in using context clues
	2. Expand vocabulary
	3. Review figures of speech and introduce new ones to enrich vocabulary
	4. Homonyms—review and introduce new ones
	5. Synonyms—review and introduce new ones to expand vocabulary
	6. Use of dictionary and glossary
	  a. Guide words
	  b. Accent marks
	  c. Diacritical marks
	    1. Review â, ä, û, å, oo, oo, ëe
	    2. Review long and short vowels
	    3. Introduce schwa, half-long o
	    4. Introduce italic u, i, a, e
	    5. Introduce ' in omitted vowel
	    6. Respellings
	7. Phonetic analysis
	  a. Review consonant sounds
	  b. Review pronunciation of diacritical marks
		Continue development in the following areas:
		A. Main idea
		B. Sequence
		C. Reading for details
		D. Appreciating literary style
		E. Drawing conclusions
		F. Enriching information
		G. Evaluating information
		H. Forming opinions and generalizing
		I. Interpreting ideas
		J. Using alphabetical arrangement
		K. Using dictionary or glossary skills
		L. Interpreting maps and pictures
		M. Skimming for purpose
		N. Classifying ideas
		O. Following directions
		P. Outlining
		Q. Summarizing
		R. Reading for accurate detail
		S. Skimming
		Introduce and teach:
		A. Discrimination between fact and fiction	

Table 2–5. *Continued*

Word-Study Skills	*Comprehension and Study Skills*	*Locating and Using Information (Study Skills)*

c. Review phonograms
8. Structural analysis
  a. Compound words
  b. Words of similar configuration
  c. Prefixes
    1. Review *un-, im-, dis-, re-*
    2. Introduce *in-, anti-, inter-, mis-*
  d. Suffixes
    1. Review *-en, -ment, -less, -ish, -ly, -ful, -y, -ed*
    2. Introduce *-sp, -or, -ours, -ness, -ward, -hood, -action, -al*
  e. Principles of syllabication
    1. Review rules already taught
    2. Consonant blends and digraphs are treated as singular spunds, and usually are not divided (*ma-chine*)
  f. Application of word analysis in attacking words outside the basic vocabulary
	B. Perceiving related ideas
	C. Strengthening power of recall
	D. Using encyclopedias, atlas, almanac, and other references
	E. Using charts and graphs
	F. Using index and pronunciation keys
	G. Reading to answer questions and for enjoyment of literary style	

Table 2–5 *Continued*

	Word-Study Skills	*Comprehension and Study Skills*	*Locating and Using Information (Study Skills)*

Sixth Grade	*Word meaning:*
	A. Antonyms—review and give practice in
	B. Homonyms—develop ability to use correctly
	C. Classify words of related meaning
	D. Enrich word meaning
	E. Review use of synonyms
	F. Use of context clues in attacking new words
	G. Expand vocabulary
	H. Become aware of expressions that refer to place and time and develop skill in interpreting such expressions
	I. Use dictionary and glossary
	  1. Further ability to use alphabetical-order guide words, and pronunciation key
	  2. Review diacritical marks—introduce circumflex-breve as in *sŏft*
	  3. Review spelling
	Word analysis:
	A. Phonetic analysis
	  1. Review consonant sounds
	  2. Diacritical marks—interpreting
		Continue development in the following areas:
		A. Main ideas
		B. Sequence
		C. Reading for details
		D. Appreciating literary style
		E. Drawing conclusions
		  1. Predicting outcomes
		  2. Forming judgments
		  3. Seeing relationships
		F. Extending and enriching information
		G. Interpreting pictures
		H. Evaluating information
		I. Interpreting ideas
		J. Using facts to form opinions, generalizing
		Introduce the skills of
		A. Enriching imagery
		B. Discriminating between fact and fiction
		C. Strengthening power of recall
			Review skills in the following:
			1. Alphabetical arrangement
			2. Use of dictionary and glossary
			3. Use of encyclopedia, almanac, and other references
			4. Interpreting maps and pictures
			5. Skimming for a purpose
			6. Classifying ideas
			7. Following directions
			8. Summarizing
			9. Outlining
			10. Reading for accurate detail
			11. Using index and pronunciation keys
			12. Using charts and graphs
			13. Reading to answer questions and for enjoyment of literary style
			Introduce the following skills:
			1. Use of facts and figures
			2. Use of headings and type style—especially use of italics
			  a. To give importance to a word or expression in a sentence

Table 2–5 *Continued*

Word-Study Skills	Comprehension and Study Skills	Locating and Using Information (Study Skills)

pronunciation symbols
3. Review vowel sounds principles
B. Structural analysis
  1. Review compound words
  2. Review hyphenated words
  3. Review prefixes
    a. Review *un-, im-, dis-, re-, in-, anti-, inter-, mis-*
    b. Introduce *trans-, pre-, fore-, ir-, non-*
  4. Review suffixes
    a. Review *-en, -ment, -less, -ish, -ly, -ful, -y, -ed, -shy, -or, -er, -ous, -ness, -ward, -hood, -ation, -al*
    b. Introduce *-able, -ance, -ence, -ate, -est, -ent, -ity, -ic, -ist, -like*
  5. Review principles of syllabication
  6. Review accented syllables
  7. Apply word analysis in attacking words outside the basic vocabulary
		b. To show that a sentence has a special importance to the plot of the story
		c. To set off a special title used in a sentence or a reference
		3. Use of an index
		4. Use of library
		5. Use of table of contents
		6. Taking notes
		7. Reading of information material
		8. Reading poetry

Source: Adapted from G. Kaluger and C. J. Kolson, *Reading and Learning Disabilities* (Columbus, Ohio: Charles E. Merrill, 1969).

ESTIMATING READING COMPREHENSION

Once an instructional level in word recognition has been estimated, the teacher may want to determine the child's reading in context and comprehension skills. The directions for developing an informal test to tap these areas are presented in some detail in the following outline. The teacher should use personal judgment in deciding how much of this test to administer. For some children, it may be necessary to administer only one or two levels to ascertain if the child's comprehension level is equal to his or her skills in word recognition. In other cases, the teacher may desire a more comprehensive probe of the student's skills.

1. Selection of a standard basal series
    a. any series that goes from preprimer to the sixth level.
    b. materials that the child has not previously used.
2. Selection of passages from the basal reader
    a. Choose a selection that makes a complete story.
    b. Choose selections of about 50 words at the preprimer level; 100 words at the primer, first, and second levels; and 100–150 words at the upper levels.
    c. Choose two selections at each level: plan to use one for oral reading and one for silent reading, and take the selection from the middle of the book.
3. Construction of questions
    a. Build five questions for each selection at the preprimer level; six questions for each selection at primer, first, and second levels; and ten questions for each selection at level three and above.
    b. Avoid "yes" and "no" questions.
    c. Include a vocabulary in the questions at the same level as the vocabulary in the selection.
    d. Construct three kinds of questions at each level in about the following percentages: factual, 40 percent; inferential, 40 percent; vocabulary, 20 percent.
4. Construction and preparation of test
    a. Cut and mount the selections on oaktag *or*
    b. Note the pages in the book, put the questions on separate cards, and have the child read the selection from the text itself.

Since the child's word-recognition level would have been determined by one of the previously mentioned word-recognition tests, the teacher can begin this test of comprehension one or two levels below the child's instructional level in word recognition. The child is asked to read the first selection aloud, the teacher noting errors in the oral reading.

The following types of errors or miscues are frequently noted as children read aloud. A common way of coding these is shown to the right.

Type of Error or Miscue	Example
Omissions - of letter, word(s), punctuation	Jane and Bob (were) riding.
Reversals	saw
	He /called\ loudly. /
Substitutions	~~think~~ *Thank* (think)
Dialect difference	(d) be He ~~has~~ gone
Insertion of words or letters	old strange ∧ man
Nonword substitution	(s)tran The ~~train~~
Word-by-word reading or long pauses	down/the/street
Repetition that corrects a previously incorrect word	(c) Saturday Today is Sunday
Repetition that abandons a previously correct word	(ac) Saturday Today is Sunday
Repetition of incorrect substitution	(uc) Saturday Today is Sunday
Child asks for assistance	He |called|

ANALYSIS OF ORAL READING MISCUES[1]

The assessment procedures described to this point will provide teachers with a number of ideas for instruction. However, each classroom has within it a small number of boys and girls whose reading problems are so persistent that addi-

1. We use the term "miscue" rather than "error" for much the same reasons as those articulated by K. S. Goodman (1969); that is, the term "miscue" is less judgmental and avoids the implication that good reading cannot involve departures from the printed text (expected responses).

tional, more intensive analysis is required. This statement is based on the belief that children's errors or miscues are not random or capricious, except in the most unusual circumstances. On the contrary, such miscues occur in systematic patterns that can be identified by careful analysis of the child's oral reading. A major goal of such qualitative miscue analysis is to derive ideas on what strategies the child is using that result in the obtained performance patterns. Miscue analysis is helpful in stimulating teachers to develop hypotheses concerning the particular ineffective or inefficient strategies being utilized by the child in the oral reading act. Once the teacher has detected the pattern of the miscues presented by the child, appropriate instructional efforts can follow.

It is recognized that the complete and comprehensive analysis of each oral reading miscue of a particular child would be too time-comsuming for everyday classroom use. For example, the complete coding of the miscues of an average reader would call for approximately 2000 separate decisions. While such detailed analyses may be necessary for research purposes, we believe that a less detailed analysis can provide the classroom teacher with necessary and valuable insight. Teachers interested in the more comprehensive program for oral miscue analysis are referred to K. S. Goodman (1969), Y. M. Goodman (1972), and Weber (1968, 1970).

A word of caution on the use of miscue analytic procedures is appropriate. Good readers do not maximally utilize every cue presented in the printed page; that is, they do not make letter-by-letter discriminations, attending to each feature of each letter or even each word. In fact, some authorities (K. S. Goodman, 1969; F. Smith, 1971) have made strong cases that the really effective and efficient reader is one who is able to derive meaning from the printed page with a minimum use of cues. Thus a good reader forms hypotheses about how the sentence, the paragraph, the story will end. Subsequent reading behavior serves to confirm or disconfirm those hypotheses, which then become part of the "meaning" derived from the page, or become modified, respectively. Accordingly, teachers should not be overly concerned if, on occasion, a child emits a response that is at variance with the printed page. The teacher is properly concerned, however, when the miscues are of a nature and a frequency that the child's comprehension is impaired. Miscue analysis can help the teacher discover what faulty strategies and consistently misleading patterns or rules the child uses that interfere with the reading performance.

Table 2–6 presents the common miscue types. They are of interest to the teacher, but they provide insufficient detail as to the strategies that underlie their use. We suggest that teachers use Table 2–7 to further refine their examination of how the child responds to graphic symbols. In actual practice, teachers will find that the overwhelming number of miscues are substitutes of

Table 2– 6.   Analysis of Oral Reading Miscues: Response Types

Response Type	Description	Example
Omission	The child omits a word or words.	the big red ball/the big ball*
Insertion	The child adds a word or words.	the big ball/the big red ball
Sequence or order	The child makes a response that is expected elsewhere in the text—either immediately preceding or following (horizontal miscue), or immediately above or below the stimulus word (vertical miscue)	John and Harry/John and Harry found the dog./found the Harry
Substitution†	The child substitutes a word other than the text indicates. (If the child makes a substitution on the first occurrence of the stimulus word, then on later occurrences makes the expected response, no further analysis is required—see self-correction below.)	The dog ran/The dog red
Sounding out	The child makes several tentative partial responses, voiced or unvoiced.	Patty will play/Patty will p—
Self-correction	The child makes any of the above response types, then spontaneously corrects himself.	That is good/What is—that is good
Dialect	The child makes any of the above, but in accordance with the rules of his dialect.	The boys were scared/The boy be scared

* In each example, the printed text or expected response precedes the diagonal line; the child's miscue or the observed response follows.
† For more detailed analysis of substitutions, see Table 2–9.

one kind or another (D'angelo and Wilson, 1979). Hence a closer look at substitution miscues (Table 2–7) is warranted.

Table 2–7 has been organized to indicate that most children's reading substitutions fall readily into graphic, syntactic, and semantic categories. These categories are, of course, not mutually exclusive; any printed word has graphic, syntactic, and semantic characteristics; and a child may use faulty strategies that apply to these characteristics singly or in combination.

An additional point about Table 2–7 is worth making. It is not accidental that the miscue characteristics are analogous to the aspects of language—phonology, syntactics, and semantics. We point this out again to underline the intimate relationship of the reading act to the child's language proficiency (see the previous section in this chapter, also Chapter 8).

In performing a miscue analysis, teachers structure the situation much as they would in administering an informal reading inventory. In fact, if adequate

Table 2–7.   Analysis of Substitution Miscues

Type of Substitution Analysis*	Example†	Hypothesis or "What the Teacher Does Next"
I. Graphic analysis		
a. No discernible similarity (no shared letters)	king/lady	Probe whether the child is just guessing. Child may have virtually no word-attack skills (test further with commercial or teacher-made word-analysis test).
b. Words similar in overall configuration	leg/boy	Child may be utilizing configural clues—this is a strength that needs to be built on and supplemented with other word-analysis skills.
c. Reversal of single letter	bad/dad	Recheck child's ability to discriminate between b and d, also between other pairs, such as p and q. Provide left-right activities, also specific exercises for discrimination training. See also section on grammatical inappropriateness.
d. Reversal of two or more letters	was/saw	Provide activities as indicated in "c."
e. Beginning letters similar	play/plant	Child is correctly utilizing initial consonant blend cue. He needs to be encouraged to utilize middle and ending graphic cues, also to attend to context. Check other initial letters.
f. Middle letters similar	good/food	Same as "e" except with middle letters.
g. Ending letters similar	that/what	Same as "e" except with ending letters; also extra exercises with "wh" and "th" letters.
h. Single letter omission, deletion, or substitution	very/every	Child needs to be encouraged to look at entire word, also help on using syntactic and semantic.
i. Similar root word; suffix/prefix miscue	toys/toy	Check for presence of dialect; then activities dealing with singular and plural; also encourage attention to word endings.

* Category types are not mutually exclusive.
† In each example, the printed text or expected response precedes the diagonal line; the child's miscue or the observed response follows.

protocols have been kept from a previous administration of an IRI, the teacher may be able to perform usable analyses without asking the child to orally read again. If no IRI protocols are available, the teacher asks the child to read several paragraphs at the instructional level, marking a double-spaced copy with an appropriate code. The miscues emitted by the child are then subjected to an analysis as follows. Using Table 2–6, the teacher categorizes the types of responses made by the child. Special note is made of the child's efforts at

Table 2–7. *Continued*

Type of Substitution Analysis*	Example†	Hypothesis or "What the Teacher Does Next"
II. Syntactic analysis		
a. Beginning position in sentence	The boy .../Who ...	Check whether child can discriminate between these words when they occur later in the sentence; if so, he is relying heavily on syntactic cues (which is good), but needs more help on word analysis skills.
b. Middle or ending position in sentence	Mary ran far/Mary ran fast	Child is using syntactic and semantic features of the sentence (good); needs help as in "I.e."
c. Grammatical appropriateness (substituted word has same privilege of occurrence as stimulus word? Sentence grammatical up to and including miscue?)	John found his pet/John found his play	Child relying on initial letter cue (good), but is not showing grammatical awareness. Does child have mastery of oral language? If so, further testing and activities with cloze technique and "guess the end of the sentence game" might be used.
III. Semantic analysis		
a. Stimulus word and child's response unrelated or only partially related	Peter could/Peter cold	Child is using fairly sophisticated word-analysis skills (teacher can build on this), but needs sequential sentence speaking and reading opportunities. Other activities as in "II.c."
b. Meaning of child's response acceptable in sentence, but not related to stimulus sentence or paragraph	Jerry went home/Jerry went away	Child is thinking about the internal meaning of the sentence (good), but is not relating it to the meaning of the story. Child lacking word-analysis skills.

"sounding out" (these efforts are invaluable in helping the teacher derive hypotheses concerning the child's word-attack strategies; in fact, the child should be encouraged to "sound out" for this reason), self-correction (which similarly provides valuable insight into how the child monitors personal performance, and whether he or she utilizes feedback effectively), and dialect considerations. This latter issue is dealt with in Chapter 8 and will not be further explicated, except to say that the child's dialect will affect the interpretation given to graphic, syntactic, and semantic miscues; in fact, the presence or absence of a dialect will determine whether certain departures from the expected responses should be considered miscues at all.

Next, each miscue is analyzed according to its graphic, syntactic, and semantic characteristics. By noting the relative proportion of miscues in each category, the teacher can form a rough idea of whether the child's difficulty is more of the word-analysis type (mostly graphic miscues) or whether the child has linguistic or cognitive difficulty in forming hypotheses about the meaning of the material being read (such difficulty showing up more in syntactic and semantic miscues). We strongly urge teachers to attend closely to this latter miscue type, for it is our belief that linguistic and cognitive aspects of reading have been generally ignored by teachers.

Once the miscue analysis has been completed, the teacher will find it useful to summarize the results on a record sheet such as the one presented in Table 2–8. The use of this record sheet should make it apparent at a glance where the child's faulty strategies seem to cluster. The teacher will then have a sound basis for beginning instruction designed to build on strengths and to

Table 2–8. Sample Record Sheet for Oral Reading Miscues

Name _____ Age _____ Grade _____ Date _____
Sample of Reading Material on Which Analysis Is Based _____
Number of Words in Sample _____

Response Type Number of Occurrences	*Response Type Number of Occurrences*
Omission _____	Sounding Out _____
Insertion _____	Self-Correction _____
Sequence _____	Dialect _____
Substitution _____	

Substitution Analysis

Graphic analysis		*Syntactic analysis*	
a. No similarity	_____	a. Beginning position	_____
b. Configuration	_____	b. Middle or ending	
c. Single-letter reversal	_____	position	_____
d. Several letters reversed	_____	c. Grammatical	
e. Beginning letters similar	_____	appropriateness	_____
f. Middle letters similar	_____	Total syntactic miscues	_____
g. Ending letters similar	_____	*Semantic analysis*	
h. Single-letter miscue	_____	a. Meaning unrelated	_____
i. Root word	_____	b. Story meaning distorted	_____
Total graphic miscues	_____	Total semantic miscues	_____

redress weaknesses. The reading protocol should be readily available as instruction is planned.

TEACHING THE CHILD WITH A READING PROBLEM

Once the teacher has a clear picture of precisely where a child's difficulty in reading lies, an appropriate instructional strategy must be developed. This strategy will be implemented with the child on a trial basis, and if the child begins to make progress, the teacher will continue to utilize that approach. However, if discernible learning does not take place, it is appropriate to return to a previous point in the Instructional Cycle (see Chapter 1)—that is, retest the child with a view to generating an alternative hypothesis as to which approach might work with that child.

TASK ANALYSIS

Frequently, the teacher will find that a child is deficient in a word analysis or comprehension skill that had been previously taught. In such cases, it is helpful to analyze the skill in question to determine if it can be broken into component parts that can be separately and successfully taught to the child. Such an approach is called task analysis. In undertaking a task analysis of a given reading skill, the first step is to state clearly the objective of the task. This objective then needs to be scrutinized on the basis of the following criteria:

1. *Significance.*   How important is it for the child to master this skill? Is it basic or trivial? Is it necessary?
2. *Relevance.*   How relevant is this skill to the other things the child needs to learn or has learned?

Having determined that the task to be taught is a significant and relevant one, the teacher then identifies the subskills that are necessary for performing the target task. Once the subskills have been delineated, the teacher asks, "What does the child have to be able to do to perform each of the subskills?" The answer to this question leads to the development of subskills. This procedure is repeated until the teacher arrives at a subskill level where the child is able to perform the tasks. This type of analysis is called a *descending* analysis, because it starts with a target task and works backward to subsidiary tasks. The procedure of developing a descending task analysis is outlined in Figure

Teacher Does　　　　　　　　　　　　　*Teacher Asks*

Step I - Statement of Target Task

Is it significant?

Is it relevant?

Step II - Statement of Subskills

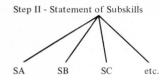

SA　　SB　　SC　　etc.

Are these subskills necessary
for performing target tasks?

Are these subskills sufficient
for performing target tasks?

Are these subskills relevant
for performing target tasks?

Are there any missing or
redundant subskills?

Can the child perform any of
these tasks?

Step III - Statement of Subskills

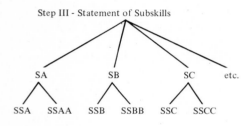

SA　　　　SB　　　　SC　　etc.

SSA　SSAA　SSB　SSBB　SSC　SSCC

Are these subsubskills necessary
for performing subskill tasks?

Are these subsubskills sufficient
for performing subskill tasks?

Are these subsubskills relevant
for performing subskill tasks?

Are there any missing or
redundant subsubskills?

Can the child perform any of
these tasks?

Continue further differentiation
into subskills until a level is
achieved where the child can
perform all the tasks.

**Figure
2–2.** Descending
Task Analysis

2–2. When the level is found at which the child can perform all the tasks, the teacher first reviews these tasks with the child. Actual instruction begins at the next higher level.

The following section presents a sample word-attack task analysis (Figure 2–4) and a comprehension analysis task (Figure 2–5). Note that these task analyses are developed in terms of the generalization (or rules) that the child must be able to utilize in order to perform the task. The generalization at each level is enclosed in a box.

Word-Attack Task Analysis

In this example, Figure 2–3, the objective is to help the child master the necessary skills, so that when the child sees a "y" preceded by a consonant at the end of a word, he or she will know what sound is represented by that "y." Using a descending task analysis, this target skill has been broken down into subskills and sub-subskills. The child is first tested on all tasks at the lowest level of the task analysis, or the sub-subskill level. Does the child know each

Figure 2–3. Example of Word-Attack Task Analysis

Target Skill Level

> When I meet another word that ends in y with a consonant before it: in a one-part word, the y will probably have the "long i" sound; in a two-or more part word, the y will probably have the "long e" sound.

Known words about which subskill level generalizations have been made

dry   funny   city   elementary
shy   berry   happily

Observations necessary
All are one-, two-, or more part words.
When I say the one-part words, each has a "long i" sound at the end.
When I say the two-or more part words, each has a "long e" sound at the end.
When I look at these words, each as a y at the end with a consonant before it.

Subskill Level

> When I meet another one-part word that ends in y with a consonant before it, y will probably have a "long i" sound.

known words about which subskill level generalizations have been made

my   cry
dry   shy
fly

Observations necessary
All are one part words.
When I say these words, each has a "long i" sound at the end.
When I look at these words, I see a y at the end with a consonant before it.

> When I meet two-or more part word that ends in y with a consonant before it, the y will probably have a "long e" sound.

Known words about which subskill level generalizations have been made

funny   many   city
silly   pony   happily
foggy   berry   elementary

Observations necessary
All are two or more part words.
When I say these words, each has a "long e" sound at the end.
When I look at these words, I see a y at the end with a consonant before it.

Sub-subskill Level

> When I see another one-part word that ends in y with a consonant before it, it will probably rhyme with....

> When I see another two-part word that ends in *any*, it will probably rhyme with....

> When I see another two-part word that ends in *erry*, it will probably rhyme with....

> When I see another two-part word that ends in *itty*, it will probably rhyme with....

> When I see another two-part word that ends in *illy*, it will probably rhyme with....

> When I see another two-part word that ends in *oggy*, it will probably rhyme with....

> When I see another two-part word that ends in *unny*, it will probably rhyme with....

> When I see another two-part word that ends in *ony*, it will probably rhyme with....

> When I see another two-part word that ends in *anny*, it will probably rhyme with....

Level at which child can perform all tasks and make all required generalizations

Known words

my   cry   fly   shy
by   dry   try   sly
      fry   why

Observations necessary
All are one part words.
When I say these words, they all rhyme.
When I look at these words, I see a y at the end with a consonant before it.

Known words

many   any

many	berry (very)	silly	kitty (city)	foggy	pony	funny
any	ferry	hilly	witty	soggy	Tony	bunny
	merry	Willy	gritty	groggy		sunny
	Sherry	frilly				
	Perry					

Observations All are two part words.
All have any, erry, illy, itty, oggy, ony, unny at the end and rhyme within those various rhyming elements.

* Adapted from Tobia, S., Elliott, B. and Rubenstone, C. Developed under the direction of M. S. Johnson at Temple University Laboratory School, Psychology of Reading Department, 1978.

set of one- and two-part words? Can the child make the indicated observations? If the child does not know the words or is unable to make the observations, he or she is taught to do so. Then the child is encouraged to make the generalizations shown in the boxes at the sub-subskill level. Only when the child can make these generalizations does the teaching move up to the next level—the subskill level. The procedures of testing and teaching words, observations, and generalizations are repeated at this level. When the child demonstrates mastery at the subskill level, he or she is ready to be exposed to tasks at the target skill level. When the child can make the generalization enclosed in the box at the top of Figure 2–3, the program is complete. The child can successfully figure out the sound of the "y" at the end of one- and two-part words.

Comprehension Task

In this example, Figure 2–4, the objective is to get the child to the point where he or she will be able to use temporal sequence clues to determine the logical order of a series of events in a story. Here again, a descending task analysis has been developed to show the levels of prerequisite tasks necessary to successfully perform the target task.

Some comments are necessary to provide perspective for this task analysis. First, sequence "clue words" have been categorized as "exact" and "nonexact." The categorizing of these clue words should help the student draw conclusions about the use of the clue words in determining sequence, since exact words (first, last) require a slightly different approach than do nonexact words (next, later).

Furthermore, the model presented in Figure 2–4 focuses only on the exact words (except at the target task level, which draws both categories together). The approach to teaching for the two categories is virtually the same. The main difference lies in the need for elaborate use of context clues when dealing with nonexact words. This technique does become evident in target task level procedures.

Additionally, at the sub-subskill level, only one subgroup of exact words is illustrated (again because it is the same basic procedure for all subgroups). Numerical clue words, such as first and second, are the focus of the procedures. Although most children come to school already familiar with the concept behind these words, it is necessary to review them in relation to the reading and sequencing task.

Finally, it should be noted that interpretative skills, background experience, and semantic knowledge is necessary in utilizing both the exact and nonexact words. Therefore, the developmental level of the student should be considered before a target skill such as this one is presented.

Figure 2–4. Example of Comprehension Task Analysis

Target Skill Level

> When I meet any clue words or phrases that tell me *when*, I can use them to determine sequence.

Known words about which Level 2 *generalizations have been made*
Baseline words—"exact" and "nonexact" clues

Observations necessary
All words or phrases tell me *when*.
Some words are "exact" clue words and some are "nonexact".

Subskill Level

> When I meet any "exact" clue words or phrases that tell me *when*, I can use them to determine sequence.

Known words about which Level 1 *generalizations have been made*
Baseline words—"exact" clues

> When I meet any "nonexact" clue words or phrases that tell me *when*, I can use them to determine sequence.

Observations necessary
All are words or phrases that tell *when*.
All are "exact" clue words or phrases.

Known words
Baseline words—"nonexact" clues

Observations necessary
All are words or phrases that tell *when*.
All are "nonexact" clue words or phrases.

Sub-Subskill Level

> When I meet . . . I know they tell me *when*, and I can use them to determine time order.

Known words
first
second
third
fourth
fifth
etc.

> When I meet . . . I know they tell me *when*, and I can use them to determine time order.

Known words
today   last
tomorrow   finally
yesterday   etc.

> When I meet . . . I know they tell me *when*, and I can use them to determine time order.

Known phrases (words)
in the beginning
day before yesterday
at the end
next to last
etc.

> When I meet . . . I know they tell me *when*, and I can use them to determine time order.

Known words
next   before
then   later
after   etc.
now

> When I meet . . . I know they tell me *when*, and I can use them to determine time order.

Known phrases
by then
last week
later that day
etc.

Level at which child can perform all tasks and make all required generalizations

Monday	January	noon	1978
Tuesday	February	midnight	etc.
Wednesday	March		
Thursday	April		
Friday	May	6:00	
Saturday	June	6:15	
Sunday	July	7:30	
	August	etc.	
	September		
	October		
	November		
	December		

* Adapted from Tobia, S., Elliot, B., and Rubenstone, C. Developed under the direction of M. S. Johnson, Temple University Laboratory School, Psychology of Reading Department, 1978.

TEACHING COMPREHENSION SKILLS

As mentioned earlier, merely being able to recognize words is insufficient for receiving communication from the printed page. Understanding what the words, sentences, and paragraphs mean is the main purpose of reading. It follows, then, that the teaching of comprehension skills is a major objective for every teacher.

Fortunately, there has been substantial research on comprehension in the last few years. Furthermore, the number and quality of commercial materials designed to improve comprehension have also increased recently. The teacher who is serious about helping children understand what they read is thus in a better position than ever before.

The use of questions to improve comprehension can help children understand and remember what they read. Asking the child questions *before* he or she reads a passage, as in a Directed Reading Activity, helps the child focus attention on the information in the text that will help him or her answer the questions. However, this approach can direct the child's attention away from those parts of the narrative that do not contain information needed to answer questions. If, on the other hand, the child is told that he or she will be questioned *after* reading a passage, the child may try to remember as much as possible about all of the passage. The teacher must ascertain whether the child can attend to the passage without the need for specific guidance.

Ruddell (1974) has developed a model of teacher questioning that facilitates moving the pupil's thinking from the literal or factual memory level toward the higher cognitive processes. These sequential steps have been summarized by Singer (1978) and are summarized in Table 2–9.

Pupil responses to inferential, as opposed to factual, questions tend to be longer and more complex and utilize the higher cognitive processes (Smith, 1978). Furthermore, the quality of pupil responses can be improved by encouraging the child to delay the response for a few seconds, to take some "think-time" before trying to answer the teacher's questions (Gambrell, 1980).

Teacher-posed questions serve as a valuable purpose in focusing the child's attention on the material and in helping the child learn the type of questions to ask himself or herself about a reading passage. The ultimate goal in reading for comprehension is not to read to answer someone else's questions, but to learn to ask appropriate questions for oneself as one reads. As noted in the earlier part of this chapter, the good reader develops hypotheses or questions as he or she reads, then reads on to see if the questions are answered the way he or she thinks they will be. Singer (1978) has called this process "active comprehension," and it occurs before, during, and after reading. Getting students to develop self-questioning skills has been found to be particularly helpful to students of low verbal ability (André and Anderson, 1978–79).

Table 2– 9.   Teacher-Student Interaction in Questioning Strategy

Teacher-Student Interaction		
Who Talks	*Function*	
Teacher	*Question*	
Student	*Response*	

Questioning Strategy

Type	Purpose	Question
Focusing	Initiate discussion or refocus on the issue.	What did you like best about story? What was the question we started to answer?
Controlling	Direct or dominate the discussion.	First, would you review the plot?
Ignoring or rejecting	Maintain current trend in discussion. Disregard a student's interest.	Would you mind if we don't go into that now?
Extending	Obtain more information at a particular level of discussion.	What other information do we have about the hero?
Clarifying	Obtain a more adequate explanation. Draw out a student.	Would you explain what you mean?
Raising	Have discussion move from factual to interpretative, inferential, or abstraction and generalization level.	We now have enough examples. What do they have in common? (Abstract) Was it always true for his behavior? (Generalization)

Response Level

Factual or literal (what the author said)
Interpretative (integration of ideas of inference)
Applied (transfer of ideas or judgment that idea is subsumed under broader generalization)
Evaluative (using cognitive or affective criteria for judging issue)

Source: H. Singer. Active comprehension: from answering to asking questions. *The Reading Teacher,* May 1978, 903. Reprinted with permission of the author and the International Reading Association.

Teaching children to generate their own questions entails the following procedures:

1. The teacher provides models of good questions (following Ruddell, 1974; or some other strategy designed to elicit higher level thinking).
2. The teacher phases out the questioning, and, depending on the ages of the pupils, uses either a picture, a title, an introductory paragraph, or another device to encourage the students to begin asking questions.
3. The questions generated by the students are used to set the purposes for reading and to encourage speculation about the main idea of the passage or story.

4. The students read the text to a point where their initial speculation is answered or intensified. At this point the teacher encourages further questioning by the students. Depending on the passage, these questions may concern generalizations, concepts, predictions of plot resolution, interpretation, character development, or making inferences.

The last two steps are repeated until the passage is completed. Throughout, the teacher's role is one of eliciting student questions, encouraging students to recognize answers to their own questions, and guiding students to ask higher level questions.

SUSTAINED SILENT READING

One goal of reading instruction is to develop in students a desire to read. Yet frequently, reading instruction is so intensive, so structured, and so "hard" that students have little or no opportunity to read material of their choice. To encourage students to develop a desire to read, as well as to consolidate learned reading skills, many teachers have scheduled a period of sustained silent reading (SSR) into the school day. The procedures and guidelines (summarized from Cline and Kretke, 1980; Gambrell, 1978; McCracken and McCracken, 1978; Minton, 1980; Moore, Jones, and Miller, 1980) are as follows:

Preparation for SSR

In large part, the success of the program depends on the following procedures to be performed *before* SSR is implemented.

1. Advertise and promote SSR well before attempting to implement it. Use bulletin boards, book displays, and letters to parents, as well as reading aloud to the class and sharing thoughts about good books with pupils.
2. Assemble reading materials of many different topics, types, and difficulty levels. Include books, news magazines, newspapers, or other appropriate reading material.
3. Develop the rules for implementing SSR. This includes deciding what time of day it should take place and where students may engage in SSR (in desks, on mats, in reading nook, in library, etc.). For very young children, the SSR period might be only five minutes in length; older pupils enjoy reading for fifteen to twenty minutes. The rules for SSR should make clear that material selection occurs *before* the actual reading time begins.

Implementation of SSR

A few precautions will enhance the probability of success for an SSR program.

1. Ensure that *everyone,* especially the teacher (no grading of tests!), reads silently and without interruption during SSR.
2. Do not allow changes of reading material during the period.
3. Reluctant or resistant readers may sit quietly at their desks; they may not walk around the room or otherwise interrupt the readers.
4. There are no book reports, questions to answer, or other follow-up activities to SSR.
5. There should be a means of sharing what has been read with the teacher or other pupils for those who wish to do so. Bulletin boards, informal commenting, or a special weekly time for promoting books may be used.
6. If possible, invite parents or other school personnel to participate in SSR when possible.

In general, SSR promotes children's reading skills and improves their attitudes toward reading. These findings are most consistent when the teacher unfailingly participates in SSR and when a good selection of reading materials is available.

TUTORING INDIVIDUAL CHILDREN IN READING

Today, adults, high school students, and even elementary pupils are often employed effectively as tutors in the schools. Even though these paraprofessionals may instruct children in basic school subjects, the primary qualifications for a tutor are not necessarily academic, a fact that is reflected in the following guidelines for selecting individuals to serve as tutors; for example, the tutor must:

1. Be dependable, for missing only one or two sessions will destroy the tutoring relationship and allow the child to regress.
2. Be patient and ready to go over material a number of times before the child has finally learned it.
3. Have an understanding of the student's problems and feelings.
4. Have integrity; for example, the tutor must be truthful and never leave the student with the impression that he or she is doing much better than is actually is the case.
5. Be capable of handling well interpersonal relations.

Beyond these qualifications, the tutor must be interested in helping children, accept responsibility readily, and follow directions.

Before a tutorial program can be initiated efficiently, certain things must be done and agreed to. First, the child's problems in reading must be assessed carefully. Second, those areas in which the tutor will work must be decided upon. Third, the approach and materials that are to be used should be selected. Fourth, the period of time to be spent on any activity should be estimated. It is very important that the tutor know exactly what is expected, what is to be done, and how to do it. Therefore, some training should be conducted before the tutor begins the program. Left to his or her own devices without proper training and supervision, the tutor may unwittingly create problems and end up being "more trouble than he or she is worth."

Record Keeping

Each tutor should be given a notebook (preferably looseleaf) in which there are three distinct kinds of pages. The first should be the Tutor's Lesson Plan. On this page, the activities, the procedures, and the amount of time to be

Name __Stanley Miller__	Date Started __10/7/76__
School __West Elementary__	Tutor __Mrs. Clark__
Grade __4__	Reading Level __Preprimer__

Description of the Problem

Stanley has a limited sight vocabulary, poor attention and concentration, and has had almost no success in school.

9:00 – 9:10 Ask ~~what~~ Stanley what he thinks will happen to the Chinese brothers. Then finish the 5 Chinese Brothers.

9:10 – 9:20 Review the Dolch Sight Vocabulary Words that he missed yesterday. Have him put those that he still doesn't know on 3" x 5" cards.

9:20 – 9:30 Use SRA Lab II Rate Builder, Red 3, as a listening exercise. Help him to set a purpose for listening. Remember to keep a record of the number of answers that he gets correct.

Figure 2–5.
Tutor's Lesson Plan

> Tutor _____ Mrs Clark _____ Student _____ Stanley Miller _____
> Date _____ 10/7/76 _____ Grade _4_ School _____ West Elementary _____
>
> Stanley ~~do~~ could think what might happen but he listened and said, "Now I know!" when we came to it. We reviewed the Dolch Words and he missed 6 of them. He asked me if he could take them home. I told him I'd check with you. He answered all the questions on the 'rate builder' correctly. This is 4 in row — he may be ready for the next color.

Figure 2–6.
Tutor's Log Sheet

devoted to each student can be listed. If special materials are required, they should be mentioned and an indication of where they may be obtained should be made. A sample lesson plan is shown in Figure 2–5.

The second kind of page that should be included in the Tutor's Notebook is a Tutor's Log Sheet. On this, the tutor may record any observations about the progress of the child on a particular day that seems pertinent. The availability of this sheet will foster ongoing communications between the tutor and the busy classroom teacher. An example is given in Figure 2–6.

Another kind of sheet is the Teacher's Note. On this page, the teacher can make comments, suggestions, and/or recommendations for changes in the Tutor's Lesson Plan. For an example, see Figure 2–7.

Figure 2–7.
Teacher's Note

> Tutor _____ Mrs Clark _____ Student _____ Stanley Miller _____
> Teacher _____ Mr Lobb _____ Date _____ 10/7/96 _____
>
> Tell Stanley that we'll need the cards for something else later. He can take them home when we are finished. Try the next color for a listening activity. Have him select another book for the oral reading.

Tutor Training

Not only must the teacher assess, prescribe, and gather materials, but also the teacher must make sure that the tutor can and does carry out the program as specified. To accomplish this, the teacher will usually have to provide the tutor with at least some minimal training (the tutor will have to be taught to complete the forms described in the previous section, to become familiar with the basic methods and strategies used by the teacher, etc.). Of course, it is not possible for the experienced teacher to transfer to the tutor all of the skills and expertise that he or she has acquired as a result of completing a four-year college program and several years of teaching; but the teacher can make sure that the tutor knows what to do and has the materials to do it.

Whenever possible, the tutor's training should be by example. The teacher should work with a child and demonstrate items of importance in a tutorial lesson, such as:

1. Qualities of good oral reading (creating interest in a story, setting purposes, anticipating outcomes, etc.).
2. Various ways to use flashcards for drill.
3. Teaching the child to trace words correctly, if this technique is used.
4. Selecting, or helping the child to select, an appropriate book.
5. Using a positive (reinforcing) attitude in all activities.
6. Keeping comprehensive records.
7. Various materials; their location and use.
8. Physical surroundings (e.g., adequate lighting).
9. Use of a dictionary when necessary.

During the training period, rapport between the tutor and the teacher must be established. If this is accomplished properly, the tutor will feel free to ask the teacher any question about the program. Rapport can be enhanced and maintained if, when asked a question, the teacher will carefully consider a response before answering. For example, it is far better for the teacher to say, "I'm sorry; I should have told you that," than to say, "I thought that you'd use your common sense." Negative criticism can shut off communication quickly.

Even when the tutors have received a great deal of training, problems will still arise, because a tutor cannot be expected to learn everything that he or she needs to know all at once. As a result, a tutor may make gross mistakes occasionally. For example, the tutor may try to get the child to "sound out" words that are not phonetic; or to make sure that a pupil is reading, the tutor may encourage the child to whisper or to move his or her lips when reading silently. From time to time, a tutor may inadvertently threaten a child with such statements as "If you don't do this, I won't like you" or "I can't understand why you don't know this; I've told you a hundred times!" The tutor may not recognize when a child is frustrated. There are many things, some great, some small, that can go wrong in a tutoring program, so the importance of adequate preparation, planning, tutor training, and supervision cannot be stressed too often.

If possible, tutors should be paid. Adult volunteers can fill the necessary gap; but they sometimes leave for a paying job, especially after they get some experience and can qualify for employment in a day-care center, a nursery school, or a private preschool; and they are often undependable. On the other hand, there is a wealth of untapped student talent in the school district that can serve as volunteer tutors. For example, older students can work with younger pupils ("cross-age tutoring"); and children of the same age can, and often do, tutor each other ("peer tutoring").

There exists a fairly impressive body of research that testifies to the merits of student tutoring in reading (e.g., Chiang, Thorpe, and Darch, 1980; Cloward, 1967; Lane, Pollack, and Sher, 1972; Erickson, 1971; Kopp, 1972; J. L. Thomas, 1972). This literature will be useful for those individuals desiring evidence of the value of peer tutoring in reading. Teachers who want to know the particulars involved in implementing and maintaining peer tutoring programs will find most useful the recent book by Ehly and Larsen (1980), *Peer Tutoring for Individualized Instruction.*

INVOLVING PARENTS IN READING PROGRAMS

Many teachers would like to see the parents of their classroom pupils involved in the school programs. Nowhere is this more needed than in the area of reading. Properly motivated and informed, parents can be strong partners with schools in helping children learn to read and to maintain interest in reading. Why then are parents so rarely involved?

Part of the difficulty seems to be due to fears on the part of teachers and principals. Some of these fears are that the parents are basically not interested in their children's reading; that they wouldn't come to school if invited, especially the parents who need to come; that they wouldn't understand the volunteer program; and if they did understand, they would want to control the program (Granowsky, Middleton, and Mumford, 1979).

Yet it has been found that parents are, in fact, interested in their children's reading; that they know whether their children are having reading problems or not; and that they help their children in reading to the best of their knowledge (Nicholson, 1980).

Several schools have successfully involved parents in reading programs (Granowsky et al., 1979; Criscuolo, 1979, 1980). The success of such programs seems to be due to the following factors:

1. *Making parents feel welcome at school.* This may take the form of scheduling parent conferences to accommodate parents' work responsibilities, providing a resource room where parents may browse or borrow reading materials, or arranging for parent observation and participation in reading programs.

2. *Keeping parents informed about the school's reading program.* Many parents are confused about the purpose and approach of the school's reading program. They may wonder why the alphabet is not being taught or why their child does or does not have reading homework. Perhaps a newsletter, parent brochure, bulletin board, or Parent Information Night, as well as informal means of communication can be used.

3. *Keeping parents informed about their children's reading progress.* Keeping parents informed means more than sending home a reading grade or a report card three or four times a year. Most parents want to know where their child is in learning essential skills (descriptive, criterion-referenced information). Such information can be conveyed through regular progress reports, informal notes, and parent conferences as well as the typical report card. Information about a child's progress can profitably be accompanied by specific ideas about how parents can help their children in reading. The suggestions may be general, such as reading aloud to children, helping them "sound out" hard words, or listening to them reading. Suggestions may also be specific—related to an individual child's difficulty or suggestions for reading enrichment.

VARIOUS APPROACHES TO THE TEACHING OF READING

As the preceding sections suggest, *how* a teacher uses reading materials is of crucial importance in teaching reading. It is becoming increasingly apparent that there is no one "best" approach to teaching reading. Research studies comparing the effectiveness of one approach with another have been singularly unproductive (e.g., Bond and Dykstra, 1967). Researchers and teachers alike are beginning to suspect that a particular reading method used successfully in a particular setting with a particular teacher interacting with a particular set of children cannot be transported to other settings, teachers, and children with predictable results (Guthrie, 1980). This is not to say, however, that the choice of an approach with a particular child or a particular class does not remain one of the most significant instructional decisions made by a teacher.

To make informed decisions on these matters, teachers need to know a variety of programs and procedures that are available. The provision of this information is the purpose of this section. Specifically, discussions include classroom approaches, and special remedial approaches.

CLASSROOM APPROACHES

Table 2–10 summarizes descriptions of various approaches to the teaching of reading that are used often in regular classroom settings. In a subsequent section, we will address reading approaches that are more commonly used in resource rooms or other more intensive, clinical-type settings. Classroom approaches are used for regular developmental reading programs. They can also be adapted for the amelioration of specific reading problems in one child or a group of children with similar difficulties.

Selecting Materials of Appropriate Level for Children

No matter which of the preceding approaches is selected as being the most appropriate for a particular child, it is necessary to identify materials that match the child's instructional level, where reading texts and sometimes textbooks in such subjects as social studies are clearly designated by grade level of difficculty. For the secondary level, however, and for supplementary or trade books at all levels, teachers need to be able to assess the difficulty level, or readability of the material.

One way that readability can be assessed is through the use of one of the readability formulas that have been developed (e.g., Fry, 1977). Basically these readability formulas are based on the finding that text with longer words and longer sentences is generally harder to read than text with shorter words and sentences.

While Klare (1976) found that readability is significantly related to comprehension, readability formulas do have their shortcomings. Irwin and Davis (1980) have recognized these shortcomings and have attempted to address them in their *Readability Checklist* (Figure 2–8). It should be noted that the Readability Checklist is divided into two major components—"Understandability" and "Learnability." This checklist is recommended for

Table 2–10. Classroom Reading Approaches

Type of Approach	Where Available	Advantages/Disadvantages/Special Comments
Complete Basals. These usually consist of reading texts, teacher's manual, and supplementary materials such as workbooks. They are often sequenced in a series from K to Grade 6 or 8. The instructional approach is one of introducing a controlled sight vocabulary coupled with an analytic phonics emphasis.	Holt, Rinehart and Winston Ginn 720 Series Scott, Foresman Harcourt, Brace, Jovanovich American Book Company Houghton Mifflin Rand-McNally MacMillan Harper and Row Allyn and Bacon Laidlaw	1. Lend themselves well to the 3-reading-group arrangement; less well to individualizing 2. Content usually designed for the "typical" child; often not appealing to inner-city children or rural children 3. Generally well-sequenced and comprehensive; attend to most aspects of developmental reading 4. Most have complete pupil packets of supplementary materials, saving teacher searching time 5. Sufficiently detailed and integrated that successful use is possible for a teacher lacking in confidence or experience
Synthetic Phonics Basals. Similar to above in some ways, but emphasis is on mastering component phonics skills, then putting together into words.	Open Court Reading Program Lippincott's Basic Reader Series Distar Reading Swirl Community Skills Program (SW Regional Laboratory)	Same as above 6. Evidence is that a synthetic approach to word attack is rarely utilized by good readers.
Linguistic Phonemic Approaches. Vocabulary that is used is highly controlled and conforms to the sound patterns of English (e.g., Nan, Dan, man, fan, ran, etc.). Most programs contain children's texts, teacher manual and supplementary materials.	Let's Read (Bloomfield) SRA Basic Reading Series Merrill Linguistic Readers Porgrammed Reading (Webster, McGraw-Hill) SRA Lift-Off to Reading Palo Alto Program (Harcourt, Brace, Jovanovich)	1. Content and usage in stories (especially early ones) sometimes contrived because of controlled vocabulary 2. Same as for Complete Basals

Table 2–10.   *Continued*

Type of Approach	*Where Available*	*Advantages/Disadvantages/ Special Comments*
Individualized Reading. Each child reads materials of own choice and at own rate. Word recognition and comprehension skills are taught as individual children need them. Monitoring of progress is done through individual teacher conferences. Careful record-keeping is necessary.	Trade books of many different types, topics, and levels	1. Children are interested in content 2. Promotes good habits of selection of reading materials 3. Need an extensive collection of books from which to choose 4. Teacher needs comprehensive knowledge of reading skills to make sure all are covered 5. Required record-keeping can be cumbersome
Diagnostic–Prescriptive Programs. These consist of entry-testing and exit-testing of skills related to specific skills. Students who pass entry test go on to other needed areas. Reading objectives fully stated.	*Print* Wisconsin Design for Reading Skill (National Computer Systems) Fountain Valley Reading Support System (Richard Zweig) Ransom Program (Addison-Wesley) *Non-Print, Computer Assisted* Stanford University Project Harcourt Brace CAI Remedial Reading Program	1. Skills are usually well sequenced 2. Pupils work at own pace 3. Learning may be boring, repetitive, or mechanistic 4. Provide for on-going assessment and feedback 5. De-emphasize the language basis of reading (interaction and communication with other people) 6. Only those skills that lend themselves to the format are taught
Language Experience Approach. Based on teacher recording of child's narrated experiences. These stories become basis for reading. May be based on level of group or individual child. Stories are collected and made into a "book."	Teacher-made materials	1. Relationship to child's experience is explicit 2. Firmly establishes reading as a language/communicative act 3. Provides no systematic skill development (left up to the teacher to improvise) 4. Can become reinforcing only at child's existing level, rather than pushing him or her on 5. Highly adaptable to pupils with unique needs and backgrounds

Figure 2–8.   Readability Checklist

This checklist is designed to help you evaluate the readability of your classroom texts. It can best be used if you rate your text while you are thinking of a specific class. Be sure to compare the textbook to a fictional ideal rather than to another text. Your goal is to find out what aspects of the text are or are not less than ideal. Finally, consider supplementary workbooks as part of the textbook and rate them together. Have fun!

Rate the questions below using the following rating system:

5—Excellent
4—Good
3—Adequate
2—Poor
1—Unacceptable
NA—Not applicable

Further comments may be written in the space provided.

Textbook title: _____

Publisher: _____

Copyright date: _____

Understandability

A. ____Are the assumptions about students' vocabulary knowledge appropriate?

B. ____Are the assumptions about students' prior knowledge of this content area appropriate?

C. ____Are the assumptions about students' general experiential backgrounds appropriate?

D. ____Does the teacher's manual provide the teacher with ways to develop and review the students' conceptual and experiential backgrounds?

E. ____Are new concepts explicitly linked to the students' prior knowledge or to their experiential backgrounds?

F. ____Does the text introduce abstract concepts by accompanying them with many concrete examples?

G. ____Does the text introduce new concepts one at a time with a sufficient number of examples for each one?

H. ____Are definitions understandable and at a lower level of abstraction than the concept being defined?

I. ____Is the level of sentence complexity appropriate for the students?

J. ____Are the main ideas of paragraphs, chapters, and subsections clearly stated?

K. ____Does the text avoid irrelevant details?

L. ____Does the text explicitly state important complex relationships (e.g., causality, conditionality, etc.) rather than always expecting the reader to infer them from the context?

M. ____Does the teacher's manual provide lists of accessible resources containing alternative readings for the very poor or very advanced readers?

N. ____Is the readability level appropriate (according to a readability formula)?

Learnability

Organization

A. ____Is an introduction provided for in each chapter?

B. ____Is there a clear and simple organizational pattern relating the chapters to each other?

C. ____Does each chapter have a clear, explicit, and simple organizational structure?

D. ____Does the text include resources such as an index, glossary, and table of contents?

E. ____Do questions and activities draw attention to the organizational pattern of the material (e.g., chronological, cause and effect, spatial, topical, etc.)?

F. ____Do consumable materials interrelate well with the textbook?

Reinforcement

A. ____Does the text provide opportunities for students to practice using new concepts?

B. ____Are there summaries at appropriate intervals in the text?

C. ____Does the text provide adequate iconic aids such as maps, graphs, illustrations, etc. to reinforce concepts?

D. ____Are there adequate suggestions for usable supplementary activities?

E. ____Do these activities provide for a broad range of ability levels?

F. ____Are there literal recall questions provided for the students' self review?

G. ____Do some of the questions encourage the students to draw inferences?

H. ____Are there discussion questions which encourage creative thinking?

I. ____Are questions clearly worded?

Motivation

A. ____Does the teacher's manual provide introductory activities that will capture students' interest?

B. ____Are chapter titles and subheadings concrete, meaningful, or interesting?

C. ____Is the writing style of the text appealing to the students?

D. ____Are the activities motivating? Will they make the students want to pursue the topic further?

E. ____Does the book clearly show how the knowledge being learned might be used by the learner in the future?

F. ____Are the cover, format, print size, and pictures appealing to the students?

G. ____Does the text provide positive and motivating models for both sexes as well as for other racial, ethnic, and socioeconomic groups?

Readability analysis

Weaknesses

1) On which items was the book rated the lowest?

2) Did these items tend to fall in certain categories?

3) Summarize the weaknesses of this text.

4) What can you do in class to compensate for the weaknesses of this text?

Assets

1) On which items was the book rated the highest?

2) Did these items fall in certain categories?

3) Summarize the assets of this text.

4) What can you do in class to take advantage of the assets of this text?

Source: J.W. Irwin and C.A. Davis. Assessing readability; the checklist approach. *Journal of Reading,* November 1980, 129–130. Reprinted with permission of the authors and the International Reading Association.

use because each item has been included on the basis of empirical evidence linking that question to reading, understanding, and retention.

SPECIAL REMEDIAL APPROACHES

The following teaching techniques are often used in schools or classes that specialize in children with reading disabilities. A regular classroom teacher would not usually be expected to use any of these clinical approaches in their entirety. However, they can be modified and adapted to meet the needs of specific children.

The Fernald (VAKT) Approach

If a child has a severe word-learning difficulty, and visual–auditory approaches have been unsuccessful, a modification of the Fernald (1943) Word Learning Technique is recommended. Although several authors refer to Fernald's remedial technique for teaching disabled readers as a kinesthetic method, the system is actually multisensory, involving four modalities simultaneously [i.e., visual, auditory, kinesthetic, and tactile (or VAKT)]. The approach is cognitive, for the words learned always originate with the reader and have contextual or meaningful association.

Fernald, who opened a clinic school at UCLA in 1920, was concerned with the emotional components of failure to learn. "The child who fails in his school work is always an emotional problem" (1943, p. 7). The circular aspect of this dilemma was approached in two ways: by analyzing the problem and by reconditioning the student. Both are positive approaches to remediation that call the child's attention to what he has already learned and assure him that he can learn any words that he wants to learn. To maintain a positive learning climate the following are avoided: (1) emotionally laden situations, (2) the use of methods associated with previous failure, (3) embarrassing situations, and (4) references to the child's problems. Poor readers are divided into two groups: total or extreme disability and partial disability. The VAKT method is used with children from both groups when the disability is failure to recognize words.

Perception of the word as a whole is basic to the Fernald method. The child begins remediation by story writing, initially about anything that interests him, and later concerning his various school subjects. The child "asks" for any word he does not know. It is written for him, learned by him, and used immediately in his story. What he has written is typed for him so that he may read it while its content is still fresh in his mind. For children with extreme disability, almost every word is necessarily taught.

Stage I uses a multisensory approach. As the child requests a word, it is written or printed for him with black crayon in blackboard-size script on a piece of heavy paper. He traces the word with firm, two-finger contact (tactile-kinesthetic), and says the word aloud in syllables (auditory) as he traces. He sees the word while he is tracing (visual), and hears it as he says it (auditory). He repeats the process until he can write the word correctly twice, without looking at the sample. When tracing or writing, the word is always written as a unit, without stopping. If he errs, the child begins again with the first step. Copying a word by alternately looking at the sample and writing a few letters is forbidden. After the lesson, the words are filed alphabetically, to provide a record or source of the words learned.

After a period of tracing, the tactile phase is discontinued and Stage II is begun. Here the child learns a new word by following the looking, saying, and writing steps of Stage I. Vocabulary is still learned in context and involves VAK. There is no arbitrary time limit for the tracing period and usually the child tends to drop tracing of his own accord.

Stage III dispenses with the kinesthetic mode, and the child learns a new word merely by looking at the sample and saying it to himself.

Stage IV is achieved when the child has the ability to recognize new words by their similarity to words or to parts of words that he has already learned (i.e., when he can generalize his reading skills). Teaching phonics is not considered necessary, for this generalizing process presumably occurs without phonetic analysis. At this stage the child reads to satisfy his curiosity.

The amount of reading necessary before discontinuing remediation and returning the child to the regular classroom reading situation depends on the educational level he must reach. Older children spend more time in Stage IV, as they do not return to the regular instructional setting until they are able to read well enough to make progress at their own instructional level.

In addition to those already stated, Fernald holds several principles:

1. Children are never read to; they must do their own reading.
2. The child never sounds out words, unless he does it while scanning a paragraph for unknown words before beginning to read that paragraph.
3. At any stage, material must be suited to the child's age and intelligence.

Careful scheduling is important, as the teacher cannot plan to work with one child unless all of the other children are involved in some purposeful activity. The child's resentment at being taken away from gym or art also might outweigh any positive accomplishment. It should be emphasized that the Fernald approach (VAKT) is basically a word-learning technique, and the child should have directed reading instruction in a group, or individually, to develop comprehension skills.

The Gillingham (Orton) Phonics Approach
(Gillingham and Stillman, 1970)

This is a remedial, phonics-oriented reading program based on the theoretical work of Orton. The systematic approaches to reading, spelling, and writing are adapted to all levels from age 6 through high school. This "alphabetic system" is based on the premise that children who fail to read by group methods do so because group programs rely upon visual–receptive strength. In contrast, Gillingham's training system stresses auditory discrimination abilities with supplementary emphasis on kinesthetic and tactile modalities. While phonetic methods help the child to synthesize what he or she sees with what he or she hears, visual perception is used minimally.

Gillingham's synthetic approach is essentially a formal skill-building program. Teachers are encouraged to follow the manual if success is to be expected. The entire program is built upon eight basic linkages that form the association of auditory, visual, and kinstetics stimuli. Once the child has mastered basic sound production, he or she is introduced to phonograms (one letter or a group of letters that represents a phonetic sound). Once the phonograms have been mastered, they are used in drill procedures.

The teaching procedure begins with the introduction of the short "a" sound plus several specified consonant sounds. When these have been learned by the method above, blending is begun. Several phonogram cards are placed side by side. Individual sounds are produced in succession and with increasing speed until a fluid rate is achieved. The day following the initiation of the blending procedure, word analysis begins. This is achieved on an auditory level with the teacher sounding the word, and the child identifying the letters he or she hears. This process leads directly to the Simultaneous Oral Spelling process, in which the teacher says the word, the child says the word, names the letters, then writes the letters as he or she names them. This procedure is always used in the production of phonetically pure words.

One of the stipulations of the early program is that the child is given no other printed materials. If the child remains in a regular class while receiving remedial help, all other subject material must be presented auditorially. After blending has been established with all of the phonetic sounds, a reader or primer may be introduced. Books are carefully screened to assure that all words included are phonetic and thus suitable for blending. He is then introduced to basic phonetic rules, including syllabication and accent (all of which are included in the manual). When the child is able to synthesize and analyze any combination of phonetic syllables, nonphonetic syllables are introduced and memorized as whole syllables.

Gillingham's program for developing skills combines the use of phonetic study as well as experiences and language stories. Tracing, copying, and dictation are used simultaneously to achieve different purposes. Tracing is useful in learning the formation of letters and establishing a letter sequence for spelling. Copying develops visual memory; after practicing this, a child must produce a model that has been removed from sight. The purpose of dictation is to lengthen the auditory attention span and promote the association between auditory stimuli and visual imagery.

Initially, Gillingham felt that children who were capable of learning by visual methods should do so. However, in "Correspondence" (1958, pp. 119–122), she noted the difficulties children have with spelling and concluded that the kinesthetic and auditory stimuli provided in her program would prevent such difficulties. Therefore, she advised that all children be exposed to the "Alphabetic System."

The success of this system seems dependent upon its use with children whose auditory discrimination is unimpaired. It is essential that the child's strengths as well as weaknesses be diagnosed. To extend its effectiveness, meaningful interpretations and activities must be introduced despite the admonitions of Gillingham.

Both Dechant (1964) and Gates (1947) have been critical of this system. Their concerns center on the lack of meaningful activities, the rigidity of the teaching procedures, and the tendency to develop labored reading. If valid, these points would certainly limit the usefulness of the system as a total reading program. Interestingly, Harris (1968) noted that even though this approach has been used for many years, he had been unable to locate any comparative research on it.

Color Phonics System (Bannatyne, 1966)

This system consists of a set of individual letters and letter combinations printed on small cards; the letters are color coded in such a way that once the principle of the coding has been learned, the child can immediately identify each sound. The system is intended for use with almost every inadequately reading child, although in a few cases specific training in visual–spatial concepts is necessary. Color phonics is, of course, not recommended for children with color blindness or color agnosia.

The Color Phonics system systematizes the irregular orthography of the English language. The color codings are not as numerous as those in Words in Color. All the consonants and the two consonant combinations *ph* and *qu* are printed in white on charcoal gray, while the vowels, including diphthongs, are printed in color sounds on a white ground. Each letter is mounted on a plaque on the back of which is a picture of some object or situation that represents the key word printed underneath. Each key word contains the appropriate underlined phoneme. The color-coded approach is unique because the letters can be sequenced and each phoneme can be identified from the name of the color itself. For example, the phoneme *ee,* as sounded in green, is printed in a green color, and the phoneme *ow,* as sounded in brown, is printed in brown, and so on.

The Color Phonics system is quite compatible with the gradual introduction of particular phonemes and phonograms, as suggested in the Gillingham method. The system is not broken up into an extended series of separate exercises. The system operates independently of books. Suitable books can be introduced, once the teacher feels that the child has regained sufficient self-confidence to tackle suitable reading material. Although the system is not rigid, there are certain broad stages that are adhered to in the teaching process.

The system is best used in a one-to-one situation with nonreading children who have auditory sequencing and/or auditory–memory problems. It is a teaching *aid* and should be used with other programs. The technique does not depend on a great deal of organization of verbal content; instead, it requires the student to provide his or her own content. This is of value when using the system with older children who might react negatively to a system with organized verbal contents, such as Words in Color.

EXAMPLES OF SPECIFIC REMEDIAL TECHNIQUES IN READING

The following list of remedial techniques can aid the teacher in helping certain children overcome specific difficulties in reading. The teacher should carefully file remedial activities so that they can be used again and again. In a few years it is possible to collect a significant number of specific exercises that can be used for individual follow-up to a group reading lesson.

Problem Area

I. General word recognition (basic sight vocabulary)

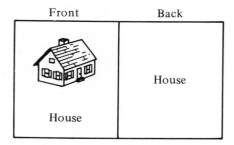

Suggested Remedial Activity

1. The picture dictionary. The child makes a scrapbook that is indexed with the letters of the alphabet. Pictures can be drawn or cut out of magazines. As the child learns a word, he or she pastes a picture on the page that has that letter. For example, the word "car" would go on the C page. This has advantages over commercial picture dictionaries because it contains the words that the child is learning and the child is making it. Most useful with nouns.

2. Picture cards and tracing. On one side of the card a picture is placed with a word underneath it; on the other side the word is printed. The teacher presents the card with the word and picture side up and pronounces the word. Then the child pronounces the word. Then the child pronounces and traces the word until he or she can recognize the word without seeing the picture. The words can be reviewed from time to time and used as an independent drill. Most useful with nouns.

3. Matching words with pictures. This can be used with words other

Problem Area

Suggested Remedial Activity

than nouns. For example, a clear picture of a child running can be used to help teach the word "run." On the back of the card, the picture is reproduced and the child is given three words and must match the word and the picture.

4. Labeling. Attach labels to the door, closet, window, pictures, bulletin board, and other things in the room so that the child will begin to associate the written symbol with the object.

5. Tachistoscope. Cut a piece of oak-tag or cardboard to a 5- by 8-inch size. Fold down the top and bottom about ½ inch to hold the word cards. Cut a window in the center to expose the word. Attach a shutter to the outside. Make up word cards with basic sight vocabulary words on them. These can be flashed by quickly opening the shutter. If the child misses a word, it can be reexposed so that the child will be able to apply word-attack skills.

6. Phrase cards. Short phrases, then longer phrases should be introduced. These can be used in the tachistoscope exercise.

II. Reversals
   A. Word

1. Place the word on a 5- by 8-inch card in crayon. Have the pupil say the word, trace it, and say it again. The child should do this a number of times and then be given an opportunity to read it in a sentence.

2. Hold up a card that is covered with a sheet of paper. Move the sheet of

Problem Area	*Suggested Remedial Activity*
	paper to the right so that the letters are exposed in the proper sequence.
	3. Use a card with the word printed on it and color lightly the first letter.
	4. Place some design (e.g., a diamond) to call the child's attention to the first letter.
B. Letter	1. Place the letter on a 3- by 5-inch card and have the child trace it until he or she is ready to write it correctly, then have the child practice writing it. This can also be done at the chalkboard.
	2. Use pictures illustrating words that begin with the letters the child reverses. For example, for the letters "b" and "d," use a picture of a boat and a duck. Place the picture of the duck to the left of the "d." Paste the picture of the boat next to the lower part of the "b" and to the right of it.
	3. Stories may be used to differentiate letters frequently reversed: This is b b is on the line b is tall like a building b looks to the right
III. Initial sounds Note: Check teacher's manuals of readiness and primary-level reading books for further suggestions	1. Dictate a series of three or four words that begin with the same sound. Have the child write the letter that represents the initial sound.
<table><tr><td rowspan="3">h</td><td>ard</td></tr><tr><td>and</td></tr><tr><td>ouse</td></tr></table>	2. On 3- by 5-inch index cards, place an "x" on the left side and three or four phonograms on the right. The child is asked to give the initial sound and then the whole word.
	3. Picture dictionary. See item 1.

Problem Area	Suggested Remedial Activity
	4. Rotating wheel. Two cardboard circles, one smaller than the other, can be fastened together so that they rotate freely. On the larger one place common phonograms, on the smaller one place initial consonants. By rotating the larger circle, initial consonants can be combined with other phonograms.
IV. Final sounds Note: Teacher's manuals from linguistically based reading series have many suggestions for developing this skill	1. Make a rhyming book to illustrate word families. 2. Ask the child to give a rhyming word for the one the teacher has just pronounced. These can be placed on the chalkboard and the parts that sound alike can be underlined. 3. Make up cards with an initial consonant on the left and an ending on the right. Have the child blend the initial sound with the ending to make new words.

```
┌─────────────────────────────┐
│   b                         │
│   l                         │
│   m           end           │
│   s                         │
└─────────────────────────────┘
```

Problem Area	Suggested Remedial Activity

V. Medial vowel sounds	1. Develop practice exercises that make the child focus attention on the medial vowel sound in the word, as:
	  a. The cat sat on a (rig, rog, rug).
	  b. The cat sat on a r___g.
	2. Make key cards with the vowel colored to call attention to the sound
	b*a*t b*e*t b*i*t b*o*t b*u*t
	(Bot is a nonsense word, but being so, the child may remember it because it is unique.)

VI. Endings	1. Place three columns of words on cards (or the chalkboard), and ask the child to pick out the one that has a different ending from the other two.

Problem Area	*Suggested Remedial Activity*
VII. Context clues	1. This teaches the child to anticipate meanings. If a new word, such as "toys" is to be introduced, write a sentence like, "Jim saw many _____ in the window of the store." Ask what he might have seen that starts with a "t." (The teacher should read the sentence and have the child simply respond with the word "toys.")
We ride to school on a _____(bus). At night I go to _____ (bed).	2. Write a sentence on the chalkboard with only one word that the child does not know the meaning of but can infer through the context. Ask the child to read the sentence silently. When the child has read it, ask if he or she knows what the last word is. If the child is having difficulty, structure further questions until he or she can infer the right word.
Mary is wearing a new — dress. bless. class.	3. Sentences can be constructed with a number of choices. Have the child underline the correct one to complete the sentence.
I carry my home. I like to live in water. I am in this room. What am I?	4. The teacher or the children can make up riddles. These can be put on spirit-duplicating masters or on the chalkboard. The children must infer the meaning from the context.
VIII. Letter discrimination *put* *hat* porch hold ball hot pot pot doll hat pass have	1. Place a list of words on the chalkboard and have the child (or children) underline the words that begin with the same letter as the first one.
IX. Phonemic and word discrimination	1. Tell the child (or children) that you are going to read a list of words.

Problem Area	*Suggested Remedial Activity*
	Most of them will begin alike (e.g., boat). Every time they hear a word that does not begin like boat, they should clap their hands.
	2. Tell the child (or children) to shut his or her eyes. Pairs of words are read and the child must tell if they sound exactly alike or are different.
	3. Follow step 2 with exercises on beginning sounds.
	4. Follow step 2 with exercises on final sounds.
	5. Pronounce a word and its beginning sound. Ask the child to give some more words that begin with the same beginning sound.
	6. Follow step 5 with exercises with ending sounds.
X. Compound words	1. Give the child a list of compound words and have the child separate them.
	2. Give the child two lists of words and have him or her draw lines from the right column to the left to make compound words.
XI. Root words	1. Present a list of words with variant endings and have the child circle the root word.
	2. Present the child with a list of words and a list of endings. Tell the child to make up as many *real* words as he or she can using the endings.
XII. Suffixes	1. Write a sentence on the chalkboard with a derived form of a word in it. Have the child find the root word and then explain how it alters the meaning of the whole word or what the meaning of the suffix is.

Problem Area	*Suggested Remedial Activity*
	a. Start with words that do not change their spelling when a suffix is added.
	b. Introduce spelling variations one at a time and provide practice before moving to another one.
XIII. Prefixes	1. Write sentences on the chalkboard containing words with prefixes. Ask the child to locate the root word. Ask the child to explain what the new word means.
Jim locked the door. Jim ——locked the door.	2. Write sentences on the chalkboard. Below each one write the same sentence but leave space for a prefix on one word. Ask the child what prefix can be added to make the sentence mean the opposite.
XIV. Vocabulary development	1. Use any opportunities to introduce new words in discussion and call attention to them, e.g., "The sign over the main door of the school is 'exit.' What do you think it means?"
	2. Develop a modified crossword puzzle. In early grades the first letter should be given.
	3. Have the children develop their own crossword puzzles.
	4. Have the children give words which they associate with the stimulus word, e.g., *volcano:* hot, lava, mountain, etc. Discuss the relationships among the words given.
XV. Classification	1. Prepare a list of words that can be separated into general classifications and have the child group them, e.g., *vegetables—house—transportation:* carrot, floor, car,

Problem Area	*Suggested Remedial Activity*
	airplane, tomato, helicopter, door, potato, train.
	2. Prepare lists of three or more words. Have the child cross out the one that doesn't belong.
XVI. Sequence	1. Cut up or draw a series of pictures that make a complete story when arranged in the proper sequence. Have the child complete the exercise.
	2. Prepare strips of paper with single sentences on each one. Ask the child to arrange them to tell a complete story.
	3. Write out directions for making something in a scrambled order. Have the child number the steps in the order in which they should happen.
	4. Cut comic strips apart and have the child put them back together in appropriate sequence.
XVII. Following directions	1. Give the child a picture with specific directions as to how it should be colored and have the child finish it.
	2. Give a child a series of oral directions and have him or her carry them out in the order in which you gave them; start from the simple and gradually become more complex.
XVIII. Main ideas	1. Read the children a short story. Write a list of phrases on the chalkboard and have them pick out the one that best tells the main idea. (In some cases, the phrases must be read to the children.)

Problem Area	*Suggested Remedial Activity*

Suggested Remedial Activity

2. Read a story to the children and have them make up a title and tell why it is a good one.

3. Exercises similar to 1 and 2 above can be done with the child reading the story and completing the exercise independently.

4. Older students may be asked to choose details from the story that support the main idea. Diagrams may be used to represent this:

Main Idea

Early humans discovered fire in different forms.

Supporting Details

lightning   hot lava of   spark from
            volcanoes   stones
                          rubbed
                          together

XIX. Cause-effect

1. Perform actions such as turning the light switch off. Ask children what happened and why. Establish the cause-effect relationship.

2. As part of a story activity, read a causal statement and have the children give the effect.

3. Have the child match causes with effect.

XX. Comparison/contrast

1. Show the child two pictures that have some similarities to each other. Have the child tell how they are alike and different.

2. Tell how two characters in a story are alike or different.

3. Older students may make a comparison/contrast chart.

3

PROBLEMS IN WRITTEN COMPOSITION

Donald D. Hammill   Mary Poplin

Writing is a highly complex method of expression involving the integration of eye-hand, linguistic, and conceptual abilities. Because of this, it is one of the highest forms of communication and hence is usually the last to be mastered. As an expressive form of a graphic symbol system used for conveying thoughts, ideas, and feelings, writing may be considered to be "the other side of the coin" from reading, which is the receptive form of that system.

The term "writing" refers to a variety of interrelated graphic skills, including: (1) *composition,* or the ability to generate ideas and to express them in an acceptable grammar, while adhering to certain stylistic conventions; (2) *spelling,* or the ability to use letters to construct words in accordance with accepted usage; and (3) *handwriting,* or the ability to physically execute the graphic marks necessary to produce legible compositions or messages. For convenience, in this book, we have arbitrarily decided to divide the material on writing into three chapters. The first of these chapters will deal with problems relating to composition; the next chapter will handle spelling difficulties; and the third chapter will discuss the problems of legibility.

The contents of the present chapter then will discuss the nature of written composition, means by which it can be assessed, and instructional procedures for improving ability in this important area.

THE MAJOR ELEMENTS IN WRITTEN COMPOSITION

Written composition includes at least three interrelated elements: a cognitive component, a linguistic component, and a stylistic component. When these are combined with two additional elements, handwriting and spelling, the result is a comprehensive concept of the entire writing process. A brief description of each of the components involved in composition follows. With minor exception, these descriptions are essentially the same as those observed by Hammill and Larsen (1978).

COGNITIVE COMPONENT

The cognitive component refers to the ability to write logical, coherent, and sequenced written products. The actual piece may be a creative story, a personal or professional letter, an essay, or a factual accounting of events; however, regardless of its content, the passage must be formulated in such a way that it is readily understandable to a reader. The maturity of the product is usually evident if the writer employs titles, paragraphs, definite endings, character development, dialogue, or humor, or if she or he expresses some philosophical or moral theme. The cognitive component is not as easily defined as are the other components, but a product that is immature in its development of expression is frequently viewed as being "sloppy" in the presentation of ideas, disjointed in thought sequence, lacking in theme, or simply difficult to understand. Because the cognitive aspects of writing are often vague and subjective, teachers have tended to overlook this aspect of writing. This is regrettable, for if a person does not write conceptually, effective written communication is virtually impossible.

LINGUISTIC COMPONENT

The linguistic component is the use of serviceable syntax and semantic structures. The selection of suitable words, tenses, plurals, subject-verb correspondences, and cases is essential to good writing. Particular vocabulary items and grammatical forms will vary somewhat from person to person, social class to social class, geographical area to geographical area, and ethnic group to ethnic group. However, in most cases, the grammar and vocabulary employed by individuals is equally efficient in conveying a writer's meaning. For example, one person may write "I grew a lot this year," while another might write "I growed a lot this year." Even though the two individuals are using different grammatical rules in expressing the past tense of "grow," the sentences that are generated convey identical thoughts. Linguistically speaking, neither rule is right nor wrong. If some people consider one form to be "better" than another, the reasons are likely to be rooted in sociological factors and personal preference. Yet if writers wish to be "accepted" by the majority of readers who encounter their passages, some standards of linguistic usage must be maintained.

Relative to this point, Otto, McMenemy, and Smith (1973) note that today there are at least five levels of English usage: the illiterate, the homely, the informal standard, the formal standard, and the literary. Illiterate usage is characteristic of "uncultured" individuals, is rarely accepted in the classroom, and is targeted for correction, e.g., "he done," "didn't have no," "them books." The homely level is more acceptable to most people than the illiterate but is not quite as accepted as standard forms of English. Often these homely forms are regional in nature and usually are tolerated but rarely sanctioned by the school, e.g., confusion between "lie" and "lay," and "like" and "as." Informal standard English is the level of colloquial speech and writing used by most educated persons. It is employed in conversations and correspondence with friends and relatives but generally not with strangers or in formal situations. The grammatical forms characteristic of this level are intended for everyday use and are considered by most individuals to be both functional and acceptable. Otto et al. suggest that this level should be the language of the classroom and the goal for most elementary students. The final two levels, formal standard English and the literary, are reserved for special occasions and purposes. Both are characterized by the absence of colloquial expressions, more than the usual attention devoted to the tone of the words, and agreement in number, tense, and case, e.g., "I *shall* be there." The structure used at the literary level raises the use of the English language to an art form, e.g., "Fourscore and seven years ago . . ." (literary form) for "Eighty-seven years ago . . ." (informal standard form).

STYLISTIC COMPONENT

The stylistic component refers to the use of "accepted" fashions or rules established for punctuation and capitalization. The rules governing punctuation and capitalization must be acquired by students before they can write effectively. In most instances, children quickly recognize that capital letters are used to give stress to words of special significance and that commas separate thoughts within a sentence.

Many of the rules governing the use of style are arbitrary in nature, based in tradition, and do not necessarily facilitate meaning. The place of the period in relation to the quotation marks in the following sentence is an example of this point: Mary said, "I saw the boy." Whether the period is placed inside or outside of the quotation marks does not affect the meaning of the sentence. Other rules, however, are essential to understanding the sense of sentences and passages. For example, the meaning of the sentence, "In reading, comprehension will be impaired greatly by poor vocabulary development," is altered considerably if the comma is omitted. Without the comma between "reading" and "comprehension," the sentence has no rational meaning.

Obviously, efficient and consistent use of the rules of punctuation and capitalization enhance the quality of a written product. In some instances, it is an absolute necessity in conveying the meaning of written communications.

ASSESSING DIFFICULTIES IN WRITTEN COMPOSITION

One goal of assessment in written composition is to identify individuals who are unable to write well enough to meet the minimum standards required for their personal daily needs. Once the pupils are identified, an equally important goal is to determine the specific problems in written composition that are in need of remediation. For the most part, when assessing the student's skills for the purpose of planning an instructional program, the teacher should rely upon the use of informal procedures or standardized instruments.

The effort to assess written composition begins with deciding which skills are to be evaulated and in what order they are to be assessed. The teacher will find these decisions are easier to make if he or she has available a scope-and-sequence chart such as the one provided in Table 3–1.

In this chart, the scope covers capitalization, punctuation, vocabulary, word usage, grammar, sentence construction, and paragraph construction. These are the major aspects in the writing curriculum. The specific skills and the order in which they are to be assessed (or taught) is represented in the sequence. In this particular case, the skills in the sequence are grouped according to grade levels.

The contents of the chart suggest the breadth of skills that can be assessed by the teacher but do not indicate the precise evaluation procedures to be used. Because this is the case, teachers must rely on subjective interpretation of children's written-work samples, on criterion-referenced tests that they have constructed for their own use, and on teacher-made checklists.

Consider the case where a second-grade child is suspected of having a writing problem involving composition. If the individual conducting the evaluation were interested in the pupil's mastery of capitalization, he or she would have to consult the chart to identify the capitalization forms that are characteristically taught in school between kindergarten and the end of the second grade.

Examples of the child's written work could then be evaluated in terms of these expected forms to learn which have been acquired by the child, which are insecurely mastered, and which are missing altogether. The main defect with the analysis of work samples is that the samples selected for evaluation may not adequately represent the child's writing weaknesses and strengths. For example, often in executing spontaneous written products, such as essays or stories, some children write only sentences that contain the grammatical forms that they know how to use. Therefore, error analysis of their work may result in a distorted view of the skills that they have and have not acquired. Put another way, if error analysis is to work well, the products that are to be evaluated must include adequate opportunities for all types of errors to occur and to be observed. Because this may or may not be the case where spontaneously written products are concerned, the teacher may want to use additonal procedures.

The teacher could generate a sentence (i.e., a test item) that contains the particular element being evaluated (e.g., the capitalization of proper names, the use of a colon to separate the hour from minutes, or the use of a comma to set off introductory clauses). Presumably, one or two sentences would be developed to correspond with each item on the chart. Next, the sentences would be typed in such a manner that the specific element being tested would be left unpunctuated (or punctuated incorrectly). The list of sentences could then be presented to the child, who is asked to correct any errors that he or she recognizes in the sentences. Example sentences might include:

1. The boy's name was bill.
2. School is out at 3 30.
3. After the movie was over Mary went to the store.

In the first sentence, children who strike out the "b" and replace it with a "B" are telling the teacher that they understand the capitalization rule that pertains to first names. Those who insert a semicolon after "Mary" on the third sentence, who see nothing wrong with the sentence, or who place a comma after "movie" are showing that they do not apply the rule concerning the punctuation of introductory clauses. The educational implications of the children's performance on such a criterion-reference device are obvious—teach them the forms that they do not know and give them ample, meaningful opportunities to practice their newly acquired knowledge.

Table 3–1. Scope and Sequence of Skills in Written Composition

	Grade 1	Grade 2	Grade 3
Capitalization	The first word of a sentence The child's first and last names The name of the teacher, school, town, street The word "I"	The date First and important words of titles of books the children read Proper names used in children's writings Titles of compositions Names of titles: Mr., Mrs., Miss	Proper names: month, day, common holidays First word in a line of verse First and important words in titles of books, stories, poems First word of salutation of informal note, as "Dear" First word of closing of informal note, as "Yours"
Punctuation	Period at the end of a sentence which tells something Period after numbers in any kind of list	Question mark at the close of a question Comma after salutation of a friendly note or letter Comma after closing of a friendly note or letter Comma between the day of the month and the year Comma between name of city and state	Period after abbreviations Period after an initial Use of an apostrophe in a common contraction such as *isn't, aren't* Commas in a list
Vocabulary	New words learned during experience Choosing words that describe accurately Choosing words that make you see, hear, feel	Words with similar meanings; with opposite meanings Alphabetical order	Extending discussion of words for precise meanings Using synonyms Distinguishing meanings and spellings of homonyms Using the prefix *un* and the suffix *less*

Grade 4	Grade 5	Grades 6, 7, and 8
Names of cities and states in general Names of organizations to which children belong, such as Boy Scouts, grade four, etc. Mother, Father, when used in place of the name Local geographical names	Names of streets Names of all places and persons, countries, oceans, etc. Capitalization used in outlining Titles when used with names, such as President Lincoln Commercial trade names	Names of the Deity and the Bible First word of a quoted sentence Proper adjectives, showing race, nationality, etc. Abbreviations of proper nouns and titles
Apostrophe to show possession Hyphen separating parts of a word divided at end of a line Period following a command Exclamation point at the end of a word or group of words that make an exclamation Comma setting off an appositive Colon after the salutation of a business letter Quotation marks before and after a direct quotation Comma between explanatory words and a quotation Period after outline Roman numeral	Colon in writing time Quotation marks around the title of a booklet, pamphlet, the chapter of a book, and the title of a poem or story Underlining the title of a book	Comma to set off nouns in direct address Hyphen in compound numbers Colon to set off a list Comma in sentences to aid in making meaning clear
Dividing words into syllables Using the accent mark Using exact words which appeal to the senses Using exact words in explanation Keeping individual lists of new words and meanings	Using antonyms Prefixes and suffixes; compound words Exactness in choice of words Dictionary work; definitions; syllables; pronunciation; macron; breve Contractions Rhyme and rhythm; words with sensory images Classification of words by parts of speech Roots and words related to them Adjectives, nouns, verbs—contrasting general and specific vocabulary	Extending meanings; writing with care in choice of words and phrases In writing and speaking, selecting words for accuracy Selecting words for effectiveness and appropriateness Selecting words for courtesy Editing a paragraph to improve a choice or words

Table 3–1. *Continued*

	Grade 1	Grade 2	Grade 3
Word Usage	*Generally in oral expression* Naming yourself last Eliminating unnecessary words (my father he); use of *well* and *good* Verb forms in sentences: is, are did, done was, were see, saw, seen ate, eaten went, gone came, come gave, given	*Generally in oral expression* Double negative Use of *a* and *an; may* and *can; teach* and *learn* Eliminating unnecessary words (this here) Verb forms in sentences: rode, ridden took, taken grow, grew, grown know, knew, known bring, brought drew, drawn began, begun ran, run	Use of *there is* and *there are; any* and *no* Use of *let* and *leave; don't* and *doesn't; would have,* not *would of* Verb forms in sentences: throw, threw, thrown drive, drove, driven wrote, written tore, torn chose, chosen climbed broke, broken wore, worn spoke, spoken sang, sung rang, rung catch, caught
Grammar	Not applicable	Not applicable	Nouns: recognition of singular, plural, and possessive Verbs: recognition

100

Grade 4	Grade 5	Grades 6, 7, and 8
Agreement of subject and verb	Avoiding unnecessary pronouns (the boy he . . .)	Homonyms: *its, it's; their, there, they're; there's, theirs; whose, who's*
Use of *she, he, I, we,* and *they* as subjects	Linking verbs and predicate nominatives	Use of parallel structure for parallel ideas, as in outlines
Use of *bring* and *take*	Conjugation of verbs, to note changes in tense, person, number	Verb forms in sentences:
Verb forms in sentences:	Transitive and intransitive verbs	beat, beat, beaten
blow, blew, blown	Verb forms in sentences:	learn, learned, learned
drink, drank, drunk	am, was, been	leave, left, left
lie, lay, lain	say, said, said	lit, lit, lit
take, took, taken	fall, fell, fallen	forget, forgot, forgotten
rise, rose, risen	dive, dived, dived	swing, swung, swung
teach, taught, taught	burst, burst, burst	spring, sprang, sprung
raise, raised, raised	buy, bought, bought	shrink, shrank, shrunk
lay, laid, laid	Additional verb forms: *climb, like, play, read, sail, vote, work*	slide, slid, slid
fly, flew, flown		
set, set, set		
swim, swam, swum		
freeze, froze, frozen		
steal, stole, stolen		
Nouns, common and proper; noun in complete subjects	Noun: possessive; objective of preposition; predicate noun	Noun: clauses; common and proper nouns; indirect object
Verb in complete predicate	Verb: tense; agreement with subject; verbs of action and state of being	Verb: conjugating to note changes in person; number, tense; linking verbs with predicate nominatives
Adjectives: recognition	Adjective: comparison; predicate adjective; proper adjective	Adjective: chart of uses; clauses; demonstrative; descriptive; numerals; phrases
Adverbs: recognition (telling how, when, where)	Adverb: comparison; words telling how, when, where, how much; modifying verbs, adjectives, adverbs	Adverb: chart of uses; clauses; comparison; descriptive; *ly* ending; modification of adverbs; phrases
Adverbs modifying verbs, adjectives, other adverbs	Pronouns: possessive, objective after prepositions	Pronoun: antecedents; declension chart—person, gender, case; demonstrative; indefinite; interrogative; personal; relative
Pronouns: recognition of singular and plural	Prepositions: recognition; prepositional phrases	Preposition: phrases
	Conjunction: recognition	Conjunction: in compound subjects and predicates; in subordinate and coordinate clauses
	Interjection: recognition	Interjection: placement of, in quotations

Table 3–1. *Continued*

	Grade 1	Grade 2	Grade 3
Grammar			
Sentences	Write simple sentences	Recognition of sentences; kinds: statement and question Composing correct and interesting original sentences Avoiding running sentences together with *and*	Exclamatory sentences Use of a variety of sentences Combining short, choppy sentences into longer ones Using interesting beginning and ending sentences Avoiding run-on sentences (no punctuation) Learning to proofread one's own and others' sentences

		Noun: antecedent of pronouns; collective nouns; compound subject; direct object; indirect object, object of preposition
		Verb: active and passive voice; emphatic forms; transitive and intransitive, tenses; linking verbs
		Adverbs: as modifiers; clauses; comparing adverbs; adverbial phrase, use of *well* and *good*
		Adjectives: as modifiers; clauses; compound adjectives
		Pronouns: agreement with antecedents; personal pronoun chart; indirect object; object of preposition; objective case, person and number; possessive form
		Preposition: in phrase
		Conjunction: coordinate; subordinate; use in compound subjects; compound predicates; complex and compound sentences
Command sentences	Using a variety of interesting sentences: declarative; interrogative; exclamatory; and imperative (*you* the subject)	Development of concise statements (avoiding wordiness or unnecessary repetition)
Complete and simple subject; complete and simple predicate	Agreement of subject and verb; changes in pronoun forms	Indirect object and predicate nominative
Adjectives and adverbs recognized; pronouns introduced	Compound subjects and compound predicates	Complex sentences
Avoiding fragments of sentences (incomplete) and the comma fault (a comma where a period belongs)	Composing paragraphs with clearly stated ideas	Clear thinking and expression (avoiding vagueness and omissions)
Improving sentences in a paragraph		

Table 3–1. *Continued*

	Grade 1	Grade 2	Grade 3
Paragraphs	Not applicable	Not applicable	Keeping to one idea Keeping sentences in order; sequence of ideas Finding and deleting sentences that do not belong Indenting

Source: Adapted from W. Otto and R. McMenemy, *Corrective and Remedial Teaching* (Boston: Houghton Mifflin, 1980); H. Greene and W. Petty, *Developing Language Skills in the Elementary School* (Boston: Allyn and Bacon, 1967).

If this criterion-referenced approach is attempted, special care should be taken to make sure that the vocabulary used in the sentences is well known to the children being evaluated. A child who cannot comprehend the meaning of a written sentence certainly cannot be expected to punctuate it properly. If the teacher has any reason to suspect that the child cannot read the sentences, the child should be asked to tell in his or her own words what the sentence means. If the pupil is unable to do this, the sentence should be reworded utilizing an appropriate vocabulary.

Also, the teacher will want to adhere very closely to the developmental sequence found in Table 3–1, for it indicates the order in which grammatical forms are usually taught in the schools. Using the three sentences above as examples, teachers would find that children are generally taught (1) during kindergarten and first grade that the first and last names of a person are capitalized, (2) between second and fifth grades that colons separate hours from minutes, and (3) between fourth and sixth grades that commas are used to set

Grade 4	Grade 5	Grades 6, 7, and 8
Selecting main topic	Improvement in writing a paragraph of several sentences	Analyzing a paragraph to note method of development
Choosing title to express main idea	Selecting subheads as well as main topic for outline	Developing a paragraph in different ways: e.g., with details, reasons, examples, or comparisons
Making simple outline with main idea	Courtesy and appropriateness in all communications	Checking for accurate statements
Developing an interesting paragraph	Recognizing topic sentences	Use of a fresh or original approach in expressing ideas
	Keeping to the topic as expressed in title and topic sentence	Use of transition words to connect ideas
	Use of more than one paragraph	Use of topic sentences in developing paragraphs
	Developing a four-point outline	Improvement in complete composition—introduction, development, conclusion
	Writing paragraphs from outline	Checking for good reasoning
	New paragraphs for new speakers in written conversation	Use of bibliography in report based on several sources
	Keeping list of books (authors and titles) used for reference	

off an introductory clause. This information is of considerable value for teachers who must prepare special programs for individual children, because it enables them to sequence both the goals that underlie training and the activities that are to be used to ameliorate deficiencies according to most desirable levels.

The assessment of the content of a composition is considerably more difficult, although the problems are hardly insurmountable. The experienced teacher can probably read a child's essay and score it properly according to the criteria specified in the Carlson Analytical Originality Scale (Carlson, 1965) (see Table 3–2). This scale requires that the teacher rate the child's written content on five dimensions—its story structure, novelty, emotion, individuality, and style.

Of course, since the ratings tend to be subjective, they are only as good as the talent and experience of the individual doing the evaluation. Therefore, it is important to take a few precautions to minimize the evaluator's subjectivity

Table 3–2. Carlson Analytical Originality Scale Scoring Key for Scoring Original Stories

Name of child _____   Name of teacher _____

Story type _____   Total score on scale _____

Scale Division A—Story Structure		*Scale Division C—Emotion*	
1. Unusual title	0 1 2 3 4 5	22. Unusual ability to express emotional depth	0 1 2 3 4 5
2. Unusual beginning	0 1 2 3 4 5	23. Unusual sincerity in expressing personal problems	0 1 2 3 4 5
3. Unusual dialogue	0 1 2 3 4 5	24. Unusual ability to identify self with feelings of others	0 1 2 3 4 5
4. Unusual ending	0 1 2 3 4 5	25. Unusual horror theme	0 1 2 3 4 5
5. Unusual plot	0 1 2 3 4 5	*Scale Division D—Individuality*	
Scale Division B—Novelty		26. Unusual perceptive sensitivity (social and physical environment)	0 1 2 3 4 5
6. Novelty of names	0 1 2 3 4 5	27. Unique philosophical thinking	0 1 2 3 4 5
7. Novelty of locale	0 1 2 3 4 5	28. Facility in beautiful writing	0 1 2 3 4 5
8. Unique punctuation and expressional devices	0 1 2 3 4 5	29. Unusual personal experience	0 1 2 3 4 5
9. New words	0 1 2 3 4 5	*Scale Division E—Style of Stories*	
10. Novelty of ideas	0 1 2 3 4 5	30. Exaggerated tall tale	0 1 2 3 4 5
11. Novel devices	0 1 2 3 4 5	31. Fairy tale type	0 1 2 3 4 5
12. Novel theme	0 1 2 3 4 5	32. Fantasy-turnabout of characters	0 1 2 3 4 5
13. Quantitative thinking	0 1 2 3 4 5	33. Highly fantastic central idea of theme	0 1 2 3 4 5
14. New objects created	0 1 2 3 4 5	34. Fantastic creatures, objects, or persons	0 1 2 3 4 5
15. Ingenuity in solving situations	0 1 2 3 4 5	35. Personal experience	0 1 2 3 4 5
16. Recombination of ideas in unusual relationships	0 1 2 3 4 5	36. Individual story style	0 1 2 3 4 5
17. Picturesque speech	0 1 2 3 4 5		
18. Humor	0 1 2 3 4 5		
19. Novelty of form	0 1 2 3 4 5		
20. Inclusion of readers	0 1 2 3 4 5		
21. Unusual related thinking	0 1 2 3 4 5		

Source: R.K. Carlson, *Sparkling Words: Two Hundred Practical and Creative Writing Ideas* (Geneva, IL: Paladin House Publishers, 1973).

and to increase his or her reliability. Whoever is designated to evaluate the quality of the ideas expressed in children's written work should take steps to calibrate the judgments by acquiring a set of "internalized norms." This can be done by standardizing the topics of the written pieces that are to be assessed. For example, if the examiner is called upon most often to assess the work of children in grades three through six, he or she should select three topics, e.g., "My Favorite Television Show," "The Place I'd Most Like to Visit," "The Person I Admire Most," and have a sample of ten to twenty representative students at each grade level write a short composition on each topic. Reading approximately sixty essays all on the same topic will usually equip the examiner with a better-than-intuitive knowledge of what constitutes average, below-average, and above-average quality with regard to a given topic and will probably enable the examiner to complete Carlson's scale items with some assurance.

In addition to informal procedures, teachers can use standardized tests to measure written composition, especially when the purposes for testing require the quantification of results. Almost all achievement test batteries commonly used in the schools today include at least one subtest that measures some aspect of composition. (See Comprehensive Test of Basic Skills; California Achievement Tests; Stanford Achievement Tests; Metropolitan Achievement Tests; SRA Achievement Series.) The findings of these tests are helpful in screening but have limited diagnostic value. For the most part, they test only word usage ability (grammar) and do this using contrived (unnatural) testing formats. They do not involve the analysis of students' spontaneously composed stories.

The Test of Written Language (Hammill and Larsen, 1978) is a standardized test of written composition that can be used for diagnostic purposes. The TOWL is made up of seven subtests, the results of which yield information about:

1. *Word usage*—the use of standard verb tenses, plurals, pronouns, and other grammatical forms
2. *Style*—the use of generally accepted conventions regarding punctuation and capitalization
3. *Spelling*—the ability to phonetically spell regular and irregular words
4. *Thematic maturity*—the ability to construct a meaningful story on a given theme
5. *Vocabulary*—the level of words used in a spontaneously composed story
6. *Thought units*—the total number of complete sentences used in the written story
7. *Handwriting*—the legibility of the written story

With the exception of Spelling and Handwriting, these subtests tap aspects of written composition.

The TOWL results can be used to identify students who have problems in writing, especially when those problems involve composition, to pinpoint specific areas of deficiency, and to conduct research. The results can be recorded on the Profile Sheet to facilitate interpretation (See Figure 3–1).

TOWL

TEST OF WRITTEN LANGUAGE

Donald D. Hammill & Stephen C. Larsen

Name _Nicholas E._

School _Durant Jr. High_   Grade _8th_

Teacher's Name _Betty Cleland_

Examiner's Name _Mary Cronin_

Examiner's Title _Educational Diagnostician_

Referred by _Mr. Bagley - School Counselor_

TOWL PROFILE CHART

Scaled Scores	VOCABULARY	THEMATIC MATURITY	SPELLING	WORD USAGE	STYLE	THOUGHT UNITS	HANDWRITING	Scaled Scores
20	·	·	·	·	·	·	·	20
19	·	·	·	·	·	·	·	19
18	·	·	·	·	·	·	·	18
17	·	·	·	·	·	·	·	17
16	·	·	·	·	·	·	·	16
15	·	·	·	·	·	·	·	15
14	·	·	·	·	·	·	·	14
13	·	·	·	·	·	·	·	13
12	·	·	·	·	·	X	·	12
11	·	·	·	·	X	·	·	11
10	X	·	·	·	·	·	·	10
9	·	X	·	X	·	·	·	9
8	·	·	X	·	·	·	·	8
7	·	·	·	·	·	·	·	7
6	·	·	·	·	·	·	·	6
5	·	·	·	·	·	·	·	5
4	·	·	·	·	·	·	X	4
3	·	·	·	·	·	·	·	3
2	·	·	·	·	·	·	·	2
1	·	·	·	·	·	·	·	1

Notes

	Year	Month	Day
Date Tested	78	11	13
Date of Birth	65	4	7
Age	13	7	6

Principal Subtests	Raw Scores	Grade Equivalents	Scaled Scores
Vocabulary	42	___	10
Thematic Maturity	7	___	9
Spelling	20	___	8
Word Usage	21	___	9
Style	18	___	11
Total for Principal Subtests			47
Written Language Quotient (WLQ)*			96

Supplemental Subtests	Raw Scores	Grade Equivalents	Scaled Scores
Thought Units	18	___	12
Handwriting	2	___	4

*Does not include the Supplemental Subtests

Additional copies of this form are available from PRO-ED, 5341 Industrial Oaks Boulevard, Austin, Texas 78735.

Figure 3–1. TOWL Profile Sheet

The TOWL was standardized on a thirteen-state sample of 1800 school-aged children attending grades two through eight. Normative data are available for each six-month age interval between 7–0 and 14–6. For measuring the written composition ability of adolescent students, those between the ages of 11 and 18½, we recommend using the appropriate subtests of *The Test of Adolescent Language* (TOAL) (Hammill, V. Brown, Larsen, & Wiederholt, 1980).

TEACHING WRITTEN COMPOSITION

The term "composition" refers to the syntactic and semantic aspects of a child's written product. It is manifested in the ability to capitalize and punctuate, to use vocabulary and grammatical forms, and to construct sentences and paragraphs. Obviously, a certain level of competence in all these abilities is essential if a child is ever to use writing as a means of self-expression. Before attempting to remedy problems in any of these areas, teachers must first be aware of (1) the goals of individualized instruction in writing, (2) the language-experience approach to teaching composition, (3) the scope and sequence of the specific skills usually taught, and (4) the instructional activities that can be used to help a child attain a desired level of competence.

Goals of Individualized Instruction

The goals of instruction in composition are threefold. The first goal is to teach students at least the minimum competencies that they will need to succeed in the school curriculum. The second goal is to instruct them in those writing abilities that will be required for success outside the school (letter writing, completion of forms, note taking, etc.). The third goal is to teach them to express their creativity in writing poetry, fantasies, and stories. Each of these goals is important and the teacher should keep them in mind when planning an intervention program for a particular student.

The Language-Experience Approach to Teaching Composition

In general, teachers usually use a variation of the language experience approach to teach conceptual writing. In using this technique, the teacher's knowledge of a particular child's background and interests serves as the basis of instruction. The teacher begins by recording a student's verbal description of objects and events on a chart or board. Contents of the chart are discussed with the child, and attention is called to the various mechanical and compositional aspects of written expression, as well as to the relationships existing between the child's experiences and between oral and written language. Gradually, the student assumes more and more responsibility for the writing of personal expressions. At first, the child is asked to write only those words that the teacher knows are well within his or her speaking vocabulary. Eventually, the child is asked to write complete compositions reflecting thoughts about some interesting topic or experience. The theme of these essays can be provided by the teacher or, as is more often the case, by the student.

At all times, the student is encouraged to write creatively; and the emphasis of instruction is always on the quality of ideas expressed and on motivation for writing. In time, the more mechanical and rule-governed aspects of writing are introduced; but care is taken to make sure that the increasing curricular focus on these skills does not interfere with the child's desire to write creatively. This approach to teaching conceptual writing is most effective when it is integrated with the teaching of other areas in the language arts curriculum (reading, spelling, penmanship, etc.). Readers who want more information on using the language-experience approach to teach writing are referred to Parts II and III of Fernald (1943); Chapters 6, 8, and 9 of J. Smith (1967), and Chapters 7–9 of Burns et al. (1971).

"Proofreading," the reading of a written product for the purpose of identifying errors, is an integral part of all approaches to teaching composition. Students are usually taught to proofread soon after they begin to read and write original compositions. Children can proofread their own work, the work of other pupils, or special pieces containing selected errors that have been composed by the teacher. Regardless of the material to be proofread, students will find the following questions designed by Burns et al. (1971, pp. 241–242) to be helpful guides to developing proofreading ability:

1. Listen and look at each group of words to be sure it is a good sentence. Make sure that you kept your sentences apart.
2. Listen and look for mistakes in punctuation. Be sure that you have put in punctuation marks only where they are needed. Did you end sentences with the mark required?
3. Listen and look for mistakes in using words correctly. Be sure that you have said what you mean and that each word is used correctly with other words. Is there any incorrect verb or pronoun usage?
4. Look for mistakes in using capital letters. Did you capitalize the first words and all important words in the title? Did you begin each sentence with a capital letter?

5. Look for misspelled words. Use the dictionary to check the spelling of any word about which you are not sure.

6. Check for legibility of writing and directions about spacing, title, and the like.[1]

Scope and Sequence for Skills in Written Composition

In teaching written expression, the teacher must have a clear understanding of the theoretical basis and the specific sequence of skills that make up the instructional program that is to be used. The teacher can use this information as a guide for assessing a child's strengths and weaknesses in that program and also as a framework for planning short- and long-term objectives. The easiest way to obtain the needed knowledge about a particular approach is to prepare and study a scope-and-sequence chart in which the skills and conceptual ideas incorporated in the program are depicted. Fortunately, the authors of many programs provide teachers with scope-and-sequence data for their materials.

The theoretical constructs (i.e., the major aspects of the curriculum) are represented in the "scope" of the chart, while the skills of a particular construct and the order in which they are to be taught are displayed in the "sequence." An example of a scope-and-sequence chart that is useful for assessment and remedial purposes in writing was presented in Table 3–1. The scope of this curriculum comprises capitalization, punctuation, vocabulary, word usage, grammar, sentence construction, and paragraph construction. These categories represent the major conceptual ideas involved in the program. The skills that make up these categories are grouped according to grade levels (i.e., the sequence). This chart serves as a guide for identifying the skills that need to be taught, for deciding the order in which the skills are to be introduced, for recording an individual's progress and for facilitating systematic instruction.

The procedures for using a scope-and-sequence chart to assess skills in writing have already been described. Having used these procedures to determine the skills that a particular child does not have, for example, the use of a period after initials and abbreviations (punctuation skills found at the third-grade level in Table 3–1), the teacher is ready to plan an appropriate course of instruction.

Instructional Activities

Once suitable scope and sequence has been acquired and a child's skill deficiencies have been identified, the teacher is ready to choose instructional activities that are appropriate to the student's needs and situation. The activities described in the remainder of this chapter are representative of those

1. P.C. Burns et al., *The Language Arts in Childhood.* © 1971 by Houghton Mifflin Company.

which can be used to teach punctuation, capitalization, vocabulary, word usage, grammar, and sentence and paragraph construction. When applied to children having problems in writing, these activities should be used in conjunction with the language-experience approach discussed earlier.

Punctuation and Capitalization.   The strategies for teaching punctuation and capitalization are basically similar. For example, to teach skills in either area, the teacher (1) utilizes the language-experience approach to collect passages of the student's written work, (2) calls attention to each incidence in the essay where punctuation or capitalization is required, (3) discusses the need to use the skill to enhance meaning, (4) shows how to use the required skill properly, (5) provides activities for practice, and (6) arranges an opportunity for the pupil to demonstrate competence in spontaneous writing. To facilitate instruction in punctuation and capitalization, the teacher may want to use variations of the following activities. For example, students can:

1. Match items on a list of punctuation marks with possible functions (stop, yield, etc.). *Examples:*
   period = stop
   comma = yield
2. Punctuate and/or capitalize written passages. *Example:* billys cat was lost but it was found quickly.
3. Proofread the work of their classmates and underline possible errors. The papers can be returned to the classmates for correction, or the students who did the proofreading may correct the error.
4. Write passages dictated by the teacher. The sentences dictated should involve various examples of punctuation and capitalization.
5. Be taught to listen for drops in the teacher's voice when he or she is dictating. These drops indicate the end of a sentence or the need for a comma. Young students can clap their hands when they recognize a point where a punctuation mark should be placed.
6. Be told to write sentences demonstrating a particular kind of form. *Example:* Write a sentence as if you were talking to Mr. Smith (quotation marks).

Vocabulary, Word Usage, and Grammar.   These are related abilities; therefore, they can often be taught simultaneously using similar instructional activities. A child's vocabulary is the supply of words that he or she comprehends and uses in speaking and writing. The goal of vocabulary-development activities is to increase this supply of words in number and complexity. Word usage, on the other hand, refers to the "appropriateness" of the child's selection of vocabulary in terms of accepted standards. This differs from grammar, in that grammar is the way in which words are structured or organized to form a complete thought. An example will illustrate these differentiations more clearly:

I am not going to school.	(The basic sentence)
I am not *attending* school.	(Improvement due to vocabulary)
I *ain't* going to school.	(Unacceptable usage—ain't)
I am going *not* to school.	(Incorrect organization of words— grammatical error)

One of the most important issues in the discussion of vocabulary, word usage, and grammar is the consideration of the student's oral language and past experiences. In no instance should the teacher expect a student's written composition to reflect a vocabulary, a usage pattern, or a grammar that the child does not use in speaking. Therefore, it is important for the teacher dealing with these aspects of written expression to allow the student to utilize those forms with which he or she is familiar. For example, in preparing experience charts, the student's own words and structure should be recorded. An attempt to remedy these kinds of problems in written language must be preceded and accompanied by remediation in oral language. Information on teaching oral language is found in Chapter 8.

The following list is an accumulation of suggested activities to increase *vocabulary* skills. They are drawn from Greene and Petty (1967), Burns et al. (1971), Otto and R. J. Smith (1980), and our own experience.

1. List on the board new words encountered in classroom and out-of-school activities.
2. Read stories, descriptions, poems, etc., aloud to the students and follow up with group discussions.
3. Have a student go on "word hunts" outside the classroom. Most students will enjoy collecting words from billboards, warning signs, traffic signs, etc. These may also be used as the child's weekly spelling list.
4. Discuss and use words appearing in reading material.
5. Let the student keep a list of words that he or she likes or wants to use. As an alternative, the child can write the new words on an index card and file them with others in a "word box."
6. Make lists or charts of special-interest words, such as those related to football, television, and cooking.
7. Build words from root words by adding prefixes, suffixes, etc.
8. List words that rhyme with others and discuss their meanings.

9. Suggest topics for oral written expression whereby students must employ the new vocabulary items.
10. Utilize word games, such as Scrabble.
11. Find synonyms and antonyms for new words.
12. Have students take turns bringing in new words for the day.
13. Use dictionary drills and emphasize proper use of reference books.

It is important for the teacher interested in remedying *word-usage* problems to select only a few items to attack at any one time. A list of common "errors" to be eliminated is that of Pooley (1960), Table 3–3. The teacher can utilize this list in targeting the particular usages to be attacked. The most important factor in correcting word usage and grammatical errors is to provide ample opportunity for the student to utilize the correct forms in oral expression. The following list provides some suggested activities to increase efficiency in word usage.

1. Provide frequent opportunities for practice. Repetition should be emphasized.
2. Utilize the tape recorder in oral language activities.
3. Provide usage activities throughout the day, not only during a language time.
4. Rephrase students' incorrect usage in situations where it will not prove embarrassing.
5. Have students clap, etc., when they hear a usage error in a selection.
6. Give students opportunities to mark incorrect usage in written expressive tasks.
7. Play games substituting correct and incorrect usage in sentences.
8. Dramatize characters in plays utilizing different usage forms.
9. Attend primarily to those most socially unaccepted usage forms.

Grammatical skills will be susceptible to most of the approaches mentioned for vocabulary and word usage. Initial instruction in the various grammatical structures will be best taught through oral and written examples and repetition. Following instruction in the simple sentences and questions using the noun + verb, noun + verb + noun, etc., the teacher will want to include instruction, group activities, and games that experiment with noun and verb phrases and, later, with clauses. For example,

The dog ran.
The big dog ran.
The big gray dog ran.
The big gray and white dog with a red collar . . .
. . . ran over the hill.
. . . ran over the green hill toward them.

Table 3– 3.   Word-Usage Errors to Be Eliminated in Elementary Grades

1. The elimination of all baby-talk and "cute" expressions.
2. The correct uses in speech and writing of *I, me, he, him, she, her.*
3. The correct uses of *is, are, was, were* with respect to number and tense.
4. Correct past tenses of common irregular verbs such as *saw, gave, took, brought, bought, stuck.*
5. Correct use of past participles of the same verbs and similar verbs after auxiliaries.
6. Elimination of the double negative; *we don't have no apples,* etc.
7. Elimination of analogical forms: *ain't, hisn, hern, ourn, theirselves,* etc.
8. Correct use of possessive pronouns: *my, mine, his, hers, theirs, ours.*
9. Mastery of the distinction between *its,* possessive pronoun, and *it's,* contraction of *it is.*
10. Placement of *have* or its phonetic reduction to *v* between *I* and a past participle.
11. Elimination of *them* as a demonstrative pronoun.
12. Elimination of *this here* and *that there.*
13. Mastery of use of *a* and *an* articles.
14. Correct use of personal pronouns in compound constructions: as subject (*Mary and I*), as object (*Mary and me*), as object of preposition (to *Mary and me*).
15. The use of *we* before an appositional noun when subject; *us* when object.
16. Correct number agreement with the phrases *there is, there are, there was, there were.*
17. Elimination of *he don't, she don't, it don't.*
18. Elimination of *learn* for *teach, leave* for *let.*
19. Elimination of pleonastic subjects: *my brother he; my mother she; that fellow he.*
20. Proper agreement in number with antecedent pronouns *one* and *anyone, everyone, each, no one.* With *everybody* and *none,* some tolerance of number seems acceptable now.
21. The use of *who* and *whom* as reference to persons (but note, *Who did he give it to?* is tolerated in all but very formal situations; in the latter, *To whom did he give it?* is preferable).
22. Accurate use of *said* in reporting the words of a speaker in the past.
23. Correction of *lay down* to *lie down.*
24. The distinction between *good* as adjective and *well* as adverb, e.g., *He spoke well.*
25. Elimination of *can't hardly, all the farther* (for *as far as*), and *Where is he* (*she, it*) *at?*

Source: R. C. Pooley, Dare schools set a standard in English usage? *English Journal,* 1960, 49, 179–180. Copyright © 1960 by the National Council of Teachers of English. Reprinted by permission of the publisher and the author.

Exercises such as these can often be extended into the absurd and not only incorporate new vocabulary but also provide for enjoyable class interactions. Burns et al. (1971, p. 21) provide twelve items in which students should be instructed so that they can manipulate grammatical structures and patterns to create sentence variations. These are quoted below with the permission of the authors. They will provide a useful guide in sequencing of instruction.

  1. Elements (as adverbs) can be recorded:
     Marie stood by quietly.   Quietly Marie stood by.

2. Indirect objects may be rearranged:
He gave a ball to John.   He gave John a ball.

3. The use of "there" provides an alternative:
A visitor was upstairs.   There was a visitor upstairs.

4. Adjectives can be used:
The cat is dirty.   The dirty cat . . . (or The cat that is dirty . . .)

5. Possessives may be formed:
Bill has a dog.
The dog is gentle. } Bill's dog is gentle.

6. Comparisons may be made:
John is strong.
Tom is stronger. } Tom is stronger than John.

7. Relatives (such as *that, which, who, whom*) can be utilized:
The girl played the piano.
The girl is my sister. } The girl who played the piano is my sister.

8. Appositives can be employed:
Clara is my youngest sister.
She went to California. } Clara, my youngest sister, went to California.

9. Noun phrase complements may consist of a "that clause"; infinitive clause ("for . . . to"); or gerundive clause (genetive or possessive form), such as:
That Bill arrived late bothered Sue.
For Bill to arrive late bothered Sue.
Bill's having arrived late bothered Sue.

10. Coordination:
The phone rang.
No one answered it. } The phone rang, but no one answered it.

11. Subordination:
The man was strong.
He was tall.
He was handsome. } The man was strong, tall, and handsome.

The wind was strong.
The leaves fell to the ground. } The leaves fell to the ground because (as, since, when) the wind was strong.

12. Sentence connection:
I am not going to the movie
I am going to the dance. } I am not going to the movie; however, I am going to the dance.

Activities employed to develop grammatical skills for children with learning problems will primarily be oral. Some examples of suggested activities are listed below:

1. Repeat and expand or elaborate child's utterances to form more complete or complex sentences.
2. Give students ample opportunities to participate orally in class:
   —describing objects or events
   —retelling a story
   —discussing an experience or activity

In the list by Burns et al., items 5–8 and 10–12 involve some type of sentence combining. When used as an instructional technique, sentence combining has been shown to be extremely effective in enhancing children's ability to write syntactically (Mellon, 1969; O'Hare, 1973; Hunt and O'Donnell, 1970) as well as to read with comprehension (Combs, 1977).

The sentence-combining technique is easy to use, especially with older children, who find it motivating. In part, this is because there is no one correct way to combine sentences; many combinations are equally acceptable.

A resource for all who would plan sentence-combining activities is the book by Strong (1973), *Sentence Combining: A Composing Book.* The following examples of the technique are from his work. [2]

Main Drag, Saturday Night
1. The cars come cruising up Broadway.
2. The cars are glittering.
3. The paint is harsh.
4. The paint is metallic.
5. The paint is highly waxed.

The student is told:
1. As you combine sentences, listen to them; say them aloud in several ways; experiment with new structures.
2. In the beginning, at least, write out all the transformations you can think of for each cluster; then choose the one you like best.
3. In a special notebook, write out the final transforms for each string; use the notebook daily.
4. Compare your transforms with those of the other students; discuss which transformations sound best; try to figure out why.
5. Look for the patterns that show up over and over as you make your combinations; you'll also see patterns of spelling and punctuation as you work.
6. Go beyond the lists that are given in the text by following the Suggestions; in other words, *keep writing.*

Examples of how students may combine the first five sentences in the "Main

2. W. Strong, *Sentence Combining: A Composing Book* (New York: Random House, Inc., 1973), pp. x, 7.

Drag, Saturday Night" series into two sentences follow. The emphasis is on forming transformations, not on combining the sentences into a single correct way.

Transformation 1

The glittering cars come cruising up Broadway. Their paint is harsh, metallic, and highly waxed. . . .

Transformation 2

The cars that glitter come cruising up Broadway. Their metallic paint is harsh and highly waxed. . . .

Sentence and Paragraph Construction.   To be competent in forming written sentences and paragraphs, children have to coordinate all the skills involved in punctuation, capitalization, vocabulary, word usage, and grammar. In addition, they must organize content as well. West (1966) has prepared a list of problems that are commonly associated with children's sentence construction. These include: fragments, run-on sentences and comma splices, sentences that are too simple or too complex, misplaced or dangling modifiers, pronouns without proper referents, lack of variety in sentence structure, pronoun–antecedent and subject–verb disagreements, overuse of expletives and passive voice, and tense-sequence problems. Each of the errors will have to be attended to individually by applying and/or adjusting instructional activities such as those that follow. The teacher should:

1. Have students arrange a string of written words that will form a sentence. *Examples:*

    | fast | the | dog | black | ran |
    | The | black | dog | ran | fast. |

2. Have students mark errors in given sentences or have them mark, correct, and rewrite the incorrect portions.

3. Have students complete partially written sentences. *Examples:*

    Mary went to the store to buy _____.

    Mary went to the store to buy _____, _____, and _____.

    Mary went _____.

4. Do much group work in composing (e.g., experience charts, writing letters to classmates, etc.).

5. Begin conceptual writing instruction with one-word composition, progress to simple sentences, and gradually increase the number and complexity of the sentences used in the exercises.

6. Encourage and provide opportunities for students to dictate letters and stories.

7. Utilize dictation and proofreading exercises in the writing program.

8. Give students a group of written statements comprising both com-

plete sentences and fragments; ask them to select those that are fragments.

9. Have students underline subject and verb as clues to determining which are complete sentences and which are fragments.
10. Have students match predicate and verb phrases.
11. Give students an outline or form for a sentence to be constructed. *Examples:*

Noun	*Verb*	*Noun*	*Noun*
John	gave	Bill	the ball.

12. Have students practice using connectives, such as *and, but, for, which, when, because,* etc. *Examples:*

Willie was tired, _____ he got up early this morning.
Susie ran well, _____ Judy won the race.

Once a student can compose complete sentences, the teacher should begin instruction on paragraph formation. Four major points should be stressed in teaching children to write paragraphs: the content to be expressed, the topic sentence, the order and flow of sentences and ideas within the paragraph, and the concluding sentence. Activities for each are provided below. The teacher may:

1. Collect statements made by students during a discussion, write them on the board, and have the students select those that go together.
2. Let students order the statements selected above.
3. Give students selections whereby they must locate inappropriate sentences in paragraphs.
4. Give students paragraphs that contain appropriate but poorly sequenced sentences; have the students rearrange the sentences into a more meaningful order. The teacher may want to see if the young pupil can tell an experience in sequence or arrange comic strips and tell a story from the frames before attempting this task.
5. Utilize opportunities, such as class or school newspapers, to motivate students to compose.
6. Employ dictation and proofreading activities.
7. Introduce students to the concept of outlining.

In conclusion, teachers should be ever mindful that in using any of the activities described in this chapter, care must be taken to ensure that students are required to perform only those tasks in which they can experience some degree of success. As the child succeeds, the complexity of the tasks can be increased gradually until eventually the child will have mastered the targeted skills or areas completely.

The authors wish to conclude this chapter by referring the reader to a new resource: *Evaluating and Improving Written Expression* (J. Hall, 1981). This practical guide for teachers is advertised as "a step-by-step approach to analyzing and building writing skills, from idea to finished composition." Teachers, and others, who assess and teach written composition—as well as handwriting and spelling—will not be disappointed in this work. The book is replete with activities designed to develop creative and practical writing, organizational skill, sentence structure, and mature vocabulary.

4

IMPROVING SPELLING SKILLS

Donald D. Hammill

Spelling is the forming of words from letters, in both written and oral forms, according to accepted usage. The written form is by far the more important to children; however, proficiency in spelling, while highly prized, is frequently unattained in language arts instruction. Most children are taught by means of a school-wide spelling program and readily become fluent spellers. However, many others, with comparable mental ability and interest, do not learn to spell adequately. When deficiencies are first observed, the teacher should immediately take steps to help the child overcome the problem. This chapter is designed to aid teachers to better understand spelling skills, and to acquire information about appropriate assessment techniques and various development and remedial teaching programs directed toward improvement in spelling.

ASSESSING SPELLING SKILLS

When a child fails in spelling, the teacher immediately needs the answers to several pertinent questions:

1. Does the child have sufficient mental ability to learn to spell?
2. Are the child's hearing, speech, and vision adequate?
3. What is the child's general level of spelling ability?
4. Are there areas of specific weakness in spelling?
5. What systems, techniques, or activities might be used to remedy difficulties?

The answers to questions one to four are crucial and prerequisite to answering question five. In most cases, there will be no question as to the pupil's mental or sensory adequacy, and the teacher can proceed directly to assessing the child's spelling deficiencies. This section is devoted to a discussion of procedures that might be used to assess spelling readiness and specific spelling skills.

ASSESSING SPELLING READINESS

There is a temptation to refer to spelling readiness in the broadest of terms; e.g., the child should be motivated to learn to spell or he should have adequate auditory and visual memory. Unfortunately, such terms are so indefinite that they are of little value to teachers. Although R. M. Smith (1968), Frostig and Maslow (1973), Westerman (1971), and many others believe on a theoretical level that "auditory and visual reception," "auditory and visual memory," "auditory and visual discrimination," "association of auditory and visual stimuli," "motor expression," and "vocal expression" are skills basic to successful spelling, the assessment of spelling readiness confined to these broad, possibly hypothetical categories is not profitable. For instance, there is no doubt that in some "abstract" sense, the ability to associate auditory and visual stimuli is involved in some ill-defined way in the act of spelling; however, the practical question remains: Which particular associative tasks are prerequisites to spelling? Clearly, not all associations are important. The ability to associate letters with their sounds is likely to be helpful, while the ability to associate spoken words with pictures is probably less critical to spelling. It is important for teachers to note that when attempts have been made to empirically study the relationships of tests of psycholinguistic processes, sensory modalities, and perceptual abilities to tests of spelling, the resultant correlation coefficients have been consistently too small to have any educational usefulness. Readers who have a particular interest in this topic are referred to the review of thirteen relevant studies on pages 48–50 in Newcomer and Hammill (1976).

For most school children, teachers should consider average mental ability and adequate hearing and sight as the primary prerequisites for spelling. Pupils exhibiting normal intelligence, language, sight, and hearing who fail in spelling should be subjected to a thorough teacher evaluation using procedures discussed in this chapter. But this assessment should focus on a study of the child's performance in tasks directly related to spelling, rather than on "underlying" psycholinguistic processes. To our knowledge, the precise constellation of skills that are predictive of spelling success are as yet mostly unknown or unresearched.

NORM-REFERENCED SPELLING TESTS

The norm-referenced standardized tests that are available to teachers range widely regarding the types and breadth of information provided. Most achievement tests yield information only on a child's general spelling ability and some yield information on several different spelling skills. The latter devices are frequently called diagnostic tests. For the most part, these tests usually involve selecting correctly spelled words or writing dictated words.

The main shortcoming of most achievement tests with which many teachers are familiar is that they yield a single score which is compared to a set of standardized norms and which results in a grade equivalent. Although this information is useful for some purposes such as determining the spelling level of a particular school or school district or identifying poor spellers, it often is not helpful to teachers. Examples of these tests include the spelling subtests from the popular achievement batteries, e.g., the Wide Range Achievement Test (Jastak and Jastak, 1965), the Metropolitan Achievement Tests (Durost et al., 1971), and the Iowa Tests of Basic Skills (Lindquist and Hieronymous, 1956).

Diagnostic tests, on the other hand, are designed to provide information about an individual's functioning ability in several different areas. Unfortunately, there are few diagnostic spelling tests available, and none of them permit the measurement of all the abilities that comprise spelling. To the extent that the diagnostic tests fail to do this, the teacher must supply his or her own information, gathered from employing the informal evaluation techniques presented in the next section. One of those multiability tests of spelling are discussed below.

A norm-referenced diagnostic test, called the Test of Written Spelling, has been developed by Larsen and Hammill (1976). The sixty words that comprise the test were chosen because they appear in each of the ten spelling series that are used most often in the schools. Thirty-five of these words are "predictable," in that their spelling is consistent with certain phonological (i.e., phoneme–grapheme correspondence) rules or generalizations (e.g., had, spring, pile, salute, legal); and twenty-five words are "unpredictable," in that their spelling conforms to no useful phonological or morphological rules (e.g., people, knew, eight, fountain, community). Test results can be interpreted in terms of the student's mastery of the predictable words, the unpredictable words, or the total number of words.

The test is standardized on a nationwide sample of 4544 children who share the national characteristics relative to geographic location, sex, and urban–rural residence. Studies indicate that the TWS is reliable (i.e., internally consistent) at all grade levels between two and nine (coefficients in the 80s and 90s), and that its results correlate strongly with the spelling subtests of the

Durrell Analysis of Reading Difficulty (.90), Wide Range Achievement Test (.80), California Achievement Test (.80), and the SRA Achievement Series (.69).

In general, norm-referenced tests with the most complete standardizations offer little information that a teacher can use to plan individual programs. On the other hand, the tests that attempt to provide a more complete analysis of an individual's spelling ability tend to have inadequate standardizations. The teacher, therefore, has the option of using a test with a comparatively sound research base but offering little instructionally relevant information, or of using a test that attempts to tap more components of spelling but has no reported reliability.

The teacher should be selective in the type of tests used and should consider the following three suggestions:

1. Know what the test measures and what its limitations are before giving it to the child: for example, what type of children were used for the standardization and what is the reported reliability and validity of the test.
2. Be prepared to supplement the test where possible with other formal measures.
3. Use informal evaluation techniques whenever specific information about the child's spelling abilities is required, and as a guide to planning a remediation program.

CRITERION-REFERENCED TESTING IN SPELLING

Norm-referenced tests such as those just mentioned usually comprise statistically selected items because they are built to be relatively short, highly reliable measurement devices. Criterion-referenced tests, on the other hand, are constructed to include a broad spectrum of items, reflecting most, if not all, of the elements that make up the skill being measured. Builders of criterion-referenced measures are not unduly concerned with the statistical characteristics of the items being chosen. The purpose of criterion-referenced testing in educational practice is not to determine where the child stands relative to other children but to identify those components of the ability being assessed that are in need of training. While these tests may or may not be accompanied by rough norms, they will invariably be quite suitable for item analysis.

This type of assessment helps the teacher to determine a child's instructional level while also measuring progress toward the task goal. The following advantages to this approach are suggested by Westerman (1971). Criterion-referenced tests:

1. Indicate the skills the child has and those the child needs.

2. Provide an objective measure of progress as the child moves from task to task.

3. Are designed by the teacher and are based upon what content is to be taught and who is to learn it.

While there are many more or less criterion-referenced measures of spelling from which the teacher may choose, only one will be presented in this book, Kottmeyer's (1970) Diagnostic Spelling Test (see Table 4–1). The test is administered using a dictation format; e.g., the examiner says to the children, "Not. He is *not* here," after which they write the word "not."

Table 4– 1.   Diagnostic Spelling Test

Give list 1 to any pupil whose placement is second or third grade.
Give list 2 to any pupil whose placement is above third grade.
Grade scoring, list 1:

Below 15 correct:	Below second grade
15–22 correct:	Second grade
23–29 correct:	Third grade

Any pupil who scores above 29 should be given the list 2 test.
Grade scoring, list 2:

Below 9 correct:	Below third grade
9–19 correct:	Third grade
20–25 correct:	Fourth grade
26–29 correct:	Fifth grade
Over 29 correct:	Sixth grade or better

Any pupil who scores below 9 should be given the list 1 test.

	List 1
Word	*Illustrative Sentence*

1. not—He is *not* here.
2. but—Mary is here, *but* Joe is not.
3. get—*Get* the wagon, John.
4. sit—*Sit* down, please.
5. man—Father is a tall *man.*
6. boat—We sailed our *boat* on the lake.
7. train—Tom has a new toy *train.*
8. time—It is *time* to come home.
9. like—We *like* ice cream.
10. found—We *found* our lost ball.
11. down—Do not fall *down.*
12. soon—Our teacher will *soon* be here.
13. good—He is a *good* boy.
14. very—We are *very* glad to be here.
15. happy—Jane is a *happy* girl.
16. kept—We *kept* our shoes dry.

Table 4–1. *Continued*

	List 1
Word	Illustrative Sentence

17. come—*Come* to our party.
18. what—*What* is your name?
19. those—*Those* are our toys.
20. show—*Show* us the way.
21. much—I feel *much* better.
22. sing—We will *sing* a new song.
23. will—Who *will* help us?
24. doll—Make a dress for the *doll*.
25. after—We play *after* school.
26. sister—My *sister* is older than I.
27. toy—I have a new *toy* train.
28. say—*Say* your name clearly.
29. little—Tom is a *little* boy.
30. one—I have only *one* book.
31. would—*Would* you come with us?
32. pretty—She is a *pretty* girl.

	List 2
Word	Illustrative Sentence

1. flower—A rose is a *flower*.
2. mouth—Open your *mouth*.
3. shoot—Joe wants to *shoot* his new gun.
4. stood—We *stood* under the roof.
5. while—We sang *while* we marched.
6. third—We are in the *third* grade.
7. each—*Each* child has a pencil.
8. class—Our *class* is reading.
9. jump—We like to *jump* rope.
10. jumps—Mary *jumps* rope.
11. jumped—We *jumped* rope yesterday.
12. jumping—The girls are *jumping* rope now.
13. hit—*Hit* the ball hard.
14. hitting—John is *hitting* the ball.
15. bite—Our dog does not *bite*.
16. biting—The dog is *biting* on the bone.
17. study—*Study* your lesson.
18. studies—He *studies* each day.
19. dark—The sky is *dark* and cloudy.
20. darker—This color is *darker* than that one.
21. darkest—This color is the *darkest* of the three.
22. afternoon—We may play this *afternoon*.
23. grandmother—Our *grandmother* will visit us.
24. can't—We *can't* go with you.
25. doesn't—Mary *doesn't* like to play.

Table 4–1. *Continued*

Word	List 2 Illustrative Sentence
26. night	—We read to Mother last *night*.
27. brought	—Joe *brought* his lunch to school.
28. apple	—An *apple* fell from the tree.
29. again	—We must come back *again*.
30. laugh	—Do not *laugh* at other children.
31. because	—We cannot play *because* of the rain.
32. through	—We ran *through* the yard.

Word	List 1 Element Tested
1. not 2. but 3. get 4. sit 5. man	Short vowels
6. boat 7. train	Two vowels together
8. time 9. like	Vowel-consonant-*e*
10. found 11. down	*ow–ou* spelling of *ou* sound
12. soon 13. good	Long and short *oo*
14. very 15. happy	Final *y* as short *i*
16. kept 17. come	*c* and *k* spellings of the *k* sound
18. what 19. those 20. show 21. much 22. sing	*wh, th, sh, ch,* and *ng* spellings and *ow* spelling of long *o*
23. will 24. doll	Doubled final consonants
25. after 26. sister	*er* spelling

Table 4–1. *Continued*

	List 1
Word	Element Tested
27. toy	]——*oy* spelling of *oi* sound
28. say	]——*ay* spelling of long *a* sound
29. little	]——*le* ending
30. one 31. would 32. pretty	]——Nonphonetic spellings

	List 2
Word	Element Tested
1. flower 2. mouth	]——*ow–ou* spellings of *ou* sound *er* ending, *th* spelling
3. shoot	]——Long *oo*, *sh*
4. stood	]——Short *oo*
5. while	]——*wh* spelling, vowel–consonant-*e*
6. third	]——*th* spelling, vowel before *r*
7. each	]——*ch* spelling, two vowels together
8. class	]——Double final consonant, *c;* spelling of *k* sound
9. jump 10. jumps 11. jumped 12. jumping	]——Addition of *s, ed, ing;* *j* spelling of soft *g* sound
13. hit 14. hitting	]——Doubling final consonant before adding *ing*
15. bite 16. biting	]——Dropping final *e* before *ing*
17. study 18. studies	]——Changing final *y* to *i* before ending
19. dark 20. darker 21. darkest	]——*er, est* endings

Table 4– 1. *Continued*

Word	List 2 Element Tested
22. afternoon 23. grandmother	Compound words
24. can't 25. doesn't	Contractions
26. night 27. brought	Silent *gh*
28. apple	*le* ending
29. again 30. laugh 31. because 32. through	Nonphonetic spellings

Source: Teacher's Guide for Remedial Reading by William Kottmeyer,
© 1970, with permission of McGraw-Hill, Inc.

After the child has completed the test, the number of correct spellings are totaled and first interpreted in a norm-referenced fashion using the data offered just below the heading "Directions for Diagnostic Spelling Test." They are next interpreted in a criterion-referenced manner. For example, if the child misspelled "not," it is likely that he or she has not yet mastered the phonological rule governing the short vowel /o/. Analysis of the child's errors on the test should result in the development of a relatively data-based remedial program.

INFORMAL ASSESSMENT PROCEDURES

Information gleaned from the informal assessment of children's spelling behavior will be of considerable value to teachers in planning individualized programs of study. This evaluation is based primarily on the teacher's direct observation of a child's behavior in a variety of spelling situations and on an analysis of many samples of a pupil's spelling work. In short, informal assessment is actually directed, structured, and/or analytic observation.

Preliminary assessments may be made by the teacher's careful scrutiny of the child's spelling lessons and work habits. In particular, Linn (1967, pp. 62–63) suggests that teachers evaluate pupil performance in terms of the following questions. Can the child recall the letter and sound symbols quickly and accurately? Can he produce them on paper correctly? Can he fuse the sound parts of words together into whole words? Does he reverse letters in sound parts? Can he remember what the teacher has written on the board a few minutes after it is erased? Does he learn words when he hears the letter sequence rather than when he sees it? Does he appear to block out or not hear sounds? Can he write the correct symbol for single sounds when they are dictated to him orally? Can he identify sounds? Errors in these areas are clues to specific spelling problems.

Brueckner and Bond[1] have systematized informal observations by suggesting the following guidelines for teachers to use:

1. Analysis of Written Work, including Test Papers
   a. Legibility of handwriting
   b. Defects in letter forms, spacing, alignment, size
   c. Classification of errors in written work, letters, or tests
   d. Range of vocabulary used
   e. Evidence of lack of knowledge of conventions and rules
2. Analysis of Oral Responses
   a. Comparison of errors in oral and written spellings
   b. Pronunciation of words spelled incorrectly
   c. Articulation and enunciation
   d. Slovenliness of speech
   e. Dialect and colloquial forms of speech
   f. Way of spelling words orally:
      (1) Spells words as units
      (2) Spells letter by letter
      (3) Spells by digraphs
      (4) Spells by syllables
   g. Rhythmic pattern in oral spelling
   h. Blending ability
   i. Giving letters for sounds or sounds for letters
   j. Technique of word analysis used
   k. Quality and error made in oral reading
   l. Oral responses on tests or word analysis
   m. Analysis of pupil's comments as he states orally his thought process while studying new words
3. Interview with Pupil and Others
   a. Questioning pupil about methods of study

1. L. J. Brueckner and G. L. Bond, The diagnosis and treatment of learning difficulties. In E. C. Frierson and W. B. Barbe (Eds.), *Educating Children with Learning Disabilities* (New York: Appleton-Century-Crofts, 1955). Reprinted by permission.

      b. Questioning pupil about spelling rules
      c. Questioning pupil about errors in convention
      d. Securing evidence as to attitude towards spelling
4. Questionnaire
      a. Applying checklist of methods of study
      b. Having pupil rank spelling according to interest
      c. Surveying use of written language
5. Free Observation in Course of Daily Work
      a. Securing evidence as to attitudes towards spelling
      b. Evidence of improvement in the study of new words
      c. Observing extent of use of dictionary
      d. Extent or error in regular written work
      e. Study habits and methods of work
      f. Social acceptability of the learner
      g. Evidences of emotional and social maladjustment
      h. Evidences of possible physical handicaps
6. Controlled Observation of Work on Set Tasks
      a. Looking up the meanings of given words in dictionary
      b. Giving pronunciation of words in dictionary
      c. Writing plural forms and derivatives of given words
      d. Observing responses on informal tests
      f. Estimating pupil scores when using a variety of methods studying selected words

    Of course, it is useful for teachers to know which words the child cannot spell. Therefore, each child who has difficulty in spelling should have his or her own list of frequently misspelled words. Since some words are more likely to be misspelled than others, the teacher should at some time assess the child's performance on the list of 100 demons, or commonly misspelled words.[2]

    Teachers should select words from the list that correspond to the child's grade level. The demons are:

ache	families	neither	sandwich
afraid	fasten	nickel	scratch
against	fault	niece	sense
all right	February	ninety	separate
although	forgotten	ninth	shining
angry	friendly	onion	silence
answered	good-bye	passed	since

2. From A. Kuska, E. J. D. Webster, and G. Elford, *Spelling in Language Arts 6* [Ontario, Canada: Thomas Nelson & Sons (Canada) Ltd., 1964.] Reprinted by permission of the publisher, Thomas Nelson & Sons (Canada) Limited.

asks	guessed	peaceful	soldier
beautiful	happened	perfectly	squirrel
because	happily	piano	stepped
beginning	here's	picnic	straight
boy's	holiday	picture	studying
buried	hungry	piece	success
busily	husband	pitcher	taught
carrying	its	pleasant	their
certain	it's	potato	there's
choose	kitchen	practice	through
Christmas	knives	prettiest	valentine
clothes	language	pumpkin	whose
climbed	lettuce	purpose	worst
course	listening	quietly	writing
double	lose	rapidly	yours
easier	marriage	receive	
eighth	meant	rotten	
either	minute	safety	
enemy	neighbor	said	

Once the misspelled words are determined, they may be taught by rote or the misspellings can be subjected to error analysis.

For each child with a spelling problem, a careful analysis of errors should be made to discern if a pattern of errors exists. For analysis and error tabulation, use both material dictated from spelling lists and material provided by uncorrected continuous prose, such as a story a child has made up. Edgington[3] has provided a sample of types of errors that exist in children's spelling work:

Addition of unneeded letters (for example, *dresses*)
Omissions of needed letters (*hom* for *home*)
Reflections of child's mispronunciations (*pin* for *pen*)
Reflections of dialectical speech patterns (*Cuber* for *Cuba*)
Reversals of whole words (*eno* for *one*)
Reversals of consonant order (*lback* for *black*)
Reversals of consonant or vowel directionality (*brithday* for *birthday*)
Reversals of syllables (*telho* for *hotel*)
Phonetic spelling of nonphonetic words or parts thereof (*cawt* for *caught*)
Wrong associations of a sound with a given set of letters, such as *u* has been learned as *ou* in *you*
"Neographisms," or letters put in a word which bear no discernible relationship with the word dictated.
Varying degrees and combinations of these or other possible patterns

3. From R. Edgington, But he spelled them right this morning, *Academic Therapy Quarterly*, 1967, *3*, 58–59. Used with permission of the author and publisher (Academic Therapy Publications, San Rafael, California).

TEACHING CHILDREN TO SPELL

Since pupils vary considerably in intellectual capacity and specific areas of weakness, spelling programs and remedial techniques should also vary with regard to level, theoretical orientation, vocabulary, manner of presentation, and format. The teacher cannot expect that a single spelling series will be suitable for all pupils. Therefore, he or she should have knowledge of an assortment of instructional alternatives. This section will review briefly several developmental and remedial systems and a few game activities which might facilitate spelling competence if employed effectively.

DEVELOPMENTAL METHODS

A long-standing and sometimes confusing controversy exists among authorities regarding the teaching of spelling. [See Yee (1966) for a detailed discussion of the topic.] Teachers should be aware of this debate because many of the spelling materials and methods used today reflect the controversy. Very simply, the conflict centers on the relative merits of using rules to enhance spelling competence. Some educators recommend the teaching of spelling rules that utilize a phonetic or sound–letter approach (Hanna and Moore, 1953; Hodges and Rudorf, 1965). They have found support in the work of Hanna, Hanna, Hodges, and Rudorf (1966), who programmed a computer with rules and made it "spell" 17,000 words, which it did with remarkable (50 percent) accuracy. Thirty-seven percent of the words were spelled with only a single error. A review of this project is in Hanna, Hodges, and Hanna (1971).

Others point out that English spelling forms are linguistically so irregular that spelling should be taught using almost no rules whatsoever. Still others suggest the limited use of teaching of rules (Archer, 1930; Horn, 1957). Spelling instruction, following this latter view, involves a gradual accumulation of necessary and practiced words and includes the introduction of rules whenever warranted.

Whatever the merits of the arguments may be, most of the developmental spelling series in common use today seem to adhere to the idea that American English spelling is sufficiently rule-governed that a basic linguistic approach can be utilized. By linguistic approach, we mean one that emphasizes the teaching of phonological, morphological, and syntactic rules or word patterns. Justification for this statement is based on the detailed survey of spelling instructional methodologies reported by Hammill, Larsen, and McNutt (1977). They contacted a nonselected group of 100 third- through eighth-grade teachers and asked them to specify the particular methods that they used to teach spelling. In all, these teachers were instructing 2956 students residing in 22 states.

The three basal spelling series utilized most often by teachers in this sample were *Spell Correctly* (Benthul, Anderson, Utech, Biggy, and Bailey, 1974), used with 26.0 percent of the children; *Word Book* (Rogers, Ort, and Serra, 1970), used with 16.7 percent of the sample; and *Basic Goals in Spelling* (Kottmeyer and Claus, 1972), used with 14.2 percent of the students. Various other spelling programs were employed with 29.6 percent of the student sample, while the teachers reported that 13.4 percent of the children were recieving no specific spelling instruction.

The authors of the three most-used basal spelling series in this sample all maintain that their method of teaching spelling is based on "linguistic theory." This being the case, a brief description of linguistics would probably be useful. Linguistics, the study of language, may be subdivided into four discrete but related topics: (1) phonology, the study of speech sounds; (2) morphology, the meaningful units of speech; (3) syntax, the rules that govern sentence formation or word order; and (4) semantics, the process by which a global understanding is gained from the presented language. While linguistic theories usually encompass all four areas of study, when they are applied to teaching spelling, two elements appear to receive a majority of the emphasis: phonology and morphology. A more specific explanation of these two areas follows.

Phonolgy refers to speech sounds with the term "phoneme" being of prime interest. A phoneme is a group of sounds that are so similar that they are considered equivalent. Although there may be slight variations in the production of a phoneme, for all intents and purposes it is a single speech sound with various letters or groups of letters being capable of representing the same phoneme. There are approximately thirty-six phonemes in our language. Graphemes are the letter or combination of letters that represent a phoneme. For example, the phoneme /k/ may be represented by the grapheme "k," "c," or "ck."

Morphology refers to the smallest units of meaningful speech, morphemes. A morpheme may be a word (e.g., *boy*, because it cannot be broken into smaller units that yield meaning) or even a single letter (e.g., the plural marker /z/ in boys). Morphology includes the inflections and changes in words that alter their meanings (e.g., prefixes and suffixes).

While each of the three most-used basal spelling series utilizes aspects of linguistic theory, this should not imply that the series are identical. To aid in identifying some of the differences, a brief description of the three spelling series follows.

The words for each unit in the *Spell Correctly* series are divided into basic lists and enrichment lists which are topical or thematic in organization. The basic words constitute approximately 90 percent of the words most students use in their daily writing, with each group or list focusing on one particular spelling pattern. The patterns generally are phonological (e.g., short *a* words) or morphological (e.g., prefixes that mean "not") in nature. In addition to the general spelling lessons, *Spell Correctly* integrates many skills from a language arts curriculum (e.g., dictionary skills) as well as containing various enrichment or extension activities for the more able student.

The authors of the *Word Book* program state that the presented words are grouped according to their particular spelling patterns: rhyming patterns (bit, fit, hit), nonrhyming patterns (did, dig, dip), and vowel-changing patterns (pat, pet, put). Additionally, the words of the core vocabulary comprise 80 percent of the spelling needed by an elementary child, while the upper levels emphasize words that are important to adult living. It should perhaps be noted that the authors do not state how the core words or the words needed for adult living were chosen. Emphasis is also placed on integrating various communication skills (e.g., speaking and listening skills). Unlike the other two series, many of the units in the *Word Book* program emphasize various topics not related to spelling (e.g., Going to Bed on Time, Nature in the Spring, A Wise Constitution).

As with *Spell Correctly, Basic Goals in Spelling* presents basic word lists and word lists for enrichment. The basic words were chosen because research revealed that they are commonly used in the writing vocabulary of pupils at each level. While morphological relationships are included, the stress according to the series authors is on sound–symbol relationships, indicating the importance of phonology. Rather than having the teacher state spelling rules for the students to memorize, the authors of the programs stress the importance of allowing the students to observe similarities of sound and spelling in words and to formulate generalizations, or rules, on their own.

That the authors of this system and the others previously described have depended heavily on linguistic theory to develop their programs is even more evident when one examines the scope-and-sequence charts in which the skills supposedly being taught are depicted. The charts associated with the *Basic Goals in Spelling* series will serve as an example and are reproduced in Tables 4–2 and 4–3.

REMEDIAL TECHNIQUES FOR SPELLING

Many students exposed to the traditional, classroom-based spelling programs reviewed in the previous section do not reach expected levels of achievement. With these students, the teacher may decide to try a remedial approach. Remedial techniques differ considerably from the developmentally oriented classroom basal series in that the student is taught on a one-to-one relationship or

Table 4–2. Linguistic Skills Taught in the Primary Grades

Skills Taught	Examples of Vocabulary	
	Grade 2	Grade 3

Auditory Recognition of Phonemes

Consonant sounds:

1. The eighteen key consonant sounds: *b, d, f, g, h, j, k, l, m, n, p, r, s, t, v, w, y, z.*

    Key pictures: ball, dog, fish, girl, hat, jug, kite, lamp, moon, nail, pig, rabbit, sun, top, vase, wagon, yarn, zebra

2. The *sh, ch, wh, th,* and *ng* sounds.

    Key pictures: shoe, chair, wheel, three, ring

    Short vowel sounds

    Key pictures: apples, elephant, Indian, ostrich, umbrella

Graphemic Representation of Phonemes

Skills Taught	Grade 2	Grade 3
Consonant sounds:		
1. The regular consonant sounds	bed, hat, sun, yes	must, trip, ask, zoo
2. The *sh, ch, ng, wh,* and *th* sounds	fish, much, sing, which, this, with	shoe, child, sang, while, those, thank
3. The *nk* spelling of the *ngk* sounds		drunk, drank
4. The *x* spelling of the *ks* sounds	box, fox	next
5. The *c* spelling of the *k* sound	cold	cup
6. The *c* and *k* spellings of the *k* sound	cat, kept	ask, cake
7. The *ck* spelling of the *k* sound	duck, black	chicken, clock
8. The *s* spelling of the *s* and *z* sounds	sun, as	
	gas, has	
9. The *gh* spelling of *f*		laugh
10. Silent consonants	doll, hill, who, know, would	bell, grass, walk, catch, wrote, night
Vowel sounds:		
1. The short vowel sound regularly spelled in initial or medial position	am, did	bad, send, stop
2. The long vowel sound spelled by		
a. a single vowel at the end of a short word in open syllables	go, be	paper, table

Table 4– 2.

Skills Taught	Examples of Vocabulary	
	Grade 2	Grade 3
b. two vowels together	meat, rain	soap, cream, train
c. vowel–consonant–silent *e*	home, ride	game, side, snake
3. Other long vowel spellings		
a. the *ow* spelling of long *o*	snow, grow	window
b. the *ay* spelling of long *a*	day, play	always, yesterday
c. the final *y* spelling of long *e*	baby, very	city, study, sorry
d. the final *y* spelling of long *i*	my, why	cry, try
4. Additional vowel sounds and spellings		
a. the *oo* spelling of *u̇* and *ü*	good, soon	cook, shoot
b. the *ow* and *ou* spellings of the *ou* sound in *owl* and *mouse*	down, house	flower, ground
c. the *oy* spelling of the *oi* sound	boy, toy	
d. vowel sounds before *r*		
the *er* spelling of *ǝr* at the end	over, teacher	ever, another
the *or* spelling of *ǝr* at the end		color
er, ir, or, and *ur* spellings of *er*	her, bird, work, hurt	person, third, word, turning
the *or* and *ar* spellings of *ôr*	for	horse, warm
the *ar* spelling of *är*	car	star, party
5. Unexpected spellings		
a. unexpected single vowel spellings	from, off, cold	kind, full, cost
b. unexpected vowel-consonant-silent *e*	give, done	whose, sure
c. unexpected spellings with two vowels together	been, said	bread, great, friend
d. other unexpected vowel spellings	they, eye	aunt, says, could
6. The *le* spelling of the *ǝl* sound		people, table
Using Morphemes to Make Structural Changes		
1. The *s* or *es* plural	cats, cows	cups, buses, dishes
2. Changing *y* to *i* before *es*		cry, cries
3. The *s* or *es* for third person singular	lives, lives	jumps, races, misses
4. The *s* to show possession	yours, ours	
5. The *d* or *ed* ending for past tense	played	asked, laughed
6. The *ing* ending with doubled consonant with dropped silent *e*	blowing	reading, thinking clapping, beginning skating, moving

Table 4–2. *Continued*

	Examples of Vocabulary	
Skills Taught	*Grade 2*	*Grade 3*
Using Morphemes to Make Structural Changes		
7. The *er* noun agent ending	singer, player	painter, builder
8. The *er* and *est* endings	old, older	high, higher, highest
Devices to Aid Spelling Recall		
1. Syllabication	yel low, go ing	bas ket, ta ble
2. Recognizing compounds	today	airplane, something
3. Recognizing rhyming words	pet, get	hand, land
Miscellaneous		
1. Homonyms	to-too-two	its-it's, eight-ate
2. Antonyms	last-first	cry-laugh
3. Alphabetizing	periodic activities requiring the use of the first, second, third, fourth, and fifth letters	

Source: "Linguistic Skills Taught in the Primary Grades," reprinted by permission of the publisher from *Basic Goals In Spelling*, 3rd ed., Teacher's Edition, Grade 2, by William Kottmeyer and Audrey Claus. Copyright © 1972 by McGraw-Hill, Inc.

in small groups, and the activities often incorporate kinesthetic elements in varying degrees.

With children who are targeted for remedial training, the teacher may find it useful to consider the general suggestions offered by Petty and Jensen (1980). In addition to encouraging the development of favorable attitudes toward spelling and good study habits, they recommend the following activities for teaching the "slow speller."

1. Emphasize the importance of the words the student is to learn. Teach a minimum list and make certain that the words on it are as useful as possible.

2. Teach no more words than the pupil can successfully learn to spell. Success is a motivating influence, and the poor speller has probably had much experience with failure in learning to spell the words in the weekly lessons.

3. Give more than the usual amount of time to oral discussion of the words to be learned. In addition to making certain the children know

Table 4–3. Linguistic Skills Taught in the Intermediate Grades

	Examples of Vocabulary		
	Grade 4	Grade 5	Grade 6

Graphemic Representation of Phonemes

Of consonant phonemes:

	Grade 4	Grade 5	Grade 6
1. The regular consonant sounds	sad	belt	fact
2. The *sh, ch,* and *ng* consonant sounds	ship rich hang	shade chest among	shelf chain gang
3. The voiced and unvoiced *th* sounds	bath those	sixth either	thread leather
4. The *ch* spelling of the *k* sound	schoolhouse	echo	orchestra
5. The *wh* spelling of the *hw* sounds	wheel	whistle	whale
6. The *g* spelling of the *g* or *j* sound	frog bridge	gate damage	cigar pledge
7. The *c* spelling of the *k* or *s* sound	cage circus	cool princess	cabbage juice
8. The *ck* spelling of the *k* sound	luck	attack	ticket
9. The *x* spelling of the *ks* sounds	fix	expect	expedition
10. The *qu* spelling of the *kw* sounds	queen	quarter	acquaint
11. The *nk* spelling of the *ngk* sounds	monkey	trunk	plank
12. The *ph* spelling of the *f* sound	elephant		alphabet
13. Silent consonants	answer	ghost	delightful

Of vowel phonemes:

	Grade 4	Grade 5	Grade 6
1. The short medial vowel regularly spelled	cap	bunch	slept
2. The long sound spelled with vowel-consonant-silent *e*	bone	prize	blaze
3. The long sound spelled with two vowels together	tie	beads	coach
4. The long sound regularly spelled in open syllables	hotel	locate	soda
5. The various spellings of vowels before *r*	born	artist	skirt
6. The *ou* and *ow* spellings of the *ou* sound	cowboy	shower	surround
7. The *ow* spelling of the $\bar{o}$ sound	unknown	crow	narrow

Table 4–3. *Continued*

	Examples of Vocabulary		
	Grade 4	*Grade 5*	*Grade 6*

Graphemic Representation of Phonemes

	Grade 4	*Grade 5*	*Grade 6*
8. The *oo* spelling of the *ŭ* and *ü* sounds	hook stood	loose choosing	bloom shook
9. Unexpected spellings	bush true	lose grew	wolf route
10. The *oi* and *oy* spellings of the *oi* sound	noise enjoy	join voice	spoil voyage
11. The *o, al, au,* and *aw* spellings of the *ô* sound	north tall	crawl chalk	author naughty
12. The spellings of the *əl* and *l* sounds	castle jungle	model central	carnival barrel
13. The *y* spelling of the *ē* sound	busy	worry	crazy

Using Morphemes to Make Structural Changes

	Grade 4	*Grade 5*	*Grade 6*
1. The *d* or *ed* ending	recalled untied	excited earned	continued contracted
2. The *s* or *es* ending	socks chimneys churches	beads beaches	insects sandwiches
3. The irregular plurals	feet		calves geese
4. The changing of *y* to *i* before *es*	bodies	colonies	pantries
5. Forming plurals of nouns which end in *o*			pianos potatoes
6. The *ing* ending	interesting	bending	stretching
7. Doubling a final consonant before *ing*	stepping	chopping	snapping
8. Dropping the final silent *e* before *ing*	trading	ruling	shaking
9. The *er* and *est* endings	paler palest	cleaner cleanest	tinier tiniest
10. The *ly* ending	finally	especially	dreadfully
11. The number suffixes	fifteen fifty	thirteen sixty	
12. Suffixes to change the part of speech	kindness friendly	playful improvement	harmless attractive
13. Prefixes to change root or root-word meanings	unlock replace	exchange promote	dishonest incorrect

Table 4–3. *Continued*

	Examples of Vocabulary		
	Grade 4	*Grade 5*	*Grade 6*
Devices to Aid Spelling			
1. Syllable division of vowel-consonant/consonant-vowel words	bottom	contest	costume
2. Syllable division of vowel/consonant-vowel words	hotel	select	museum
3. Syllable division of vowel-consonant/vowel words	cabin	salad	proper
4. Remembering unexpected spellings	minute	gloves	thread
5. Choosing the correct homonym	whole	hymn	principal
6. Spelling compounds by parts	upstairs	watermelon	schoolmate

Source: "Linguistic Skills Taught in the Intermediate Grades," reprinted by permission of the publisher from *Basic Goals In Spelling*, 3rd ed., Teacher's Edition, Grade 6, by William Kottmeyer and Audrey Claus. Copyright © 1972 by McGraw-Hill, Inc.

the meanings of the words, ask questions about structural aspects of the words.

4. Pay particular attention to pronunciation. Make certain the pupil can pronounce each word properly and naturally.
5. Strengthen pupil's images of words by having them trace the forms with their index fingers as you write them on the board.
6. Note bad study habits. Show how the habit is harmful and may prevent success in spelling.
7. Check and perhaps modify the child's method of individual study.
8. Provide a wide variety of writing activities that necessitates using the words learned. (pp. 456–457)

Having considered carefully the recommendations of Petty and Jensen, the teacher is ready to select a particular remedial strategy. The following are examples of specific teaching techniques in spelling that can be used for remediation.

1. Fernald's (1943) multisensory approach is reported to be highly successful with some children. The child traces the letters (tactile—kinesthetic), sees the tracing (visual), says the letters aloud (vocal), and

hears what he or she says (auditory). For this reason, the approach is often referred to as the VAKT (visual–auditory–kinesthetic–tactile) technique.

Fernald's techniques are usually reserved for clinical use with children who have serious problems in spelling. This is somewhat unfortunate; for although the activities are highly individualized, they can easily be adapted to work in a regular classroom as well as in a remedial group. When teaching remedial spelling, Fernald recommends that teachers adhere strictly to the following procedures:

a. The word to be learned should be written on the blackboard or on paper by the teacher.
b. The teacher pronounces the word very clearly and distinctly. The children pronounce the words.
c. Time is allowed for each child to study the word.
d. When every child is sure of the word, it is erased or covered; and the child writes it from memory.
e. The paper should be turned over and the word written a second time.
f. Some arrangement should be made so that it is natural for the child to make frequent use, in written expression, of the word he or she has learned.
g. Finally, it is necessary that the child be allowed to get the correct form of the word at any time when he or she is doubtful of its spelling.
h. If spelling matches (spelling "bees") are desired, they should be written instead of oral.

In her book, Fernald described in detail just how each of these steps is to be carried out, what verbal instructions are given to the child, and how spelling vocabulary lists are used to select the "foundation" words that should be taught first. Of all the approaches to the remedial teaching of spelling, this one is perhaps the most popular.

2. The Gillingham alphabetic system (Gillingham and Stillman, 1970) stresses the child's ability to build sounds into words through the application of visual, auditory, and kinesthetic associations, sometimes called the "language triangle." The child links a sound with a letter form, establishes a visual memory pattern for a particular word, and then reinforces that pattern by writing the word.

3. The sensory approach has been advocated by Montessori (1965a) and many other educators. The basic procedure involves some system of color-cueing for vowels, consonants, and sight words that must be memorized. Words may be traced over, used orally in a sentence, visu-

ally studied, traced, and sounded out, until the word can be spelled and written independently.

4. The phonovisual method (Schoolfield and Timberlake, 1960) is a phonetic system that provides direct training in visual and auditory discrimination. Wall charts are used to orally introduce consonants and vowels. The introduction of consonant and vowel sounds is well organized and pictures on the charts provide the pupil with familiar visual images to associate with the letter sound.

5. Shaw (1971) has formulated a teaching system for the self-motivated older student or the adult who wishes to improve his or her spelling ability. He reduces spelling remediation to six basic methods: [3]
   a. Mentally see words as well as hear them.
   b. Pronounce words correctly and carefully.
   c. Use a dictionary.
   d. Learn a few simple rules of spelling.
   e. Use memory devices.
   f. Spell carefully to avoid errors.
   The relevance of these six strategies is described in detail in his book, along with numerous related training activities.

This section on training is concluded by referring the reader to Hansen's (1978) chapter in *The Fourth R: Research in the Classroom*. In this work, she reviews the research relating to three categories of behaviorally oriented methods for remedying spelling. Although all of these direct teaching procedures are useful, only one is described here because of the limits of space. The "cover-copy-compare" tactic comprises four steps:

> . . . first, the student analyzes a word and notes its distinctive features; then, he or she writes the word while saying each letter silently; next, he or she covers the word and writes it once again from memory; finally, the student compares the written word to the original to see if it is spelled correctly. The pupil repeats the process until he or she spells each word correctly without referring to the model (p. 108–109).

GAME SUPPLEMENTS FOR SPELLING INSTRUCTION

The teacher will find the literature replete with games and other activities reported to be beneficial as supplements to a spelling program. While games provide diversification on the method of presentation and help to foster interest in the teaching effort, the experienced teacher knows that they are intended as supplements and not as substitutions for a spelling program. Several examples of spelling games follow.

3. From p. 14 in *Spell It Right!*, second edition by Harry Shaw (Barnes & Noble Books) Copyright © 1961, 1965 by Harry Shaw. Reprinted by permission of Harper & Row, Publishers, Inc.

Tongue Twisters.	Objective: Awareness of initial consonants.
Direction:	Think of a sentence in which most of the words start like "Funny father."
Example:	1. *Funny father fed five foxes.* 2. *Polly Page put a potato in her pocket.*
Variation:	The teacher writes the child's twister on the board.
Direction:	How are many of these words similar? Draw a line under the similar parts. Help the children see that most of the words start with the same sound and letter.

Bingo. For grades three to six. Fold paper into sixteen squares. Children are asked to give a word. A scribe writes the word on the board or challenges the donor to spell the word. The children all write the correctly spelled word on any of one of the sixteen squares. When all the squares are filled, a child is selected to come forward. With his or her back to the board, the child spells any one of the words a selected caller gives. Each correctly spelled word enables the class to place a marker on the corresponding Bingo square. The first child to complete a row or a diagonal calls "Bingo" and wins the game. The teacher keeps a list of the words called and checks off the winner. These Bingo squares may be kept for repeated playing.

Treasure Hunt.	A team game for grades two to six. Select teams, set a time limit of two minutes, and write a base word on the board at the head of each team's column.
Direction:	Each child can write only one word, a new one or a corrected one. At a given sign, the first child from each team races to the board and writes any word that can be made with letters in the base word. Each child races back, hands the chalk to the next child, and goes to the end of the line. Continue until the teacher calls time. The group with the longest correct list in a specified limit is the winner.

Example:	The given base word is *tame.*
	Children may write: tam
	             am
	             me

Anagrams.	Children can make anagram or scribble games for independent activities.
Variations:	1. Make words by adding a letter in vertical or horizontal order.

Example:	C a t
	  o v e r
	      e
	      r
	      y

2. Start with a common word. Change one letter each time the word is spelled. Example: dime—dome—home—hope. Each player must have a scribe to record the peer's completed word, or record his or her own words. Winners are those who can complete the greatest numbers of correctly spelled words. Teachers act as final judges of correct spelling.

Telegraph. Objective: Quick thinking and correct spelling. A team game for grade five.

Establish a goal of six or ten points for game, and a time limit of four slow counts or four seconds for the hesitant speller.

Direction: Each child is given one or two letters of the alphabet. The teacher pronounces a word to team one. The letters of the telegraph begin to respond in proper order. If the response is correct, they get one point and another word to transmit.
The opposing side gets a word when
1. a member of the team has failed to give a letter in the four-second time limit or by four counts;
2. if the completed word was misspelled;
3. someone on the team "helped" to spell the word.

Example: The word is battle. The letters respond in proper order, b a t t l e.

Scoring: One point is scored for each correctly spelled word; a game is eight or ten points.

Variation: A group game for primary grades
1. Letters used or needed for the spelling of the teacher's list are printed on 2- by 6-inch cards. Each child receives a card. The teacher pronounces a word. The telegraph letters take their places in the proper order at the front of the room.

2. Letters may be placed in a chart holder or on the blackboard ledge.

The teaching of spelling, a tool subject, should be integrated as much as possible into the total language arts program. Too often, however, the activities, methods, and materials used to teach spelling have little or no relationship to the rest of the language arts program. Westerman (1971) notes that frequently one set of words is used in teaching reading, another set in spelling (usually designed to meet the needs for different sound patterns), and still other sets for speaking and listening. A coordinated program, on the other hand, is more efficient for the teacher and motivating for the child.

5

CORRECTING HANDWRITING DEFICIENCIES

Donald D. Hammill

No matter how well conceived a composition may be, it is useless if it is so illegible that it cannot be read. At one time or another, we have all had the experience of hastily jotting down a good idea and later being unable to decipher the writing. If we frequently cannot read our own handwriting, consider the dismay of those individuals who occasionally have to read what we write. The frustrations that teachers encounter as a result of having to read the all-too-often unreadable compositions of students is but another reason why good handwriting is a desirable ability. To be understood, it is essential that some care be taken in the physical preparation of compositions. Also, legible handwriting is simply good manners, a courtesy that the readers have the right to expect.

This discussion on correcting handwriting deficiencies is divided into two major parts. The first part describes procedures for measuring handwriting and determining specific deficiencies. The second part is devoted to describing activities and programs that are helpful in remedying poor handwriting.

MEASURING HANDWRITING

The discussion pertaining to the measurement of handwriting has three sections: (1) assessing handwriting readiness, (2) assessing general handwriting competence, and (3) assessing specific errors in handwriting.

ASSESSING HANDWRITING READINESS

We do not agree with the concept of "handwriting readiness." We doubt, for example, that copying geometric shapes or developing laterality (handedness), ocular control, and visual perception of forms not involving words or letters have much to do with proficiency in handwriting. In fact, much research supports this suspicion (Wiederholt, 1971; Harris and Herrick, 1963). All the so-called prerequisite, readiness skills can probably be developed naturally without any specific instruction as a consequence of teaching children to write letters, words, and phrases directly. However, since many educators do consider these to be readiness skills for writing, they deserve some mention. A list of possible readiness skills and techniques for their evaluation follows:

1. Visual–motor integration
   a. coordination
      (1) "Imitation of Movement" (Kephart, 1971). These tasks require the child to transfer a visual pattern into a motor pattern.
      (2) Eye–Hand Coordination subtest of the Frostig Developmental Test of Visual Perception (Frostig et al., 1964)
   b. Copying
      (1) Slingerland's (1970) test: Far point, subtest 1; Near point, subtest 2
      (2) Copying subtest from the Metropolitan Readiness Test
      (3) Spatial Relations subtest from the Frostig DTVP
   c. Ocular control. Roach and Kephart's (1966) Purdue Perceptual–Motor Survey
   d. Left–right progressions
      (1) Put two dots on the blackboard. Does he connect them from left to right?
      (2) When given paper and pencil tasks does he begin at the left side of the page?
   e. Small-muscle coordination
      (1) Observe the child stringing beads, using a pegboard, holding his pencil
      (2) Review the child's school records. Did the kindergarten, first-grade, or second-grade teachers comment that he had poor small-muscle coordination?
2. Laterality
   a. Handedness
      (1) Case history of handedness
      (2) Keep a record of the activities for which he uses his right or left hand

        (3) Ask the child to pretend he is
           (a) Eating
           (b) Brushing his teeth
           (c) Throwing a ball
           (d) Writing

Then have him actually do these things with the appropriate utensils. A child will often use his dominant hand for the pretended activities and his nondominant hand that he was forced to use for the real activity in instances where the child was switched.

        (4) Observe the child in the classroom and have the mother keep a record at home of which hand he prefers for
           (a) Throwing a ball
           (b) Picking up objects
           (c) Coloring
           (d) Cutting

   b. Eyedness
      (1) Fold a 9- by 12-inch paper in half two times. Tear off a corner for a peephole. Have the child hold it in both hands at waist level, arms outstretched. Tell him to fixate on a small object on eye level at midline. Then have the child lift the paper and look through the peephole. The eye used to sight the object may be said to be dominant.
      (2) Have the child sit at his desk and mark an "X" abour ¼ inch high on a sheet of paper. Give him a small tube, 3 or 5 inches long, made of a rolled sheet of paper. Have him hold the tube in both hands and look at the "X" through the tube. Then ask him to bring the tube slowly back close to his eye without losing sight of the "X." Notice to which eye he brings the tube. Do this several times.

  3. Tactile
   a. Use figures (letters and numbers) cut from sandpaper. Place several into a bag. Ask the child to reach into the bag and identify, by touch alone, the figure he has drawn.

To us, the skills mentioned above are decidedly offtask as far as writing readiness is concerned. Because of this opinion, we prefer a more direct approach to handwriting assessment, one that can be used to identify young children who are likely to become poor writers later in their school life and to pinpoint the specific areas of writing readiness that are in need of training. To achieve these purposes, the teacher can use the Writing subscale of the Basic School Skill Inventory (Hammill and Leigh, 1983).

The Basic School Skill Inventory (BSSI) was developed to measure fundamental school-related skills in children aged 4–0 through 6–11. It was constructed primarily on the results of extensive interviews with kindergarten and first-grade teachers. In these interviews, the teachers were asked to describe the actual behaviors that seemed to distinguish between children who were "ready" for school and those who were not. The behaviors that related to writing were singled out and used to form the Writing subscale of the BSSI.

The BSSI can be used either in a norm-referenced fashion (i.e., to identify children who are "low in writing readiness" and thereby need special help) or in a criterion-referenced fashion (i.e., to decide what skills are to be taught and in what order). To use the scale, the teacher selects a particular child to be assessed, finds the time at school or home to read each item carefully, and using personal knowledge about the child's classroom performance relative to the item, decides whether or not the pupil can do the task. The child is not taken aside and "tested" unless the teacher lacks sufficient familiarity with the pupil's writing behavior to answer the questions, or the scale items. The ten items that comprise the subscale are reproduced in Table 5–1.

Table 5–1.   Writing

    Materials: primary pencil
                   lined primary writing paper
                   card containing a common word
                   chalkboard

The items on this subscale measure the child's proficiency in using a pencil and paper. The items focus on those abilities and skills directly involved in writing letters, words, and sentences. The child may use either manuscript or cursive writing for each of the items.

1. *Does the child write from left to right?*
   To earn a pass on this item, a child should demonstrate some consistent knowledge of left-right progression in writing. Letters or words may be illegible, poorly formed, misspelled, or otherwise inadequate and still be recorded as a pass if, in the execution of his/her written efforts, the child proceeds in a left-to-right sequence. This sequence does not even have to be on a straight line; diagonal writing is permissible, as long as it is basically left to right.

2. *When writing, does the child exhibit an easy three-finger grasp near the tip of the pencil?*
   For most children, writing is accomplished most easily when the pencil is grasped with the thumb and the next two fingers. Using either hand, the child should hold the pencil loosely near the pencil tip in a proper manner.

3. *Can the child write his/her first name?*
   The intention of this item is to determine whether the child can write (manuscript or cursive) his/her first name on command. The letters do not have to be properly formed nor does spelling have to be exactly correct. The result must, however, be recognizable as being the child's actual name. Writing one's name from a model is not acceptable here.

4. *Does the child maintain a proper sitting and writing position?*
   Observe whether the child keeps his/her head reasonably erect, uses the non-writing hand to hold the paper in a steady position, maintains an appropriate distance between eyes and paper, and generally assumes a proper posture when writing.

5. *When given a common word on a card, can the child copy the word correctly on his/her own paper?*
   Place a card containing a common word with at least three letters on the child's desk. The pupil must copy the example correctly to receive credit for the item. The letters in the word must be recognizable and in proper order.

6. *When a common word is written on the chalkboard, can the child copy it correctly on his/her own paper?*
   Copying from the chalkboard is an activity required of pupils throughout the school years. Write a common word containing at least three letters on the chalkboard in the size and type of print you would typically use. While sitting at his/her usual location in the room, the child must copy the word correctly. The copied word must be correctly spelled, although quality of handwriting is not a consideration on this item.

7. *When writing, can the child stay on the line?*
   This is a relatively difficult task for many children. In scoring the item, you are concerned with the child's skill at organizing and spacing the letters squarely on the line, not with the legibility or quality of the letters themselves.

8. *Can the child write his/her last name?*
   To receive credit for this item, a child should make a solid attempt at writing his/her last name. The name may be misspelled and some of the letters may be reversed or poorly formed. The child receives credit for producing a recognizable version of his/her last name without copying from a model.

9. *Can the child write letters upon request by the teacher?*
   Ask the child to write each of the following letters as you say them: a, b, e, h, m, t. While the letters do not have to be perfectly formed, all six letters must be clearly legible in order for the child to receive credit.

10. *Can the child write simple words dictated by the teacher?*
    Select three simple words which are definitely in the child's vocabulary. Ask the child to write each word after it is dictated. You may repeat words or use the words in context if necessary. To pass the item, the child's effort must yield a recognizable version of each of the three words. However, the words do not have to be correctly spelled, nor must the letters be perfectly formed or spaced.

11. *When sentences or instructions are written on the chalkboard, can the child copy them correctly on his/her own paper?*
    Write the following sentence, using the size and type of print you would typically use, on the chalkboard: *The dog is brown.* The child must copy the sentence as it appears on the board. Spelling, capitalization, punctuation, and word order must be correct. The child should receive credit even though the letters may be poorly formed and spaced, if the sentence has been properly copied otherwise.

12. *Can the child write simple sentences dictated by the teacher?*
    Create a simple sentence containing no more than four words which are in the child's vocabulary. Ask the child to write the sentence after you say it in a natural, conversational manner. Do not pause between words to enable the child to write each word after it is presented. You may repeat the sentence if the

Table 5–1.   *Continued*

child does not appear to understand or remember it. To receive credit, the child must write each of the words in the correct sequence from left to right. Spelling, capitalization, punctuation, and penmanship should not be considered in scoring the item.

13. *Does the child use correct capitalization and punctuation in writing?*
    Ask the child to write the following two sentences as you dictate them: *I have a ball. The ball is red.* Since the purpose of this item is to determine if the child possesses beginning skills pertaining to capitalization and punctuation, you may repeat the sentences, pausing between words if necessary, to enable the child to write each word as you say it. The child passes the item if he/she capitalizes the first word in each sentence and places a period at the end of both sentences. Scoring of the item is not affected by the child's spelling or quality of handwriting.

14. *Can the child spell simple words correctly?*
    Ask the child to write each of the following words: *in, cat, make.* Say each word to the child, use the word in a simple sentence, and then repeat the word (e.g., "in . . . The boy is *in* the house . . . in"). Although the quality of formation of letters is not important, the child must produce clearly recognizable letters in the correct sequences for all three words to pass the item.

15. *Can the child write a complete sentence consisting of at least four words?*
    This item pertains to the child's ability to compose a grammatically and syntactically correct sentence. Ask the child to write a story containing at least four sentences. To receive credit, the child must write at least one complete sentence in which at least four words are used with correct grammar and sentence structure. Spelling, penmanship, capitalization, and punctuation do not have to be correct. However, the child's response must clearly include at least four words used properly as a complete unit containing a subject-predicate relationship.

16. *Can the child write a simple story consisting of at least three sentences?*
    To pass this item, the child must be able to independently compose a story which contains a minimum of three sentences. Although the sentences do not have to be grammatically or syntactically perfect, they must be related to some extent in theme or topic. Credit should be awarded even if the relationship among the sentences is minimal (e.g., "Tom is my brother. He is big. He likes ice cream."—In this story, all three sentences relate to the topic of Tom). Spelling, capitalization, punctuation, and handwriting quality do not affect scoring on this item.

17. *Does the child share information or ideas with others through meaningful and purposeful writing?*
    To receive credit on this item, the child must demonstrate the ability to independently and spontaneously use his/her writing skills, regardless of level, to communicate with other people. The child may do this, for example, by writing letters to other children, writing stories for family members, writing notes to the teacher or other students, or in any other manner in which the writing activity is self-initiated and self-directed. Writing letters or stories to fulfill class assignments should not be counted.

Source: The Basic School Skills Inventory (Austin, TX: Pro-Ed, 1983). Reprinted by permission of authors and publisher.

ASSESSING GENERAL HANDWRITING COMPETENCE

The experienced teacher has no difficulty in identifying children whose handwriting is below average for their age. But new teachers or teachers who wish to quantify their observations will find the following techniques helpful.

A popular informal device for assessing the cursive and manuscript handwriting of pupils in grades one through high school is Zaner-Bloser's Evaluation Scale (1974). To administer this test, the teacher writes a particular sample sentence on the chalkboard. After several practice efforts, the pupils copy the example on a piece of paper. They are allowed two minutes to complete the task. Papers are collected and assigned to one of three groups ("good," "medium," or "poor") on the basis of the teacher's judgment. Each paper is then matched against a series of five specimen sentences that are appropriate to the child's grade placement. Each of the sentences represents a different quality of penmanship, ranging from "high for grade" to "poor for grade." The use of the specimen sentences permits teachers to make rough estimates about the adequacy of a child's penmanship compared with youngsters in the same grade. Two examples of Zaner-Bloser's evaluation sentence charts, one for manuscript and one for cursive writing, are provided in Figures 5–1 and 5–2. A critical review of this and other legibility scales is provided by Herrick and Erlebacher (1963), and Starkel (1975).

On those occasions when a norm-referenced test of overall handwriting is needed, we recommend using the Handwriting subtest from the *Test of Written Language* (Hammill and Larsen, 1978). Here handwriting ability is estimated by classifying samples of students' spontaneous writing, using graded examples as guides. Norms are based on the analysis of the written products of a national, representative sample of 1700 students attending grades two through eight.

Use of these assessment devices will permit only the grossest evaluation of a child's handwriting. For example, they allow the examiner to determine if the pupil's penmanship skills are seriously behind, level with, or appreciably above peers, but they do not yield the kinds of specific information about the child's handwriting that can be used to formulate a remedial program. To derive maximum value from this procedure, teachers must subject the child's written products to a thorough analysis of errors.

ASSESSING SPECIFIC ERRORS IN HANDWRITING

Having determined, through direct observation or through the use of one of the scales just mentioned, that a problem does exist, the teacher can use Freeman's (1965) checklists as a guide to error analysis. (He offers one checklist for manu-

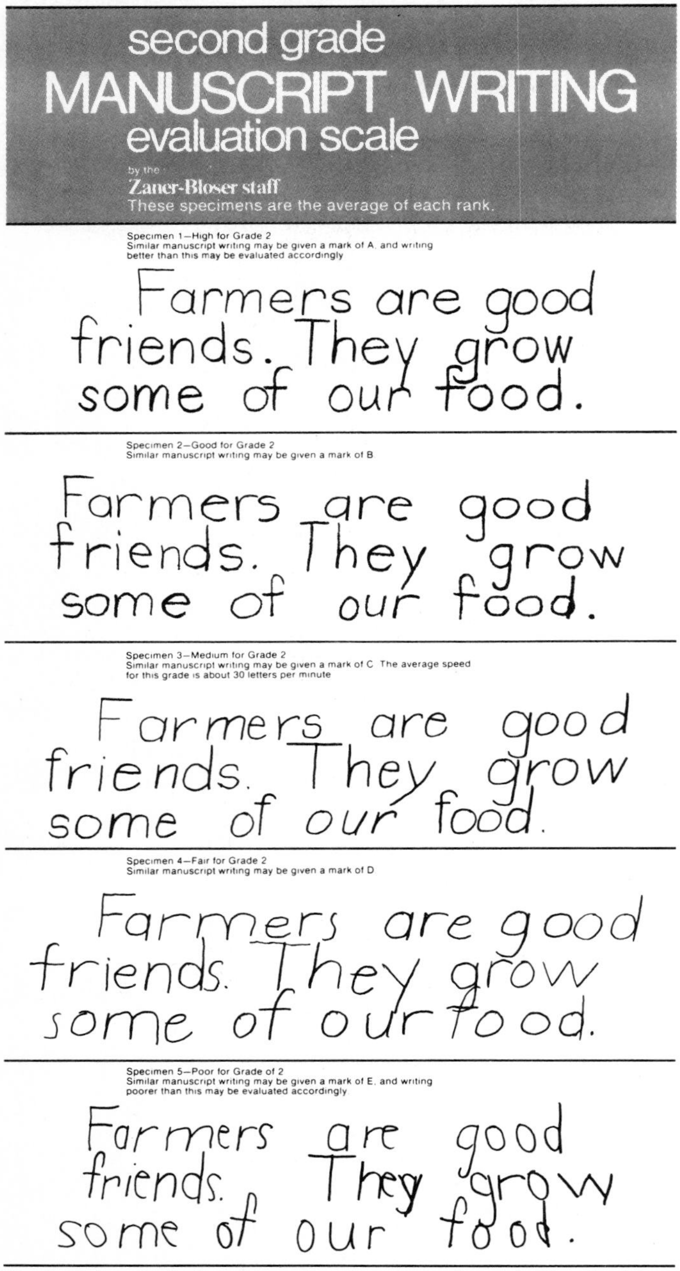

second grade
MANUSCRIPT WRITING
evaluation scale
by the
Zaner-Bloser staff
These specimens are the average of each rank.

Specimen 1—High for Grade 2
Similar manuscript writing may be given a mark of A, and writing better than this may be evaluated accordingly

Farmers are good friends. They grow some of our food.

Specimen 2—Good for Grade 2
Similar manuscript writing may be given a mark of B

Farmers are good friends. They grow some of our food.

Specimen 3—Medium for Grade 2
Similar manuscript writing may be given a mark of C. The average speed for this grade is about 30 letters per minute

Farmers are good friends. They grow some of our food.

Specimen 4—Fair for Grade 2
Similar manuscript writing may be given a mark of D

Farmers are good friends. They grow some of our food.

Specimen 5—Poor for Grade of 2
Similar manuscript writing may be given a mark of E, and writing poorer than this may be evaluated accordingly

Farmers are good friends. They grow some of our food.

Figure 5–1. Evaluation Scale for Manuscript Writing

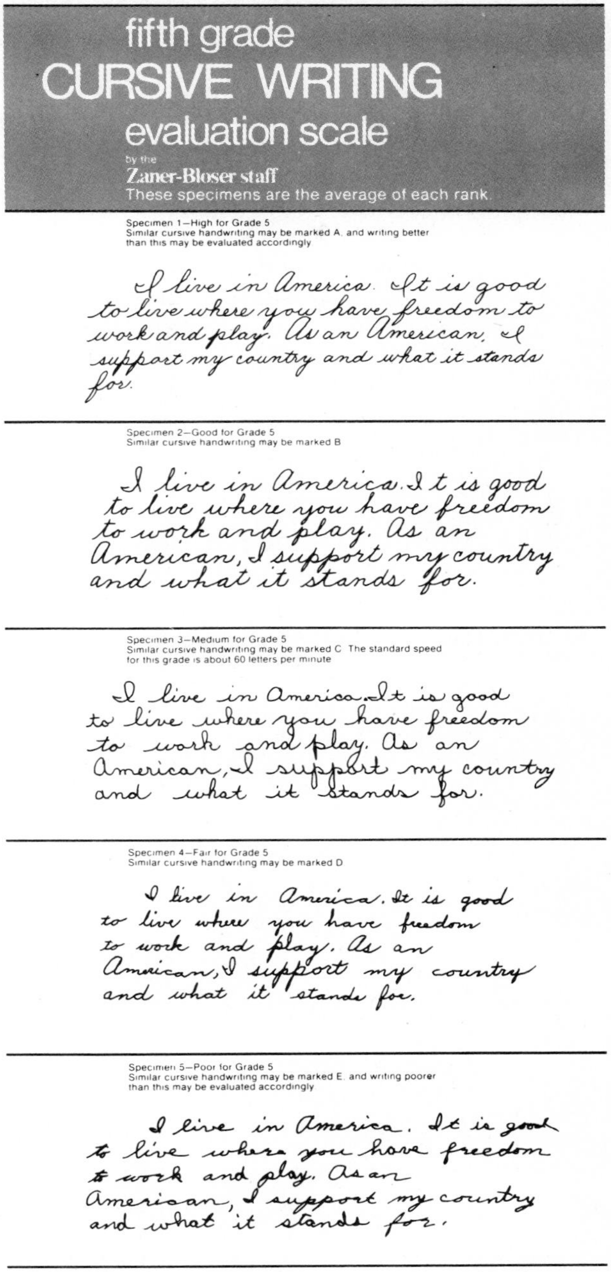

Specimen 1—High for Grade 5
Similar cursive handwriting may be marked A. and writing better
than this may be evaluated accordingly

I live in America. It is good to live where you have freedom to work and play. As an American, I support my country and what it stands for.

Specimen 2—Good for Grade 5
Similar cursive handwriting may be marked B

I live in America. It is good to live where you have freedom to work and play. As an American, I support my country and what it stands for.

Specimen 3—Medium for Grade 5
Similar cursive handwriting may be marked C. The standard speed
for this grade is about 60 letters per minute

I live in America. It is good to live where you have freedom to work and play. As an American, I support my country and what it stands for.

Specimen 4—Fair for Grade 5
Similar cursive handwriting may be marked D

I live in America. It is good to live where you have freedom to work and play. As an American, I support my country and what it stands for.

Specimen 5—Poor for Grade 5
Similar cursive handwriting may be marked E. and writing poorer
than this may be evaluated accordingly

I live in America. It is good to live where you have freedom to work and play. As an American, I support my country and what it stands for.

Figure 5–2. Evaluation Scale for Cursive Handwriting

Used with permission from *Creative Growth with Handwriting*. Evaluation scale, fifth grade. Copyright © 1974. Zaner-Bloser, Inc., Columbus, Ohio.

script and another for cursive.) These checklists, reproduced in Table 5–2, direct the teacher's attention to such aspects of penmanship as letter size, proportion, formation, spacing, and slant.

While the use of these checklists will provide the teacher with some valuable information, they yield no data about the particular letters that are illegible. Therefore, when engaged in a complete analysis of the errors in a child's handwriting, the teacher should keep in mind the work of Newland (1932), who studied the handwriting of 2381 people and analyzed the errors they made. He identified the most common illegibilities made in cursive handwriting by elementary-school pupils and classified the errors into twenty-six major groups. Surprisingly, almost half of the illegibilities were associated with the letters *a, e, r,* and *t.* If teachers are familiar with these common errors, they will find it easier to recognize them in their pupil's written work. The ten most common errors were:[1]

1. Failure to close letters (e.g., *a, b, f*) accounted for 24 percent of all errors.
2. Top loops closed (*l* like *t, e* like *i*) accounted for 13 percent.
3. Looping nonlooped strokes (*i* like *e*) accounted for 12 percent.
4. Using straight-up-strokes rather than rounded strokes (*n* like *u, c* like *i*) accounted for 11 percent.
5. End-stroke difficulty (not brought up, not brought down, not left horizontal) accounted for 11 percent.
6. Top short (*b, d, h, k*): 6 percent.
7. Difficulty crossing *t*: 5 percent.
8. Letters too small: 4 percent.
9. Closing *c, h, u, w*: 4 percent.
10. Part of letter omitted: 4 percent.

Newland's (1932) research concerning common errors can easily be incorporated into a simple criterion-referenced assessment procedure that can be used to identify the letters that are illegible in a child's writing and to estimate the particular kinds of errors being made in the formation of those letters. For example:

1. The first step is to obtain a sample of the child's ability to write the letters that are most likely to be illegible. To do this, the teacher might have the child write five to ten *a*'s in a row in cursive, then an equal number of *b*'s, of *e*'s, *h*'s, *m*'s, *n*'s, *o*'s, *r*'s, and *t*'s. These particular letters are selected because the research suggests that they are the ones

1. From T.E. Newland, An analytical study of the development of illegibilities in handwriting from the lower grades to adulthood. *The Journal of Educational Research, 26,* 1932, 249–258.

Table 5–2. Helping in Analyzing and Grading Handwriting

Name

Your Manuscript Handwriting has been thoughtfully analyzed and rated according to the chart below. Any item checked in Section I is outstandingly good and worthy of mention. If an item in Section II is checked, it is faulty and needs improvement. To improve your manuscript handwriting, you will want to study both lists and then review the lesson giving special attention to all items checked—the good ones, to be continued; the faulty ones, to be corrected.

Section I   Good

☐ Appearance of work
☐ Size
☐ Quality of line
☐ Vertical writing
☐ Form of letters
☐ Spacing
☐ Alignment
☐ Proportion
☐ Figures
☐ Margins

Section II   Room for Improvement

Position of Hand, Arm, Body, or Paper
☐ Incorrect

Size of Writing
☐ Too large
☐ Too small
☐ Varying in size
☐ See your text

Proportion
☐ Not primary (half to whole relationship)
☐ Changing
☐ See your handwriting aid

Quality of Pencil Line
☐ Too heavy
☐ Too light
☐ Varying
☐ Kinky (looks slow)
☐ Wild and uncontrolled

Slant of Writing
☐ Too slanting
☐ Not vertical (back slant)
☐ Irregular (too many different slants)

Figures
☐ Poor figures

Manuscript Handwriting Grading Slip

Form of Letters
☐ Poor circles
☐ Places illegible
☐ Poor straight strokes
☐ Parts of letters disconnected
☐ Capital letters weak

Spacing
☐ Within letters
☐ Between letters
☐ Between words
☐ Between lines
☐ Too wide
☐ Crowded
☐ Irregular
☐ Poorly arranged on page
☐ Margins uneven

Alignment of Letters
☐ Off the line in places
☐ Low letters uneven in height

Fluency
☐ Too fast
☐ Too slow

Table 5–2. Continued

Name	Section II Room for Improvement	Cursive Handwriting Grading Slip
Your Cursive Handwriting has been thoughtfully analyzed and rated according to the chart below. Any item checked in Section I is outstandingly good and worthy of mention. Any item checked under Section II is faulty and needs improvement. To improve your handwriting, you will want to note the items checked and then review the lesson giving special attention to them—the good ones, to be continued; the faulty ones, to be corrected.	Position of Hand, Arm, Body, or Paper ☐ Incorrect	☐ Uneven in height ☐ Capital and loop letters uneven ☐ Minimum letters vary ☐ Intermediate letters vary
	Size of Writing ☐ Too large ☐ Too small ☐ Varying in size ☐ See your text	Form of Letters ☐ Angular letters ☐ Letters too round ☐ Letters too thin ☐ Places illegible ☐ Beginning strokes poorly made ☐ Ending strokes poorly made ☐ Poor loop letters ☐ Upper ☐ Lower
Section I Good ☐ Appearance of writing ☐ Margins ☐ Slant of writing ☐ Quality of pen or pencil line ☐ Spacing in and between words ☐ Letter forms ☐ Size of writing ☐ Alignment of letters ☐ Figures ☐ Proportion	Proportion ☐ Not primary (half to whole relationship) ☐ Not upper grade ☐ Changing ☐ See your handwriting aid	Capital letters weak ☐ Too small ☐ Too large ☐ Small letters need strengthening ☐ Disconnected letters in words ☐ Down-strokes not uniform
	Quality of Pen or Pencil Line ☐ Too heavy ☐ Too light ☐ Varying ☐ Kinky (looks slow)	Figures ☐ Poor figures
	Slant of Writing ☐ Too slanting ☐ Too nearly vertical ☐ Irregular	
	Alignment of Letters ☐ Off the line in places	

Name _____

Section I Good

☐ Appearance of writing
☐ Margins
☐ Slant of writing
☐ Quality of pen or pencil line
☐ Spacing in and between words
☐ Letter forms
☐ Size of writing
☐ Alignment of letters
☐ Figures
☐ Proportion

Section II Room for Improvement

Position: This refers to the position of the hand, arm, body, or paper. Incorrect

When position is checked on the grading slip, it means one of four things:

1. Position of your body is incorrect.
2. Position of the paper is incorrect.
3. Position of your hand and arm is incorrect.
4. You are holding the penholder or pencil wrong.

How can we tell this by looking at your writing?

If your writing is too nearly vertical or too slanting, there is something wrong with position. Either the body position is not right, the paper is being held at the wrong slant, or you are not writing in front of your eyes and pulling the down-strokes toward the center of your body (for the left-hander, pull down-strokes toward the left elbow).

If the bottoms of the letters are shaded, there is too much pressure being put on the pen or pencil at the bottom of each letter. The pen or pencil is being held incorrectly. Position and slant go hand in hand. If your paper and body are in the correct position, and if you write directly in front of your eyes and pull all of the down-strokes or slant-strokes toward the center of your body, the slant of your writing will be accurate, uniform, and regular.

Fluency
☐ Too fast
☐ Too slow

Spacing
☐ Within letters
☐ Between letters
☐ Between words
☐ Between lines
☐ Too scattered (wide)
☐ Crowded
☐ Irregular
☐ Poorly arranged on page
☐ Margins uneven

An Explanation of the Cursive Handwriting Grade Slip

On nearly every writing paper there are some good features. It is the intent of this "Good" section on this grading slip to pick out the good features and commend the pupil. This tends to instill confidence in his own ability to write. Any of these ten items that are checked good are representative of the best things on the paper.

Source: F. W. Freeman, *Reference Manual for Teachers. Grades One Through Four* (Columbus, Ohio: Zaner-Bloser, 1965), pp. 21–23. Used with permission of the author and publisher.

that are most often produced in a defective, unreadable fashion. The child's paper might look like the following:

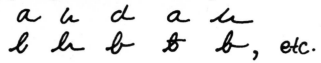

2. An alternative to step 1 might be to take an example of the child's spontaneous or elicited written work and circle the *a*'s, *b*'s, *e*'s, *h*'s, etc.
3. The next step is to evaluate the way a pupil forms letters according to the criteria listed below:

	Wrong	*Right*
1. *a* like *o*	*o*	*a*
2. *a* like *u*	*u*	*a*
3. *a* like *ci*	*ci*	*a*
4. *b* like *li*	*li*	*b*
5. *d* like *cl*	*cl*	*d*
6. *e* closed	*e*	*e*
7. *h* like *li*	*li*	*h*
8. *i* like *e* with no dot	*e*	*i*
9. *m* like *w*	*m*	*m*
10. *n* like *u*	*u*	*n*
11. *o* like *a*	*a*	*o*
12. *r* like *i*	*r*	*r*
13. *r* like *n*	*n*	*r*
14. *t* like *l*	*l*	*t*
15. *t* with cross above	*t̄*	*t*

If the manner in which the child forms the letters differs from that suggested in the column marked "right," one can assume that illegibility will be increased. The handwriting examples under the "wrong" column indicate the most common errors made in the formation of the eight letters. These particular errors are often referred to in the language arts literature as the fifteen handwriting demons and are purported to cause or contribute to most of the illegibilities in children's cursive writing.

The procedures outlined in this section will enable teachers to identify (1) the students who need help in handwriting, (2) the general areas requiring attention (slanting, spacing, etc.), (3) the individual letters being misformed, and (4) the specific kinds of errors causing the illegibilities. It is this kind of information that teachers can use to individualize remedial programs for children.

REMEDYING PROBLEMS IN HANDWRITING

The remainder of this chapter is devoted to discussing how handwriting can be taught to students who exhibit difficulty in developing proficiency in the skill. Before presenting the specifics of a remedial program, it is desirable for the reader to have some background information on several topics that relate to the teaching of handwriting in general.

BACKGROUND INFORMATION CONCERNING HANDWRITING INSTRUCTION

Before describing selected procedures for teaching handwriting, several points should be mentioned. Teaching handwriting to left-handed children presents a few special problems, although in general the techniques used with right-handed pupils will suffice with slight variation. Readers are referred to the work of Petty and Jensen (1980), Lerner (1976), or Cohen and Plaskon (1980) for discussions of the modifications for left-handed pupils. Current thinking dictates that a child who is definitely left-handed should be allowed to write with the preferred hand. Forcing the child to use the right hand is not recommended.

Often teachers are undecided whether to teach manuscript or cursive initially. Lerner (1976) has briefly summarized the arguments for each.

> The arguments for beginning with cursive writing are that it minimizes spatial judgment problems for the child and that there is a rhythmic continuity and

wholeness that is missing from manuscript writing. Further, errors of reversals are virtually eliminated with cursive writing; and by beginning with the cursive form in initial instruction, the need to transfer from one to another is eliminated. Many children with learning disabilities find it difficult to make the transfer to cursive writing if they have first learned manuscript writing.

The advantages of manuscript writing are: it is easier to learn since it consists of only circles and straight lines; the manuscript letter form is closer to the printed form used in reading; and some educators feel it is not important for a child to transfer to cursive writing at all since the manuscript form is legal, legible, and thought by some to be just as rapid (p. 255).

The research suggests that in most cases it does not matter which style is taught, although the common practice is to begin with manuscript and to introduce cursive at about the third-grade level.

The concept of handwriting readiness should be considered carefully before planning an instructional program for any child. Most children are "ready" to begin to write before they reach their sixth birthday and enter school. In point of fact, children usually start reading and writing during the preschool years as a natural consequence of daily interaction with the print that is omnipresent in their environment. Thus, there are probably no true readiness abilities that children must learn before they can learn to write, although there are doubtlessly a few prerequisites. For example, children do not have to be able to scribble circles before they are able to learn to write the letter O; but children must be able to see, to grasp a pencil, and to think of an idea before they can learn to write. Of equal importance, they must possess a desire to write. When these abilities are present, instruction in writing can begin formally with every likelihood of success. When these basic abilities are lacking, it is unlikely that they will be developed by a traditional school "readiness" program.

We feel that the most efficient way for children to learn to write is to teach them to write directly, with a straightforward approach. They will learn to write in a left-to-right direction, to discriminate one letter from another, and to use a pencil to form legible letters best as a result of practice in writing. Perceptual-motor training, tracing geometric shapes, walking board exercises, and activities that do not involve letters are offtask and should be avoided; unless, of course, they are being done for their own sake, to improve general eye-hand coordination or to amuse the children. Fortunately, some readiness programs that are available commercially do emphasize the skills of early writing; and these should be sought out and used.

TEACHING HANDWRITING

In teaching handwriting, it is often useful to have a scope and sequence of skills in mind. The scope-and-sequence chart enables the teacher to identify skills to be taught and their order of presentation. Graham and Miller (1980)

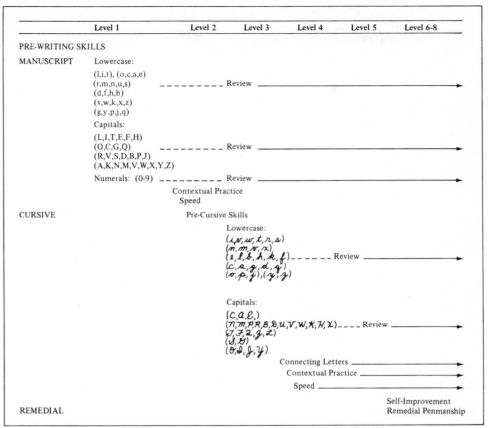

Figure 5–3. Handwriting Scope and Sequence

Source: S. Graham, and L. Miller. Handwriting research and practice. *Focus on Exceptional Children*, 1980, p. 6.

present an eight-level handwriting scope-and-sequence chart. In this chart (presented as Figure 5–3) each level represents approximately one school year. They point out that "depending upon the student's characteristics and the severity of the handicapping condition, the rate of progression though the curriculum may be either decelerated or accelerated" (p. 5).

After targeting a level and a letter for training, the teacher is ready to intervene. The procedures for teaching handwriting skills necessary for legible writing are subdivided by Reger et al. (1968, pp. 220–224) into four developmental levels.[2] The teacher should begin with Level I and move to Level IV as

2. Material in this section was drawn from *Special Education: Children with Learning Problems* by Roger Reger, Wendy Schroeder, and Kathie Uschold. Copyright © 1968 Oxford University Press, Inc. Used with permission.

the pupil masters the skills. It should be noted that while this sequence could be used as a program for all pupils, it is intended for use with children who experience difficulty in handwriting. Most children will respond adequately to one of the developmental systems described later in this chapter.

Level I—Introductory Movements

Using the chalkboard as a prop, the teacher discusses how the movements of writing are made; for example, "First we go up and then we go down." The teacher demonstrates on the board. Or she says, "We go away from our body and then towards our body." The children make the movement at the board while they look at the teacher's model but not at the board as they draw. They say "up" when they are going up and "down" when they are going down. The movements should be rhythmic and free flowing. The children should stand at least six inches from the board. Supplementary chalkboard activities are provided by Ramming (1968).

After the child has had several days of practicing the movement on the board following the procedure above, the auditory clue is eliminated and the child makes the movement on the board while looking at the model but not at his or her hands. Then the outlined procedures are repeated, this time on paper or large newsprint, using crayon. Reger et al. (1968, p. 221) suggest the movements shown in Figure 5–4.

The teacher will also want to keep in mind Spalding and Spalding's observation (1962, p. 74) that only the six different pencil strokes shown in Figure 5–5 are necessary for making lowercase manuscript letters. One or two of

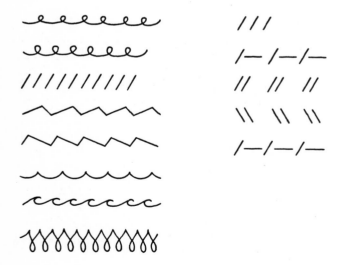

Figure 5– 4.   Introductory Movements

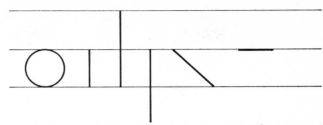

Figure 5– 5.   Pencil Strokes Needed for
Lowercase Letters

From R. B. Spalding and W. T. Spalding, *The Writing Road to Reading* (New York: William Morrow, 1962), p. 74. Used by permission of the authors and publishers.

these movements can be introduced each week in conjunction with Reger's exercises. If a child has difficulty with any of the movements, additional practice should be given as often as possible. Before introducing a new movement, the previous ones should be reviewed.

Level II—Introducing movements on the Chalkboard

The same procedures are repeated, but the child is allowed to look at the paper. It should be kept in mind that: (1) the child should have correct posture when performing the movements; (2) the slant of the paper should be correct, and dependent on the hand used; (3) the hand position should be proper. Teachers can usually find detailed descriptions of the proper positions for writing in the teacher manuals that accompany the various commercially available writing programs.

The movements on paper should be done first on paper with 1-inch spaces. The letters should be three spaces high initially, then two spaces, and finally one space high. The teacher can line the paper with felt-tipped markers, using blue for the top line, green for the middle line, and red for the bottom line. This helps the children stay on and within the lines. Serio (1968) is a source of information regarding writing materials, especially pencils and paper with colored lines.

Level III—Movements for Cursive Writing

Follow the procedures set forth under Level I using the movements shown in Figure 5–6. Begin on the chalkboard and eventually progress to newsprint using crayon or marker.

Spalding and Spalding (1962) offer an alternative by suggesting that cursive writing is an adaptation of manuscript and that it is only necessary to teach five connecting strokes (Figure 5–7).

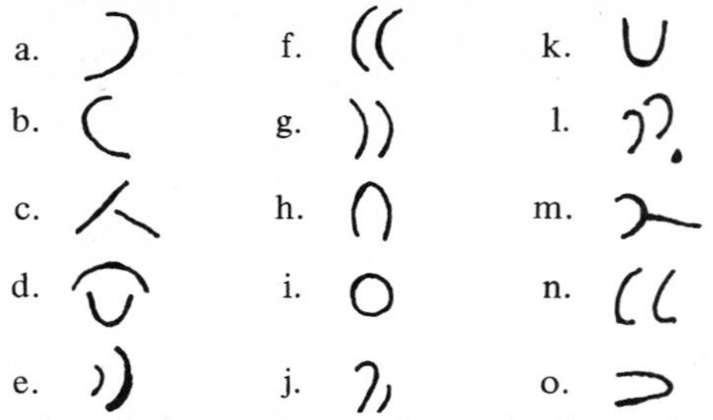

a.   ⟩

b.   C

c.   ⋏

d.   ⌢̣

e.   ⟩⟩

f.   ⟨⟨

g.   ⟩⟩

h.   ∩

i.   ○

j.   ⟩⟩

k.   ∪

l.   ⟩⟩.

m.   ⟩

n.   ⟨⟨

o.   ⊃

Figure 5–6. Movements for Cursive Writing

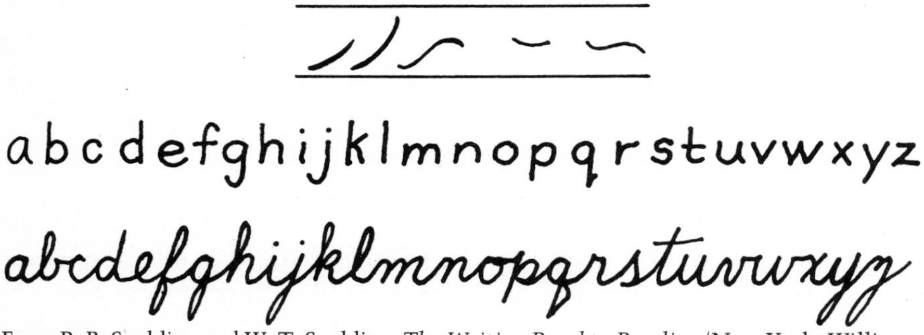

Adapted from W. M. Cruickshank, F. A. Bentzen, F. H. Ratzeburg, and M. Tannhauser, *A Teaching Method for Brain-Injured and Hyperactive Children* (Syracuse, N.Y.: Syracuse University Press, 1961)

a b c d e f g h i j k l m n o p q r s t u v w x y z

abcdefghijklmnopqrstuvwxyz

Figure 5–7.
Cursive Writing

From R. B. Spalding and W. T. Spalding, *The Writing Road to Reading* (New York: William Morrow, 1962), pp. 88–89. Used by permission of the authors and publisher.

Level IV—Movements for Writing

Using letters, progress from the chalkboard (repeating the procedures stipulated under Level I), to 1-inch-lined paper where three lines have been drawn with red, green, and blue markers, and finally progress to regular lined paper. Materials for this level include: (1) Overlays with each letter made on the transparency with felt-tipped marker, blank overlays, and overhead projector. (2) The different parts of the letter are made in different colors with markers to show the various movements. (3) To show the direction of the letters, such as *s*, *z*, and others, cinematic materials are used. A Polaroid filter mounted on a clear plastic wheel that is motorized is placed over the transparency. The letters then move from left to right, or right to left, to show the child the direction of the letter.

In general, the following sequence is appropriate for teaching at this level:

1. Name the letter.
2. Discuss the form of the letter while the child looks at it.
3. On a blank overlay, make the letter for the children.
4. Using the Polaroid filter wheel, show the children the direction of the letter.
5. Develop the kinesthetic feel for the form of letters by using sunken and raised script letterboards (may be purchased from the American Printing House for the Blind).
6. The child makes the letter while looking at the model.
7. Eyes are on the model, not the hand.
8. Help the child compare his or her work with the model.
9. Oral clues may be given to help the child who has difficulty with the letter, or the child's hand may be held as he or she makes the letter. Some children may need to write the letter in salt or sand (on a salt tray).
10. Have the child write the letter on the chalkboard without the model.
11. Have the child write the letter on newsprint without a model, eyes averted.
12. Have the child write on paper with eyes on the paper.

In following this sequence, 1-inch-lined paper should be used with the writing space divided into three parts (by colored markers). If the top line is always blue, the middle line green, and the bottom line red, the teacher can then say to the child "Start on the red line, go up to the blue line, come down to the red line," depending on the letter. The lines should be dark and heavy so the child will be able to stay within them.

The teacher puts a model of the letter on the child's paper, and the letter form and direction are discussed. The position of the paper for left- and right-handed children is demonstrated, and each child's paper is checked for proper positioning. Masking tape or marks on the desk are used to show the child how he or she should position the paper.

The writing posture is discussed and demonstrated: elbow on the desk, nonwriting hand holding the paper, fingers on the pencil correctly, feet on floor, proper head tilt. Before each writing assignment, the correct habits for writing should be reviewed.

The child traces the model of the letter and makes a row of letters. The teacher should watch the child carefully to determine the success with the letter and to decide where he or she needs help. The child is then taught to write within the 2-inch-lined area, next uses 1-inch lines, and finally writes on regular primary paper. The same procedure as mentioned above should be followed.

When the child has succeeded in writing the letters accurately, he or she should be taught to connect letters and then to write simple words. As the child progresses, simple sentences should be copied and gradually the child should be encouraged to attempt to write without copying. It is at this point that handwriting becomes an expressive language ability. The time of the writing period will vary from class to class and from child to child. If one child can tolerate writing only one line, he or she should write only that much. If another child can write a whole page, he or she should be allowed to do so. The sequence just outlined is basically a remedial one and can be supplemented by activities drawn from Gillingham and Stillman (1970), Spalding and Spalding (1962, 1970), and Johnson and Myklebust (1967).

The "applied behavioral analysis" technique is particularly productive when specific errors in handwriting have been noted and selected for improvement. For example, the teacher may have decided as a result of observation or testing that the child's difficulty is centered in letter illegibility, improper spacing, sloppiness, slowness, and/or unacceptable slanting. One of these problems, probably the one that is the most annoying to the teacher, is chosen as the target for retraining; and the principles of ABA are implemented. The dynamics of managing an ABA program are based on the ideas expressed in the behavior-modification section in Chapter 7. Individuals interested in this approach should read the section referred to as well as Lovitt's (1975b) description of how the technique has been used to help improve children's handwriting skills.

The experienced teacher will recognize readily that the procedures just outlined probably cannot be used with all the children in a regular class. They are best reserved for use in special remedial classes with an enrollment of six to ten pupils or with those few pupils in the regular class who are developing problems in writing. Although this book is primarily concerned with the management of children with problems, the teacher must have considerable knowledge of the "developmental" teaching systems. For example, in teaching handwriting to a whole class of children, one system may work quite efficiently with 80 percent of the pupils, another system with the remaining 20 percent. By using several developmental systems, remedial procedures may not be necessary at all. In 1960, four companies, Zaner-Bloser, Palmer, Scale, and Noble and Noble, accounted for 50 percent of all instructional materials in the United States for teaching handwriting. As they are all similar, only one set of materials, Noble and Noble, will be described.

The Noble and Noble program, *Better Handwriting for You*, contains a series of eight workbooks and teacher editions prepared by Noble (1966). Books 1 and 2 present manuscript writing and Books 3 through 8 deal with cursive writing. There is a transitional book between Books 2 and 3 that begins with manuscript and introduces cursive. Throughout, the teacher is given instructions regarding management of the left-handed pupil, correct position for holding the pencil, proper positions for the paper, and correct positions for writing on the chalkboard or at the desk.

In the first book, uppercase and lowercase letters and numbers are introduced. Numbers and arrows are used to teach the sequence and direction of strokes necessary to write the various graphic forms. Models and ample opportunity to copy them are provided in the workbooks. In Books 7 and 8, devices are presented whereby the pupil can evaluate the quality of his or her writing; the child is presented with the 15 handwriting demons, or the errors that cause most illegibilities, and the 100 spelling demons.

A program comprising of six programmed texts with several unique features is provided by Skinner and Krakower (1968). The first three deal with the formation of capital and lowercase letters and numbers; the remainder are concerned "with the evaluation of handwriting, and the practical uses of both manuscript and cursive writing" (p. 1). The paper in the workbook is specially treated so that a correct mark appears yellow with a gray dot in it, while an incorrect mark is all yellow. This use of color allows the pupil to monitor his or her own work for correctness. Every attempt is made to present the writing exercise within a relevant and varied framework. Therefore, the writing activities include the filling out of bank deposit forms, library cards, and applications for Social Security numbers, among other exercises. The authors have made a concerted effort to provide interesting and relevant activities and as a result their program offers a marked contrast to others.

6

PROBLEMS IN MATHEMATICS ACHIEVEMENT

Nettie R. Bartel

After decades of neglect, the teaching of mathematics to children with particular difficulty in this subject seems to be suddenly fashionable. For many years, the priority in teaching children with learning problems was clearly given to the teaching of reading. Important as reading is, we are now beginning to see that basic mathematical skills and especially the cognitive operations (such as ability to classify) underlying those skills are basic to adequate functioning in our society. This realization has led to a virtual explosion of new programs, kits, and techniques for teaching the child who has difficulties in mathematics. Research on mathematical processes and mathematics instruction has not yet caught up to the need for new programs—a lag that we hope will be redressed soon.

In this chapter, an overview is provided for establishing the goals of a mathematics program. Attention is then directed toward the question of pupil readiness for mathematics instruction. This is followed by a description of why children have difficulty in mathematics. The fourth section is concerned with assessing mathematical problems; it includes a section on standardized mathematics testing and a fairly detailed set of procedures to be utilized by the teacher in the diagnostic instructional cycle. A final section on record keeping concludes the chapter.

ESTABLISHING GOALS IN MATHEMATICS

Any mathematical activity should be undertaken only if it is responsive to some goal or objective that has been established for a particular child or for a group of children. Teachers will find many sources that will help to articulate the goals of the mathematics program: curriculum guides; professional publications, scope-and-sequence charts accompanying commercial materials, Bloom's Taxononomy of Educational Objectives (1956), and the landmark 1963 report of the Cambridge Conference on School Mathematics.

For our purposes, we have developed the following set of broad mathematical goals:

1. Development of problem-solving ability (including convergent, divergent, logical and creative thinking).
2. Development of understanding of basic mathematical concepts and terms.
3. Development of the ability to understand and perform measurements of distance, weight, temperature, quantity, area, speed, volume, and money with conventional and Metric units, where appropriate.
4. Development of the ability to perform basic mathematical computations.
5. Development of an understanding of how mathematics computation and concepts are utilized in real-life situations.

This last goal is included in recognition of the fact that, for most persons, mathematics will serve as a tool in daily living. For example, in a study conducted by the author with graduate students in Special Education, newspapers and radio and television news programs were analyzed for prerequisite mathematical understandings. To fully comprehend such material, it was found that individuals needed to know the following:

1. Understanding of money relationships (including large sums).
2. Understanding of measurements—temperature, speed, distance, weight or quantity, and area (listed in order of frequency).
3. Understanding of time—past, present, future; and by the hour, day, week, month, season, year and decade.
4. Understanding of computations with whole numbers, fractions, decimals, and percentages, including ratios.

Moreover, Norton and Norton (1936) cited the following mathematical requirements as most representative of daily living:

1. Basic addition, subtraction, multiplication, division
2. Common fractions
3. Measurements—length, volume, weight
4. Use of money—buying and selling
                    borrowing and repaying
                    rent and mortgages
                    insurance
                    budget

Recent technological developments with calculators make this a highly likely item to be used in daily living; hence, children need to be familiarized with their existence and use.

MATHEMATICAL READINESS

Insufficient readiness may seriously affect the performance of a child at any level of arithmetic functioning. This being the case, some children are unable to learn to count because they do not have a clear notion of one-to-one correspondence. Some children fail to master long division because they have not yet learned to multiply. Therefore, this section discusses readiness as it relates both to beginning instruction in mathematics and to the more advanced mathematical functioning.

BASIC READINESS

Basic to the development of arithmetic-related abilities is the child's ability to classify. *Classification* refers to the grouping of objects according to some common distinguishing characteristic. In order to do this, the child must be able to discriminate between objects on the basis of some relevant aspect of color, size, shape, or pattern. The ability to make these discriminations is usually attained by a child sometime between two and seven years, during the period which Piaget has called the pre-operations period (Piaget, 1965). Initially, motor actions, then internalized behaviors, are utilized in the child's coming awareness of various classifications (Piaget and Inhelder, 1963). In accordance with the general Piagetian principle of actions preceding perceptions, children should be encouraged to enact as many concepts as possible and to manipulate two- and three-dimensional objects in the initial stages of classificatory behavior. During the latter part of this period, acquisition of language is believed to facilitate the ability to classify.

The ability to classify may be assessed a number of different ways. Children may be shown an array of objects and asked "Which does not belong?" when all items except the one share a common characteristic: for example, "Which does not belong . . . dog, cat, tree, bird?" Since three of the items share the category "animal," the correct answer is "tree." The Sesame Street jingle, "One of these things is not like the others; one of these things doesn't belong" is exemplary of the kind of exercise that helps to establish whether a child has learned to classify. It should be recognized that classification tasks vary greatly on difficulty, depending on the characteristic that must be discriminated and the salience of that characteristic.

Learning the concept of *one-to-one correspondence* is essential for subsequently learning to count and for mastering addition and subtraction. The concept underlies such seemingly intuitive abilities as placing the correct number of table settings for a given number of people or for distributing candies or other treats on the basis of one or two per child. Whether the pupil understands one-to-one correspondence or not can be quickly established by asking him or her to give each child in a row a piece of paper or to get enough pencils for each child in a reading group. Teaching children the idea of one-to-one correspondence should begin with situations in which there are only two objects in each set. Gradually, the numbers to be corresponded are increased. Only when one-to-one correspondence in a wide variety of settings has been firmly established should the children be instructed in many-to-one correspondence. Initially, items in each set should be identical. Later, children can be asked to match dissimilar objects, such as matching pieces of bubble gum with pennies. Pictures of objects are introduced only when the youngster has developed a firm grasp of the concept and had demonstrated success with concrete objects.

Seriation or *ordering* in its simplest form can be accomplished by a two- or three-year-old child who successfully places a series of rings of graduated sizes on a cone. More complex seriation tasks involve lining up disks of graduated diameter or height in ascending order. More difficult are tasks that require the child to seriate on the basis of numbers in a series of sets—sets of one, two, or three objects in order. It is apparent that ability to seriate underlies the entire number system. Work in seriation can most meaningfully be done with three-dimensional objects. The Montessori materials, the Stern materials, and the Cuisenaire rods (discussed later in this chapter) offer excellent training in seriation and ordering. Lacking any of these materials, the teacher can teach seriation with bottles, crayons, pencils, or cards of varying sizes.

In additon to the linear seriation described above, children also need to become familiar with *temporal seriation.* This refers to the idea that some things or events or processes precede others in an orderly fashion. Children may initially be introduced to notions of temporal seriation through awareness of morning and afternoon and through sequencing of classroom activities. The mastery of temporal seriation is basic to any mathematical operation that has more than one step—such as adding two-place numbers. For this reason, it is important that children firmly grasp this concept before formal mathematics is introduced. (A complete task analysis of temporal seriation or sequence may be found in the Reading chapter of this book, Table 2–6).

The child's *understanding of space and spatial representation* has both perceptual and cognitive aspects. Perceptual aspects are dealt with in Chapter 9; hence, it is sufficient to state here that a firm grasp of spatial relations is important not only for traditional geometry (geometric forms), but for understanding sets and fractions, and the basic arithmetic processes of addition, subtraction, multiplication, and division. Here again, according to Piaget, motor actions should precede strictly perceptual tasks (Piaget and Inhelder, 1963). Visual-perceptual activities should be supplemented with opportunities for tactual explorations of objects.

Before meaningful formal instruction (counting, adding) in arithmetic can occur, the child must have achieved *flexibility* and *reversibility* of thought, as well as the concept of *conservation*. Flexibility of thought is demonstrated by the child's ability to see that colored geometric shapes can be sorted first in the basis of one criterion, namely color, then shifted to another criterion, shape, and finally to possibly a third criterion, size. Flexibility also characterizes the conceptual process of observing that an individual or object belongs to several categories and subcategories at once; a person may be both a mother and a daughter, or two cups of water equal both one pint and half a quart. Flexibility is also necessary for a child to recognize that 10 equals 5 + 5, but it may also equal 4 + 6 or 9 + 1.

Reversibility is essential for the child to grasp the relationship between addition and subtraction; e.g., 5 + 4 = 9 and 9 − 4 = 5. In younger children, reversibility can be readily demonstrated with the Cuisenaire and Stern materials. Only with considerable experience in the manipulation of objects can the child achieve a firm grasp of the concept that no matter how objects are arranged they can always be returned to their original pattern. Thus, if ⦙ · ⦙ is rearranged to ˙. ˙., its basic value is still the same, and it can be reversed back.

The concept of conservation, closely related to that of reversibility, refers to the fact that the number of units within an object or set remains the same regardless of changes made in the shape of the unit or the arrangement of the set (Figure 6–1). The familiar Piagetian experiments of the ball of clay rolled into a long roll, or of water poured into a tall, thin glass versus a low, wide glass are examples of conservation. While the question of whether conservation can be directly taught is debatable, allowing the child plenty of opportunity to manipulate clay and to rearrange units of sets will permit reinforcement of the notion of conservation.

Figure 6– 1.
Amount of Water in the Two Containers Is the Same; Amount of Clay in the Two Shapes Is the Same

To assess the child's readiness for formal instruction in mathematics, it is suggested that the teacher engage the child in a set of tasks such as those described in Table 6–1.

READINESS FOR MORE ADVANCED MATHEMATICS

Readiness for higher-level mathematical operations was the topic of a study reported by Brownell (1951). The particular type of mathematics task that he investigated was division by two-place divisors. Prior to the study, he identified the mathematics skills that children must have in order to perform the division task. The specific subskills that he considered prerequisite for "readiness" for two-place divisor division are the following:

1. Multiply a two-place number by a digit:

    $$\begin{array}{r} 23 \\ \times\ 6 \\ \hline \end{array}$$

2. Add, to the extent of carrying in multiplication:

    $$\begin{array}{r} 48 \\ +48 \\ \hline \end{array}$$

3. Subtract, without and with borrowing:

    $$\begin{array}{r} 323 \\ -\ 21 \\ \hline \end{array} \qquad \begin{array}{r} 323 \\ -\ 27 \\ \hline \end{array}$$

4. Divide, in the sense of knowing the algorithm: $3\overline{)\,7\,}$.

Next, Brownell developed a Test of Readiness for Division by Two-Place Divisors—a test of skills 1 to 4 above. Using 80 percent correct as a criterion, he concluded that almost half of the children were "not ready" to begin instruction in two-place division. Yet their teachers already had begun such instruction.

This study is illustrative of the need for establishing the criteria for "readiness" clearly. Whether one is dealing with initial mathematics instruction or with the introduction of a more advanced topic, the teacher's effectiveness and efficiency is enhanced by appropriate timing in the presentation of teaching tasks. The real test of "readiness" for a given mathematical topic is

Table 6–1. Assessment of Prerequisite Cognitive Abilities

Cognitive Ability	Examples of How Child Demonstrates Ability		
	Orally State	Demonstrate With Object	Match/Select/Other
Classification			
by function	Can child state why a toy car does not belong in an array of toy furniture?	Can child arrange groups of objects by function, e.g., all transportation by air, land, water?	Can child match pictures of items that "go with" other items by function, e.g., mitten with hand, boot with foot?
by color	Can child state why red block does not belong with blue blocks?	Can child group objects by color?	Can child match objects by color?
by size	Can child state why large flag does not belong in group of small flags?	Can child arrange objects into groups by size?	Can child select "large" or "small" object in group?
by shape	Can child state why circles do not belong in group of squares?	Can child group objects by shape?	Can child identify several circular shaped, rectangular shaped, objects in the room?
by several criteria simultaneously	Can child state differences between prearranged groups of blue squares, red squares, blue squares, red circles?	Can child sort objects on basis of simultaneous criteria of size and function, size and shape, color and shape, etc.?	Can child select which one "does not belong" in array employing two criteria at once?
Seriation			
linear	Can child state basis of linear serial array based on increasing size?	Can child arrange objects in order of increasingly intense color?	Can child select item missing in a serial array?
unit	Can child state relationships between sets of 1, 2, 3, 4, etc.?	Can child develop sequence of objects or numerals, based on units in each?	Can child count to 10 or 20? Can child tell which numeral contains more—4 or 6, 3 or 8, etc.?
temporal	Can child state what he did first in a simple task, what last?	Can child follow simple directions, e.g., "First put the block in the box; next put the penny beside the tray"?	Is there informal evidence of child's developing temporal sense—e.g., does child

Table 6–1. *Continued*

Cognitive Ability	Examples of How Child Demonstrates Ability		
	Orally State	*Demonstrate With Object*	*Match/Select/Other*
temporal (*cont.*)			know which task is doen after recess without being told?
one-to-one correspondence	Can child state the number of pencils that will be required in a group of three children?	Can child "order" milk for the class lunch based on the number in attendance? Does he or she know how to distribute the milk when it's received?	Can child pair boots or mittens with the owner?
understanding of spatial relations	Can child state which object is over, under, in or beside with respect to another object?	Can child match geometric objects to openings into which they fit?	Can child distinguish between right and left?
Conservation			
of shape	Can child state if, and why, a ball of clay is the same mass whether rolled into a ball or into a rope?	Can child show that a ball of clay can be made into a rope and back into a ball again?	Can the child do same task at left, except (a) break clay into smaller pieces and put back into a ball and (b) flatten clay like a pancake and put back into ball?
of liquid	Can child state which glass contains more water?	Can child demonstrate equality by pouring more or less water into glasses?	Can child do task at left when water from one glass is poured into several smaller ones?
of number	Can child state which now has more blocks?	Can child make equal numbers in these rows?	Can child recognize that the number of pencils is the same whether they are packed in a box or scattered on a desk?

not whether that topic comes next in the workbook but whether the pupils have mastered the prerequisite skills (as demonstrated in Brownell's study) or have achieved the cognitive operations underlying the topic to be introduced. Establishing the state of a child's readiness is an important component of mathematical diagnosis, and is dealt with next.

CAUSES FOR DIFFICULTY IN MATHEMATICS

When a child demonstrates difficulty in mathematics performance, the teacher will want to undertake a preliminary appraisal of possible reasons for the problem. This initial appraisal is usually informal in nature and highly subjective. At this point, the teacher is attempting to generate hypotheses about the possible reasons for the difficulty; he or she will then try to confirm these initial hypotheses using more objective means. Depending on what is discovered, the teacher may refine, reformulate, or implement an intervention on the basis of that first hypothesis. Descriptions of some of the more general reasons underlying mathematics difficulty are presented below.

1. *Ineffective instruction* probably accounts for more cases of problems in arithmetic than any other factor. Children who are the victims of poor teaching can frequently be identified by their relatively good performance in arithmetic concepts that are usually acquired incidentally (size relationships or value of coins) compared with skills that are usually acquired as the result of specific instruction ("carrying" in addition or long division). Remediation is usually effective if it is planned on the basis of a diagnosis of specific deficits.

2. *Difficulties in abstract or symbolic thinking* will intefere with the child's ability to conceptualize the relationship between numerals and objects that they represent, the structure of the number system (base of 10), and relationships between units of measurement. Teachers of children with these difficulties frequently turn in frustration from attempting to get the child to master concepts to emphasizing the rote manipulation of numerals. This may create a facade of arithmetic competence, when in fact the child does not understand what he or she is doing.

3. *Reading problems* frequently characterize those children who perform well on tests of computation or on oral story problems, but who do poorly in typical workbook or standardized test situations in which they must be able to read the problem to understand which mathematical process to perform.

4. *Poor attitudes or anxiety* about mathematics may inhibit the performance of some children. Careful observation on the part of the teacher may provide the first indication that this is at the root of the child's problem. Does the child avoid mathematics? Does the child "play sick" when it is time for mathematical activities? The teacher may also wish

to use one of the instruments developed for assessing attitudes toward arithmetic. An example of one such instrument is presented later in the chapter in Table 6–3.

ASSESSMENT OF MATHEMATICS PERFORMANCE

To engage in appropriate and efficient instruction, the teacher must employ a set of assessment procedures that permit him or her to have a detailed picture of each child's strengths and weaknesses in mathematics. Most teachers discover quickly that the standardized survey type of mathematics achievement tests yields little information. Therefore, it becomes necessary for the teacher to study in depth the areas of difficulty pointed out by the survey test. For example, the child who is shown to be having computational difficulties is given a much more detailed inventory of computational problems. The teacher appraises the child's performance on the various computation tasks to determine the types of errors that trouble the child. Further probing of the child's errors is done through intensive analysis of written work and/or through an oral interview in which the child "thinks out loud" while solving problems. The entire process can be conceived of as a search on the part of the teacher for the faulty concepts and strategies being used by the child. Initial testing is gross and provides only the most general clues to the teacher. Successive assessment efforts, based on clues obtained from previous testing, help the teacher to "zero in" on the child's difficulty. Having discovered the problem, the teacher then plans an intervention to correct the difficulty. If the child shows improvement, the teacher may conclude that the problem was correctly identified and followed by appropriate instruction. Continued failure by the child must lead to reexamination of the diagnostic process and/or of the subsequent instruction.

THE USE OF STANDARDIZED TESTS

A teacher could establish a child's overall performance level by having the child "try out" in various mathematics texts, programs, or instructional systems. We believe, however, that it is much more efficient and reliable to administer a norm-referenced test that will give the teacher a general idea of the child's functional level in mathematics. Such survey tests may be of either the group-administered or individually administered type. Some of the most

Table 6– 2. Commonly Used Standardized Survey Tests of Arithmetic Achievement

Test (Author)	Grade Level	Reliability Coefficient	Skills Measured	Special Features
California Achievement Test (Tiegs and Clark, 1970)	1–9	.70–.97	1. Computation 2. Concepts and problems 3. Total	May be used diagnostically Weak students may obtain fair scores by guessing
Iowa Test of Basic Skills—Arithmetic (Lindquist and Hieronymous, 1956)	1–9	.89–.91	1. Arithmetic concepts 2. Problem solving 3. Total	Convenient Much verbal content
Metropolitan Achievement Tests—Arithmetic (Durost et al., 1971)	3–9	.82–.95	1. Computation 2. Problem solving 3. Concepts 4. Total	Traditional
Stanford Achievement Series in Arithmetic (Kelly et al., 1964)	1–10	.77–.89	1. Concepts 2. Computation 3. Application	Traditional
SRA Achievement Series in Arithmetic (Thorpe, Lefever, and Naslund, 1969)	1–9	.80–.96	1. Concepts 2. Reasoning 3. Computation 4. Total	Provides handbook for diagnostic analysis
Wide Range Achievement (Jastak and Jastak. 1965)	1–10	.94–.97		Individually administered Takes only 5–10 minutes

widely used survey tests of mathematical functioning are presented in Table 6–2.

The authors of a few mathematics programs provide their own placement tests to help teachers establish the child's entry level into the program. Of course, such tests are usually applicable to only that program.

Even for children whose survey test performance indicates grade-level or near-grade-level functioning, we recommend that the teacher check the errors made by the pupil to see whether the child's performance is reasonably even across the various types of mathematics problems; it is possible to obtain a fairly average score by excelling in one area, say addition, even if performance in another area, say multiplication, is very poor. The analysis of errors and error patterns has been found to be particularly helpful for pupils who are new to the teacher.

Table 6–3.   Evaluation of Attitudes Toward Arithmetic

Check (X) only the statements that express your feeling toward arithmetic.

_____ 1. I feel arithmetic is an important part of the school curriculum.

_____ 2. Arithmetic is something you have to do even though it is not enjoyable.

_____ 3. Working with numbers is fun.

_____ 4. I have never liked arithmetic.

_____ 5. Arithmetic thrills me and I like it better than any other subject.

_____ 6. I get no satisfaction from studying arithmetic.

_____ 7. I like arithmetic because the procedures are logical.

_____ 8. I am afraid of doing word problems.

_____ 9. I like working all types of arithmetic problems.

_____10. I detest arithmetic and avoid using it at all times.

_____11. I have a growing appreciation of arithmetic through understanding its values, applications, and processes.

_____12. I am completely indifferent to arithmetic.

_____13. I have always liked arithmetic because it has presented me with a challenge.

_____14. I like arithmetic but I like other subjects just as well.

_____15. The completion amd proof of accuracy in arithmetic gave me satisfaction and feelings of accomplishment.

Before scoring your attitude scale, place an (X) on the line below to indicate where you think your general feeling toward arithmetic might be:

11	10	9	8	7	6	5	4	3	2	1
Strongly Favor				*Neutral*				*Strongly Against*		

To help the teacher establish whether a child's difficulty is related to fear or dislike of mathematics, we have included an example of a test of attitudes toward mathematics (Table 6–3).

Table 6–3 is designed to show attitudes for or against arithmetic. Individals will usually have both favorable and unfavorable feelings toward arithmetic. By adding all responses and dividing by the total number of responses, the teacher can secure a general average for each individual. Each test item will provide data for pupil guidance. For example, a pupil may like the logical aspects of arithmetic (No. 7) but be afraid of word problems (No. 8).

Each item on the test has a scale value (see below). Have pupils total the scale values of all items they checked on the test, and divide by the number of items checked. This will yield an average scale value score to be compared with where the student placed himself on the "general feeling toward arithmetic" line above.

Test Item	Scale Value	Test Item	Scale Value	Test Item	Scale Value
1	7.2	6	2.6	11	8.2
2	3.3	7	7.9	12	5.2
3	8.7	8	2.0	13	9.5
4	1.5	9	9.6	14	5.6
5	10.5	10	1.0	15	9.0

Source: Wilbur H. Dutton ad L. J. Adams, *Arithmetic for Teachers*, 1961. Reprinted by permission of Prentice-Hall, Englewood Cliffs, N.J.

While standardized survey tests are used to answer the questions "What is the child's relative status in mathematics?" the standardized diagnostic" tests deal with "What is the child's status in the various areas of mathematics, e.g., addition, subtraction, fractions, etc.?" A number of tests that have been commercially developed for appraising a pupil's performance in greater detail are listed in Table 6–4. Although these tests are purported to be "diagnostic," none of them provides sufficient opportunity to probe strengths and weaknesses adequately. They are helpful, however, for identifying broad areas that need further analysis. The type of analysis that is most effective for the detailed probing of children's mathematical difficulties can only be done by the teacher.

TEACHER-MADE DIAGNOSTIC INVENTORIES

The teacher's first step in developing an inventory is to choose the content to be assessed. One way to do this is to study the scope-and-sequence chart of the mathematics program that is being used in the school (most mathematics series present these near the beginning of the teacher's manual) or from Table 6–5. The contents of the table have been organized in such a way as to enable the teacher to quickly identify, on the basis of a child's grade level, what mathematics skills and capabilities he or she should have. For example, if the child is in second grade and is having difficulty with subtraction, the teacher looks in column 2 of part V of the table. The table (based on commonly used commercial texts and curriculum guides) indicates that the child should understand the properties of subtraction, be able to conceptualize subtraction as the inverse of addition, be able to use the number line to subtract, be able to use both vertical and horizontal notation, be able to subtract up to two-place numbers without regrouping and two-place numbers with regrouping. Of course, the teacher may wish to include more difficult items on the inventory in order to establish whether the child has skills beyond those usually developed in second grade.

The next step is to establish whether the child has the necessary underlying concepts and capacities required for the subtraction tasks. Here the teacher

Table 6–4. "Diagnostic" Tests of Mathematics Performance

Test	Skills Measured	Grade Level	Special Features
Fountain Valley Teacher Support System in Mathematics (1976)	1. Numbers and operations 2. Geometry 3. Measurement 4. Application 5. Statistics/probability 6. Sets 7. Functions 8. Logical thinking 9. Problem solving	K–8	Criterion-referenced Self-scoring Areas of weakness keyed to math text or program
Basic Educational Skills Inventory in Math (1972)	All mathematical areas	Elementary	Criterion-referenced Keyed to a retrieval system that refers teacher to materials designed to develop skills that the child missed
Patterns Recognition Skills Inventory (Sternberg, 1976)	Levels of readiness for all areas of math Reasoning skills	Ages 5–10	Concept-referenced diagnostic inventory Requires no reading by student Developmentally sequenced
Diagnostic Tests and Self-Helps in Arithmetic (Brueckner, 1955)	1. Computation with whole numbers 2. Operations with fractions, decimals, percentage 3. Measurement	3–8	Each diagnostic test is correlated with corrective self-help exercises
KeyMath Diagnostic Arithmetic Test (Connelly, Nachtman, and Pritchett, 1976)	1. Content 2. Operations 3. Applications	K–6	Convenient and attractive to administer Requires almost no reading or writing Not really diagnostic (not enough items), but useful for identifying problem areas
Individualized Criterion-Referenced Testing (Educational Progress)	All mathematical areas	1–8	Diagnostic and prescriptive Correlative to five major math programs

Table 6– 5. Typical Scope and Sequence of Elementary Mathematics

	K	1	2	3	4	5	6
I. *Readiness for Mathematics*							
Classification	•	•	•	•	•	•	•
One-to-one correspondence	•	•	•	•	•	•	•
One-to-many correspondence			•	•	•	•	•
Seriation or ordering	•	•	•	•	•	•	•
Space and spatial representation	•	•	•	•	•	•	•
Flexibility and reversibility	•	•	•	•	•	•	•
Conservation	•	•	•	•	•	•	•
II. *Mathematical Concepts*							
Same, equal, as much as	•	•	•	•	•	•	•
More than, greater, greatest, larger, largest	•	•	•	•	•	•	•
Bigger, biggest, longer, longest	•	•	•	•	•	•	•
Less than, fewer, fewest, smaller, smallest	•	•	•	•	•	•	•
Shorter, shorter, most, least	•	•	•	•	•	•	•
Enough, not enough, more than enough	•	•	•	•	•	•	•
Left, right		•	•	•	•	•	•
Above, below, up, down, next to, between		•	•	•	•	•	•
Putting together, add, plus		•	•	•	•	•	•
Take apart, take away, subtract, minus		•	•	•	•	•	•
How many in all? How many are left?		•	•	•	•	•	•
Odd, even			•	•	•	•	•
Open, closed			•	•	•	•	•
=, >, <		•		•	•	•	•
Factors, primes, multiples							•
III. *Sets*							
Definition	•	•	•	•	•	•	•
Elements of sets	•	•	•	•	•	•	•
Kinds of sets							
Identical	•	•		•	•	•	•
Equal and equivalent	•	•		•	•	•	•
Unequal and nonequivalent						•	•
Empty set		•	•	•	•	•	•
Union of sets (addition)		•	•	•	•	•	•
Subset (subtraction)		•	•	•	•	•	•
Intersection of sets						•	•
VI. *Whole Numbers*							
Abstracting idea of cardinal number from equivalent set	•	•	•	•	•	•	•
Counting: one through ten	•	•	•	•	•	•	•
Concepts and counting: numbers above ten		•	•	•	•	•	•
Concept of zero	•	•	•	•	•	•	•
Skip counting by twos, threes, fives, tens		•	•	•	•	•	•

Table 6–5. *Continued*

			Grade				
	K	1	2	3	4	5	6
V. *Operations on Whole Numbers: Addition and Subtraction*							
Properties							
Closure and nonclosure		•	•	•	•	•	•
Commutatively and noncommutativity		•	•	•	•	•	•
Associativity and nonassociativity		•	•	•	•	•	•
Inverse relation of addition and subtraction		•	•	•	•	•	•
Ways of conceptualizing							
Union of sets or forming of subsets		•	•	•	•	•	•
Number line		•	•	•	•	•	•
Addition and subtraction with zero		•	•	•	•	•	•
Addition and subtraction with horizontal notation		•	•	•	•	•	•
Addition and subtraction with vertical notation		•	•	•	•	•	•
Addition and subtraction without regrouping							
One-place numbers	•	•	•	•	•	•	•
Two-place numbers		•	•	•	•	•	•
Three-place numbers			•	•	•	•	•
Numbers with more than three digits				•	•	•	•
Addition and subtraction with regrouping							
Two-place numbers			•	•	•	•	•
More than two-place numbers				•	•	•	•
Column addition		•	•	•	•	•	•
VI. *Operations on Whole Numbers: Multiplication and Division*							
Properties							
Commutativity of multiplication				•	•	•	•
Associativity of multiplication					•	•	•
Distributive property of multiplication and division over addition					•	•	•
Inverse relation of multiplication and division				•	•	•	•
Ways of conceptualizing							
Union of sets or partitioning into equivalent sets				•	•	•	•
Repeated addition or successive subtraction				•	•	•	•
Arrays				•	•	•	•
Number line				•	•	•	•
Multiplication and division with horizontal notation				•	•	•	•
Multiplication and division with vertical notation				•	•	•	•
Use of zero in multiplication and division				•	•	•	•
"One" as the identity element				•	•	•	•
Multiplication and division with 10's, 100's, etc.					•	•	•
Computation without regrouping							
One-place factor or divisor, one-place sums, dividend				•	•	•	•
One-place factor or divisor, two-place sums or dividends				•	•	•	•
Computation with regrouping							
One-place factor or divisor, two- or three-place sums or dividends					•	•	•

Table 6–5. *Continued*

	K	1	2	3	4	5	6
Two-place factors or divisors, any number sums or dividends					•	•	•
Three- or four-place factors or divisors							•
Multiple multiplication				•	•	•	•
VII. *Fractions*							
Definition		•	•	•	•	•	•
Ways of conceptualizing							
Number line			•		•	•	•
Arrays or subsets			•		•	•	•
Geometric figures		•	•		•	•	•
Computation							
Addition and subtraction of simple fractions with common denominators					•	•	•
Addition and subtraction of simple fractions with mixed denominators						•	•
Addition and subtraction of mixed fractions with common denominators					•	•	•
Addition and subtraction of mixed fractions with mixed denominators						•	•
Multiplication and division							•
Decimal fractions							•
VIII. *Measurement*							
Measurement of length (inch, foot, yard, mile, metric)		•	•	•		•	•
Measurement of area (English and metric units)						•	•
Measurement of weight (ounce, pound, ton, metric units)					•	•	•
Measurement of liquids (cup, pint, quart, metric units)	•	•	•	•		•	•
Dry measures (quart, peck, bushel, metric units)					•	•	•
Measurement of quantity (dozen, gross)					•	•	•
Measurement of temperature (Fahrenheit, Celsius)					•	•	•
Measurement of time (clock, calendar)	•	•	•	•		•	•
Measure of money (coins, paper bills)	•	•	•	•		•	•
IX. *Geometry*							
Geometric shapes (circle, square, rectangle, triangle)	•	•	•	•		•	•
Spatial relationships	•	•	•	•		•	•
Point, line, line segment, ray, intersection					•	•	•
Parallel line, curved line, straight line						•	•
Radius, diameter					•	•	•
Angles, arc degrees							•
Closed-line plane, open-line plane							•
Area and perimeter						•	•
Three-dimensional shapes (sphere, cube, cone)						•	•

Grade

is referred to Figure 6–2, which outlines the general hierarchical interrelationships between and among various areas of mathematical functioning. In each case, the source of an arrow may be considered to be a necessary prerequisite for full mastery of the capability to which the arrow is pointing. Thus, in the subtraction example, the child would need to have evidenced the readiness capabilities of Box A and mastery of basic mathematical concepts and vocabulary of Box B. (For fuller development of these, the reader is referred to the preceding section on Readiness and to Part II, Mathematical Concepts of Table 6–5.)

An alternative approach is to conduct a task analysis and/or concept analysis of each of the terminal skills desired in the subtraction area. The reader is referred to Chapter 2 for an explication of these procedures. (For an excellent description of how to proceed with a mathematical task analysis, see also Reisman, 1972; 1977.)

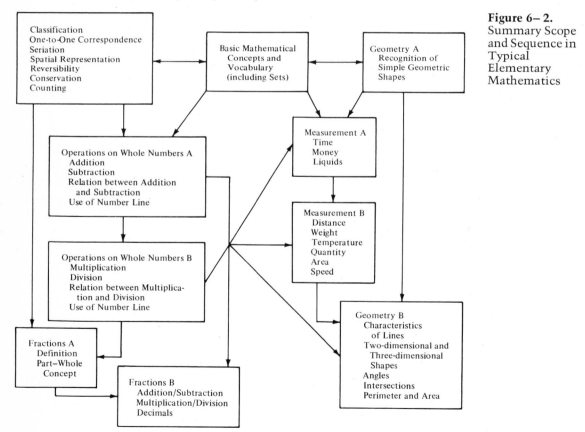

Figure 6– 2.
Summary Scope and Sequence in Typical Elementary Mathematics

The final step in determining what should go into the diagnostic inventory is to decide in what form and under what conditions the child is supposed to be able to perform the task. This decision should be stated in *precise, observable* terms. (See Chapter 1 for a fuller discussion on the stating of objectives.)

Now the teacher is ready to begin to write the actual items. They may be adapted from commercial texts, or workbooks; or the teacher may write them. An example of a subtraction inventory, adapted from Burns (1965), and limited to the vertical format, is presented in Table 6–6.

Table 6– 6.   Sample Analytical Inventory: Subtraction

Problem Type	Exercises for Child to Complete			
Basic subtraction facts without zero	1. 4 − 2	2. 8 − 1	3. 17 − 3	4. 15 − 6
Basic subtraction facts involving zero		5. 7 − 7	6. 9 − 0	
Higher-decade subtraction fact requiring no regrouping		7. 79 − 6		
Higher-decade subtraction fact requiring regrouping		8. 75 − 9		
Higher-decade subtraction fact, with difference in ones' place		9. 25 − 23		
Higher-decade subtraction fact; zero in ones' place in minuend		10. 20 − 3		
Subtraction of ones and tens with no regrouping required		11. 47 − 24		
Three-digit minuend minus two-digit subtrahend; no regrouping		12. 169 − 45		
Subtraction of ones, tens, hundreds; no regrouping		13. 436 − 215		
Two-digit minuend minus two-digit subtrahend; regrouping tens and ones in minuend required		14. 46 − 38	15. 72 − 34	
Three-digit minuend minus two-digit subtrahend; regrouping tens and ones in minuend required (zero in difference)		16. 272 − 64		
Three-digit minuend minus two-digit subtrahend; regrouping hundreds and tens of minuend required		17. 528 − 54		
Subtraction of ones, tens, hundreds; regrouping tens and ones in minuend required		18. 742 − 208	19. 750 − 374	

Table 6– 6.   *Continued*

Problem Type	Exercises for Child to Complete					
Subtraction of ones, tens, hundreds; regrouping hundreds and tens in minuend required	20.	$\begin{array}{r} 724 \\ -\ 183 \end{array}$	21.	$\begin{array}{r} 307 \\ -\ 121 \end{array}$		
Subtraction of ones, tens, hundreds; regrouping entire minuend required	22.	$\begin{array}{r} 531 \\ -\ 173 \end{array}$				
Four-digit minuend minus three-digit subtrahend; regrouping entire minuend required	23.	$\begin{array}{r} 1076 \\ -\ 247 \end{array}$	24.	$\begin{array}{r} 5254 \\ -\ 968 \end{array}$	25.	$\begin{array}{r} 5805 \\ -\ 978 \end{array}$
Subtraction of ones, tens, hundreds, thousands; regrouping hundreds, tens, and ones of minuend required	26.	$\begin{array}{r} 4553 \\ -\ 1258 \end{array}$				
Subtraction of ones, tens, hundreds, thousands; regrouping entire minuend required	27.	$\begin{array}{r} 9563 \\ -\ 2687 \end{array}$				
Five-digit minus four-digit subtrahend; regrouping entire minuend required	28.	$\begin{array}{r} 23238 \\ -\ 3879 \end{array}$				
Five-digit minuend minus four-digit subtrahend; regrouping entire minuend (involving zeros) required	29.	$\begin{array}{r} 10000 \\ -\ 7192 \end{array}$				
Five-digit minuend minus five-digit subtrahend; regrouping entire minuend required	30.	$\begin{array}{r} 30503 \\ -\ 19765 \end{array}$				

To further probe the child's understanding of concepts underlying subtraction proficiency and to assess ability to perform subtraction problems in a variety of formats and contexts, Burns (1965) has suggested a series of follow-up exercises. These are presented in Table 6–7.

THE ORAL INTERVIEW

All existing evidence shows that most computational errors are caused by children's problems with number facts or by their using faulty algorithms. Diagnosis of difficulty with number facts can usually be discovered and confirmed by an examination of the child's written work. However, to establish the faulty rules or strategies that the child is using in the computational procedures, it is frequently necessary to engage the child in an oral interview. The oral interview may be used to search for the child's error strategies, or it may be used to confirm (or disconfirm) the "hunches" that the teacher has derived from an examination of the child's written work. Because of the time-consuming nature of the oral interview, the teacher will want to confine its use

Table 6–7. Follow-Up Exercises for the Analytical Test of Subtraction

1. Make a dot drawing to represent the fact that 17 take away 8 leaves 9.
2. What subtraction fact does this drawing illustrate?

12 cookies in all

⌒000000000000⌒

left   eaten

3. Show on the number line how the answer to 31 minus 12 might be found.
4. Start at 57 and count down by 5's to the first number in the thirties. To do this, say, "57, 52, 47," and so on.
5. Write three different ways to read the number statement, $24 - 8 = 16$ (as "8 from 24 leaves 16").
6. What is the result when zero is subtracted from a number?
7. What is the result when a number is subtracted from itself?
8. What pairs of one-digit numbers would make each a true sentence?

   $\square + \square = 9$ $\square + \square = 11$ $\square + \square = 13$

9. What basic subtraction fact helps you to subtract 6 from 53?
10. Start with 13, subtract 6, add 3, subtract 4, subtract 3. Where are you?
11. There is a two-digit minuend and a one-digit subtrahend whose difference is 9. What might they be?
12. Think the answers to the following questions. Then write the answers.
    a. 7 from 18 leaves how many?
    b. 68 and how many more equals 72?
    c. The difference bewteen 77 and 24 equals what number?
    d. Is 19 minus 12 equal to 7?
    e. When 203 is taken from 526, what is left?
    f. Is 60 from 388 equal to 328?
    g. Does 65 minus 9 equal 56?
    h. If you think 36 from 64, what do you get?
    i. How many are left if 19 is subtracted from 52?
    j. 525 is how much less than 3478?
13. In subtracting 1 ft 3 in. from 3 ft 1 in., to what name would you change one of the measures?
14. When 16 is subtracted from 51, to what number name is the 51 changed?
15. Do the following subtractions, using numerals and words.

    a. $20 = 2$ tens 0 ones $=$ b. $31 = 3$ tens 1 one $=$
         $\underline{- \ 3} = \quad$ 3 ones$=$ $\underline{- 17} = $ 1 ten 7 ones $=$

    c. $500 = 5$ hundreds 0 tens 0 ones $=$
         $\underline{- 125} = $ 1 hundred 2 tens 5 ones $=$

16. Use the words hundreds, tens, and ones to show the renaming of 413 in subtracting 187 from 413.
17. What do the digits at the top of the work mean?

				9 1̶0̶
3 13		6 12		4 10
a. 4̶3̶	b.	7̶2̶4̶	c.	5̶0̶0̶
$-$ 18		$-$ 183		$-$ 125
25				

Table 6–7. *Continued*

18. Write the number sentence for this word problem. There are 527 pupils in the Madison School, of whom 283 are boys. How many girls are there?

19. How can an equivalent addition question be written for the subtraction question $42 - 26 = n$?

20. Does $n + 17 = 42$ represent an addition or a subtraction situation?
    Does $n - 17 = 25$ represent a subtraction situation?

21. For each addition statement, write the subtraction statement that "undoes" it. The first one is done for you.
    $6 + 4 = \qquad 36 + 7 = \qquad 58 + 17 =$
    $10 - 6 = 4$
    $\quad$ or
    $10 - 4 = 6$

22. Write the missing numeral for each of the following statements:
    $19 - \square = 7 \qquad \square - 47 = 24 \qquad 36 - 28 = \square$

23. Subtract $6.98 from $10.00.

24. Subtract. Check your answers by subtracting the difference from the minuend. Check again by adding the difference and the subtrahend.
    $$\begin{array}{cccc} 162 & 806 & 1422 & 8461 \\ \underline{75} & \underline{436} & \underline{766} & \underline{7298} \end{array}$$

Source: P. C. Burns, Analytical testing and follow-up exercises in elementary school mathematics. *School Science and Mathematics, 1965, 65,* 34–38. With permission.

to "hard-core" problems. The procedures described below have been adapted from Cawley (1976) and Lankford (1974), as well as from the authors' experience.

1. *Select one problem area at a time.* The problem selected should be sequentially prior to the others in a task analysis or on Figure 6–2. For example, if a student is having difficulty in both addition and multiplication, clear up the addition problems first. Once this has been accomplished, the child will need to be retested on written multiplication before oral probing in that area. It may be that correction of the faulty addition strategy modifies the difficulty in multiplication.

2. *Begin with the easiest problems first.* To help give the child a sense of confidence, present the child first with a problem that he or she probably can perform correctly. Then provide examples that are of increasing difficulty (for the child).

3. *Tape or keep a written record of the interview.* If tape is used, the child should be told that his or her explanations are being recorded. A similar explanation should be given if a written record is made.

4. *The child simultaneously solves the problem in written form and "explains" what he or she is doing orally.* The teacher must remember

that the oral interview is a diagnostic exercise, not an instructional lesson.

5. *The child must be left free to solve the problem in his or her own way without a hint that he or she is doing something wrong.* Avoid giving clues or asking leading questions. If the child directly asks whether the answers are correct, the teacher should tell the child to concentrate on "telling in his or her own words" how he or she is solving the problem.

6. *Avoid hurrying the pupil.* Depending on the complexity of the operations being diagnosed, the oral interview can take from 15 to 45 minutes.

ANALYSIS OF ERRORS

The identification and interpretation of a child's errors, whether evidenced in written work or in the oral interview, is the basis on which the teacher develops an appropriate instructional program. It is important, therefore, for the teacher to be proficient in the analysis of pupil errors. This section identifies some of the common types of errors made by pupils (see Table 6–8) and provides some examples of error analyses. Errors made in verbal problem solving are dealt with in the next section.

In a recent study, Lepore (1974) investigated the types of computation errors made by 79 mildly handicapped children aged 12 to 14 on 38 problems in addition, subtraction, multiplication, and division. As can be seen in Table 6–9, the type of error most frequently made was that of "renaming" (sometimes called "regrouping" or "borrowing" or "carrying"). Procedural errors were also well represented, as were errors due to lack of knowing the number facts required for the computations. While we hesitate to draw firm conclusions from this study (because we do not know how representative it is), we believe it can increase the efficiency of a classroom teacher by providing clues to the types of errors to look for first. An additional caution is that it is highly likely that types of errors made by students reflect the type of mathematics instruction that those students have been exposed to. (This information is not provided in the Lepore study cited above.) Therefore, we urge teachers to keep records of the types of difficulty encountered by pupils of a given type at a given level in a given mathematics program.

A more systematic analysis of error types, easily adapted for classroom use, was reported by Roberts (1962). The "failure strategies" employed by children usually fall into one of the categories outlined in Table 6–10.

Roberts found in his group of third-graders that the most common type of error was in use of a defective algorithm. Only the lowest-functioning children made errors of another type—and these were random responses.

Table 6–8.   Types of Arithmetic Habits Observed in Elementary School Pupils

Addition

Errors in combinations	Errors in reading numbers
Counting	Dropped back one or more tens
Added carried number last	Derived unknown combination from familiar
Forgot to add carried number	one
Repeated work after partly done	Disregarded one column
Wrote number to be carried	Error in writing answer
Irregular procedure in column	Skipped one or more decades
Carried wrong number	Carrying when there was nothing to carry
Grouped two or more numbers	Used scratch paper
Split numbers onto parts	Added in pairs, giving last sum as answer
Used wrong fundamental operation	Added same digit in two columns
Lost place in column	Wrote carried number in answer
Depended on visualization	Added same number twice
Disregarding column position	
Omitted one or more digits	

Subtraction

Errors in combinations	Deducted from minuend when borrowing was
Did not allow for having borrowed	not necessary
Counting	Ignored a digit
Errors due to zero in minuend	Deducted 2 from minuend after borrowing
Said example backwards	Error due to minuend and subtrahend digits
Subtracted minuend from subtrahend	being same
Failed to borrow; gave zero as answer	Used minuend or subtrahend as remainder
Added instead of subtracted	Reversed digits in remainder
Error in reading	Confused process with division or
Used same digit in two columns	multiplication
Derived unknown from known combination	Skipped one or more decades
Omitted a column	Increased minuend digit after borrowing
Used trial-and-error addition	Based subtraction on multiplication
Split numbers	combination

Multiplication

Errors in combinations	Confused products when multiplier had two or
Error in adding the carried number	more digits
Wrote rows of zeros	Repeated part of table
Carried a wrong number	Multiplied by adding
Errors in addition	Did not multiply a digit in multiplicand
Forgot to carry	Based unknown combination on another
Used multiplicand as multiplier	Errors in reading
Error in single zero combinations, zero as	Omitted digit in writing product
multiplier	Errors in carrying into zero
Errors due to zero in multiplier	Counted to carry
Used wrong process—added	Omitted digit in multiplier
Error in single zero combinations, zero as	Split multiplier
multiplicand	Wrote wrong digit of product

Table 6–8. *Continued*

Multiplication	

Errors due to zero in multiplicand	Multiplied by same digit twice
Error in position of partial products	Reversed digits in product
Counted to get multiplication combinations	Wrote tables
Illegible figures	
Forgot to add partial products	

Division	

Errors in division combinations	Used remainder without new dividend figure
Errors in subtraction	Derived unknown combinations from known
Errors in multiplication	one
Used remainder larger than divisor	Had right answer, used wrong one
Found quotient by trial multiplication	Grouped too many digits in dividend
Neglected to use remainder within problem	Error in reading
Omitted zero resulting from another digit	Used dividend or divisor as quotient
Counted to get quotient	Found quotient by adding
Repeated part of multiplication table	Reversed dividend and divisor
Used short division form for long division	Used digits of divisor separately
Wrote remainders within problem	Wrote all remainders at end of problem
Omitted zero resulting from zero in dividend	Misinterpreted table
Omitted final remainder	Used digit in dividend twice
Used long division form for short division	Used second digit or divisor to find quotient
Said example backwards	Began dividing at units digit of dividend
	Split dividend
	Counted in subtracting
	Used too large a product
	Used endings to find quotient

Source: G. T. Buswell and Leonore John, *Diagnostic Studies in Arithmetic* Chicago: Univeristy of Chicago Press, 1926). Used with the permission of the publisher.

Table 6–9. Analysis of Computation Errors

Type of Error	Addition	Subtraction	Multiplication	Division
Procedural	5	16	144	58
Number facts	12	60	55	16
Regrouping	33	232	42	
Omissions and reversals	16	35	4	
Gaps (problems combining one-place with two- or three-place numbers)	7	19		
Use of zero	0	84	25	11
Add/subtract errors in multiplication/division problems			17	2

Source: Adapted from Lepore (1974).

Table 6–10.   Failure Strategies Employed by Elementary Pupils

| | Example | |
Strategy	Problem	Pupil Response
Wrong operation (the pupil performs an operation that leads to an incorrect result)	38 −11	$\begin{array}{r} 38 \\ -11 \\ \hline 49 \end{array}$
Obvious computational error (the pupil makes an obvious error in basic number facts)	42 × 3	$\begin{array}{r} 42 \\ \times\,3 \\ \hline 146 \end{array}$
Defective algorithm (the pupil makes procedural errors as he tries to apply the correct process)	562 −387	$\begin{array}{r} 562 \\ -387 \\ \hline 225 \end{array}$
Random response (the pupil's response does not relate in any discernible way to the problem)	742 × 59	$\begin{array}{r} 742 \\ \times\,59 \\ \hline 123 \end{array}$

Source: Adapted from Roberts (1962).

The utilization of the child's written work and statements during an oral interview in the diagnostic-instructional sequence is illustrated in Table 6–11. In each case, what the child does and what the child says lead the teacher to a tentative hypothesis concerning the source of difficulty. Once having identified the problem, the teacher is able to make a good guess as to what instructional procedures will be effective with the child. Possible teaching strategies for each instance are exemplified in the column "What the teacher does next."

INSTRUCTION IN MATHEMATICS

Once the child's performance has been analyzed in detail, instruction can begin. The nature of decisions to be made by the teacher shifts now to considerations of materials, methodologies, and approaches. This section begins with a discussion of a few principles that will assist the teacher in making sound instructional decisions. This is followed by descriptions of several instructional approaches which lend themselves to use with children having particular difficulty in mathematics. Because of the particular difficulty experienced by many children with verbal problem solving, this aspect of instruction has been singled out for special attention. A final section on one aspect of instruction—record keeping—concludes this chapter.

Table 6–11. Sample Inventory of Subtraction of Whole Numbers: Error Analysis*

Problem Presented	What the Child Writes	What the Child Says (Oral Interview)	Error Analysis Teacher's Hypotheses	What the Teacher Does Next
7 − 3	7 − 3 2	7 take away 3 = 2.	Doesn't know number fact.	Present same problem in another form (rule out random error). Check other subtraction facts. Provide practice with physical objects, worksheets, number line, flashcards, games, etc. Retest before going to more difficult subtraction.
15 − 6	15 − 6 11	6 take away 5 is 1; 1 stays the same.	Faulty algorithm; doesn't understand integrity of minuend and subtrahend; doesn't know number fact.	Check further to see if child always subtracts smaller number from larger. Review addition and subtraction at enactive and iconic level (Bruner) with one-digit numbers, then two-digit. Have child respond orally before returning to written form.
85 − 3	85 − 3 52	3 from 8 is 5; 3 from 5 is 2.	Problem worked left to right; problem with place value (subtracting ones from tens).	Review place value at the enactive, iconic, and symbolic levels; provide practice with subtraction algorithm in simpler two-digit problems.
85 − 9	8¹5 − 9 86	The 8 goes down here; then you have to change the 5 to 15, then subtract 9 from 15.	Problem worked left to right; doesn't understand effect of regrouping ones on tens	Provide experience with place value—manipulating bundles of straws (1's, 10's, 100's), pocket chart, or Stern materials; then provide workbook pictorial practice. Finally, rework symbolic problem.

Table 6–11. *Continued*

Problem Presented	What the Child Writes	What the Child Says (Oral Interview)	Error Analysis Teacher's Hypotheses	What the Teacher Does Next
91 − 83	⁹1 −83 —— 1	Since you can't take 3 from 1, the answer is 1; also because 8 from 9 is 1.	Problem in regrouping; possible problem in number fact.	Review place value (tens and ones);* perform several problems of this type on the pocket chart, or with Cuisenaire rods. Provide successful experience on problems of this type before returning to numerical form.
523 − 284	4⁵¹²¹³ −2 8 4 ———— 2 4 9	This 2 (in tens place) should be 12, that makes this 5 a 4. Now 12 − 8 = 4 and 4 − 2 = 2. To take 4 away over here (ones column) you make the 3 to a 13; 13 − 4 = 9; change 12 to 11.	Sequence is the problem here. The child performed all the steps correctly but in the wrong order.	Practice right-to-left sequence in problems not involving regrouping. Use place-value box or chart to show why sequence affects results.
300 − 157	³⁰⁰⁰ − 1 5 7 ———— 0 5 3	You have to get ones from the three because there aren't any here (pointing to 0's); 3 take away 2 makes the 3 a 1. Now we have 10 ones, and 10 tens, and we can subtract.	Relationship of empty sets of ones to tens to hundreds a problem. Child doesn't understand conversion from one unity to another.	Provide child with experience in converting tens to ones and hundreds to ones. (It might be very effective to use dollars, dimes, and pennies first; then use the paper-and-pencil model). First provide practice using only tens and ones together, then hundreds and tens together, then hundreds and ones together, finally conversions involving all three units in one problem.

* For an excellent discussion and numerous examples of error analysis, the reader is referred to R. B. Ashlock, *Error Patterns in Computation: A Semiprogrammed Approach* (Columbus, Ohio: Charles E. Merrill, 1972).

IMPORTANT PRINCIPLES INVOLVED IN INSTRUCTION

Before actually implementing an intervention in math, the teacher should be familiar with two of the more important principles associated with teaching material in this subject area: (1) the place of the discovery method and (2) the use of flexibility in programming.

The Place of the Discovery Method

More than any other issue, the field of mathematics education has been dominated by a discussion of the extent to which teachers should use a "discovery approach" in teaching. The widespread adoption of this style of teaching is based on the belief that children learn more thoroughly and better retain principles and concepts that were acquired through a "discovery" process rather than through didactic instruction on the part of a teacher. Although Jerome Bruner of Harvard University has been a leading advocate of the discovery approach, other individuals have articulated it as well (Schulman, 1967; Kersh, 1965; Worthen, 1967). In using the discovery method, the teacher limits the number of cues that are given to the child to assist the child in solving a particular problem. The cues that are withheld might be process cues, e.g., telling the child to do such-and-such, or product cues, e.g., giving "hints" as to where to look for the answer.

The debate over the discovery method takes on particular significance when one is talking about the instruction of children who have problems in mathematics performance. One could define such children as those for whom cues that were sufficient for their peer group are not sufficient. That is, whatever the quantity and type of cues that made it possible for their classmates to learn did not work for this group. To advise further cue reduction for these children, then, seems almost irresponsible. Should children with mathematics problems be presented only with expository-type teaching? Although there is no research evidence one way or the other, we believe such a course to be unwise. *All* children, including those with learning difficulties, should be exposed to a variety of teaching styles and instructional approaches. Naturally, we do not advocate persisting with an approach that has been manifestly ineffective. What we are asserting is that there is more than one way to teach mathematics to children, and discovery learning should not be ruled out for any child. Similarly, to rely exclusively on the discovery method seems to us to be just as foolhardy. Optimum learning appears to take place when the teacher behavior is indirect but supportive, and when the child is in an active as opposed to a passive learning mode (Becher, 1980). This appears particularly to be the case in the development of the cognitive prerequisites to formal mathematics learning.

Figure 6–3. Proposal for Relating Three Modes of Experience to the Acquisition of an Underlying System of Knowledge and Skills

Cognitive Development		Categories of Behavior (Modes) From Which Information May Be Extracted		Informational Coding (Alternatives Specified by:)
Knowledge	Skills			
Diagonal	Checkerboard Drawing Speaking	Contingent experience { Direct / Directed (instructional)		Reinforcement consequent upon one's acts (learning theory)
Chair	Sitting Drawing Describing	Observational learning { Observation / Modeling (instruction)		Modeled alternatives (social learning theory)
Objects	Locomotive			
Events	Prehensive	Symbolic Systems { Communication / Instruction		Coded alternatives (cognitive theory)
Space	Linguistic			
Time	Mathematical Iconological			

Information extraction processes

Flexibility in Using Instructional Approaches

As stated in the preceding section, the effective teacher utilizes more than one approach, depending on the child, the task, and the situation. Olson (1972), noting that children can acquire the same knowledge when instructed in different modes, has presented a model that relates mode of experience to the acquisition of an underlying system of knowledge and skills (Figure 6–3). Note that a child may acquire the concept of the diagonal, for example, by direct or directed reinforced experience; by observing someone demonstrate the concept; or by verbal instruction through a symbol system (in this case, the English language). Olson's proposal has enormous implications for the teacher of mathematics (and to all teachers). If he is correct, teachers have considerably more choice than they may have thought they had in selecting an instructional mode. Thus, at times they may select procedures derived from learning theory (reinforcement consequent upon one's acts), at other times from social learning theory (modeled alternatives), or from cognitive theory (coded alternatives).

The same general thinking underlies a series of research studies and a mathematical development project at the University of Connecticut (Cawley, 1971, 1976). Cawley and his coworkers have postulated an *interactive unit model* (see Table 6–12) that refers to the interaction of teacher and pupil in the mathematics teaching–learning situation. The instructional requirements for the teacher vary from constructing something, presenting something, saying something, or writing something. The child, when interacting with the teacher, can construct something, identify something, say something, or write something. The various combinations of teacher input and student output are sixteen in number. This flexibility permits maximum discretion on the part of the teacher in planning for individuals or groups of children. Thus, if a child is a nonreader, for example, there are still twelve other ways that he or she and the teacher can interact in the instructional setting.

The teacher can evidence flexibility in mathematics instruction in other ways, such as permitting pupils to have a choice in selecting the materials with which they wish to work or encouraging pupils to use unusual or alternative algorithms in working mathematical problems. Most textbook-prescribed algorithms are based on convention and on "efficiency," but there are equally acceptable ways of performing the same operation. For example, students having an inordinate amount of difficulty with subtraction involving borrowing (see Table 6–11.) may wish to use the alternative algorithm known as the "equal addition method" (Ashlock, 1972). Thus, the problem is

$$773$$
$$- 254$$

Table 6–12. Project MATH Interactive Unit (Example Selected: Teaching the Concept of "Open" and "Closed")

| | | INPUT, usually by teacher (T) | | |
		constructs	presents	states	writes
OUTPUT, usually by pupil (P)	constructs	T demonstrates "open" and "closed" with containers; P models with containers.	T presents containers to P; P opens or closes items as requested.	T states "open" or "closed"; P must form open or closed figure with yarn.	T writes "open" or "closed" on chalkboard; P closes or opens containers.
	presents	T constructs examples of open and closed containers; P points to his own sample that matches T's.	T presents containers or pictures to P; P selects open or closed as requested.	T states "open" or "closed"; P points to appropriate picture.	P circles workbook picture that has "open" printed at top of page.
	states	T constructs examples of open and closed containers; P correctly says "open" or "closed," as required.	T presents open and closed items to P; P states whether they are open or closed.	T asks P to name open and closed objects in the room.	P reads word from board, then states which items correspond.
	writes	T constructs examples of open and closed containers; P correctly writes "open" or "closed," as required.	T presents pictures of open and closed items to P; P writes "open" or "closed."	T describes items; P writes "open" or "closed."	T writes "open" or "closed" at top of page; P writes word under pictures.

Definitions	
Construct (do)	To pile, build, arrange, manipulate two- or three-dimensional objects or materials.
Present (see)	To display in fixed representations either two- or three-dimensional stimuli.
Identify (see)	To point to or otherwise mark nonsymbolic options in a multiple-choice task.
State (say)	To orally state.
Graphically symbolize (say)	To write with symbols (letters/numerals) or to draw.

Source: Adapted from J. F. Cawley, *Learning Disabilities in Mathematics: A Curriculum Design for Upper Grades* (unpublished manuscript, University of Connecticut, Storrs, Conn., 1976).

The solution by this method is

$$
\begin{array}{r}
77^13 \\
- 2_65 4 \\
\hline
5 1 9
\end{array}
$$

The rationale for this approach is the principle of compensation: whatever is added to the minuend must be added to the subtrahend. Thus, 10 ones are added to the minuend; 1 ten is added to the subtrahend to compensate. Then, subtraction proceeds normally.

APPROACHES TO TEACHING MATHEMATICS

As stated in the introductory section to this chapter, there has been a great increase in the number of instructional mathematics materials available to teachers. This section will briefly describe some of the current approaches that have potential applicability for children with problems in mathematics achievement.

Basal Math Texts

For many years, the use of basal texts has been the most common way of teaching mathematics. Generally the materials consist of pupil texts, pupil workbooks, and teacher's manuals. Sometimes additional supplementary materials are available, such as spirit duplicator masters, charts for recording pupil progress, or quizzes or tests to establish whether a child is ready to begin a new section. Among the best of the elementary basal math series are:

Growth in Mathematics (Harcourt Brace)
Essentials of Math (Ginn)
Modern School Math: Structure and Use (Houghton Mifflin)
Math for Individual Achievement (Houghton Mifflin)
Skillseekers (Addison-Wesley)
SRA Mathematics Program (Science Research Associates)
Individual Math Improvement Series (Bobbs Merrill)

Math Kits

Increasing numbers of publishers have produced mathematics instructional programs in the form of kits or packages with various components.

Table 6–13. Summary Descriptions of Instructional Math Kits

Title and (Publisher)	Comments
Basic Computation Skills Series 1,2,3 (Holt, Rinehart)	Self-administered diagnostic tests prescribing work on Study-Do sheets. Record sheets. Teacher's guide.
Computational Arithmetic Program (1–6) (Pro-Ed)	Sequenced, computational lessons. Considerable data base provided. Primarily intended for remedial use. Behavioral orientation.
Diagnosis: An Instructional Aid (Science Research Associates)	Survey and diagnostic tests (probes). Prescription guides. Remediation activities. Management system for teaching pupil progress.
Distar: Arithmetic I, Arithmetic II (K–2) (Science Research Associates)	Direct instructional method. Teacher and pupil books. Take-home workbooks.
Foundations for Math: Basic Math Skill Development (Teaching Resources)	Emphasizes skill development.
Fundamentals Underlying Numbers (Teaching Resources)	
Individualized Math System (Rev.) (1–8) (Ginn)	"Program" consists of reusable laminated pages. Pre- and post-tests. Prescriptive tests.
Math: An Activity Approach (6–9) (Science Research Associates)	Individualized. 188 games and activities from whole numbers through statistics. New skills, review of old skills. Application.
Mathematics Involvement Program (K–6) (Science Research Associates)	Individualized. Multilevel. Manipulative emphasis. Numerous reinforcement and enrichment activities. Over 200 activity cards.
Math—Series 300 to 800 (3–8) (Educational Progress)	Individuals work at own rate and level. Concepts and skill sequence based on most widely used texts. Activity cards. Audio tapes. Student record keeping.
Project MATH (K–6) (Educational Development Corp)	Multiple option curriculum. Interactive units based on teacher/learner: input/output.
Skill Modes in Math (4–Adult) (Science Research Associates)	Self diagnosis. Self teaching. Student activity and practice cards. Record books.

Usually these consist of activity cards for daily lessons, teacher's guides, and materials for pupil activities. A summary of such kits is presented in Table 6–13. (All of these kits were developed in the latter 1970s or early 1980s).

Special Approaches

A few educational approaches have been developed for children who require a more concrete, less abstract approach to mathematics. There are three of these—the Montessori Approach, the Cuisenaire–Gattegno Approach, and Stern's *Structural Arithmetic* Approach. Each of these is briefly described next.

Montessori Materials
(Montessori, 1964, 1965a, 1965b)

Theory and Rationale. The Montessori approach encompasses the entire physiological and psychological development the child. Montessori (1965a) has organized her didactic materials into three major areas: motor education, sensory education, and language. The learning of arithmetic is seen as integrally related to the education of the senses, and most of the sensory training materials are readily adaptable for arithmetic activities. Montessori advocates a careful sequential development of basic numerical concepts rather than presenting "certain preliminary ideas" in haste (Montessori, 1965a, p. 165).

Training Techniques. The Montessori materials are designed to be self-teaching. The basic materials include sets of solid cubes, cylinders, rods, prisms, and other geometric shapes and plane geometric forms; they also include counting boxes, sandpaper numerals, arithmetic frames and heads, counting frames, and bead chains. The materials may be used for learning seriation and ordering, one-to-one correspondence, shape and size, volume and length, counting, place value, addition, subtraction, multiplication, division, and factors.

To illustrate how the Montessori materials are employed for teaching basic arithmetic concepts, the use of cylinders is described. The materials themselves consist of four sets of cylinder boxes, each containing ten cylinders. The cylinders illustrate: (1) same height, change in diameter; (2) corresponding changes in height and diameter; (3) same diameter, change in height; and (4) opposite changes in diameter and height. One set at a time, the cylinders are removed from the box and randomly arranged. Through a series of trials and errors, the child replaces each cylinder until he or she finds the proper fit between the space in the box and the cylinder. The child may also line up the cylinders in order of ascending or descending height or diameter without the use of the boxes.

The purposes of the activities are to observe and make comparisons between objects in terms of one or two dimensions—height and diameter. The child also learns seriation and ordering.

Program Evaluation. The work of Montessori may be considered the forerunner of developmental theory concerning motor, sensory, and intellectual development, later refined and reformulated by Piaget, Bruner, and others.

The use of concrete materials in the classroom as representations of abstract principles appears to be a major strength of the Montessori methods. However, after reviewing nineteen experimental studies of the effectiveness of this approach, L. Goodman (1974) concluded that Montessori's techniques had not yet been proved to be particularly useful.

Cuisenaire–Gattegno Rods

Rationale and Theory. The Cuisenaire rods (Davidson, 1969) are instructional aids that seem particularly relevant to a modern mathematics curriculum. They are capable of generating pupil interest and enthusiasm while promoting a dialogue between learner and teacher. The rods are based on a definition of mathematics as a process of observation and a discovery of relationships. They were designed for the purpose of teaching conceptual knowledge of the basic structure of mathematics, rather than simply the manipulative skills. The teacher's role in the setting provided by the rods is to observe and ask questions about what the children are discovering for themselves, rather than to instruct or explain. It would appear that a child who works out facts and ideas for himself or herself will learn and retain them better. Using rods, a kindergartener is introduced to algebraic equations and a basic appreciation of place value and the number system. The rods were invented by George Cuisenaire in 1953, and have been further developed by Caleb Gattegno.

Training Techniques. There are 291 Cuisenaire rods, made of wood, and varying in length and color. The rods combine color and length to embody algebraic principles and number relationships. They are 1 centimeter square in cross section and from 1 to 10 centimeters long. There are five color families. The red rods represent the quantities of 2, 4, and 8; the blue–green rods, 3, 6, and 9; the yellow rods, 5 and 10; the black rod, 7; and the white cube, 1.

Since the rods have no numerals on them, children who have not yet developed an adequate number background can use the materials to explore logic as well as relationships between quantities. Children who possess basic number awareness can work with the rods in terms of the principles identified with particular operations.

Introduction of the rods at any given grade level is done in the following four stages: (1) independent exploration; that is, the child is permitted to "play" with the rods; (2) independent exploration and direct activities with the rods, in which relationships are observed and discussed without the use of mathematical notation. The following aspects of mathematics are explored at this point:

Equivalence
Trains (sequences)
Patterns
Greater than and less than
Staircase (seriation)
Complements
Trains of one color
Transformations
Odds and evens

(3) directed activities in which mathematical notation is introduced and used without assigning number value to the rods. Opportunities for independent exploration are still needed; (4) directed activities in which the use of mathematical notation is extended and number values are assigned to the rods. Independent exploration will go beyond the directed activities.

Care should be taken to use rods for proper purposes, that is, discovery and verification. The method would be valueless if children were unable to do sums without the help of the rods. As soon as the situation is well understood, the child must be encouraged to work it out mentally.

Four booklets that accompany the rods treat such topics as cardinality, ordinality, factors, equivalence, permutations, transformations, complements, various forms of measurement, inequalities, proportions, basic whole numbers and rational number operations, and number properties. While the booklets are concerned with various aspects of basic mathematics, they cannot be considered a complete program.

Although these materials can be used in grades kindergarten through six, they are usually emphasized through grade three. They may be used with an entire class, a small group, or an individual child. They have been successfully utilized with children possessing a varied range of abilities: the deaf, mentally retarded, gifted, and emotionally disturbed, as well as with other children who need visual and tactile reinforcement for effective learning.

Program Evaluation. Research on the Cuisenaire–Gattegno materials has not been conclusive, but it has indicated that the rods are at least as effective as more traditional mathematics approaches. In addition, these materials minimize drill and rote learning and promote discovery and understanding by the individual child according to his or her own developmental level. Student interest and enthusiasm is usually high. The concreteness of the materials and their manipulation by a tactile modality make them particularly useful for children with whom a traditional mathematics program has been unsuccessful.

The Cuisenaire rods have been criticized on the grounds that children become too dependent on them and are unable to function at a symbolic, abstract level without them. However, used judiciously in conjunction with other models and approaches, the Cuisenaire rods have a place as supplemental materials in a modern mathematics curriculum for children with learning problems.

Structural Arithmetic (Stern, 1965)

Rationale. This system is based on the assumption that arithmetic is the basis for the further study of mathematics and science; it presumes that mathematical concepts can and must be developed at the beginning of school life. Furthermore, the program assures mastery in computation by developing an insight into number relationships. This is achieved by having the child experiment with concrete materials that reveal the structure of our number system.

The goals of this approach are to develop mathematical thinking and nurture an appreciation for its exactness and clarity. Mathematical thinking can only develop if the child has obtained insight into the characteristic structure of the entire set of concepts to which specific addition or subtraction facts belong, or if the child has developed insight into structural relationships that make transfer of learning possible. All experiments in *Structural Arithmetic* are designed to develop concepts that lead the child to arrive at generalizations essential to the understanding and mastery of arithmetic.

Structural Arithmetic hopes to achieve its goals through the following approaches:

1. By the use of concrete materials which allow the child to discover a number fact.
2. By following a carefully arranged sequence of experiments through which the child advances step by step from simple number concepts to the mastery of arithmetical computation and problem solving.
3. By presenting functional illustrations in the workbooks which help the child reconstruct any forgotten number fact.

It is hoped that the child will experience the following achievements resulting from use of structural materials:

1. Immediate success in arithmetic. (There will be a carryover from work with concrete materials to ability to do abstract figuring.)
2. Development of self-reliance. (The child can check answers and make corrections; the child will become accustomed to always checking for correctness.)
3. Preparation for the mathematical thinking necessary in the later development of mathematics.

Training Techniques. The materials for *Structural Arithmetic* (SA) are packaged in four kits, appropriate for kindergarten level and grades one through three. Materials for each grade include a teacher's manual, pupils' workbooks, and manipulatable materials (number markers, number guide, number track, number stand and accompanying slides, pattern board, unit box with unit blocks, subtraction shield, number cases, and a box of 100 cubes).

The approach in SA is based on measuring. The numbers are represented by blocks that measure 1 unit, 2 units, 3 units, and so on. With these devices the child can discover all existing number relations by himself or herself. He or she finds out by measuring not only what block combinations yield 10, but also discovers processes of carrying and borrowing, multiplying and dividing. They are as well adapted for use with groups as for individual instruction.

Problem solving is an important part of SA. Pupils are prepared step by step for solving problems. They begin by listening carefully to oral problems and then demonstrate the problems with the manipulative materials. In SA 1, problems are presented by pictures without any printed words. In this way, a child's lack of reading ability will not hold him or her back. Word problems are introduced in SA 2 and used through SA 3. The vocabulary is kept simple throughout. In addition to work with structural materials, most of the lessons contain suggestions that teachers may use to provide an opportunity for pupils to do oral computation. Mastery tests appear at the end of each workbook and are also used throughout the SA program.

Each lesson is planned in the teacher's guide to help the teacher set up experiments that guide pupils to make appropriate discoveries and generalizations. From each experiment the pupils are to gain insight into an arithmetical procedure. To check whether the demonstration was successful, the teacher should present examples that the children can solve without the structural materials or pencil and paper. Following this the children continue using the topic of the day's experiment in their workbooks. There are provisions for additional experiments for the child who is having difficulty, and enrichment activities for the child who wishes to work independently.

Program Evaluation. *Structural Arithmetic* is a complete mathematics program that is flexible, well organized, and concrete. The teacher's guide is very thorough and includes detailed teaching suggestions. The program has been successful with mildly retarded and learning disabled children, as well as in regular classes. The materials are nonconsumable.

VERBAL PROBLEM SOLVING

Several authors have noted that there is much more to verbal problem solving than merely deciding on the correct computational procedure and performing the computation. Solving problems potentially involves questions of judgments concerning reasonableness and practicality, as well as other considerations. McGinty and Meyerson (1980) have schematically portrayed the way in which solving problems in mathematics is related to problem solving in everyday life. (See Figure 6–4) Cawley, Fitzmaurice, Shaw, Kahn, and Bates (1979) make much the same point when they note that many problems appropriately posed in the mathematics program involve no computation at all. They also show that some students are able to "solve" the rather contrived typical mathematics problems, but are not able to solve real-life problems. Such problems, they observe, entail an integration of computational skill, concept analysis, selection and deriving of relevant information, and decision making (p. 37). An adequate problem solving program in mathematics prepares students for real-life problem solving, which often involves numbers. Some of these numbers (such as Social Security numbers, telephone numbers or utility readings) may not require computation, but will require problem-solving skills for their successful use in day-to-day living. Such skills would involve map-reading skills, writing and keeping track of checks, indexing and cross-referencing, comparison shopping, measuring in standard and metric measures, computing interest, and understanding such things as rental forms requiring different kinds of deposits.

Probably no area of mathematics performance causes more difficulty for students than verbal problem solving (Carpenter, Corbitt, Kepner, Lindquist, and Reys, 1980a, b). It is not known what all the causes for poor problem-solving ability are, but they almost certainly include the following:

1. *Lack of practice.* Some teachers do not fully recognize the complexity of problem solving, and fail to teach it in a systematic way. Considerable time must be alloted for the successful development of problem-solving skills.

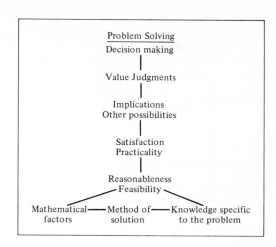

Figure 6–4. Aspects of Problem Solving

2. *Inadequate development of underlying capabilities.* Task analysis and research have indicated that the following are related to ability to solve mathematical problems:

a. *Ability to perform required computations is a necessary subskill.* Pace (1961) found that an understanding of the four fundamental operations (addition, subtraction, multiplication, division) is vital for problem solving.

b. *Ability to read with understanding.* That reading problems are frequently implicated in problem-solving difficulties is exemplified by Heddens and Smith (1964). This study found that the typical commercial mathematics text has a readability level above that of the assigned grade level. The reading aspect of mathematical problems is further affected by the fact that many words have a different meaning in a mathematical context than in everyday life. For example, "set" in mathematics refers to a grouping of items; in ordinary usage it is a verb, as in "set the table." Even if the child can read the word "set," it does not follow that the child knows its mathematical usage. Other such special terms include "order," "base," "power," and "roots." Treacy (1944) found that poor problem solvers had trouble with a number of reading skills, particularly those that had to do with interpreting vocabulary.

c. *Ability to estimate answers.* Checking the "reasonableness" of an obtained answer requires the ability to estimate. Poor problem solvers tend not to be proficient in this skill. (Carpenter, et al., 1980a).

Table 6–14.   Suggested Steps in Verbal Problems Solving

	Problem A	Problem B
	Mary has 3 apples. Betty has 2 oranges. Peter has 4 apples. How many pieces of fruit do the girls have?	Bill has 7 quarters, 3 dimes, and 4 pennies. How much money will he have left if he spends 45 cents for candy?
A. Preview: read the problem		
1. Identify unknown words	None	None
2. Identify words with unusual usages	None	None
3. Identify any "cue" words, e.g., "total," "in all," "how many were left"	None	"How much . . . have left"
B. Re-reading: information processing		
1. Identify what is given		
a. Is renaming required?		
i. unit conversion	No	Quarters and dimes to cents
ii. categorization (superordinate, subordinate categories)	Apples and oranges to fruit	No
b. Is sufficient information given?		
c. Is irrelevant or distracting information given?	"Peter has 4 apples."	
2. Identify what is asked for; formulate hypothesis		
a. What process is required? (comparing, combining, etc.)	Combining	Conversion, combining, separating
b. What unit or category is required (minutes, inches, apples, dollars, etc.)	Fruit	Dollars and cents
C. Refine hypothesis: operations analysis		
Decide what operations need to be performed	Combining: addition	Combining: Addition, then separation: subtraction
Possible strategies:		
1. Substitute easier numbers in the problem	Not applicable	Bill has (10 cents). How much money will he have left if he spends 5 cents for candy? Solution pattern: subtract money spent from original amount of

Table 6–14. *Continued.*

	Problem A	Problem B
	Mary has 3 apples. Betty has 2 oranges. Peter has 4 apples. How many pieces of fruit do the girls have?	Bill has 7 quarters, 3 dimes, and 4 pennies. How much money will he have left if he spends 45 cents for candy?
		money, or; original money − money spent = *required answer.* Now substitute numbers from Problem B.
2. Use manipulative objects, number line, or doodles drawn on paper to help "visualize" the problem.		
D. Write the mathematical sentences	3 + 2 = *required answer*	$7 \times .25 = a$ $3 \times .10 = b$ $4 \times .01 = c$ $a + b + c = d$ $d − .45 = required\ answer$
E. Perform the operation	3 + 2 = 5	$7 \times .25 = 1.25$ $3 \times .10 = .30$ $4 \times .01 = .04$ $1.75 + .30 + .04 = 2.09$ $2.09 − .45 = 1.64$
F. Check the answer		
1. Recheck reason and computation.	Repeat steps A–E	Repeat steps A–E
2. Estimate the answer and compare to obtained answer.	Will vary	Will vary
G. State the result In terms of E (above) In terms of B.2.b (above)	The girls now have 5 pieces of fruit.	Bill will have $1.64 left.

Source: Adapted from K. Kramer, *The Teaching of Elementary School Mathematics* (Boston: Allyn and Bacon, 1970); J. F. Cawley, Learning Disabilities in Mathematics: A Curriculum Design for Upper Grades (unpublished) manuscript, University of Connecticut, Storrs, Conn., 1976); and from author's experience.

d. *Acquisition of prerequisite concepts and cognitive structures.* There is reason to believe that the capacities described in the section on "Readiness" are necessary for children to solve mathematical problems. For example, Steffe (1968) reported that ability to conserve was related to problem-solving performance.

e. *Ability to organize required problem-solving steps in sequence.* Although the evidence is mixed as far as the necessity for teaching specific problem-solving steps to most children (Wilson, 1967; Lerch and Hamilton, 1966), we advocate the use of such procedures for children who are having inordinate difficulty. The procedure to be followed is outlined in Table 6–14.

How does a teacher find appropriate verbal problems for children with mathematical difficulty? Some of these children have reading problems; some have computational difficulties; others are unable to deal with extraneous information or are unable to discern whether they have sufficient information to solve a given problem. Cawley et al. (1979) have suggested that teachers develop a matrix that incorporates those dimensions of problem solving that seem to be problematic for the children in question. For example, if the teacher has children who have poor reading ability and variable computational skills, a matrix such as Figure 6–5 can be constructed, with separate matrices for problems in addition, subtraction, and so on.

A child who has a second-grade reading level, but computational mastery with two-digit numbers (no regrouping) would be given problems from cell E. As the child's reading level improves, but computational skills stay constant, verbal problems at a higher reading level but constant comprehension level (cells F, G, H) would be given to the child. If the child's computational level improves, but reading level does not, problems written for cells I and M would be given to the child. Using a matrix such as this permits making verbal problems individualized and relevant to the needs of specific children.

Level of Computational Difficulty	2nd Grade	3rd Grade	4th Grade	5th Grade
1 digit	A	B	C	D
2 digit No regrouping	E	F	G	H
2 digit Regrouping	I	J	K	L
etc.	M	N	O	P

Reading Level ──────►

Figure 6–5. Sample Problem-Solving Matrix

RECORD KEEPING FOR DIAGNOSTIC TEACHING

Employment of the diagnostic, analytic procedures outlined in the previous sections obviously calls for precise record keeping. The teacher will want to keep at least two kinds of records for each child's performance in mathematics. The first type is in the form of a summary checksheet for a group of children or for an entire class and is used to plan individual and group activities. A portion of such a table is shown as Figure 6–6.

Checksheets such as this can be used to keep a record of when each child has finally achieved mastery of given areas or mathematics achievement. During the period from when the child is first instructed in a given performance area until the time that he or she achieves mastery, more detailed record keeping is required. Take the example of a child who has just been introduced to a new unit on long division. The objective is to teach the child to perform division problems of the type

$$3 \overline{)7965} \quad \text{(one-digit divisor, no remainder)}$$

Figure 6– 6. Summary Checksheet

Name of Pupil	One-place whole numbers without carrying	Two-place whole numbers without carrying	Three-place whole numbers without carrying	Two-place whole numbers with carrying 10's	Three-place numbers with carrying 10's	Three-place numbers with carrying 10's, 100's	Mixed digit addition with carrying	Simple fractions common denominators	Mixed fractions common denominators	Simple fractions mixed denominators	Mixed fractions mixed denominators	Decimals–one decimal point	Decimals–two or more decimal points
Mary B.	9/26	10/4	10/14	1/21	1/30	2/14	5/10						
Tommy S.	9/2	9/30											

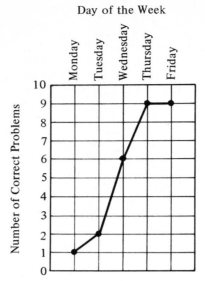

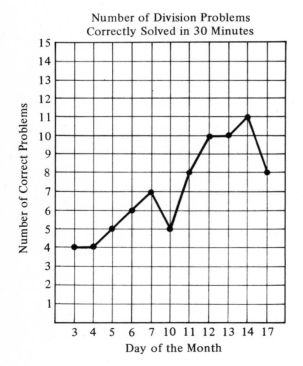

Figure 6–7. Example of Untimed Number-Correct Record Keeping

Figure 6–8. Example of Rate-per-Minute Record Keeping

Each day the child is presented with ten problems of this type. A record of his or her performance might look as shown in Figure 6–7. After the child has demonstrated adequacy in performing division problems of this type, the teacher might wish to encourage a child to work more quickly by recording the performance on a rate-per-minute index, or as the number performed in a given number of minutes. An example of this type of recording is given in Figure 6–8.

7

EVALUATING AND MANAGING CLASSROOM BEHAVIOR

Linda Brown

Teachers are expected to manage most of the behavior problems that arise in their classrooms. Of these problems, aggressive behaviors are the most apparent, in that they involve such things as fighting, stealing, or destroying property. They are obviously harmful to the children involved and they certainly disrupt the ongoing educational program. Passive behaviors, such as withdrawing, refusing to begin or complete work, or crying are less obvious; but they, too, prevent the affected child from participating fully in the academic and social activities of the classroom. Dealing with both passive and aggressive behaviors consumes the teacher's time and attention. Time is also devoted to managing numerous less serious, but not necessarily less aggravating problems, such as throwing spitwads, swearing, poking classmates, or running noisily through the corridors. We are confident that teachers can evaluate and manage the vast majority of these problems.

This chapter will present a variety of strategies that teachers can use to handle the problem behaviors, large and small, that occur every day in their classrooms. The assessment techniques described in the first section emphasize an ecological model that encourages teachers to approach a problem behavior directly and to pay special attention to situational and environmental influences that may contribute to the difficulty or aggravate it. An eclectic selection of management techniques presented in the second section will help the teacher manage or change problematic behavior patterns observed in the class or alter ecological variables determined to be important aspects of such behaviors.

ASSESSING PROBLEM BEHAVIORS

The evaluation of school-based behavior problems is a responsibility that usually is shared by classroom teachers and school psychology personnel. In some instances such evaluations are the sole responsibility of teachers, especially during the initial stages. The assessment unit of this chapter has been designed to assist classroom teachers in that evaluation process. In the first part of this section, we describe and present a rationale for ecological assessment, a model which we believe is well suited to behavioral evaluations. In the second part, we describe eight specific assessment strategies for teachers to use in measuring problem behaviors.

AN ECOLOGICAL FRAMEWORK FOR ASSESSING
PROBLEM BEHAVIORS

Teachers often observe behaviors that interfere with a student's school learning or that are symptomatic of emotional distress. For example, Jim cries every morning while on the school bus, unusual behavior for a fourth-grade student; Mary cuts high school English repeatedly but attends her other classes regularly; Willie is given to spitting on other people and pulling out patches of his hair; Nellie is friendless, frequently involved in fighting and teasing episodes, and is verbally abusive to her classmates; Sarah constantly talks out in class and almost never is in her seat; and David is abnormally reticent and withdrawn.

In any of these instances, when a student is suspected of being emotionally or behaviorally disordered or of exhibiting behavioral problems related to a learning difficulty, school personnel will need considerable information about the problem before they can make placement, diagnostic, or educational decisions. When the situation is thought to be serious, the teacher will want to prepare a written description detailing the precise behaviors that are of concern and the situations in which these behaviors occur. The teacher will need to document through objective means the presence and severity of the difficulty and to probe the areas of perceived difficulty more fully and systematically. Such documentation may be necessary to qualify a youngster for special services, to help the teacher set priorities for those behaviors requiring immediate attention, or to demonstrate that behavioral change has occurred as a result of treatment.

It is important that this information be gathered within an ecological frame of reference. Ecological assessment allows an examiner to evaluate a student's status in the various ecologies or environments in which the student functions. This type of evaluation is rapidly gaining popularity in the public schools, and many states now require that students identified as emotionally disturbed be evaluated in an ecological manner.

We advocate ecological assessment because it avoids at least two of the problems inherent in more traditional evaluations. First, ecological assessment obviously provides a much broader and more natural picture of the target child than one obtained from conventional evaluations that typically remove the child from the classroom and that are conducted in an isolated, sterile environment such as a testing room or the school psychologist's office. Ecological assessment also differs radically in its assumptions about the nature of behavioral difficulties. While traditional evaluations assume that the child is or has the problem, ecological assessment assumes that many factors other than child-centered ones may cause or aggravate behavioral problems.

No behavior occurs in a vacuum. It is possible that a so-called problem behavior is, in fact, "normal," but that a particular perception of that behavior is deviant. For instance, a teacher who is unfamiliar with six-year-olds may perceive normally busy first-graders as hyperactive and make referrals on that basis. We know that teachers' evaluations of behavior can affect their subsequent academic evaluations and that estimates of academic competence can affect behavioral evaluations (L. Brown and Sherbenou, 1981). Students of average or above-average academic ability seem to be given greater behavioral latitude than their less academically competent peers. It also is possible for elements of an environment to exacerbate problem behaviors. A classic example is provided by the student (or teacher!) who becomes restless and troublesome in a hot, noisy classroom. It should be apparent that the source of the problem may lie within the environment and not within the child. Only through ecological assessment can any of these suppositions be validated. "Ecological assessment can be very versatile; it can permit the exploration of positive, as well as negative, elements of the classroom or school" (Wallace and Larsen, 1978, p. 141).

Several environments may be tapped during ecological assessment. Among these are the school, the home, and the community, as well as the child's interpersonal environment and his or her internal ecology. Within the school setting, which is the environment we are most concerned with in this chapter, a teacher can assume that students change ecologies each time they change classes, teachers, or academic content or format within the same classroom. An example of the latter might be moving from a supervised reading group to an art interest center or even to independent reading activities. Presumably the requirements for success vary in each of these ecologies. One environment may require a great deal of verbalization (a language-experience reading group) while another requires silence (the library); one may require independence and creativity (an exploratory interest center) while another requires strict conformity and adherence to established rules and regulations (a chemistry lab or woodworking shop). It would not be unusual for a student to function in all of these very different environments during a typical school day.

Ecologies also may be discerned on the basis of the perceptions being recorded. The activities taking place in a reading group no doubt look very different through the teacher's eyes than through the students' eyes. Most teachers involved in ecological assessment will want to seek the perceptions of the target student and that student's teacher(s), parent(s), and peers. If the student in question is participating in a work-study program, the teacher may want to gather information from supervisors or co-workers in that environment.

In the Behavior Rating Profile (BRP), an ecological assessment battery which will be described in detail later, L. Brown and Hammill (1978) propose a two-dimensional model that includes a variety of perceptions that are evaluated within several environments or ecologies. Following this model, which is presented graphically in Figure 7–1, the teacher would decide which ecologies it is important to assess and whose perceptions should be sought. Data then would be gathered from these sources and assembled into an ecological profile.

Laten and Katz (1975) have defined five phases in conducting an ecological assessment. These include (1) assimilating referral data, (2) identifying ecological expectations, (3) organizing behavioral descriptions, (4) summarizing data,

Relationship of BRP Components to
Type of Respondent and Ecology

BRP COMPONENT	RESPONDENT				ECOLOGY		
	Student	Teacher(s)	Parent(s)	Peers	Home	School	Social-life
Student Rating Scale: Home	X				X		
Student Rating Scale: School	X					X	
Student Rating Scale: Peer	X						X
Teacher Rating Scale		X				X	
Parent Rating Scale			X		X		
Sociogram				X			X

Figure 7–1. Relationship of BRP Components to Type of Respondent and Ecology

Source: Reprinted with permission of the authors and publisher of L. L. Brown and D. D. Hammill, *The Behavior Rating Profile* (Austin, Texas: Pro-Ed, 1978).

and (5) establishing goals. In each of these phases, data are gathered from all relevant ecologies. The instances in which the student experiences success are scrutinized as carefully as those where the pupil is experiencing difficulty: (1) The first phase, referral, involves gathering broad intake data from each of the ecologies in which the child functions. Of particular interest at this time is the degree of success which the child enjoys in each ecology. (2) The expectations or requirements that each ecology demands of the child are identified in the second phase. What level of academic proficiency is expected? What social behaviors are required? Are there any special demands? In general, the teacher attempts to learn what things the child must do in each ecology in order to succeed and meet the requirements. (3) Behavioral descriptions are organized during the third stage. What does the child do? How does he or she behave? What skills does he or she possess and use? Particular attention is given to determining the child's behaviors with regard to the expectations that were identified in the preceding phase. Descriptions of the professional skills and support services that each ecology can provide are included. (4) The data then are summarized. (5) Finally, goals are established for the child and for the professionals within each ecology. Reasonable goals for improvement are defined for the child and guidelines for the material and personnel support that will be provided in each category are established. Interested readers are referred to Laten and Katz (1975), to Wiederholt, Hammill, and V. Brown (1978), and to Wallace and Larsen (1978) for more detailed descriptions of the ecological assessment process.

EIGHT GENERAL TECHNIQUES FOR ASSESSING PROBLEM BEHAVIORS

Eight general techniques that classroom teachers can use to evaluate problem behaviors are described in this section. These include the use of (1) direct observation, (2) behavioral checklists and inventories, (3) Q-sorts, (4) interviews, (5) criteria for analyzing the physical environment, (6) procedures for examining teacher–pupil interaction in the classroom, (7) peer-nominating techniques, and (8) standardized tests of personality. By taking care to note the people from whom these techniques gather information and the environments that they seem to evaluate, teachers can tailor ecological assessment plans that satisfy their particular assessment needs.

DIRECT OBSERVATION

The most convenient method a teacher can use to measure problem behavior is to observe it directly in the classroom. Cartwright and Cartwright (1974) provide an excellent discussion of classroom observation skills. Interested readers are encouraged to consult this text. The three direct-observation techniques have been described by Hall (1971c). They are (1) automatic recording, (2) analysis of permanent products, and (3) observational recording.

Automatic Recording

Automatic recording involves the measurement of behavior by machines. For instance, in biofeedback such behaviors as pulse, heart rate, blood pressure, and galvanic skin response are measured by sensitive mechanical devices. In laboratories where animal research is conducted, such machines are used frequently to record the movements or responses of the laboratory animals. These machines are costly to purchase and to repair, and they are rigid in their functioning, usually incapable of being adapted to measure more than a single behavior or set of behaviors. For these reasons, automatic recording devices are rarely used in school settings. They are mentioned here only to familiarize teachers with their existence.

Analysis of Permanent Products

This technique is infinitely more useful to teachers. In using this approach, the teacher evaluates the product of a behavior rather than the behavior itself. For example, a student's spelling paper is the "permanent product" of taking a spelling test. The number of correctly spelled words (or correct algebra problems, complete sentences, etc.) can be counted and verified easily. While it is often used by teachers to measure pupil status or progress in academics, the technique is seldom employed to assess affective behaviors because they do not usually have permanent prodcuts associated with them.

Observational Recording

Observational recording of classroom behavior problems can be accomplished in one of six ways: (1) maintaining anecdotal records, (2) event recording, (3) duration recording, (4) interval recording, (5) time sampling, or (6) planned activity check. Data obtained from these observational techniques should be recorded in a systematic way that can be interpreted quickly and easily. Anecdotal records, of course, must be presented in narrative form. The most common way of recording data gathered through the other five

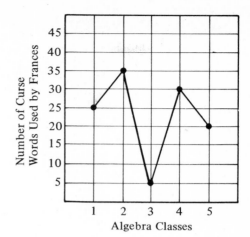

Figure 7–2.   Graph of Frances's Swearing
Behavior During Algebra Class

techniques is by graphing them, as in Figure 7–2. The teacher can easily glance
at these graphs to note trends or to see when the rate or duration of a behavior
begins to increase or decrease.

1. *Anecdotal records* provide an account of everything that is done to,
   with, for, by, or around the target child. Obviously, no individual
   teacher can take the time to gather all the anecdotal data that are
   required for a comprehensive record. Occasionally, other personnel
   such as trained volunteers, aides, or student teachers can be assigned
   some responsibility for gathering these data. Ideally, a videotape recording of the child's entire school day should be available for analysis
   but, of course, this is not practical in most situations. A coding system
   or some form of shorthand may be devised to permit the observer to
   record as much data as possible in a short amount of time and space.
   The shorthand is transcribed later into narrative form that can be understood by individuals who are unfamiliar with the coding system. A
   coded entry in an anecdotal record might look like this: "1025—sci
   ctr—X pokes SL—SL cries, X pokes more—M, SR, PR also in ctr—M
   calls △, others tell X to quit—△ comes to ctr." Translated, this means
   that at 10:25 in the science interest center, the target child (X) poked at
   Susan Lily (SL) until she cried, after which he continued poking her.
   The other children in the science center (M, SR, and PR) told the target
   child to quit poking and M called the teacher (△), who then came to the
   science center. Anecdotal records are especially useful when a teacher
   is unable to identify the pattern of the student's problem. By analyzing
   a continuous recording of the student's behavior over a period of time,
   the teacher may learn that the behavior occurs only in certain situa-

tions or at certain time periods in the day or that every occurrence of the problem behavior is followed by a positive reward, perhaps by increased teacher attention and interest. While it is possible to identify these variables from reading an anecdotal record, continuous recording is not a time-efficient measurement device for the classroom teacher to employ in most instances.

2. *Event recording* is a frequently used observational recording technique. It is, simply, a record of the number of times a defined behavior occurs. It is a behavioral frequency count. Using this technique, a teacher learns that Frances used 27 curse words during the 30-minute algebra class on Monday, 33 on Tuesday, 8 on Wednesday, 28 on Thursday, and 19 on Friday. These data are recorded in the form of a conventional graph in Figure 7–2.

3. *Duration recording* is used when a teacher is more concerned with how long a behavior lasts than with the frequency of occurrence. Knowledge of the duration of a child's temper tantrum, for instance, may occasionally be more important than a recording of the number of outbursts occurring during a given time period. Another example is provided by Linda, who has difficulty attending to the task at hand. It could be that she exhibits only one instance of offtask behavior during the independent work period; regrettably, that one instance lasts for twenty minutes.

4. *Interval recording* combines the two previously described techniques, giving the teacher a measure of both the frequency and the duration of a behavior. An observation period is divided into equal, usually short, time periods. For instance, the 5 minutes after recess may be divided into thirty 10-second intervals. The teacher observes continuously during the 5-minute session and notes whether or not the defined behavior occurs during each of the shorter intervals. For instance, if Pat talked without permission during twenty-five of the thirty 10-second intervals, the results would be reported as 83 percent of the time spent talking out. The form on which the teacher recorded Pat's talking (T) would probably look something like the following:

T_1	T_2	T_3	T_4	T_5	T_6
T_7	T_8	T_9	T_{10}	11	12
T_{13}	T_{14}	T_{15}	T_{16}	T_{17}	T_{18}
T_{19}	T_{20}	T_{21}	T_{22}	T_{23}	T_{24}
T_{25}	T_{26}	T_{27}	T_{28}	29	30

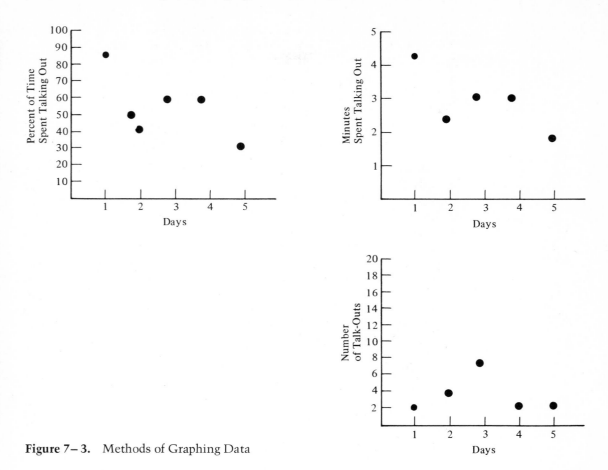

Figure 7– 3. Methods of Graphing Data

The duration of the talking could be calculated easily: Pat was talking during twenty-five 10-second intervals, or for 4 minutes and 10 seconds. Event data also could be extracted: Pat talked out twice, from the first through the tenth 10-second interval and from the fourteenth through the twenty-eighth interval. The data could be graphed in any of the three ways shown in Figure 7–3.

5. *Time sampling* is very similar to interval recording, but it is more useful because it does not require the teacher to observe continuously. The observation period again is divided into equal, usually longer, time periods. For instance, Mr. Nixon, the world history teacher, may divide his 50-minute class period into five 10-minute intervals. He then conducts a time sampling of Henry's behavior while Henry is supposed to be answering the questions at the end of Chapter 14 in the world his-

tory textbook. After (not throughout) each 10-minute interval, Mr. Nixon observes to see if Henry is answering the questions. If Henry was working (W) four of the five times that Mr. Nixon observed him, he would be recorded as working 80 percent of the time. An example of Mr. Nixon's time sampling record is as follows:

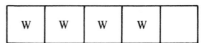

6. *Planned activity check,* sometimes called "placheck," is used to measure the behaviors of groups of children. Teachers using this technique would be interested in the percentage of students engaged in a defined behavior. Perhaps a teacher would want to do a placheck of the children working on an assignment in an interest center. The teacher first would count the number of students working and then would count the number of students actually in the interest center. If ten students were in the center and only four were engaged in the assignment, the placheck record would be 40 percent. Placheck records often are taken on a time sampling basis. For example, Mr. Nixon, the world history teacher, may do placheck every ten minutes during his 50-minute class period. If 25 students are in the class and if 24 are working at the first check, 20 at the second check, 25 at the third and fourth checks, and 5 at the final check, the placheck records would be 96, 80, 100, 100, and 20 percent, respectively. Mr. Nixon might conclude that studying behavior dropped off during the final 10 minutes of his class, particularly if this pattern continued over a period of time. He might adjust his planning to make better use of that final 10 minutes.

BEHAVIORAL CHECKLISTS AND INVENTORIES

On some occasions, the teacher may find it helpful to assess problem behaviors by using checklists and inventories. Checklist items typically relate to a variety of both normal and problem behaviors. They do not concentrate solely in behaviors that are or disturbing and disruptive. In addition, checklists are intended for use with several children, not for a single student, and they derive some objectivity from this characteristic. Teachers may find checklists particularly useful in identifying children who are passive or withdrawn or engage in other behaviors that might go unnoticed in a busy classroom. Many teachers use checklists to narrow their target behaviors or to find precise descriptions of target behaviors. Some published checklists also give teachers guidelines for determining the seriousness or severity of particular behavior problems. In this section we will describe some published checklists and inventories and present criteria for the development of informal behavioral checklists.

Published Checklists

A few published checklists are norm referenced and yield standardized results. Most provide only rough criteria for interpretation and do not have adequate reliability or demonstrated validity (Spivak and Swift, 1973). Care should be taken to limit the use of such instruments to general observation and assessment where they can be of some value despite these shortcomings. We will describe one specific battery of scales, the Behavior Rating Profile (L. Brown and Hammill, 1978), in detail. Other behavioral checklists and inventories will be described briefly and their age/grade ranges, reliability, and ecological characteristics will be summarized. Some of these instruments, and others not mentioned here, are reviewed in Buros' (1978) *Eighth Mental Measurements Yearbook.* Teachers are encouraged to consult Buros before selecting a published checklist or inventory. In addition, Borich and Madden (1977) describe and evaluate hundreds of published and unpublished measures that teachers may find helpful. They include instruments in nine classifications: about the teacher from the teacher, from the pupil, and from an observer; about the pupil from the teacher, from the pupil, and from an observer; and about the classroom from the teacher, from the pupil, and from an observer.

The Behavior Rating Profile (BRP) is an ecological assessment battery that includes five norm-referenced scales and a sociogram. The six components of the BRP are independent and individually normed measures that can be used separately or in conjunction with the other components.

The BRP was standardized on a large, national population. It is appropriate for use with students ages 6 to 18 years and with their parents and teachers. The BRP has high internal consistency reliability with both normal and deviant populations, and test-retest reliability is acceptable. Reliability coefficients consistently exceed .80. Concurrent validity of the instrument was established by research studies, and, in a study of the BRP's diagnostic validity, the six components accurately discriminated among groups of emotionally disturbed, learning disabled, and normal children. The constructs of the BRP have been empirically validated and content validity is established.

The BRP examines the home, school, and interpersonal environments of a target student from the perspectives of that student and his or her parents, teachers, and peers. Figure 7–1 depicts the relationship of the various BRP components to type of respondent and ecology. Because of its unique construction, the BRP permits a user to identify children suspected of being emotionally disturbed or behaviorally disordered, to document the degree of perceived deviance, to identify settings in which problem behaviors seem to be most prominent, and to identify individuals who have varying perceptions of a student's behavior.

There are three Student Rating Scales on the BRP: Home, School, and Peer. Each contains twenty items that have been combined into a single sixty-item response sheet. Students completing these scales are asked to classify each item as True or False.

Items on the Student Rating Scale: Home describe behaviors or situations that are found primarily at home. Examples of these items include:

1. My parents "bug" me a lot.
33. I have lots of nightmares and bad dreams.
47. I often break rules set by my parents.

Items on the Student Rating Scale: School relate to the school and classroom environment. Examples of these items include:

14. I sometimes stammer or stutter when the teacher calls on me.
29. My teachers give me work that I cannot do.
59. The things I learn in school are not as important or helpful as the things I learn outside of school.

Items on the Student Rating Scale: Peer describe behaviors involving interpersonal relationships or skills. Examples of these items include:

6. Some of my friends think it is fun to cheat, skip school, etc.
10. Other kids don't seem to like me very much.
31. I seem to get into a lot of fights.

The Teacher Rating Scale assesses the perceptions of a student's teacher(s) concerning that student's classroom behavior. The scale contains thirty items that teachers classify into four categories: Very Much Like The Student, Like The Student, Not Much Like The Student, and Not At All Like The Student. Examples of these items include:

4. Tattles on classmates.
17. Is an academic underachiever
30. Doesn't follow class rules

The Parent Rating Scale is completed by either or both of the target student's parents. Parent surrogates (foster parents, houseparents) are also appropriate respondents for this instrument. Respondents are asked to classify each of the thirty items into one of four categories: Very Much Like My Child, Like My Child, Not Much Like My Child, or Not At All Like My Child. Examples of these items include:

1. Is verbally aggressive to parents
10. Is shy; clings to parents
27. Won't share belongings willingly

The sociogram is not a checklist. It is a peer-nominating technique that has been adapted to provide peer input into the BRP. It is described here to give readers a picture of the entire BRP profile. To administer the sociogram, the teacher selects one or more pairs of questions, e.g., "Which of the girls and boys in your class would you most like to have in your class at school next year?" and "Which of the girls and boys in your class would you least like to have in your class at school next year?" Students are asked to nominate three classmates in response to each question. A unique scoring system allows the examiner to derive the same type of standard, scaled score for the sociogram as for the five BRP scales.

The examiner may administer any one or all of the BRP components. When several are administered, the resulting scaled scores can be recorded on a profile sheet. The examiner then can review the various possible relationships inherent in the profile, such as particular ecologies or respondents that are characterized by unusually high or low scores.

Some other popular behavior checklists and inventories are summarized in Table 7–1. Most of these instruments are administered to the target pupil, to the referring teacher(s), or to the student's parent(s).

Administering the school-related instruments to classmates of the target student and to several teachers may provide a broader picture of the problem behavior. Let's take the example of James, a student whose behavior is viewed as deviant by his fifth-grade teaches. Do his other teachers—the art teacher, the physical education instructor, the band director, the special education teacher—view him similarly or do their responses on a behavioral checklist reveal markedly different perceptions? If so, is this because his behavior is different in each of these settings (something that could be determined through direct observation) or is it because the teacher's requirements and expectations are different (something that could be determined through an interview)? Likewise, if James views his class as a negative experience, is this perception shared by his classmates? Do they also find the class to be negative or is James's perception unique?

Similarly, the examiner may find it helpful to ask a student's parents to complete behavioral checklists on all of their children rather than just on the target child. Do the parents view their children similarly? Do mother and father express similar feelings or does each parent express different perceptions? The same axiom may be applied to inventories completed by the target student: do brothers and sisters concur with that child's perceptions of the home ecology?

Table 7–1. Checklists and Inventories that Assess Aspects of School, Home, and Internal Ecologies

Ecology Measured	Tests	Age/Grade*	Intended Population	Respondent	Reliability*
School	AAMD Adaptive Behavior Scale, Public School Version (Nihira, Foster, Shellhaas, and Leland, 1975)	7–13 yrs.	Mentally retarded and emotionally maladjusted	Teacher	Interscorer, $\overline{X}$ = .67
School	Barclay Classroom Climate Inventory (Barclay, 1971)	3–6 grades	Normal	Student and teacher	Split-Half, .58–.90 Test-Retest, .34–.77
School	Devereux Adolescent Behavior Rating Scale (Spivak, Spotts, and Haimes, 1967)	13–18 yrs.	Normal and emotionally disturbed	Teacher	Interscorer, Median = .82
School	Devereux Elementary School Behavior Rating Scale (Spivak and Swift, 1967)	K–6 grades	Normal	Teacher	Test-Retest, Median = .87
School	Learning Environment Inventory (Anderson, 1973)	7–12 grades	Normal	Student	Alpha Coefficients, .54–.85 Test-Retest, .43–73
School	Pupil Behavior Rating Scale (Lambert, Bower, and Hartsbough, 1979)	K–7 grades	Normal	Teacher, student, and peers	None Reported

School	Behavior Problem Checklist (Quay and Peterson, 1967)	1–6 grades	Normal and emotionally disturbed	Teacher	None Reported
School	Walker Problem Behavior Identification Checklist (Walker, 1970)	4–6 grades	Normal and emotionally disturbed	Teacher	Split-Half, .98
Home	Child Behavior Rating Scale (Spivak and Spotts, 1966)	8–12 yrs.	Emotionally disturbed and emotionally retarded	Person with "intimate living arrangement"	Test-Retest, .83
Home	Family Relations Test (Bene and Anthony, 1977)	Preschool–6 grades	Normal and emotionally disturbed	Child	Split-Half, .68–.90
Home	Vineland Social Maturity Scale (Doll, 1965)	1 mo.–25+ yrs.	Normal and mentally retarded	Parent	Test-Retest, .97
Internal (Self-Concept)	Animal Crackers (Adkins and Ballif, 1973)	Preschool—1 grade	Normal	Child	Kuder-Richardson, .90
Internal (Self-Concept)	Coopersmith Self-Esteem Inventory (Coopersmith, 1968)	8–10 yrs.	Normal	Child	Test-Retest, .78–.88
Internal (Self-Concept)	Piers-Harris Children's Self-Concept Scale (Piers and Harris, 1969)	3–12 grades	Normal	Child	Kuder-Richardson, .78–.93 Test-Retest, .72.

* As reported in the Tests' Manuals.

We emphasize that even though investigations of this scope are consistent with the principles of ecological assessment, they should be undertaken only when the need is warranted. The process can be quite time consuming and there is no reason to lengthen it unnecessarily. We suggest these variations as a means of stimulating the formation of alternative hypotheses regarding problem behaviors. L. Brown and Hammill (1978) warn that "a low score [on a behavioral measure] . . . should not be interpreted flatly as a sign of deviance on the part of the child." (p. 32). It is the profile or pattern of scores that is important.

Informal Behavioral Checklists

Instead of using published checklists, teachers will find that in some instances—perhaps most—an informal behavioral checklist based on a particular classroom checklist or child is most helpful. Bower and Lambert (1971) discussed teacher-made behavioral checklists and concluded that items should describe behaviors seen specifically (1) in the target child, (2) in the target child's interaction with other students in the class, and (3) in the teacher's interaction with the target child. More recently, Wiederholt, Hammill, and V. Brown (1978) have suggested that these same three categories of behavior should be sampled by checklist items. These authors go on to recommend that a teacher-made checklist include no more than thirty items. They provide a sample teacher-made checklist, which is reproduced in Figure 7–4.

Figure 7–4. Teacher-Made Checklist for Measuring Problems in Social and Emotional Development

Teacher Checklist: This measure was designed to be used by teachers in any classroom to make them more aware of their students' behavior. This list might help identify behavior that otherwise might be overlooked or misunderstood. From here the teacher might want to take frequency counts of identified behavior, or in some other way further analyze the situation.

	Frequently	*Not Frequently*
1. Self-Image		
A. Makes I can't statements		
B. Reacts negatively to correction		
C. Gets frustrated easily		
D. Makes self-critical statements		

Figure 7–4. *Continued*

	Frequently	*Not Frequently*
E. Integrity: Cheats		
tattles		
steals		
destroys property		
F. Makes excessive physical complaints		
G. Takes responsibility for actions		
H. Reacts appropriately to praise		
2. Social Interaction A. Seeks attention by acting immaturely: thumbsucking, babytalking, etc.		
B. Interacts negatively		
C. Fails to interact		
D. Initiates positive interaction		
E. Initiates negative interaction		
F. Reacts with anger, verbally		
G. Reacts with anger, physically		
3. Adult/Teacher Relationships A. Seeks attention by acting immaturely		
B. Excessively demands attention		
C. Reacts appropriately to teacher requests		
D. Inappropriately reacts to authority figures		
4. School-Related Activities A. Attends to task		
B. Exhibits offtask behavior		
C. Interferes with the other students' learning		
D. Show flexibility to routine changes		

Date the checklist and complete one for each child. Once the checklist has been completed and reviewed a narrative report can be written with explanations and suggestions for the future. For the list to be effective, the teacher must use the results to actually make changes in the classroom.

Source: Developed by the following teachers and used with their permission: Lee Person, Becky Beck Browning, Margaret Hughes Hiatt, and Margaret Morey-Brown. Reprinted with permission of the authors and publisher of J. L. Wiederholt, D. D. Hammill, and V. Brown, *The Resource Teacher* (Boston: Allyn and Bacon, 1978).

Q-SORTS

Q-sorting is uniquely suited to ecological assessment. This technique can be used by teachers to compare two interpretations of a single set of behaviors. For example, a teacher might describe behaviors associated with reading (e.g., reads well, doesn't like to read, reads at home) or even social attributes (e.g., dates a lot, can't dance, has friends). The teacher then would compare how a child or teen-ager viewed the various items from both realistic and idealistic points of view. Commercial Q-sorts are available and teachers can easily devise Q-sorts of their own which will match the classroom situations and behaviors of particular interest to them. Directions for constructing a Q-sort and suggestions for its use will be presented in this section.

The first step in using the Q-sort technique is to devise a list of descriptor statements such as those in Figure 7–5. The items can be drawn from any setting deemed to be important or of interest: home, school, nonacademic classroom activities, interpersonal relationships, and so on. A different set of descriptions should be developed for each ecology. Although most Q-sorts have twenty-five or thirty-six items, any number of descriptor statements may be included as long as the items can be sorted into a perfect pyramid form as in Figure 7–6. The descriptor statements are written on small cards, one item per card, which are read to or by the students who are responding.

After reading through the items, students sort them onto a formboard such as the one in Figure 7–6. All the squares on the pyramidlike form must be used: none may be left blank and none may be used twice, although students may rearrange the items until they are satisfied with their responses. Students

Figure 7– 5. Parent Q-Sort Items

1. Does assigned chores.	13. Eats between meals.
2. Does homework on time.	14. Is overweight.
3. Goes to bed without problems.	15. Is destructive of property.
4. Comes home when he should.	16. Gets ready for school on time.
5. Argues with parents.	17. Makes own decisions.
6. Has friends.	18. Chooses own clothes.
7. Likes school.	19. Is unhealthy.
8. Cries or sulks when he doesn't get his own way.	20. Fights with brothers and sisters.
9. Throws temper tantrums.	21. Has a messy room.
10. Likes to watch TV.	22. Responds to rewards.
11. Likes to read.	23. Does acceptable schoolwork.
12. Plays alone.	24. Is a restless sleeper.
	25. Stretches the truth.

Reprinted with permission of the author and publisher of R. Kroth, The behavioral Q-sort as a diagnostic tool, *Academic Therapy*, 1973, *8*, 327 (Academic Therapy Publications, San Rafael, California.)

Figure 7–6. Q-Sort Formboard.

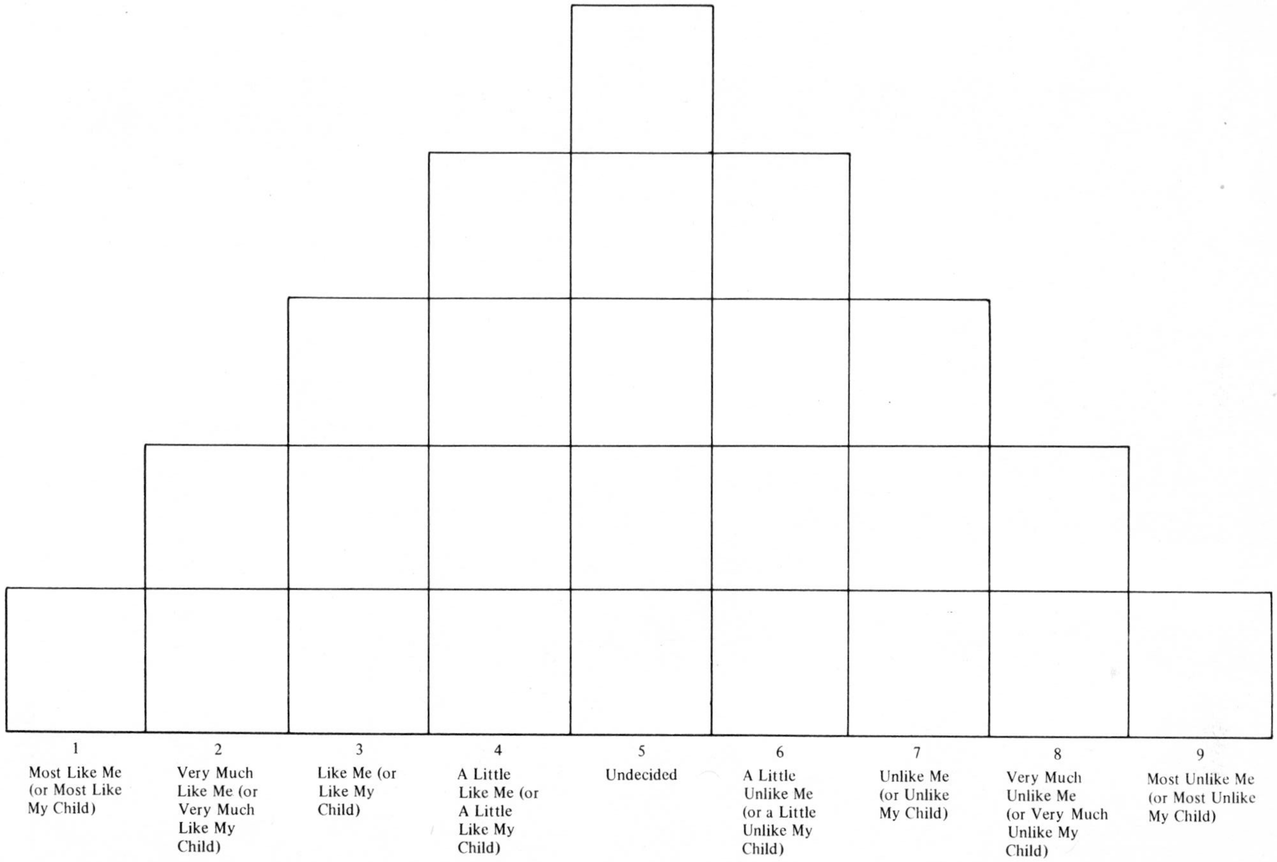

| 1
Most Like Me
(or Most Like
My Child) | 2
Very Much
Like Me (or
Very Much
Like My
Child) | 3
Like Me (or
Like My
Child) | 4
A Little
Like Me (or
A Little
Like My
Child) | 5
Undecided | 6
A Little
Unlike Me
(or a Little
Unlike My
Child) | 7
Unlike Me
(or Unlike
My Child) | 8
Very Much
Unlike Me
(or Very Much
Unlike My
Child) | 9
Most Unlike Me
(or Most Unlike
My Child) |

Reprinted with permission of the author and publisher of R. Kroth, The behavioral Q-sort as a diagnostic tool, *Academic Therapy*, 1973, 8, 327 (Academic Therapy Publications, San Rafael, California.)

sort the items twice. On the first sort they place the items into categories that reflect how they believe they really are; this is called the *real sort.* The second time, the students sort the items into the categories as they wish they were; this is called the *ideal sort.*

Students' responses are recorded on the form shown in Figure 7–7 and a simple correlation is calculated between the two sorts. For example, if a student sorted item 1 as "A Little Like Me" on the real sort, a 4 would be recorded in the first column (S-1). If the student rated the same item as "Unlike Me" on the ideal sort, a 7 would be recorded in the second column (S-2). The difference between the sorts is 3, and this is recorded in the D column. The difference squared (D^2) is 9. The D^2 column is summed and the total (ΣD^2) is substituted into the formula at the bottom of the page. This formula will yield a correlation coefficient; it will not be larger than $+1.00$ or smaller than -1.00. The farther the correlation is from $r = .00$, the greater the agreement between the real and ideal sorts.

In most instances, the teacher will be less interested in the correlation between the two sorts than in those individual items that have large discrepancies between them. Items with great discrepancies between the sorts probably describe target behaviors for intervention. If the child rates an item such as "Likes to read," as "Like Me" on the ideal sort but as "Very Unlike Me" on the real sort, the teacher may have identified an area in which the child is ready to begin work for improvement.

Kroth (1973a) has an excellent article on the uses of the behavioral Q-sort and interested teachers will want to read it. He suggests that Q-sorts could be administered to children's parents and teachers, with the real sort representing the way they believe their children behave and the ideal sort representing the way they wished their children would behave. The use of the technique in this way would permit analysis of various combinations of Q-sort responses: e.g., the child's ideal sort compared with the parent's ideal sort, the regular classroom teacher's real sort compared with the resource teacher's real sort, the child's real sort compared with the teacher's real sort, and so on. Again, particular discrepancies may be more important than the actual correlation between the sorts. If the child's regular class teacher rates "Likes to read" as "A Little Unlike My Child" and the special education teacher rates this same item as "Like My Child," a source of conflict *may* have been identified.

Q-sort items can be read to nonreaders, although this has not been particularly successful. Children who cannot read the items have great difficulty in manipulating the cards, especially when only a few slots are left on the formboard and some switching is necessary. Children who are easily frustrated also have difficulty with the Q-sort because they are forced to limit each category to a specific number of items. Most children, however, enjoy the activity and can complete it independently after brief instructions have been given.

Name of Subject _____ Sex _____ Date Tested _____

Address _____ Phone _____ Date of Birth _____

School _____ Teacher _____ Grade _____ Age _____

Name of Examinee _____ Relationship to Child _____

Card No.	Column S-1	Column S-2	D	D²
1				
2				
3				
4				
5				
6				
7				
8				
9				
10				
11				
12				
13				
14				
15				
16				
17				
18				
19				
20				
21				
22				
23				
24				
25				

$$n = 1 - \frac{\Sigma D^2}{200}$$

$\Sigma =$

Figure 7–7.
Q-Sort Record Form

Reprinted with permission of the author and publisher of R. Kroth, The behavioral Q-sort as a diagnostic tool, *Academic Therapy*, 1973, 8, 327 (Academic Therapy Publications, San Rafael, California).

INTERVIEWS

Interviewing is a versatile and useful technique in ecological assessment. It can be used to gather a great deal of information from students, parents, and other teachers. Interviews are certainly subjective in nature, and they are quite informal. Despite the informality, however, specific goals should be established before an interview is scheduled, and the interviewer should consider several possible approaches to conducting the interview.

In general, interviewers will want to begin by stating the purpose of the interview, establishing the time parameters of the conversation, and briefly introducing themselves, describing their role or position in the school. McCallon and McCray (1975) suggest that an interviewer then should:

1. Open the interview by asking factual, nonthreatening questions
2. Locate major pieces of information through unstructured lead questions
3. Make use of guide questions
4. Make an effort to locate fruitful areas of conversation
5. Use probes to obtain specific information
6. Pursue fruitful areas once they are found
7. Clarify unclear responses through further questioning
8. Follow up areas where the respondent shows emotional involvement
9. Redirect the interview to different topics when useful data are not emerging
10. Be alert to sensitive subjects and handle them diplomatically
11. Answer any direct questions posed by the respondent
12. Complete the interview before the respondent becomes tired or bored
13. Evaluate the general climate of the interview before deciding whether to take notes or otherwise record the interview.

It is possible to gather several types of information during an interview. If the current status of the target student is not known—age, grade, general background and health information—it should be established early in the interview. The student's educational situation may be explored: academic and social competence, relationships with peers or school personnel, any evaluation data that may be available from school or private sources, and unique perceptions or expectations of particular teachers. It may be helpful to gather personal information during the interview, such as students' attitudes toward the settings in which they function and the various people encountered in those environments, any hobbies or special interests, goals and aspirations, particular likes or dislikes. It also may be possible to learn more about a student's home life from an interview, particularly the attitudes and values that are present at home and the extent of cooperation that can be expected from that quarter. With adolescents, it may be fruitful to interview employers or co-workers. In all cases, it is important for the interviewer to establish a clear need for any information requested during an interview. An interview is not a fishing expedition. It is easy to become a professional voyeur, asking questions out of curiosity rather than need.

Both McCallon and McCray (1975) and Stewart and Cash (1976) emphasize the need to maintain a friendly, nondefensive atmosphere throughout the interview. They suggest the use of probe questions or remarks such as, "Can you give me an example of what you mean?" "What did you have in mind?" "You feel that . . .?" or "That's a really good idea. How do you think we can implement it?" Such remarks facilitate the gathering of information without jeopardizing an open atmosphere that may have been established. They also lay a base for future cooperative efforts that may grow out of the interview.

Interested readers are referred to Losen and Daiment (1978), McCallon and McCray (1975), and Stewart and Cash (1976) for more detailed information on the intervening process. The discussion on life space interviewing presented later in this chapter may be helpful, too.

CRITERIA FOR ANALYZING THE PHYSICAL ENVIRONMENT

Not all of the behavior problems that occur in school can be understood fully by limiting analysis of those problems to the behaviors of individual children. Many of the difficulties experienced by children are caused by elements of the physical environment of the classroom and the school. For this reason, teachers will want to examine the classroom environment for physical variables that may be stimulating or maintaining problem behaviors. Lighting, temperature, and noise level in a classroom are obvious examples. Redl (1959) identified four variables relating to physical aspects of the school's physical environment that can be manipulated to prevent or ameliorate behavior problems. These variables are space, equipment, time, and props. Careful examination of each of these variables may be indicated when teachers are assessing children's behavior problems.

The teacher first must be aware that these variables can cause or contribute to classroom behavior problems. The teacher will want to ask such questions as: Does the child need more space for a particular activity? Does the child need to move around the class more? Does the child need to work within precise boundaries? Could the problem be avoided by using (or discarding) certain pieces of equipment? If the activity were rescheduled for a different time, would the behavior problems associated with it decrease? Is attention being drwan away from a lesson or activity and focused on a nonrelevant but highly seductive item such as a noisy pencil sharpener, other classes going out to recess, or the smell of food from the cafeteria? If the answer to any of these questions is yes, the teacher will want to document the existence and severity of the problem by using one of the measurement techniques described earlier (event recording, time sampling, and so on). For instance, if the teacher believes that a child's problems are aggravated by having too much work space, the following sequence would be appropriate for both assessment and intervention. First, the teacher would define and measure the problem behavior(s). The teacher would then alter the troublesome variable. In this instance, excess space could be handled by providing the child with a study carrel or a small, well-defined study area. Using the same measurement technique used earlier, the teacher would note any changes in the target behavior after the study carrel was introduced. If no change occurs, the teacher can be relatively certain that space is not a relevant variable in the child's current problems or that the solution selected, in this instance the use of a carrel, was not effective. If changes are noted, the teacher will have a ready-made prescription to relieve the behavior problem. Each of Redl's four variables (space, time, equipment, and props) will be explained briefly below.

Space

This item refers to the amount of physical area allotted to a particular activity and the ways in which that space affects children's behaviors. Redl notes that it is difficult to hold the attention of a small group of children located in the gymnasium. Equally disruptive behaviors may arise when too many students are crowded into a small area, as when all the fifth-hour social studies classes are sent into one classroom to view a film.

Time

The period of the day when an activity is scheduled is important. Most elementary school teachers intuitively utilize this element in their planning: the bulk of the basic academic work is scheduled for the early morning, and "winding-down" activities are employed after recesses and lunch periods. A hot, sweaty child who has just returned from a stimulating game of kickball can hardly be expected to buckle down immediately to a sheet of long-division problems. Unfortunately, teachers in secondary schools have little control over scheduling. They work in a system that assumes, probably fallaciously, that high school students do not require these same considerations. Woe to the English teacher who must present the delights of Chaucer to a class in which many of the students have just returned from band practice, physical education, or lunch!

Equipment

Materials and equipment that are required for each activity should be identified and acquired before the activity is initiated. Is the necessary equipment available, is it in working order, can the students operate it? In individualized instruction, a student's ability to use equipment is an important factor in his or her ability and willingness to continue working without disruption. Such equipment can be highly motivating or highly frustrating and disruptive. In group instruction, the teacher's attention may be divided as a consequence of preoccupation with arranging or setting up materials and equipment. Students who are wondering just how much they can get by with when the teacher isn't looking are likely to begin testing classroom rules. The flow of activity is again disrupted when the teacher is forced to stop arranging equipment to manage the problem behaviors. It may be difficult to resume a steady pace. Equipment also can assume the seductive characteristics attributed below to props.

Props

Most classrooms are filled with items or "props" that teachers use to set the classroom stage. Those items which hold students' attention during a mathematics lesson do not suddenly lose their seductive charms when instruction is switched to social studies. Many of these items are more attention holding, seductive, and alluring than either the teacher or the lesson at hand. When this occurs, disruptive behaviors are sure to ensue. By the same token, disinterested behaviors will be elicited when the props supporting a lesson are not interesting and seductive. The teacher's job will be to determine those props which contribute to the program, those which detract from the program, and those which should be present occasionally and absent at all other times.

PROCEDURES FOR EXAMINING TEACHER– PUPIL INTERACTION IN THE CLASSROOM

By now it should be apparent that many of the problems in classrooms do not spring from a single cause. Rather, they are products of the interaction of two or more variables. This section will examine techniques used to measure the type and quality of teacher-child interaction. There are a number of interaction analysis instruments on the market. Four of the more prominent ones include Flanders Interaction Analysis System, the Observation System for Instructional Analysis, Dyadic Interaction Analysis, and the Florida Climate and Control System.

The Flanders interaction analysis system (Flanders, 1970) does not focus on any one child's interactions with the teacher. Instead, it codes and analyzes interactions between the teacher and all the students in the class. It is a system that is more valuable for teachers who wish to modify their own behavior in the classroom than for teachers who are interested in those few children who are exhibiting behavior problems. Flanders identifies ten behaviors, which are recorded in four-second intervals. The ten behaviors include seven teacher responses and initiations, two student behaviors, and a no-behavior or silence category. The teacher responses include: (1) accepting students' feelings, (2) praising or encouraging students, and (3) accepting/using students' ideas. Teacher initiations are: (4) asking questions, (5) lecturing, (6) giving directions, and (7) criticizing. The two student behaviors are: (8) responding to the teacher and (9) initiating talk or conversation. The final category is: (10) silence or confusion. Observational periods should be short, perhaps a maximum of thirty minutes at a time, and data should be taken for several days.

The Observation System for Instructional Analysis (OSIA) (Hough, 1967) was developed from the original Flanders system. The number of student behavior categories in OSIA was increased to equal the number of teacher behavior categories, so the instrument codes a total of 16 behavior types. OSIA was "designed to enable investigators to test hypotheses from learning (reinforcement) theory [and] . . . to distinguish between teachers who reinforce different kinds of student responses" (Gauthier, 1980, p. 20–21). A particularly helpful aspect of OSIA is the recent development of revisions devised for use during specific types of classroom instruction, such as reading, mathematics, and physical education.

Dyadic Interaction Analysis (Brophy and Good, 1969) is similar to the Flanders system in the type of behavioral contracts that are coded. However, Brophy and Good devised their instrument to identify and measure interactions between the classroom teacher and one particular student. The Florida Climate and Control System (Soar, Soar, and Ragosta, 1971) is widely used in research, but it is quite elaborate. A teacher probably would not use this system for personal purposes. In addition to coding more than fifty incidences of student and teacher interaction, the Florida system also codes variables related to the physical environment of the classroom, including the size and type of class, the nature of the classroom activity at the time of the observation, student and teacher tasks, classroom structure, seating arrangements, and the use and type of various displays in the classroom. These and other interaction analysis instruments are described and evaluated by Borich and Madden (1977).

PEER-NOMINATING TECHNIQUES

Peer-nominating techniques are the traditional means for gathering information about the way a student is perceived by classmates or age-mates. Sociometrics and other peer-nominating techniques will be discussed in this section.

Sociometrics

This way of obtaining peer ratings is a nominating technique originally developed by Moreno (1953). Sociometrics may be used to determine each child's position within the class by analyzing peer choices made by each child in the group. Thorndike and Hagen (1977) have stressed that in order to understand the individual child and the climate of the class, it is important to appraise the role of the individual child within that group.

In applying this technique to the classroom situation, each child is asked to choose one, two, or three children with whom he or she would like to engage in the activity specified in the stimulus question. This information can aid in understanding the social structure within the group. Nominations on a sociogram may be mapped as illustrated in Figure 7–8. In this example, ten children

Figure 7–8. Example of a Sociogram

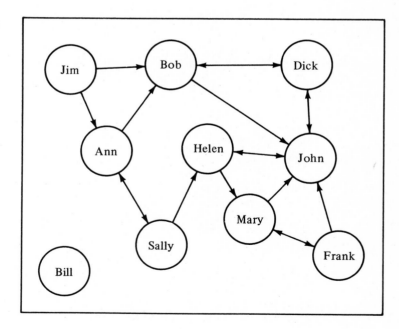

were asked to choose two children with whom they would like to work on an art project.

In examining the diagram, it becomes apparent that John was most highly desired as a partner, while Bill was an "isolate," neither making nor receiving any nominations. Jim was an unchosen member of the group; although he did choose two children, he was not selected by any member of the group.

After the teacher has determined which child is isolated or without friends, he or she may begin to seek out the causes. Frequently, the explanations are quite simple, such as being new to the class, living outside the community, or being older than the other children. The teacher can now be sensitive to structuring situations in which the isolate can interact with others. Sometimes the causes are more complicated, but when they are understood, the teacher can help the child develop necessary social, athletic, or academic skills that will enable him or her to enter into the mainstream of the group's social system. Isolation also may be the result of attitudes toward minority-group members. In that case, the teacher should focus on *group* attitudinal and behavioral changes instead of changes within the isolated member.

Another use of sociometrics, infrequently practiced, acts as feedback to the teacher's behavior. Often the teacher consciously or unconsciously praises or rebukes the same children. This habit could be corroborated or disproved by asking the class to "Write the name of the class member whom Ms. Jones likes best" or "Write the name of the class member whom Ms. Jones does not like." If the teacher receives a variety of names in response to these questions, she is not isolating the same children. If only one or two names are reported by the class, the teacher actually may be betraying personal preferences, causing the other class members to feel rejected or anonymous.

L. Brown and Hammill (1978) suggest that sociograms are most efficient in classes of at least twenty students. They also emphasize that students participating in the sociogram should have been in the class for at least six weeks in order to permit the formation of the relationships measured by the sociogram.

There has been a general feeling (e.g., Gronlund, 1981) that responses to one pair of stimulus questions should not be generalized to anticipated responses from another pair of questions. For instance, a set of questions related to cooperating on schoolwork presumably would attract different responses than a set of questions related to playing together on a kickball team. Preliminary evidence (L. Brown and Sherbenou, 1980) suggests that the distinction may not be necessary with elementary students. Their research indicates that popular, rejected, and ignored children tended to maintain their relative status across several stimulus questions, although children with middle status ranks seemed to be differentially chosen. Brown and Sherbenou also report that the reliability of sociometric responses seems to be both age and sex related. Young children in kindergarten and grade one and girls in grades five and six were less reliable respondents than other children. Fiske and Cox (1960), Hollander (1965), Lindzey and Borgatta (1954), and Reynolds (1966) have offered evidence which suggests that sociometric peer rating is one of the most dependable rating techniques. It not only assesses the present status of the group but also acts as a valuable tool for measuring the effectiveness of teacher intervention.

Most sociograms are informal measures, and evaluations of them are subjective. Their value, therefore, is directly related to the skill and experience of the person conducting the sociogram or interpreting its results. An exception to this is the sociogram of the Behavior Rating Profile (L. Brown and Hammill, 1978), which was described earlier in this chapter. Unlike other sociograms, this instrument is standardized and it yields a scaled score.

Other Peer-Nominating Techniques

Good examples of nonsociometric peer-nominating techniques are found in three of Bower and Lambert's (1971) screening instruments: Class Pictures, Class Play, and Student Survey. These instruments were developed for use with students in kindergarten through grade three, grades three through seven, and junior and senior high school respectively. No normative data or information concerning reliability and validity are available for these instruments, but the reader may find their indirect formats to be useful and interesting.

Class Pictures is individually administered. Twelve pictures containing twenty items are shown to students. Ten items depict students engaging in "maladjusted" behaviors (five with boys and five with girls) and the remaining ten items depict positive or neutral behaviors (again, five with boys and five with girls). Students then are asked which of their classmates is like the subject in each of the twenty situations. A score is derived by comparing the student's negative perceptions to the total number of times he or she was selected by peers for any role.

Class Play describes twenty hypothetical roles. Students are asked to nominate classmates for each role. Another form of the instrument, used to judge student's self-perceptions, asks them to select roles for themselves and to identify roles they think others would select for them.

In the Student Survey, students are asked to name a classmate who is best characterized by the description in each of twenty items, ten presumably describing "emotionally disturbed" behaviors and ten describing positive or neutral behaviors. This instrument also could be adapted to a self-report measure on the manner described for the Class Play.

STANDARDIZED TESTS OF PERSONALITY

Occasionally, a teacher will be provided with the results of standardized tests of personality or character that have been administered to a child. These are usually found in cumulative folders of children who have been referred to another professional in the school or to an agency specializing in disturbed or disruptive children. In assessing a referral, school counselors, psychologists, and other mental health specialists often use standardized personality measures as well as many of the observational techniques and checklists already described in this chapter. Personality tests are rarely, if ever, given by classroom teachers. However, since the results of such tests are frequently shared with them, teachers probably should have some basic information about commonly used personality measures.

One broad category of personality testing involves the use of self-report devices, e.g., sentence-completion tests or checklists completed by the child. There are several weaknesses inherent in any self-report device. Predominant among these is the ease with which the individual completing the instrument can hide or disguise feelings. Some instruments have built in "lie scales" to help offset such effects. Other instruments have adopted a projective format to elicit responses indirectly, thereby reducing any apparent need for deception that the respondent may feel.

Sentence-completion tests contain sentence stems that the child is asked to complete. Typical sentence stems might be:

The thing I like most about school is ———————————————————.

My mother ——————————————————————————————.

I am afraid when ————————————————————————————.

Personality inventories also might be included in an assessment of a problem area. These tests present the child with a series of statements ("I am happy," "People usually like me.") which the child rates as true, false, or some noncommital response ("Not sure," "Cannot say"), with a series of questions ("Are you frequently ill?" "Do you like to attend parties?") to which the child responds yes or no, or with pairs of statements which the student must choose between ("I like to play team sports," "I like to play games by myself"). Tests of this type include the Minnesota Multiphasic Personality Inventory (MMPI) (Hathaway and McKinley, 1951), the California Test of Personality (Thorpe, Clark, and Tiegs, 1953), the Bell Adjustment Inventory (1961), the Junior Eysenck Personality Inventory (Eysenck, 1965), and IPAT's Children's Personality Questionnaire (Porter and Cattell, 1075) and Sixteen Personality Factor Questionnaire (Cattell, 1967).

Locus-of-control tests, such as the Bialer Children's Locus of Control Scale (Bialer, 1961) or the Children's Intellectual Achievement Responsibility Questionnaire (Crandall, Kathovsky, and Crandall, 1965), are also classified in this category.

Projective instruments constitute another major type of standardized personality measure. Cronbach (1970) asserts that these instruments are of two types, tests in which the type of problem solving is important (stylistic tests) and tests in which the content of the solution is important (thematic tests). The Rorschach Inkblot Test (Rorschach, 1954) and the Bender Visual–Motor Gestalt Tests Bender, 1938) are stylistic. The Thematic Apperception Test (TAT) (Murray, 1943) and the Children's Apperception Test (Bellak and Bellak, 1961) are thematic in nature. In projective testing the child is presented with a stimulus such as an inkblot, a drawing, or a picture and is then asked to describe what is seen or to tell a story about the picture. Two instruments used with children, the Blacky Tests (Blum, 1958) and Buttons (Rothman and Berkowitz, 1963), use animals, a dog and a rabbit respectively, to present stories or situations that the responding student is asked to complete or resolve.

Analyses of children's drawings are also frequently included in these assessments. The Draw-A-Person (Urban, 1963) and House–Tree–Person (Buck, 1948) Tests are popular examples. Drawings from the Bender may also be used. Rough standards for interptretation are usually included in the manuals accompanying these measures. Yet, even when these are available, the results of projective testing are quite subjective. They are, therefore, highly dependent on the competence and experience of the examiner. After studying the extent to which the use of these projective tests yielded valuable information, Kessler (1966) concluded that the derived information can usually be obtained from other sources, notably from teacher assessment. For a more detailed discussion of projective testing, the reader is referred to Anastasi (1976), Kessler (1966), Thorndike and Hagen (1977), and Ullmann and Krasner (1975).

MANAGING PROBLEM BEHAVIORS

The intervention strategies about to be presented become strongly associated with specific schools of thought. For instance, the various behavior modification strategies were developed and are used primarily by individuals holding a behavioral point of view, while a technique such as life-space interviewing evolved from the work of analytically oriented professionals. Analytic professionals often scoff at the uses of behavior modification, and the behaviorists almost invariably advise against the use of analytic techniques.

To us, the division of management techniques according to discrete philosophical categories is a useless activity that will only reduce the number of tools available to today's teachers. We believe that each of the techniques described in this section has value in some situations and that all of them are well within the teacher's ability to use.

The first important aspect of an intervention plan (i.e., establishing a goal for behavioral improvement and assessing the current level of the behavior problem) has been discussed earlier. In this section six methods for managing behavior are described: behavior modification; contracting; Long and Newman's techniques for managing surface behaviors; Trieschman's strategies for managing temper tantrums; life-space interviewing; projective techniques such as role playing, play therapy, puppetry, and art and music therapy; and cognitive therapies. Commercially available programs that purport to assist in the development of children's affective domains also will be reviewed.

BEHAVIOR MODIFICATION

Rationale

Classroom management, consequence management, or behavior modification has its roots with the behavioral learning theorists Thorndike, Pavlov, Watson, and Jones. Ayllon (1965), Skinner (1957) and Ferster and Skinner (1957) expanded and refined the theory and popularized its clinical use, enabling the behavioral specialist to use it in modifying deviant behavior. Clinical experimentation with individual children and adults brought this approach into the foreground in the 1960s, with the renewed interest in the interaction between people and their environment. In short, behavior modification is a systematic, highly structured approach to altering behavior. Its use will have the effect of strengthening, weakening, or maintaining target behaviors. For a more detailed description of the specific techniques involved, the reader is referred to Hall's (1971a, 1971b, 1971c) series of pamphlets entitled *Behavioral Modification*, to Miller's (1975) *Principles of Everyday Behavior Analysis*, to Axelrod's (1977) *Behavioral Modification for the Classroom Teacher*, and to Sulzer-Azaroff and Mayer's (1977) *Applying Behavior Analysis Procedures with Children and Youth*.

Procedures

A plan to modify a target behavior comprises four phases: (1) the acquisition of baseline data, (2) the selection and implementation of a particular modification technique, (3) the verification of results, and (4) the application of the program in the classroom.

1. Taking Baseline Data. The selection of any intervention technique is predicated upon the assumption that the teacher has defined the target behavior and has taken baseline data regarding its frequency or duration. Hall's direct observation techniques described on pages 228–232 are employed often in gathering baseline information. To ensure a representative sample of a child's behavior, five measurement periods usually are devoted to collecting baseline data. The effects of intervention strategies can then be devoted to collecting baseline data. The effects of intervention strategies can then be determined objectively by comparing the baseline with subsequent increases or decreases in the targeted behaviors. The data graphed in Figure 7–2 represent baseline data.

2. Selecting a Treatment. Reinforcement and punishment are the two basic treatments in behavior modification. These will be discussed in some detail in this section. Extinction, differential reinforcement, shaping, discrimination training, generalization, modeling, and token economies will also be presented.

a. Reinforcement. A reinforcer is any event that occurs after a behavior and that increases the frequency or duration of the behavior and/or increases the likelihood that the behavior will reoccur (Hall, 1971b). A graph depicting the frequency of a behavior that is being reinforced will show an upward trend. Teachers may assume that being smiled at, receiving an A grade, or being given five minutes of free time are reinforcing events, at least to most children; but this conclusion is only justified when there is an observed increase in the behaviors which these events follow. In fact, the teacher will quickly discover that many children who exhibit problem behaviors are not reinforced by the "usual" things.

Some behaviorists will refine this definition of reinforcement by describing its negative and positive instances. For instance, the reader may have encountered the terms "negative reinforcement" (a reinforcement procedure in which something aversive or negative is removed from the environment) and "positive reinforcement" (a reinforcement procedure in which something pleasant or positive is added to the environment). These refined definitions can be quite confusing. Therefore, we have elected to use Hall's definition cited above because it is simple, practical, and straight-forward.

Observation of children will probably give the teacher ample ideas of things that are likely to be rewarding for them. Additional information can be obtained by asking individual children to complete an interest inventory or by directly asking children what they like to do. The teacher can select a potential reinforcer from the lists that have been developed. If the event proves to be reinforcing, that is, if the target behavior increases, the teacher will continue to use the reinforcer, alternating it occasionally with other reinforcers to prevent the pupil from becoming tired of "the same old thing." Overuse of a reinforcer eventually will result in satiation and in the loss of reinforcement power. If the event does not prove to be reinforcing (i.e., if the target behavior does not increase), the teacher must select another potential reinforcer from the student's reinforcement menu.

Reinforcers may be primary or secondary. Examples of primary reinforcers are the following:

food	playing ball in the gym
money	drawing paper
a drink of water	crayons
lavatory privileges	chewing gum

Secondary reinforcers usually are social rather than tangible or physical, and often gain their power from being associated with a primary reinforcer. Following are several examples:

receiving a star or an A
moving one's seat close to the teacher
verbal praise
sending a praising note home to parents
a pat on the shoulder
a hug

It should be reemphasized that one of the goals of behavior modification is to encourage a child or class of children to work for social reinforcement. Thus, whenever food or toys are given as a consequence, they must be accompanied by social reinforcement—verbal praise, a smile, or a hug. In doing this, the primary reinforcement becomes associated with social approval. Eventually, the social reinforcement will have the same effect as a tangible item.

Reinforcement can be delivered on either a ratio or an interval schedule, and in both cases the arrangement or reinforcement can be fixed or variable. With *ratio* schedules, the number of responses emitted is important. The rate of reinforcement is largely self-controlled, because the more behaviors that the students emit, the more reinforcement they will receive. For this reason, ratio schedules usually yield fairly high rates of responding. *Interval* schedules, however, deliver reinforcement after a specified amount of time has elapsed, rather than after a particular number of behaviors. Reinforcement on interval schedules is controlled by the teacher, not by the student; a set amount of time must pass before reinforcement can be delivered, regardless of the number of behaviors students have emitted. Consequently, interval schedules tend to yield low rates of responding. On a *fixed* schedule, reinforcement occurs at a regular interval or after a set number of responses. Fixed schedules are characterized by pauses in responding after reinforcement, because the children know when reinforcement will occur. Reinforcement in *variable* schedules, however, occurs at irregular intervals or after varying numbers of responses. Variable schedules therefore are characterized by fairly steady rates of responding, because the children are not certain just when reinforcement will be delivered.

Thus, reinforcement can be of four varieties: fixed ratio, variable ratio, fixed interval, and variable interval. Behaviors reinforced on *fixed ratio* schedules would result in high rates of behavior with pauses. Behaviors reinforced on *variable ratio* schedules would have high steady rates of responding. *Fixed interval* schedules would yield low rates of responding with pauses. *Variable interval* schedules would result in low steady rates of responding. Cumulative graphs of typical behavior patterns on each of these schedules are shown in Figure 7–9.

On a continuous fixed ratio schedule (CFR), every behavior or response is reinforced. This is a valuable schedule for stimulating behaviors that may not occur frequently. On the other hand, it is an inefficient means of maintaining behaviors, because the acquired behavior disappears rapidly if reinforcement ever is withdrawn. The behaviors that we exhibit in using vending machines are frequently cited as examples of those maintained on a CFR schedule. The insertion of a quarter into a pop machine almost always is rewarded with a can of soda. This is CFR: every behavior is reinforced. If the machine is broken, however, the insertion of a quarter will not be reinforced by the appearance of a can of soda. One might insert a second quarter, but it is unlikely that an individual would continue to put money into the machine. Because of this, one of the intermittent schedules described below is preferred for maintaining a behavior after it has been acquired on a CFR schedule.

On a fixed ratio schedule (FR), reinforcement follows a fixed number of responses. For example, a behavior that is reinforced on an FR-3 schedule would be reinforced after every third response (i.e., after the third, sixth, ninth, twelfth, etc., behaviors). In fact, CFR also could be called an FR-1 schedule. Piecework is an example of behaviors maintained on an FR schedule. Fruit pickers who are paid by the basket are reinforced on an FR schedule, as are children who receive free time after completing a set amount of work. An FR schedule results in high rates of behavior with pauses after reinforcement has been delivered. For instance, a student who completes three pages of problems in a math workbook and then is reinforced (by receiving a star, a smile, or an "attaboy" from the teacher) is likely to rest or take a breather before beginning the next task.

On a variable ratio schedule (VR), reinforcement follows an average number of responses. On a VR-3 schedule, reinforcement might follow any

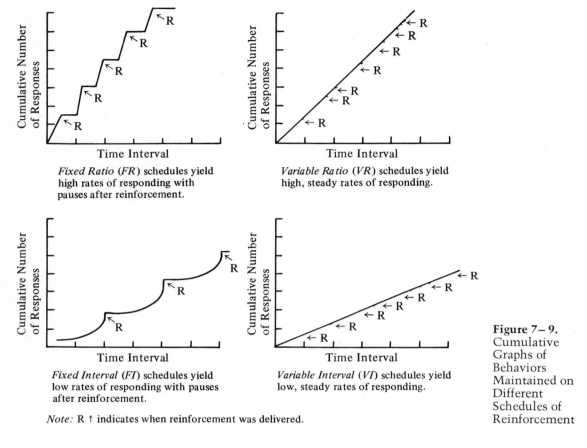

Fixed Ratio (FR) schedules yield high rates of responding with pauses after reinforcement.

Variable Ratio (VR) schedules yield high, steady rates of responding.

Fixed Interval (FI) schedules yield low rates of responding with pauses after reinforcement.

Variable Interval (VI) schedules yield low, steady rates of responding.

Figure 7–9. Cumulative Graphs of Behaviors Maintained on Different Schedules of Reinforcement

Note: R ↑ indicates when reinforcement was delivered.

behaviors, as long as the average number of responses per reinforcement is three. Gambling on slot machines is a common example of behavior that is maintained on a VR schedule. The machines are calibrated to provide reinforcement (a jackpot) after an average number of coins has been inserted. A VR schedule results in a high, steady rate of responding. Such response patterns might be seen in classes where the teacher moves around the room reinforcing the students after they have completed varying amounts of work.

On a fixed interval schedule (FI), reinforcement follows the first behavior to occur after a fixed period of time has elapsed. FI-2 minutes means that reinforcement will follow the first behavior to occur after 2 minutes, 4 minutes, 6 minutes, and so on. It does not matter if the student emits 1 behavior or 100 behaviors during the 2-minute interval; reinforcement will occur only after the allotted time has passed. The FI schedule yields a low response rate with pauses after reinforcement. Students who know that their math work-books will be checked every morning at 11:00 (FI-24 hours) are likely to work with increasing speed until that time and to stop working until the interval is about to close the next morning, again working at faster rates as 11:00 ap-proaches. On a variable interval schedule (VI), reinforcement follows the first behavior to occur after an average amount of time has passed. This schedule yields low steady rates of behavior.

Regardless of the reinforcement schedule that a teacher elects to employ, it is imperative that reinforcement be delivered as quickly as possible to avoid reinforcing the wrong behavior. The child should know why reinforcement is delivered. It will help if the teacher verbalizes this as the points, tokens, or praise are delivered: "Good, Billie! You worked quietly for two minutes." It also is important to remember that the reinforcement is delivered *only* as a consequence of the desired behavior. If free time is the reinforcer that is being used, then free time should not be available to the target child at any other time in his or her regular daily schedule.

Reinforcing incompatible responses involves regarding action that is in-compatible with the bothersome behavior. For example, a pupil talks out loud most of the morning. Instead of punishing the student for talking without permission, the teacher decides to reward the child for completing ten arith-metic problems. In order to accomplish this task and obtain the reward, the child is too busy to talk. The desired behavior is incompatible with talking aloud. Not only does this approach reduce disturbing behavior, but it also increases desirable academic performance (Table 7–2). Although reinforcing incompatible responses has not received as much emphasis as other behavior-modification techniques, it appears to be an easily applied and effec-tive procedure for classroom use.

b. Punishment.   A "punisher" is any event that follows a behavior and that decreases the frequency or duration of the behavior and/or decreases the likeli-hood that the behavior will reoccur (Hall, 1971b). The frequency graph of a

Table 7–2. Simultaneous Effects of Reinforcing Incompatible Responses

Target Behavior	Behavioral Results
Disturbing, annoying	Decrease
Desirable academic performance	Increase

behavior that is being punished will show a downward trend. Again, the assumption that such things as expulsion from school, low grades, or standing in the hall are punishing must be proved. Let's look at a brief example. Brett swears in class and his teacher decides to punish this behavior by sending him to the principal's office. If Brett's swearing increases, the teacher must assume that going to the principal's office, is, in fact, reinforcing for Brett, not punishing.

Earlier we discussed negative and positive reinforcement. The reader also may encounter descriptions of two punishment procedures. That is, punishment can be achieved by adding something aversive to the environment or by removing some pleasurable consequence. The important thing for the teacher to note is if the target behavior decreases.

The teacher will select a punishment procedure if the goal is to decrease a behavior, and if this cannot be achieved by reinforcing an incompatible behavior, a reinforcement procedure will be used to increase a behavior. Obviously, the precise definition of the target behavior is crucial to this. For instance, a teacher could elect to reinforce a child for only talking with permission, to punish the same child for talking without permission, or to do both. In the vast majority of instances, it is more desirable to reinforce than to punish a child. Whenever punishment is to be used, it should be accompanied by reinforcement if at all possible. Punishing a behavior tells the student only that the behavior is unacceptable; it does not, in any way, indicate behaviors that are considered appropriate.

The effectiveness of a punisher is governed by many of the same variables that affect reinforcers. Punishers will be more powerful if they are delivered immediately, if the student knows why they are delivered, and if delivery of punishment is contingent upon a specific behavior. In addition, punishers and reinforcers are most effective when they are not overused (e.g., when the child is not satiated).

Punishment has the effect of arresting or suppressing behavior without eliminating or extinguishing it. It is beneficial only when applied to specific acts (running out into the street) rather than to generalized situations (being a naughty child). Momentarily stopping an undesirable behavior has positive effects when it is accompanied by the demonstration and reinforcement of alternative responses.

The teacher must be aware of the possible negative effects of using punishment. The emotional side effects, such as guilt, fear, withdrawal, and frustration, may lead to other maladaptive behaviors. In addition, the punishing teacher may serve as a negative, aggressive model for other children.

c. Extinction.   Extinction occurs when a reinforcing event is withdrawn and the behavior that it followed decreases. For example, Carolee frequently talks without permission and is corrected by the teacher. If Carolee's talking without permission subsequently increases, we can assume that the teacher's corrections reinforced the unwanted behavior. Extinction would occur if Carolee's talking out behavior decreased after the teacher withdrew the apparent reinforcement (the corrections) and ignored the talking out. As teachers, we often unwittingly reinforce undesirable behaviors, as Carolee's teacher did. Extinction, then, is a tool that can be invaluable.

d. Differential Reinforcement.   Differential reinforcement involves two or more different responses: one response is reinforced and the other(s) is/are extinguished. For example, Marty frequently made self-deprecatory remarks (one response), only rarely noting something that he did well (a second response). His teacher ignored the negative remarks (extinction) and reinforced the positive remarks (by attending to them). Eventually, Marty spoke more highly of himself as a result of differential reinforcement. Differential reinforcement is valuable because its use reduces or eliminates undesirable behaviors while simultaneously encouraging behaviors considered to be appropriate.

e. Shaping.   Shaping is the differential reinforcement of successive approximations of a behavior. Let's consider the example of Karen, a first-grader who is out of her seat 60 percent of the time in the reading period. Using differential reinforcement, the teacher extinguished Karen's out-of-seat behavior (by ignoring it) and reinforced her in-seat behavior (by praising it). The goal for Karen is to be in her seat throughout the reading period. Successive approximations of this goal would be increasing percentages of time spent in her seat before receiving reinforcement, perhaps 50 percent, then 55 percent, and so on. The final goal (i.e., for her to be in seat during the entire reading period) would be achieved through a shaping process. In fact, education itself is primarily a process of shaping.

f. Discrimination Training.   Discrimination training involves a single behavior that is reinforced in the presence of one stimulus and is extinguished in the presence of other stimuli. For instance, Matt is reinforced for responding "two" when he is asked to supply the answer to "1 + 1 = ____." However, that same response ("two") is extinguished when Matt is asked to supply the answer to all other questions, such as "2 + 3 = ____" and "1 + 2 = ____." Discrimination training has also occurred with the students who learn that they may use the pencil sharpener whenever they want to in Ms. Penny's English I class but that they must get permission to use it in Mr. Schroeder's algebra class. Discrimination training also might be used to teach a retarded adolescent that kissing is acceptable with some people (e.g., with relatives) but that it is not acceptable with strangers or on the job.

g. *Generalization.*   Generalization is the occurrence of a response learned through discrimination training in the presence of a novel or unknown stimulus. Matt also has learned (through discrimination training) to respond "red" when he sees red circles and squares and to refrain from making that response when he sees circles and squares of other colors. Generalization has occurred if Matt responds "red" when presented with novel stimuli such as red triangles and does not respond "red" when presented with blue, green, or yellow triangles. Generalization is the desired outcome of any intervention plan, regardless of the methodology employed. Students must be able to generalize what is learned, or every situation they encounter will be new. The following steps will facilitate the generalization of a student's behavior from one school situation to another or from school to home.

1. Place the behavior on intermittent reinforcement (every behavior is *not* reinforced).
2. Fade the reinforcer from primary to social.
3. Have another adult (parent or student volunteer) participate in the treatment.
4. Have an extinction period, withdrawing reinforcement and returning to no treatment.
5. Contract with the student to monitor his own behavior by keeping a record and turning to it in at the end of the week for reinforcement, thinning the reinforcement schedule.
6. Use tokens to bridge the gap between primary and social reinforcement and to encourage delay in gratification. Delay in gratification should occur under natural circumstances and should not become an exercise to its own end. It is doubtful that any teacher reading this book will wait a week to pick up a paycheck, just to demonstrate the self-discipline to delay gratification!

The time requirements for this technique are great. The steps are essential, however, for successful application. Once this procedure has been practiced, its time efficiency increases markedly.

h. *Modeling.*   In modeling, verbal instructions or initiation are used to teach a child a new behavior. According to Miller (1975), instructional training, form of modeling, involves three steps: a verbal description of the desired behavior, a demonstration by the learner of the described behavior, and reinforcement following the demonstration of the behavior. Imitation training, another form of modeling, also consists of three stages: demonstration by the teacher of the target behavior, an imitation by the learner of the demonstrated behavior, and reinforcement of the imitation. Instructional training is said to take place when, for instance, the teacher says, "Please sit at your desk," the child complies, and the teacher smiles and says, "Thank you." Imitation training occurs when the teacher makes the short *s* sound, the child imitates it, and the teacher says, "Good."

Modeling also occurs when the child observes that another child who is engaging in instructional or imitation learning is being reinforced (or punished) for complying (or not complying). The child who observes that Mark is permitted to go to recess as soon as he has complied with the teacher's instructions to clear off his desk is quite likely to follow suit and clear off his desk, too (if recess is reinforcing). Likewise, the same behavior will result if he sees that the recess privilege is withdrawn from a child who failed to comply with this request.

i. Token Economies.   Reinforcers may be delivered in "token economies," settings where the children receive tokens with which they can later buy tangible items or privileges. The child completes a task (his "job"), such as correctly working five arithmetic problems or sitting quietly in the reading circle, and is paid with a token at the completion of his job. Poker chips, pieces of paper, and stars are examples of items that can be used as tokens. Tokens (like money) are then exchanged in the economy for things the child wants: 5 tokens may buy a piece of gum, 10 may buy a luncheon date with the teacher or some free time, 50 may buy a field trip, and 500 may buy a day off from school.

There are a number of advantages to a token economy system. The problem of satiation is avoided because the "store" where tokens are exchanged provides a wide variety of reinforcers on the "menu." The system also eases the problem of thinning the reinforcement schedule, because a child eventually does more work for each token. Five minutes of independent work may earn one token today. A month later, it may take six or seven minutes of independent work to earn a token. Token systems demand that the children exercise some delay of gratification while providing immediate, tangible reinforcement. They are also very natural. Children can see a variety of token systems functioning in the "real world" around them. Additional advantages and disadvantages are discussed by Iwata and Bailey (1974).

3. Verification of Results.   Most teachers will readily recognize the effects of an intervention and will not see the need to experimentally verify the results. In some instances, however, it is important to demonstrate formally that the changes achieved through a behavior modification plan are not the result of other happenings. It is possible, for instance, for Sandy's teacher to instigate a behavior modification program to reduce the girl's aggressive behavior. The behaviors may disappear, but there is no proof that the change in behavior was a result of the program which the teacher instigated or a visit by Sandy's grandmother or other variables at home. A reversal or return to baseline is one form of verification. This involves a brief interruption of the intervention program to see if the target behavior begins to approximate its previous baseline level. The program is then reinstituted and the results are verified if the behavior again changes. Many teachers object to using the reversal procedure because they believe they are "pulling the rug out from under" a pupil by reinforcing a particular behavior and then momentarily withdrawing the reinforcement. Multiple baseline is a verification procedure that avoids the problem. This procedure involves the use of the same intervention program for several children exhibiting similar behavior problems or for one child exhibiting a variety of behavior problems, e.g., cursing for Sally, Susie, and Sara, or cursing, spitting, and fighting for Sally. If similar results are achieved on each of the multiple baselines after intervention has been initiated, verification has taken place. Certainly behavior modification results of an experimental or research nature should be verified through these or other means, although the classroom teacher may find these procedures to be too cumbersome and time consuming to implement on a regular basis.

4. *Classroom Application.* There is an abundance of research reporting the significant effects of behavior modification with different populations of children. Since it is impossible here to describe all the research, several studies are cited that have particular relevance to problem children. Token economies were set up in most of these studies, where children received points, poker chips, etc., to be traded in at a specified time for desirable reinforcers.

Wadsworth (1971) investigated the efficacy of two different types of instructional approaches to increase motivation in reading for learning-disabled boys. He found that the reinforcement technique was significantly more effective than clinical tutoring in facilitating increased reading motivation and achievement. In another study (Glavin, Quay, and Werry, 1971), a token economy was established in a classroom of poorly disciplined children. It was successful in decreasing deviant behavior (such as jumping put of the seat), while simultaneously increasing attention and academic performance. Perline and Levinsky (1968) and Sulzbacker and Hauser (1968) reported similar results with mentally retarded children.

In a class of seventeen emotionally disturbed nine-year-olds, O'Leary and Becker (1967) attempted to use a token reinforcement system to eliminate deviant behaviors. They were successful in decreasing these behaviors from a range of 66 to 91 percent to a range of 3 to 32 percent. Preschool problem children were involved in a study by Allen, Turner, and Everett (1970). Using contingency reinforcement, disruptive behaviors (hitting, kicking, spitting) were significantly reduced while appropriate behaviors, such as play and motor skills, were increased. Additional classroom applications may be found in Wolpe's (1976) *Theme and Variations: A Behavior Therapy Casebook*, Kazdin's (1975) *Behavior Modification in Applied Settings*, and O'Leary and O'Leary's *Classroom Management*.

CONTRACTING

Contracting for behavioral change is a popular and effective method for giving students some responsibility for changing their own behavior. A contract is a *two-way* agreement. The child agrees to behave in a certain fashion or to do a certain task at or within a given period of time. The teacher (or parent or other school personnel) agrees to deliver specific kinds of support during the contract and a particular payoff when the contract has been fulfilled. Sample behavioral contracts are shown in Figures 7–10 and 7–11. For additional sample contracts, the reader is also referred to Kohfeldt's (1974) excellent little book, *Contracts*.

LONG AND NEWMAN'S TECHNIQUES FOR MANAGING SURFACE BEHAVIORS

Rationale

Perhaps the most succinct discussion of the management of surface behaviors is offered by Long and Newman (1971). These techniques are intended for use as "stop-gap" devices to prevent escalation of behavior problems or to avoid negative contagion. If necessary, they may be explored in depth (clinical exploitation) at a later time.

Procedures

Twelve interference techniques are described: planned ignoring, signal interference, proximity control, interest boosting, tension decontamination through humor, hurdle lessons, restructuring the classroom program, support from routine, direct appeal to value areas, removing seductive objects, antiseptic bouncing, and physical restraint. *Planned ignoring* closely resembles the extinction procedure, described in the previous section. The basic assumption is that many behaviors will disappear more quickly if they are ignored than if the teacher attempts to intervene in some way. *Signal interference* involves the use of some cue, usually a nonverbal one, which will let the student(s) know that particular behaviors should be abandoned. The "school marm" look which most teachers develop is an example of signal interference. *Proximity*

Date: SEPT. 5, 1977

STUDENT: I agree to follow these rules to student behavior: 1) when my teacher is giving instructions, I will look at her and listen 2) I will complete my workbook assignments in reading

Signed: Albert Johnson

TEACHER: I agree to help Albert by: 1) calling him by name when I am giving instructions 2) Giving him short workbook assignments he will be able to finish. I will give him a check at the end of each hour for following each rule and I will send his checklist home every Friday

Signed: Mrs J. Rhoads

PRINCIPAL: I agree to help Albert by: Having a 10 minute conference with him every Friday to discuss his progress

Signed: Pete Principle

PARENTS: I/We agree to help Albert by: Purchasing Sullivan workbooks for him. 2) He will earn 2¢ of his allowance for each check he brings home on Friday

Signed: Albert Johnson, Sr
Mary G. Johnson

Figure 7–10.
Formal
Contract

Reprinted with the permission of the author and publisher of P. Hawisher, *The Resource Room: Access to Excellence* (Lancaster, S.C.: S.C. Region V Educational Service Center, 1975).

Date: *October 12, 1974*

STUDENT: *I agree to use only good student language today. When I talk I will speak quietly.*

Signed: *Phillip Carson*

TEACHER: *Phillip* will earn the following reward: *to wear the Good Citizenship Button tomorrow*

Signed: *Mr Stanley*

Date: *November 13, 1975*

I will *not hit Susie this week*

I will *say "darn it" when I am angry*

I will _____

Signed: *Jim*

I will arrange for: *Jim to see a movie on Friday if he has 19 teacher signatures by that time.*

Signed: *Mrs Reagan, Counselor*

Monday	Tuesday	Wednesday	Thursday	Friday
JRB	JRB	JRB	JRB	JRB
LM	LM	LM	LM	LM
R Trayer	R Trayer	R Trayer	R Trayer	R Trayer
VFT	VFT	VFT	VFT	VFT

Figure 7–11.
Informal
Contracts

Reprinted with the permission of the author and publisher of P. Hawisher, *The Resource Room: Access to Excellence* (Lancaster: S.C.: S.C. Region V Educational Service Center, 1975).

control is a device that teachers have often used. The teacher's presence in a potential trouble spot is usually sufficient to stop many surface behaviors that are disrupting the program (such as whispering and note passing) and to prevent the spread of these behaviors. *Interest boosting* and *hurdle lessons* are very similar techniques. In the former, the teacher makes an attempt to demonstrate interest in the child as an individual. The latter involves individual attention, too, although it usually centers around providing academic assistance to alleviate frustration. *Restructuring the classroom program* and *support from routine* are opposite techniques. Both require that the teacher be sensitive to needs within the classroom: Do the students require a fresh outlook or will a familiar, no-surprises approach be more supportive? *Direct appeal to value areas* can be effective only when the teacher and the students share the same values or when the teacher is aware of those values that the students have internalized. *Removing seductive objects* has a direct relationship to the props which Redl discussed and which were presented earlier in this chapter. It is frequently easier to remove seductive objectives than it is to manage the behaviors that they may elicit from children. *Antiseptic bouncing* is used to remove a child from the classroom without any punitive overtones. It is a useful technique to prevent the spread of contagious behaviors such as giggling or false hiccoughing or to give an embarrassed or angry child an opportunity to regain control. Usually the child is asked to run an errand or to perform some other chore outside the class. *Tension decontamination through humor* reflects the power of a sense of humor. Many tense situations can be defused by a single good-natured or humorous remark from the teacher. The final management technique, *physical restraint,* is used on those rare occasions when a child has lost control completely. Physical restraint is intended to prevent the child from injuring himself or herself or others and to communicate the teacher's willingness to provide external control. Most teachers already use many, if not all, of these management techniques. Their power as intervention strategies will be increased if teachers will use them consciously and on a planned basis.

TRIESCHMAN'S STRATEGY FOR MANAGING TEMPER TANTRUMS

Rationale

Trieschman (1969) hypothesizes that a temper tantrum is not a single behavior but a series of events with definite stages. He identified six stages, which were given descriptive names: the Rumbling and Grumbling stage, the Help–Help stage, the Either–Or stage, the No–No stage, the Leave Me

Alone stage, and the Hangover stage. Tantrums are managed by dealing with the behaviors in each stage. If the early stages are managed appropriately, the author asserts that tantrums might occur less frequently or might possibly be prevented from occurring at all.

Procedures

During the Rumbling and Grumbling stage, the child is generally grumpy. He appears to be "dribbling (as opposed to gushing) hostility" (p. 176). The child is seeking an issue over which to throw the tantrum he has already decided to have. In many instances, the issue that the child selects is one that lacks a satisfactory solution. For instance, the child may demand that an irreparably broken toy be mended immediately. Management is aided by identifying the pattern of Rumbling and Grumbling. Frequently, the tantrum issue will have a similar time and place (e.g., right before lunch or only in the P.E. class), which will fall into a recognizable pattern. The teacher who recognizes the pattern sometimes can help the child to verbalize the problem rather than to act out the "front issue" for the problem. This is usually accomplished through life-spacing interviewing, a technique that will be discussed later.

The Help–Help stage is the first really loud, noisy stage of the tantrum. The child "has found his issue and is now signaling his need for help. The signal he uses is usually a very visible and deliberate rule-breaking act" (p. 179), which is designed to attract adult attention. The child senses that he is losing internal control and is demanding that an authority figure intervene and impose external control. Management primarily involves teaching the child to signal a need for help in a more appropriate manner, to substitute an appropriate signal for the inappropriate rule-breaking signal. It may be necessary at this point to utilize the physical restraint technique described by Long and Newman while verbalizing to the child the teacher's desire to help him control his behavior. It is best, according to Trieschman, to avoid pointing out that the child broke a rule: he knows he broke the rule, for he broke it deliberately.

The Either–Or stage represents the child's attempt to show that he or she still can control the situation by setting out either–or alternatives. The child often tries to insult the adult or authority figure who is attempting to help by making fun of the adult's personal characteristics. The most important part of the management at this stage is to model appropriate anger for the child. "Helpfully modeling reasonable anger is something a child could imitate more easily than boundless patience and complete passivity in the face of fury" (p. 186). Any either–or proposition that can be accepted should be promoted by the adult and additional alternatives also may be proposed.

The No–No stage is the one in which the child will respond negatively to any suggestion or statement by the adult. It is frequently impossible to manage a tantrum that has reached this stage, although sometimes the tantrum can be pushed back to the previous, Either–Or stage. If good rapport exists between the child and the teacher, it may even be possible to point out the foolishness of the No–No stage by stating questions in such a way that the child actually complies with your wishes by saying "No." This technique can certainly backfire, however, and should be used with extreme caution so that the child does not come to believe that the teacher is making fun of him or her or that he or she is once again "the goat." The noisy part of the tantrum usually dies down at the end of this stage.

The Leave Me Alone stage is relatively quiet and is often mistaken for a return to normal behavior. It is not. The noise is gone and the child may be more amenable to assistance from the adult, but the child is not ready to resume interaction with the world and should not be expected to do so. The child's desire to be left alone should be respected, although the adult should remain within eyeshot or earshot to assure the child that external control is still available if it is necessary. As little conversation as possible is advisable at this stage.

During the Hangover stage, two states of affairs may arise. Some children will experience a "clean drunk" after their tantrums. They have no painful memories of the tantrum and appear to have returned to normal. Other children experience a hangover and feel quite guilty and embarrassed about the incident. The memory is painful. The latter condition is desirable. If a child experiences a clean drunk, it may be possible to induce a hangover that can be exploited, probably through life-space interviewing. Signal words can be devised, as can other alternative behaviors which are more acceptable than tantruming. "Reviewing the sequence of events . . . and learning alternative coping skills is constructive" (p. 192).

LIFE-SPACE INTERVIEWING

Rationale

Life-space interviewing (LSI) is a psychoeducationally oriented technique aimed at dealing with the everyday interactional problems that occur in the classroom. Originally designed for use by teachers assigned to cope with crisis situations, LSI can be used effectively within the classroom. Rational and semidirectional in its approach, LSI attempts to structure a situation so that children can work out their own problems. The teacher's role is one of listener and facilitator in the decision making enacted by the children involved. The technique is nonjudgmental and presents immediate concrete consequences to the children without the typical value appeals that adults frequently make in reaction to behavioral outbursts.

Procedure

A description of an actual incident in which LSI was used is perhaps the most effective way of explaining the approach.

> In the middle of a handwriting lesson, Johnny and David suddenly broke out into a violent fight—cursing, yelling, and hitting each other. The teacher told the rest of the class to continue working and asked the two boys involved in the fight to come up and talk about what just happened.

The LSI approach would proceed in the following manner.

Step 1.   The teacher asks Johnny what happened, telling David that he will have equal time to explain as soon as Johnny finishes. The aim of this step is to determine each child's *perception* of what happened. The facts are not important, but rather each child's understanding of the incident. At this point the teacher simply listens.

Step 2.   Through objective questioning, the teacher tries to determine if the boys' explanations for fighting really constitute the crux of the problem. Are they fighting over the ownership of a pencil, or is this the manifestation of a deeper worry? Frequently, children bring arguments or hostilities to school that have developed at home or at recess. Questioning by the teacher is an attempt to discover how extensive the problem is, without making any interpretations.

Step 3.   After the boys have had a chance to express thoroughly their feelings about the fight and why they think it happened, they are asked what they feel they *can* (not *should*) do about it. By asking this, the values of the child are usually brought to the surface. If their suggestions for remedy are acceptable to all three involved, the interview is terminated here. A note of caution to the teacher should be made at this point: do not ververbalize. Given a structured and guided opportunity to deal with their problems, children often can reach an acceptable solution, without extensive suggestions by the teacher.

Step 4.   If the problem is not resolved at this point, the teacher takes a more direct role, pointing out the reality factors of the situation and the consequences of the behavior if it occurs again. Once more, value judgments are minimized. The teacher should not moralize about the impropriety of cursing and fighting, but say simply that the rules of the school prohibit fighting in class and explain the consequences.

Step 5.   By talking with the boys, their motivation for change can be explored. If there is no discernible remedy for the situation, the teacher can make suggestions, such as breaking the pencil in half or flipping a coin.

Step 6.   The final step is to develop a follow-through plan with the boys that includes discussing alternative procedures should the problem arise in the future. Consequences are once again clearly described by the teacher.

Redl and Wineman (1957) list two components of life-space interviewing: emotional first aid on the spot and clinical exploitation of life events. In differentiating these two, Reinert (1976) cites the example of Dennis, a young boy who is challenged in the lunchroom for unruly behavior and who subsequently becomes "unglued," fleeing the cafeteria for his classroom. If the teacher attempts to restructure the crisis situation and enable the boy to return to lunch as quickly and painlessly as possible, this is an example of emotional first aid. If, however, the teacher elected to spend the lunch hour piecing together the precipitating events and relating them to similar events involving Dennis, this would be clinical exploitation.

Emotional first aid has five subcategories. (1) *Drainoff of frustration acidity* is an attempt to remove the "sting" from unexpected disappointment or frustration. (2) *Support for the management of panic, fury, and guilt* is a means of providing temporary support for a child who is unable to deal effectively with feelings of hate, guilt, anxiety, or anger. (3) *Communication maintenance in moments of relationship decay* is an attempt to maintain a thread of communication and to prevent the child from totally withdrawing. (4) *Regulation of behavioral and social traffic* is the consistent application of rules and/or guidelines for appropriate behavior. (5) *Umpire services,* the final category, is an attempt by an impartial adult to referee difficulties between two children or within a single child.

Redl and Wineman also identified five techniques of clinical exploitation, the in-depth analysis of situations in which problem behaviors occur. (1) *Reality rub-in* is an attempt to make the child aware of what really happened in a crisis situation. (2) *Symptom estrangement* helps the child let go of inappropriate behaviors. (3) *Massaging numb value areas* is a technique to stimulate dormant values that are appropriate to a child's particular situation. (4) *New tool salesmanship* is an attempt to "sell" a child on alternative forms of behavior that are more appropriate and/or socially acceptable. (5) *Manipulation of the boundaries of the self* is an attempt to make the child aware of himself as an individual so that he will not be "sucked" unawares into roles or actions defined by others. Any one or all of these techniques may be used in LSI.

The effectiveness of the LSI approach is dependent on the attitudes and behavior of the teacher. Consciously structuring responses will facilitate positive outcomes. During the interview, a casual and polite atmosphere should be maintained, for this reduces the defensive and hostile feelings of the child or children. The teacher should sit close to the children and avoid towering above them, appearing as much as possible to be neutral and approachable.

If the teacher knows something about the incident, he or she should confront the children with this knowledge. This frequently places the problem in its proper perspective and saves time by eliminating the need for each child to give a detailed description of the event. They will readily add their own perceptions of what occurred. The teacher should avoid asking "why" questions, because many children lack the insight or verbal ability to explain their actions. By calmly stating that situations like this sometimes do occur, or that no real harm has been done, the teacher reassures the child that the teacher is not such a terrible person, enabling the child to "open up" to the teacher. Most important, the children should be listened to, helped to plan for future incidents, and given a chance to ask questions.

The advantages of this approach have been summarized by Redl and Wattenburg (1959). LSI demonstrates to children that they have alternative ways of dealing with their problems. At the same time, they are encouraged to see the consequences of their behavior in an actual life experience without being subjected to moralizing and punishment. Through neutral and supportive communication between child and teacher, hostilities, frustrations, and guilt are relieved. This can help to avoid explosive outbursts later that same day. Because the intervention is immediate, the desire for help and the motivation for change are greatly increased. Life-space interviewing frequently leads to as much growth in the teacher as in the pupils. This is particularly so when teachers and pupils come from different cultural backgrounds. Careful listening on the part of the teacher can lead to insights into the reasons underlying children's behavior.

There are, however, several limitations to this approach that must be described. First, in a class of perhaps twenty to thirty children, the immediate, time-consuming interview may not be feasible. However, if the teacher has confidence in the rationale of LSI, there is no reason why the teacher-pupil interaction cannot be delayed until recess or after school.

LSI requires expert emotional control and sensitivity on the part of the teacher. If the teacher becomes involved in the emotionalism of the problem, effectiveness is sacrificed and the technique becomes useless. There is another subtle limitation to LSI: by removing the child from a 30-to-1 classroom situation to a 2-to-1 personal interaction, the teacher may be reinforcing the negative behavior instead of changing it.

PROJECTIVE TECHNIQUES

Projective techniques frequently utilize supportive media such as puppets, dramatic plays, toys, books, art materials, and music as stimuli to encourage children to express ("project") feelings which they might not reveal in conversation or interviews. Therapies based on projective theory have been developed largely in clinical practice and are used primarily by specially trained professionals. Most have a decided neo-Freudian orientation. However, some of these techniques may be used by classroom teachers to highlight a specific problem area or to explore it in depth. In particular, role playing and puppetry are used by classroom teachers as well as some aspects of art and music therapy. Some projective techniques will be used by members of the professional support team working with seriously disturbed children who are receiving help or therapy outside the classroom. The contents of this section relate to role playing, play therapy, puppetry, and art and music therapy.

Role Playing

Role playing is another form of "let's pretend." The children act out situations that involve problems of getting along together. A distinctive version of role playing, called psychodrama, has been developed by Moreno (1946). Psychodrama is usually employed with a severely disturbed individual who is required to come upon a stage and express real or fantasized feelings and problems. There is no criticism in psychodrama, only "controlled confrontation." Participation is voluntary. Some of Moreno's psychodramatic techniques include role reversal, soliloquy, double (where a "helper" participates in the play), mirror (where one participant "apes" the actions of another), behind the back (where other participants talk about the target individual), high chair, empty chair, magic shop (where goals and aspirations are expressed), and ideal other. Psychodrama requires the use of a trained therapist because of its explosive nature; therefore, it is not recommended for use in the classroom. However, role playing as a technique for learning new behaviors and skills can be appropriately adapted to the classroom.

Interpersonal problems often find solution through acceptance of criticism or other forms of perceived punishment or rejection. Children can learn how to cope with these experiences by exploring various responses and reactions. One child can portray the role of an angry member of the class, and another child play himself or herself entering into a potential fight with that child. Through the use of suggestions from the teacher and class members, the child can learn to respond to anger more skillfully and without losing face. This technique can also help physically or mentally handicapped children face real or imagined social reactions without reverting to excessive emotional outbursts.

Harth (1966) applied role playing to a classroom of ten emotionally disturbed children from two public schools in a low socioeconomic area of a southern city. He studied the effects of the therapy on the children's attitudes toward school, their classroom behavior, and their reaction to frustration.

During a five-week period, the experimental group engaged in two role-playing sessions weekly. During this time they portrayed school personnel in various problem situations centered around school. After the experimental period, Harth found no change in either the children's attitude toward school or their reaction to frustration. However, classroom behavior of the experimental group did change from baseline information.

Although the results of this study indicate a cautious optimism, further studies are needed to demonstrate the effectiveness of this approach with various types and sizes of classes. This is not to imply that the teacher need wait for such substantiation before using role playing within the school setting.

Puppetry

Theories that utilize the construct of the "unconscious" as a potent motivator in human behavior recognize the need for expressing such feelings and bringing them to the level of consciousness. An effective way of doing this is through the use of puppetry (Woltmann, 1971), another form of psychodrama. The puppets have specific meaning to each child, who is able to project hate, anger, fears, and desires onto them in a neutral, fantasylike manner. Many of these feelings ordinarily remain suppressed because expression of them in actual life situations is often too threatening to the child. But as Woltmann states: "Puppetry carries with it the reassurance that everything on the stage is only a make-believe affair" (p. 226). To kill the bad guy is acceptable. Not only does he always come to life during the next show, but with each "killing" comes the release of suppressed rage, which often inappropriately releases itself during instructional time.

All that puppetry requires is commercial or homemade puppets and a structure than can serve as a stage. Often the children themselves can create the needed equipment. The puppet characters should combine both fantastic and realistic factors, so the child can enter easily into the activity and identify with the characters and their problems. Woltmann suggests the use of the following types of puppet actors: (1) the hero; (2) a bad mother, often appearing as a witch; (3) a bad father, appearing as a giant; (4) a little boy or girl representing the child's idealized self; and (4) an animal. Other personalities can be added as the children begin to interact in this problem-solving world of fantasy.

Initially, it is best for an adult to act as the puppeteer who follows the commands of the audience. Some children may yell out "Kill the witch! Kill her!" while others shrink away in fear. It frequently is helpful to bring a fearful child behind the stage while the acting is going to assure him or her that it is only make-believe. During the show all pupil commands should be accepted, but afterward alternative solutions to the problems revealed in the fantasy play can be discussed and acted out. Puppetry can dispel intense feelings and contribute to learning alternatives to stereotypic behaviors. The teacher should be careful to resolve any problems broached in the play so that the children have a "clean slate" and are relaxed for the next activity.

Play Therapy

The use of play therapy in the school differs in some ways from play as a psychotherapeutic technique. A primary goal in school is to increase the individual's understanding of himself or herself by relating a free situation (play) in which the child is given the opportunity to self-actualize (Alexander, 1971). According to Axline (1964), an acknowledged authority on the technique of play therapy, "the child must first learn self-respect and a sense of dignity that grows out of his increasing self-understanding before he can learn to respect the personalities and rights and differences of others" (p. 67). In psychotherapy the aim is to discover unconscious motivations by interpretative techniques. Both educational and psychotherapeutic play share several common views: (1) the relationship between therapist (or teacher) and the child is the key to emotional growth, and (2) the selection and use of various play activities aids in expressing personal and social needs. The play situation is provided because it is usually the most comfortable one for the child and the most conducive to self-expression.

Play materials are provided for the child, but their use should not be contrived by the therapist. Recommended materials are:

sandbox	basin filled with water
doll house	toy dishes
toy soldiers	toy police and fire trucks
crayons	toy animals
scissors	hammer

Ginott (1961), another early proponent of play therapy, suggests that young children who are "socially hungry" are the best candidates for play therapy. The technique seems to lose its effectiveness after about age eight, he says, pointing out that play therapy probably is counterindicated for children who are aggressive or have deviant sexual drives, children who suffer from intense sibling rivalries or extreme hostility, children who tend to steal, children who are prone to have unusually strong stress reactions, and children who engage in sociopathic behaviors.

Although these are no clear-cut procedures, Kessler (1966, pp. 376–377) restates Axline's eight basic principles of play therapy[1]:

1. The therapist must develop a warm, friendly relationship with the child.

1. From Jane W. Kessler, *Psychopathology of Childhood,* © 1966. By permission of Prentice-Hall, Inc.

2. The therapist accepts the child exactly as he is.
3. The therapist establishes a feeling of permissiveness in the relationship.
4. The therapist is alert to recognize the feelings [of the child] and to reflect the feelings back to the child so that she gains insight into his behavior.
5. The therapist maintains a deep respect for the child's ability to solve his own problems.
6. The child leads the way; the therapist follows.
7. The therapist does not attempt to hurry the therapy along.
8. The therapist establishes only those limitations that are necessary to anchor the therapy to the world of reality and to make the child aware of his responsibility in the relationship.

The effects of play therapy have been equivocal. According to Pumpfrey and Elliott (1970) and Schiedlinger and Rauch (1972), the efficacy of play therapy is still doubtful. Fleming and Snyder (1947), Fisher (1953), Axline (1947), Bills (1950), and Ginott (1961) report favorable results from play therapy in relationship to personality adjustment and reading achievement with emotionally disturbed children. In a survey of thirty-seven investigations of the efficacy of psychotherapy with children (many using play therapy), Levitt (1957) noted the absence of differences between treated children and controls. Two thirds of the children evaluated immediately after treatment and three fourths evaluated at follow-up showed improvement. The statistics were approximately the same for control groups. Levitt concludes that this study fails to support the efficacy of this approach with children. However, the decision to use or not to use play therapy depends on more than reports of efficacy studies; the time required for the process and the size of the class are practical determinants. As Newcomer summarized in her recent book, *Understanding and Teaching Emotionally Disturbed Children* (1980), ". . . it seems most likely that play therapy is not the panacea that advocates like Axline think it is. It certainly is not the best means of remediating serious reading or spelling problems, as she has indicated. However, if the teacher's goals . . . pertain to helping children develop increasingly mature and adaptive social skills, establishing a nonthreatening relationship . . ., and/or providing opportunities . . . to model better adjusted peers, it may prove a helpful technique" (p. 365).

Art and Music Therapy

The goals of art and music therapy parallel those previously expressed for play therapy, puppetry, and role playing. They encourage children to express themselves freely and without fear. Music and various art media such as paint and clay may elicit expressions of feelings that would not surface otherwise. Art and music therapy provide nonthreatening situations for children to share their feelings and to release inner tensions.

In art therapy, a wide variety of media should be available in the classroom or therapy room. Freestyle activities such as finger painting, clay sculpting, and drawing will provide unstructured avenues for expression. Denny (1977) suggests a number of goals for art therapy in the schools. Among these are encouraging spontaneous expression, building rapport by encouraging interaction with other participants, facilitating the expression of inner feelings, and exploring self-perceptions. It is not unusual for teachers to detect some of the problems that children are experiencing by examining their art work. Usually, though, this will only be a confirmation of problems that already have been identified. Teachers are cautioned *not* to use art therapy as a diagnostic tool unless they have had specific training in this area. Readers who are interested in learning more about art therapy are referred to Kramer (1971), Naumberg (1973), and Ulman and Dachinger (1977).

Music is often cited as a universal language and it certainly plays an especially important role in the social life of many adolescents. Music can have a quieting effect on unusually active children and can promote concentration, since it helps to shut out noises that might otherwise be distracting (Reinert, 2976). Aggressive behaviors can be vented through such music activities as dancing, playing drums, rhythm sticks or sandpaper blocks, and singing action songs. In addition to traditional therapeutic activities of singing, dancing, or playing musical instruments, students can be encouraged to talk or write about the feelings elicited by certain types of music or about musical content, such as historical information on certain pieces of music, composers' biographies, and so on. Readers interested in music therapy are referred to Nordoff and Robbins (1971) and to Michel (1971).

COGNITIVE INTERVENTIONS

Cognitive behavior modification and other so-called rational approaches to behavior management have gained recognition in recent years. Prominent among these approaches are Glasser's (1965, 1969) work with reality therapy, Ellis' (1962, 1970, 1974; Ellis, Wolfe, and Mosely, 1972) work with rational-emotive therapy, and Meichenbaum's (1975) cognitive behavior management.

Rationale

Each of these approaches requires that the clients, patients, or students assume responsibility not only for their own behavior, but also for the therapy programs. For instance, in reality therapy students are asked to select a better course of behavior than the ones they have been following. Throughout the process, students make value judgments regarding their own behavior and commit themselves to change. Several "better courses" may be attempted before the child falls into a comfortable and acceptable behavioral pattern. The premise is that "all patients have a common characteristic: they all deny the reality of the world around them" (Glasser, 1965, p. 6). Similar views are expressed by Ellis (1962) when he describes the "irrational" beliefs that clients hold on to, such as the "idea that it is a dire necessity for an adult human to be loved or approved by virtually every significant other person in his life" (p. 153).

Procedure

Each of these approaches sports a full-blown therapy program to which we cannot do justice in the space allowed. Interested readers should consult the authors' original work before attempting to establish such programs in their schools. We will attempt here to summarize the basic tenets of cognitively based therapies.

Ellis (1974) discusses several premises which he believes are basic to his rational-emotive therapy. Probably the most important tenet is that change must be effected in the inner language that people use to talk to themselves about their behavior, their values, and their reasons for acting in a particular way. Ellis believes that such a language change will facilitate behavior change by allowing clients to clarify their reasoning through the formation and use of hypotheses. Ellis emphasizes that the burden for the success of any intervention must be assumed by the client, although he stresses that no blame should be attached to failure and that the therapist can "sell" or market behavioral change in much the same way that one might sell an actual product. Ellis stresses that the causes of one's problems are found only on the present. He insists on practice and "homework" for clients. In general, this is highly verbal therapy and may not be appropriate for students who have language or general reasoning difficulties.

Glasser (1969) is more specific than Ellis in discussing ways that teachers can implement reality therapy in the classroom. He says that the teacher should continually ask three questions of the student: "What are you doing?" "Is your behavior helping you or those around you?" "What could you do differently?" He advocates a more behavioristic approach than Ellis and, for this reason, Newcomer (1980) suggests that reality therapy may be more useful with young children or with students whose verbal reasoning powers are limited or impaired.

Meichenbaum (1975) is even more behavioral. His methods are essentially ones of values clarification combined with social skills training. He suggests the use of basic modeling principles to help students acquire self-control over their behaviors. In general, he suggests the need to identify problem areas through discussion or role playing. Skills to be acquired are broken down into subcomponents and their verbal aspects are studied carefully. The teaching process begins following a concise explanation for why a particular skill needs to be learned. The steps of the skill are defined, modeled by the teacher, therapist or a peer, practiced by the target student through role playing and real life situations, and altered or reinforced through feedback and praise. Meichenbaum believes that many of these steps can be accomplished in group sessions, because many students lack the same (or similar) basic social skills.

COMMERCIALLY AVAILABLE PROGRAMS

Rationale

There has been a noticeable paucity of materials designed to teach affective skills, until recently when several commercial programs have become available. Most of these programs are designed to teach children such skills as how to be open to new experiences, how to cope, how to label and appropriately express feelings, and how to identify and clarify values. For instruction, they depend heavily on the use of puppetry, role playing, sociodrama, and discussion. Although most of the materials were designed with "normal" children in mind, their use need not be limited solely to this population. Teachers can use portions of the programs which seem appropriate and can integrate them with materials of their own design.

There is little empirical evidence to support the efficacy of commercially available affective programs. L. Brown (1979) studied the effectiveness of two commercial programs, Toward Affective Development (TAD) and Developing Understanding of Self and Others (DUSO), with groups of third-graders who were followed through the sixth grade. Triads of students, matched on the basis of sex, intelligence, and homeroom teacher, were randomly assigned to TAD, DUSO, or a control program of supervised free play. Several measures of behavioral and self-concept change were administered at the end of the one-year program and during each of the three following years. No significant group differences were detected on any measure, although more students who participated in the two commercial programs reported that they had fun.

Programs

Thirteen programs will be discussed briefly in this section: My Friends and Me, Human Development, DUSO-I and II, TAD, Lollipop Dragon, First Things, Dimensions of Personality, Child's Series on Psychologically Relevant

Themes, Transition, Coping With, Contact Maturity, Target Behavior, and values clarification.

My Friends and Me (David, 1977) was written for a preschool audience. Through the use of discussion, puppetry, role playing, and drawing, students go through the process of self-identification and recognition of group rights and responsibilities. There are eight units: Social Identity, Emotional Identity, Physical Identity, Intellectual and Creative Identity, Cooperation, Consideration for Others, Ownership and Sharing, and Dependence and Help.

The Human Development Program (Palomares and Ball, 1974), popularly known as Magic Circle, is one of the more widely used commercial programs for teaching affective skills. The basic premise of the program is that teacher-led discussions which take place in a structured setting (e.g., in the Magic Circle) will help students to develop richer, more meaningful interrelationships with each other. Manuals and materials are provided for students from age four to age eleven (preschool through sixth grade). Objectives of the Human Development Program include improving self-control, listening skills, and expression; learning the meaning of responsibility, fantasy, and role expectations; and developing a positive self-concept, trust, and satisfactory interpersonal relationships.

The Developing Understanding of Self and Others (DUSO) kits are designed for use with kindergarteners and first-graders (D-I) (Dinkmeyer, 1970) and for second- through fourth-graders (D-II) (1973). DUSO-I stresses the inquiry method of learning. Stories, puppetry, and discussion are used to promote the eight unit themes: (1) Undestanding and Accepting Self; (2) Understanding Feelings; (3) Understanding Others; (4) Understanding Independence; (5) Understanding Goals and Purposeful Behavior;(6) Understanding Mastery, Competence, and Resourcefulness; (7) Understanding Emotional Maturity; and (8) Understanding Choices and Consequences. Daily lessons plans for DUSO activities are presented in the manual. Role playing, puppetry, and listening are the primary activities used to develop the eight themes in DUSO II. Stimulus posters and situation cards are provided to assist the teacher in initiating discussion around these themes: (1) Towards Self-Identity: Developing Self-Awareness and a positive Self-Concept; (2) Towards Friendship: Understanding Peers; (3) Towards Responsible Interdependence: Understanding Growth from Self-Centeredness to Social Interest; (4) Towards Self-Reliance: Understanding Personal Responsibility; (5) Towards Resourcefulness and Purposefulness: Understanding Personal Motivation; (6) Towards Competence: Understanding Accomplishments; (7) Towards Emotional Stability: Understanding Stress; and (8) Towards Responsible Choice Making: Understanding Values.

Toward Affective Development (TAD) (DuPont, Gardner, and Brody, 1974) is a popular, widely used affective curriculum. It was designed for "normal" children in grades three through six, but is appropriate for guidance or remedial work. Lessons are organized into five major units that use a child's real or vicarious experiences as the basis for growing and learning. These units include Reaching In and Reaching Out, Your Feelings and Mine, Working Together, Me: Today and Tomorrow, and Feeling, Thinking, Doing. Most of the activities are verbal: brainstorming, role playing, and discussion groups. The TAD kit includes filmstrips, cassettes, posters and pictures, dittos, a "feeling wheel," and folders containing information on various careers and job opportunities.

The Adventures of the Lollipop Dragon (1970) was designed for students in the primary grades. Six filmstrips are included in the kit. They depict stories that emphasize personal relationships and interdependency (e.g., taking turns, sharing with others, and working in groups). The "hero" of the series is the Lollipop Dragon, who inhabits a small kingdom where the economy is based on the production of lollipops. The filmstrips are accompanied by records and cassettes of the stories and by a coloring book, "How the Lollipop Dragon Got His Name."

First Things (Grannis and Schone, 1970) was designed for first-, second-, and third-graders. Five themes are developed through the use of videotapes, sociodramatics, and role playing. Group interaction and the classification and expression of feelings are stressed. The themes are: (1) Who do you think you are? (2) Guess who's in a group! (3) What happens between people? (4) You got mad: are you glad? (5) What do you expect of others?

Dimensions of Personality (Linnbacher, 1969) was written for students in the upper-elementary grades (four through six). According to the manual, portions of the program may be suitable for use with low-reading junior and senior high school students as well. It purports to maintain a holistic approach to affective education through which "children will come to understand their physical, intellectual, and emotional growth better" (Reinert, 1976, p. 147). Provocative questions, posters, pictures, and cartoons are used to stimulate discussion activities.

The Child's Series on Psychologically Relevant Themes (Fasler, 1971) was designed for preschool and primary grade students. The themes are "relevant" within a psychoanalytic orientation. The kit contains six videotapes, each of which tells a story and promotes a major psychodynamic theme. The videotapes are (1) "The Man of the House," in which a young boy is the man of the house in his father's absence and must then relinquish the role when his father returns from a business trip; (2) "All Alone with Daddy," in which a young girl develops a close relationship with her father while her mother is away and then becomes jealous when the mother returns; (3) "Grandpa Died Today," in which a boy's reaction to the death of his grandfather is chronicled; (4) "Don't Worry Dear," in which a young girl is teased about stuttering and develops some immature habits such as bedwetting and thumbsucking; (5) "Boy with a

Problem," in which a young boy develops a variety of hypochondriacal symptoms because he is keeping a problem inside himself; and (6) "One Little Girl," in which a little girl learns to compensate for her weaknesses by promoting her strengths.

Transition (DePont and DePont, 1979) is intended for students from ages twelve to fifteen. It uses posters and pictures, cassette tapes with printed scripts, ditto sheets, discussion cards, and feeling word cards in a program of activities that are primarily verbal in nature and are discussion oriented. Activities are incorporated into five units: Let's Communicate, Let's Trust Each Other, Let's Express Our Feelings, Let's Understand Each Other, and Let's Discover What We Value.

The Coping With series (Wrenn and Schwarznock, 1978) was developed for junior and senior high students. It contains a large series of books depicting some typical adolescent problems. The books for group discussions. Stimulus questions are provided for the teacher or other group leader to use in initiating discussion.

Contact Maturity: Growing Up Strong (1972) was designed for junior and senior high school students with low reading abilities. It stresses a language arts approach, and one of the major goals of the program is to encourage an interest in reading. Poetry, short stories, open-ended stories, posters, and pictures are used to stimulate discussion and values clarification. Students are also encouraged to keep diaries of their daily activities and of their feelings in specific situations.

Target Behavior (Kroth, 1973b) is a commercially packaged Q-sorting kit. It contains the formboard, behavioral items, record sheets, and instructions. The materials would be used to isolate target behaviors for change or modification. The Q-sorting technique was discussed earlier in this chapter.

Values clarification is an affective program, although it is not packaged as a kit. Several authors (such as Fine, 1973, and Weinstein and Fantini, 1970) discuss the uses of a values clarification program in the classroom. The reader is referred to an excellent book, *Values Clarification* by Simon, Howe, and Kirschenbaum (1972), which describes the technique of values clarification and provides activities for the teacher to use. In essence, values clarification is a questioning procedure that "should serve to generate thought regarding what values the student holds to, how the value was acquired, what the pragmatic implications are of the value and what complementary or competing values might exist on the part of the classmates" (Fine, 1973, p. 68). Values clarification is usually most successful with older elementary students and with adolescents because the technique requires participants to be able to identify and talk about abstract concepts such as values, emotions, and feelings.

PROBLEMS IN LANGUAGE DEVELOPMENT

Nettie R. Bartel   Diane N. Bryen[1]

This chaper deals with the comprehension and production of oral language. Primary consideration is give to (1) the nature of language; (2) the acquisition of normal language; (3) formal and informal assessment of language functioning; and (4) approaches to instruction and remediation in language.

THE NATURE OF LANGUAGE

In everyday life, people use language in unified, integrated ways to communicate to others and to understand messages from others. However, in order to understand what happens when language communication occurs, it is necessary to separate the process into component aspects. First, in any given communication a specific *content* is conveyed, that is, the communicated message is about something. Secondly, that specific content is couched in a particular *form,* the form varying on the basis of the language (German, English, Chinese) that is being used. And finally, communication occurs in specific contexts to serve certain functions, that is, language *usage* depends on the goal of the speaker. These three aspects or dimensions of language are schematically portrayed in Figure 8–1.

1. Dr. Bryen's contributions are the sections "Informal Approaches to Language Assessment" and "Informal Instructional Approaches."

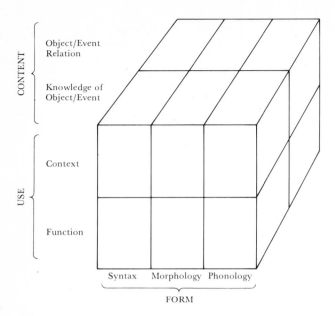

Figure 8–1.   Dimensions of Language

Each language act involves the three dimensions identified in Figure 8–1. Each event of communication involves having something to say (content), a reason to say it (use), and a way to say it (form). The effective and appropriate intergration of these aspects of language—saying the right thing in the right way in appropriate circumstances—is called communicative competence. Thus, the person with fully developed communicative competence has some ideas or content to convey and understands how to transform these ideas into specific speech sounds that comprise words and sentences. The language used depends upon the context of communication and the person's purpose in speaking. For example, we use different language in informal situations than we do in formal situations. Similar considerations underlie communicative competence in other media, such as print or pictures. In each case, questions of content, form, and use must be taken into account.

Similarly, the competent recipient of another person's communicative act must be able to relate the content of the communication to a personal background of ideas and experiences. The receiver must be familiar with the form the speaker is using—the speech sounds, inflections, intonations, grammar, etc. And finally, he or she must discern the context and function of the communicative effort. All of these considerations are involved whether the recipient of the communication is listening or reading. The dimensions of content, form, and use are so basic to understanding language that we will return to them in greater detail later in this chapter. We turn now to some additional aspects of the nature of language.

It is generally agreed by linguists that *language is a symbol system or code through which ideas about the world are communicated through a conventional set of arbitrary signals.* The "symbol system or code" in this definition means that languages involve representations or things that stand for other things; when we say "desk," we understand a learned rule or convention—namely that the word "desk" stands for or represents the object "desk." For the speaker and the listener to communicate, they must agree on such rules or conventions. The rules themselves change over time; note the difficulty we have understanding Chaucer's English. Sometimes linguistic rules evolve rapidly or change with respect to certain subgroups of a population. Thus, a "cool cat" may represent a freezing four-legged animal or it may stand for a worldly-wise young person.

The second part of the definition, "ideas about the world," refers to the fact that we communicate about our thoughts. Olsen (1970) has noted that a person cannot talk about something of which he or she knows nothing (although we've all heard people who try!) The knowledge that people have about objects and events in the world comprises the content about which they communicate.

This brings us to the part of the definition that states that language is communication of ideas. Language is not just using words for the sake of using words; it is using words to convey meaning to somebody else. Knowing what language can do (it can bring food or water; it can "spell relief"; it can express happiness or anger) is an important part of communicative competence.

Finally, language consists of a conventional set of arbitrary signals. In English, for example, speakers and listeners have agreed on the semantic convention that a certain four-legged animal found in many homes will be known as "dog," rather than say "hund," as in German. Similarly, in English syntax, one finds the convention that descriptors referring to size precede those referring to color, as in "big red ball" rather than "red big ball." While there is no intrinsic reason why one rule rather than another would be utilized in a given language, the fact is that this is the case; and observation of children's language shows that most children learn these rules quickly and accurately. Our concern in this chapter, of course, is with those children who experience difficulty for one reason or another.

There is one additional aspect of language that needs to be mentioned. This is the fact that language is *generative* in nature. The generative nature of language means that (1) users of a language can speak and understand sentences that they have never heard or used before and (2) the rules of every known language are such that an infinite number of sentences are possible.

Obviously, these aspects of language have major implications for training. For example, attempting to teach language to a child is quite different from teaching the multiplication table. In the case of the multiplication facts, all possible combinations can be presented on a matrix, and practice can occur until the child performs correctly 100 percent of the time. In teaching language, however, one can never exhaust all the possibilities. Even if one attempted to teach only one kind of simple sentence—let us say sentences of the subject–action type (e.g., "ball rolls," "dog runs," "cat jumps," "girl screams," etc.)—we would still have an infinite number of examples. Clearly, what is called for is a teaching technique that helps children discover the rules that would permit them to generate novel sentences that are appropriate for their communicative intent, and similarly to understand the intent of another speaker, even though they have never heard that particular sentence before.

This capability for producing or understanding novel utterances is part of *language competence.* Competence, the underlying knowledge that an individual has regarding a given language, is distinguished from *performance,* which is the actual expression of that competence in the understanding or producing of well-formed sentences. An individual's linguistic competence can be masked by a variety of performance variables such as poor memory, distraction, or lack of interest.

Although it would be of great educational significance to be able to directly measure a child's linguistic competence, competence itself can never be directly observed. One can only infer that it is or is not present in a child, on the basis of the child's understanding or production of sentences. As indicated above, a child's performance may be attentuated by a variety of factors. For this reason, the assessment of a child's language ability remains one of the most challenging tasks for educators.

The nature of linguistic competence—its rule-governed and generative aspects—indicate that language is not merely a set of conditioned responses or a series of stimulus–response bonds. It suggests that basic language structure, and the meaning given to expression through that structure, may not be trainable through rote and drill procedures. In fact, most children acquire basic linguistic competence by about four years of age without any formal instruction at all. The development of effective procedures for teaching children who have not acquired competence by that age is a critical, unresolved issue. Our position in this chapter is that the most promising possibility for effective instruction lies in an examination and adaptation of the circumstances under which most children normally acquire language competence. It is necessary to analyze the procedures and sequence of normal language acquisition to formulate the most promising ideas about how to instruct children with language problems. It is to such an analysis that we turn next.

THE ACQUISITION OF LANGUAGE

The careful observation of very young children, or of older children who have not developed language, makes it clear that a good deal of intellectual development occurs before the child begins to speak, typically at about age one. Myklebust refers to this preverbal period as the time when "inner language" is developed (Johnson and Myklebust, 1967). At this stage the child does not give overt evidence of language development, although he or she is beginning to organize experiences in a systematic way.

Along the same lines, Piaget (1962) has stated:

> Language is not enough to explain thought, because the structures that characterize thought have their roots in action and in sensorimotor mechanisms that are deeper than linguistics (p. 98).

Piaget and others (e.g., Moerk, 1975; Parisi and Antinucci, 1970; Sinclair-de-Zwart, 1969; Slobin, 1970, 1971) have begun to delineate the processes engaged in by the child during this preverbal period, procedures which nonetheless have implications for the child's later verbal utterances. Using the basic functions of *assimilation* (the tendency of the organism to incorporate environmental stimuli into a system of mental structures) and *accommodation* (adjusting to the environment), the child constantly searches for *equilibrium* (i.e., balance). Even the very young child is a problem solver, attempting to reconcile events in the world around him with his present state of understanding while simultaneously changing his understanding in response to actions in his environment. The child is active, not passive, and interacts with and transforms his conceptions of events. The child is not just a responder to acts and situations but is also an initiator—a fact that shows up in all observations of children's language acquisition. It is through the child's active and reactive manipulations of the environment that the beginnings of intelligence are revealed. Since thought precedes language, the nature of language must have its roots in the development of thought beginning sometime during the sensorimotor period.

Although Piaget emphasizes the organism's interaction with the environment, development can be explained only as the combination of maturation, social transmission, experience, and equilibration. Without the interrelationships among these factors, there can be no development, hence no learning. Language acquisition is thus based on cognitive development, as opposed solely to the accretion of linguistic terms.

In fact, recent research has demonstrated a rather amazing correspondence between the early stages of cognitive development (as outlined by Piaget) and the corresponding indicators of prelinguistic and linguistic behaviors (see, for example, Sinclair, 1969, 1971, 1973; L. Bloom, 1973; Nelson, 1973; Bruner, 1975; Uzgiris, 1976). Piaget has stated that the sensorimotor period is characterized by action and interaction between a child and his or her environment. This perspective of the child as an active constructor of knowledge of the world is parallel to the way the child appears to develop language as well. Several examples follow:

Cognitive Aspect	*Language Aspect*
Child develops concept of *object permanence* (believes object still exists even if out of sight).	Child develops utterances relating to *existence, nonexistence,* and *recurrence* of objects, e.g., "Cookie," "Cookie all gone," "More cookie."
Child develops schemata of *cause-effect* and *means-end* relationship.	Child says "Mommy milk" when asking mother to bring milk.

Observation of the interaction between an infant and its mother, even before there is any overt evidence of language capability on the part of the child, shows that the child and the mother follow each other's "line of regard," that is, they attend to the same things. It has been noted that even at four months of age, the child follows the mother's line of regard, a behavior that occurs even more readily when the mother draws attention to what she is doing with statements such as "Look here!" Once the mother has the child's attention, she comments on or acts upon the object or event that has their mutual attention. From the very earliest stages of infancy then, the child learns the routine *"Attend to→Act upon"* (Bruner, 1975). The usefulness of this paradigm for teaching can scarcely be overstated. Before any significant language training can occur, steps must be taken to ensure that the child is attending to what the teacher is attending. As we have seen, this routine is basic to language instruction.

While it is a truism that children learn language from hearing others speak it, only recently have researchers begun to understand the nature of the relationship between the speaker and the child that makes this learning possible.

As noted above, in the normal language learning environment, the home, the child hears comment or sees actions directed toward events to which his or her attention has been called. The comments and the actions that the child sees and hears are not arbitrary but serve as expressions of the mother's intent. Bruner (1975) has shown that even very young children grasp the notion that others (usually the mother) have intentions, and thus begin to make the first crucial distinctions between people and things. Soon thereafter the child himself expresses intent. A teacher can observe intent in a nonverbal child by noting the direction of the child's regard, by observing what satisfies him (does he stop whining when you let him have a certain toy?), by watching whether he substitutes one strategy for another (if he doesn't get results by looking at the closet where his coat and boots are, does he try walking to the door to convey the idea that he wants to go outdoors?), and finally, by noting the child's persistence.

We have discussed the issue of *intent* in some detail because of the significant role that it can play in language instruction. We have observed teachers spending valuable time attempting to get nonverbal children to distinguish between red and blue chips while the child sat at the desk sullenly ignoring the teacher; we have also seen teachers engaging groups of children in loud chants of "That is a pencil"; utterances that bore no relationship to the intent of the child and were never uttered spontaneously in an appropriate setting. What works so well in the informal circumstances of the preschooler's home is the commenting on and the acting upon events to which the child's attention has been directed. Bruner (1975) states that "Language is acquired as an instrument for regulating joint action and joint attention" and then again ". . . language is a specialized and conventionalized extension of cooperative action" (p. 2). These early interactions between the caretaker (usually the mother) and the child are strikingly similar to adult discourse, and have been called "protoconversation" or "protodialogue" (Tamir, 1979). There is evidence that these early conversations are not random exchanges but carefully controlled by the mother (Martlew, 1980).

In these early social interactions, language is used to express what the child already "knows"—what he or she has seen acted on or what he or she has heard commented on. The task of language learning, from the child's point of view, has been expressed by Slobin (1973) as follows:

> In order to acquire language, the child must attend both to speech and to the contexts in which speech occurs—that is, he must be trying to understand what he hears, and be trying to express the intentions of which he is capable. This means that he must have both cognitive and linguistic discovery procedures available—in order to formulate internal structures which are capable of assimilating and relating both linguistic and nonlinguistic data, and which are capable of realizing intentions as utterances. The emergence of new communicative intentions must bring with it the means to decode those intentions in the speech the child hears, and this makes it possible for him to discover new means for expressing those intentions (p. 186).

Recent research has shown that adults interacting with children systematically alter their linguistic behavior apparently to facilitate the child's learning of language. Among the changes in adult speech are clearer enunciation, shorter and slower utterances, higher pitch and exaggerated intonation, less syntactic complexity, more limited vocabulary use, mostly concrete references, and more directives, imperatives, and questions (summarized in de Villiers and de Villiers, 1978). In fact, recent research shows that several characteristics of mothers' speech such as utterance length significantly predict child speech six months or so later (Furrow, Nelson, and Benedict, 1979). Studies such as this are making it increasingly apparent that the linguistic environment affects language learning in important ways. This is in contrast to an earlier point of view, sometimes called "nativist," that language simply emerges with little input necessary from the environment (Hedge, 1980). Evidence from the experimental and diary data on the acquisition of several different European and Oriental languages shows that the language-learning child interacts actively in a dynamic fashion with his or her environment. This interaction may be described as a cyclical process in which acquisition is followed by application (use), and application is followed by correction, which in turn leads back to additional acquisition (MacWhinney, 1978).

From the very beginning, children use language in purposeful, intentional ways to comment on some event occurring in their environment or to make a request of some kind. For example, consider the following exchange between a mother and her eighteen-month-old son, Matthew.

Mother:	What do you want? Pop-Up? (Pop-Up is a wind-up toy.)
Matthew:	No.
Mother:	Don't you want Pop-Up?
Matthew:	Turn Pop-Up.
Mother:	Do you want to turn Pop-Up?
Matthew:	Mommy Pop-Up?

Apparently, Matthew's intent in this exchange is to request that his mother wind-up (turn) the toy, Pop-Up. However, he does not yet have sufficient mastery of his language to say "Mommy turn Pop-Up," so instead he says "Turn Pop-Up," and "Mommy Pop-Up," which taken together with his "No" in response to his mother's first question, makes his intent clear.

If Slobin (1973, p. 185) is right when he states that the appearance in a child's speech of a new formal device serves only to code a function that the child already has understood and expressed implicitly, then one would expect to see in Matthew's speech the emergence of "Mommy turn Pop-Up." In a child whose language development is not proceeding normally, the presence of an exchange like that of Matthew's (above) would signal to the perceptive teacher that the time is right to teach the child "Mommy turn Pop-Up." The rule is: *Explicit instruction of the verbal form is likely to be beneficial only when the child shows evidence of having grasped the meaning.*

It should be clear that our position is that meaning, or language content, plays a primary role in language acquisition. It is to a consideration of content that we turn next.

THE DEVELOPMENT OF LANGUAGE CONTENT (SEMANTICS)

According to Olson (1970), semantics involves the "categories, meanings, meaning components, and dimensions that correspond to the recurrent features of the world. [It] is closely tied to the referents, the objects, and the events in the environment, and it reflects the needs of the language community" (p. 257). Until a child understands, at least in rudimentary form the nature of some of those objects and events in the environment, the child has no referents for a semantic system, "a system of meaning," and hence is incapable of learning language. MacNamara (1972) put it this way: "The infant uses meaning as a clue to language, rather than language as a clue to meaning. . . . Infants learn their language by first determining, independent of language, the meaning which a speaker intends to convey to them, and then working out the relationship between the meaning and the language" (p. 1). Meaning, according to MacNamara, refers to all that a person can express by means of a linguistic code. Sentences are names for the intentions which they express. Meanings may take the form of assertions, negations, commands, and questions. They may include aspects of a person's physical environment, feelings, or ideas. In order for a speaker to express an intent, he or she must have cognitively organized the communicative intent, whether that intent is related to the physical world or to some inner state. Similarly, in order for the hearer to comprehend the communication, he or she, too, must be knowledgeable about the intended referent. Semantic comprehension and production are based on cognition—the knowledge of the intended referent—not on the rules internal to language (Olson, 1970).

This point assumes great significance when one considers the nature of the semantic decisions to be made by a speaker. For purposes of illustration,

> A gold star is placed under a small, wooden block. A speaker who saw this act is then asked to tell a listener, who did not see the act, where the gold star is. In every case, the star is placed under the *same* block, a small, round, white . . . one. However, in the first case there is one alternative block present, a small, round, *black* one. In the second case there is a different alternative block present, a small, *square*, white . . . one. In a third case there are three alternative blocks present, a round black one, a square one, and a square white one. These three cases are shown in Figure 8–2.
>
> In these situations, the speaker would say the following for case 1: "It's under the *white* one"; for case 2: "It's under the *round* one"; for case 3: "It's under the *round, white* one" (p. 264).

Olson summarizes his conclusions as follows:

1. Words are not simple names for things. If this were the case, each speaker would utilize the same word(s) in referring to the same thing. This clearly was not the case in the situation above.

	Event	Alternative	Utterance
Case 1	○	●	. . . the white one
Case 2	○	□	. . . the round one
Case 3	○	□ ● ■	. . . the round, white one
Case 4	○		. . . (look under) the round, white, wooden block that is about 1 inch across . . .

Figure 8– 2. Relation of an Utterance to an Intended Referent

Adapted from D.R. Olsen, Language and thought: Aspects of a cognitive theory of semantics. *Psychological Review*, 1970, 77, 257–273. © 1970 by the American Psychological Association. Adapted by permission of the author and publisher.

2. Words do not name intended referents. In the example cited, the gold star is under the same block, which remains the intended referent. Yet in each case the utterances differ. "Words designate, signal, or specify an intended referent relative to the set of alternatives from which it must be differentiated" (Olson, p. 264). It is as if the speaker asks himself in this instance: "What alternatives could confuse or distract the listener; what do I need to mention so that this does not occur?" The speaker puts himself or herself into the place of the listener, anticipates the comprehension task of the listener, and designates a response in terms that will be unambiguous for the listener. This consideration of the listener is necessary for communication to occur. The fact that it does occur is clear from the Olson paradigm, where the speaker is not varying responses for personal benefit (after all, the speaker *knows* where the gold star is, since he saw it being placed there) but for the benefit of the listener.

3. A given utterance does not exhaust the potential features of the referent in question. Thus, in the example, any speaker could have designated the object as "wooden" or as "small" or as "inanimate," etc. Yet none did so. Rather, they utilized those aspects or features of the referent that served to distinguish it from the distractors. Consider Figure 8–3.

In each case, where the speaker is asked to identify an event (recognize a square), he or she does so by saying "This is a square." In case 2, however, while the speaker says only "This is a square," the relevant meaning of

	Utterance	Event	Alternative	Meaning
Case 1	This is a square	☐	—	Ambiguous
Case 2	This is a square	☐	△	Four-sided
Case 3	This is a square	☐	○	Straight-edged
Case 4	This is a square	☐	○ △ ☐	Straight-edged Four-sided Symmetric

Figure 8– 3.
Learning Word
Meaning as a
Function of Alter-
natives
Differentiated

Adapted from D.R. Olsen, Language and thought: Aspects of a cognitive theory of semantics. *Psychological Review*, 1970, 77, 257–273. © 1970 by the American Psychological Association. Adapted by permission of the author and publisher.

"square" is its four-sidedness (to distinguish it from the alternative, triangle).
In case 3, the meaning of "square" has to do with its straightedged characteristic, to distinguish it from the circle. Case 4 is an example of multiple meanings
being required to distinguish it from the circle, the triangle, and the rectangle.

We have gone to considerable length on this point because of the major
implications that an adequate view of semantics has for teaching children. A
common problem arises when a child is taught a label for an object such as
"book." The child may label it correctly as such in the instructional situation
but later fail to do so when he or she must distinguish the book from items
other than those used by the teacher. The occurrence of this problem underlines the fact that language usage must be taught in a variety of situations in
which the child is required to make a variety of distinctions. Furthermore,
from the earliest learning on, children need to become aware that referents do
not go by only one name and that they may be referred to in many different
ways, depending on what the listener is likely to be confused by. Learning the
name for an object is only the first step in semantic learning; the more interesting and more functional aspects to be learned come when the child uses
the label appropriately in an unfamiliar context; and further, when the child
learns to anticipate the problem faced by the listener and can modify the
description of the referent accordingly.

Nelson (1974), in reference to concept learning, makes much the same
point when she states that concept acquisition has to do with comprehending
the referent in a functional or relational way rather than through the specification of a set of critical attributes. Nelson makes the further significant point
that learning the meaning of a concept involves two distinct procedures. The
first of these, *concept generation*, entails distinguishing reliably the referent in
question in all settings and in all contexts. That is, a book is still a book,

whether it is on a shelf, on a desk, or in the teacher's hand. The second part of concept learning refers to applying the new concept label to as-yet-unidentified exemplars. Thus, having learned that a given item is appropriately referred to as "book," the child must learn to refer to other similar items as "books" also. Furthermore, the child must refrain from referring to noninstances of books, such as collections of loose paper, as books.

Here, again, the instructional implications are apparent. A concept is not learned (i.e., its meaning in the child's mind is not fully established) until both requirements of concept learning have been met. The child must be able to discriminate the referent in question correctly in many settings and with respect to many different alternatives. Second, the child must be given experience in applying the label for the concept to other potential instances. Many games can be devised in the classroom for both these purposes.

A question that arises at this point is: What concepts or words should be taught first to the child? The question is of more than passing interest, especially when one considers the difficulty that children encounter in laboratory-type studies of acquiring such simple static concepts as those of shape or colors. Again, it is instructive to turn to observations of children's early words acquired in naturalistic settings. Nelson (1974) has made some interesting observations about children's early words. First, the words selected by the child for first utterances tend to be words that move and change. The principle the child seems to be using in selecting words from an environment that is complex and dymanic and in which the concept domain is unlimited and undefined is: *those things are similar that can be acted upon in the same way.* The concepts selected by the child are defined in terms of logical relationships rather than in terms of common elements. Rarely, if ever, does a child select as his or her first word such unvarying, static concepts as "circle," which are the favorites of curriculum developers, especially those inclined to a programming approach. The child seems to go out of the way to select dynamic, changeable events that have to do with categories of agent, object, causation, time, and space.

When does the first word appear? Because of the frequently encountered difficulty in determining the precise break between babbling behavior and the emergence of the first "true" word, we suggest following Nelson's (1973) procedure of using attainment of ten vocabulary items as definitive evidence of the beginnings of productive language, rather than looking for just the first word. The most frequently cited range for such beginnings is from 10 to 13 months of age. The typical rapidity of vocabulary growth from that point on is remarkable. McCarthy (1954) has summarized a large number of studies of vocabulary acquisition. Her data show that vocabulary growth is almost exponential, with the typical child having approximately 20 words at 15 months of age, close to 300 words at age 2, almost 1000 words at age 3, and about 3000 words by the time he or she enters school as age 6.

The number of traditional-type vocabulary studies being conducted has declined recently. It has become apparent that merely noting the presence of a word in a child's vocabulary does not tell enough about the meaning of the word to the child. Second, words are not equal in terms of what they signify for the child's language development. For example, the child who adds the words "sixty-four" and "sixty-five" to his or her vocabulary when learning to count to 100 is adding a linguistic capability that is fundamentally different in nature from the child who is adding to his or her active vocabulary the words "before" and "after." Yet, in studies that count vocabulary items, each new word counts the same as any other new word. Third, vocabulary studies in and of themselves do not provide a representative indication of the child's proficiency in semantics, since they do not address the crucial question of how word meanings are combined into sentence meanings. After all, children beyond the age of two rarely rely to any extent on one-word sentences.

Nelson (1973) has made some additional observations about children's first words. Based on an analysis of the first fifty words used by each of eighteen children, Nelson found that the most common category (accounting for about half of the different words) used by children at this age were the general nominals (e.g., ball, doggie, snow). The next most common group were the special nominals, such as Mommy or the name of a stuffed toy. Next, accounting for somewhat over 10 percent of the different words used was a category of action words, such as bye-bye, give, or come. Less common were groups of modifiers (red, outside), and personal-social words (yes, no, please). While this breakdown reflected the distribution of different words used, some of the categories are used with great frequency, for example, some words, such as bye-bye, are used repeatedly in conjunction with general and specific nominals. Of particular interest was Nelson's finding that among the nominals representing items of clothing, children select for their usage at this age only such items that they themselves can act upon (e.g., shoes, socks). Notably absent from the children's utterances were references to such items as diaper, sweater, mittens.

In a somewhat different type of analysis, Clark (1973) has reanalyzed a number of diary studies from the point of looking at the child's overextensions or overgeneralizations. Clark interpreted her findings to conclude that children overextend words frequently on the basis of such perceptual attributes of features such as shape, size, sound, movement, taste, and texture. Overextensions based on color were not found. Clark's work with its emphasis on perceptual attributes, stands in contrast to the work of Nelson (cited earlier), with its emphasis on the functions of concepts acquired by children. It is possible that different children rely on different aspects of meaning in deriving and applying conceptual learning, a fact that if true would once again exemplify the idiosyncratic nature of language development.

Bloom (1970) has given a number of examples of children using different meanings in what appear to be identical utterances. For example, the use of the utterance "Mommy sock" was found to occur in two distinct contexts: in one, to denote a genitive relationship (the sock belongs to Mommy), and in another, to show the relationship between subject and object (Mommy is putting a sock on me). Early utterances are apparently motivated by their semantic function.

Similarly, the word "no," frequently used by children, may mean, depending on context:

Negation:	"No night-night" (I don't want to go to bed.)
Rejection:	"No milk" (I don't want milk.)
Denial:	"No Teddy" (That's not a Teddy Bear.)
Lack of occurrence:	"No blanket" (No blanket in the child's bed; the child had expected to see it there.)

An additional example, from Brown (1973), shows that children use the same verb form, bare and uninflected, to mean at least four different things; for example, a child's utterance "Car go" could mean:

The name of the current action or state	(The car is going.)
A reference to the immediate past	(We went for a ride in the car.)
A statement of wish or intent	(I would like to ride in the car.)
Imperative	(Car go!)

Again, an analysis of the child's meaning is necessary to determine what language instruction the child can benefit from. The child who says "Car go" to refer to the current action of the car is ready to be instructed in "The car is going," and so forth. *A prime teaching opportunity lies in the apparent lag between a child's communicative intent and the ability to manifest that intent in an appropriate form.*

To help teachers determine the meanings of a child's utterances, we cite the following suggestions from Antinucci and Parisi (1973):

1. Observe carefully and in detail the extralinguistic context in which the child's sentences and lexical items occur. (What is the child doing when he says what he does? What is he paying attention to?)
2. Carefully observe the child's intentions.
3. Observe how the child understands sentences said to him.
4. Observe how the child combines one lexical item with another.

Dale (1976) has summarized a considerable amount of research dealing with children's acquisition of labels for a number of concepts. Such concepts include "more" and "less"; the dimensions of "big," "little," "long," "short," and "thick"; "before" and "after"; verbs and the expression of causation, e.g., "drop"; verbs of possession and transfer, e.g., "give"; color naming words;

"left" and "right"; "I" and "you"; and words for expressing concepts of expectations. He concludes that there is no single framework that covers all patterns of development of these concepts with all children: semantic development appears to be as varied as the concepts that language encodes.

THE ACQUISITION OF LINGUISTIC FORM

To this point, we have considered the cognitive and semantic underpinnings of all language development. While one can argue that all aspects of language derive ultimately from a communicative intent (either receptive or expressive) that is cognitive in nature, one can, for analytical purposes, deal separately with its formal, structured aspects. Accordingly, we direct our attention to that aspect of language that has to do with the arrangement of words into meaningful sequence—syntax. We also include a brief section on morphology, which deals with the smallest meaningful grammatical units of language, and a section on phonology, which deals with the development of speech sounds.

Syntax

During the 1960s the normal acquisition of syntactic structure was widely researched and commented on (e.g., Chomsky, 1957; McNeill, 1966, 1970; Menyuk, 1969). In addition, researchers studied extensively and longitudinally the development of sentences in three groups of children at Harvard, Berkeley, and Johns Hopkins universities. Much of what is known about the emergence of syntactic structures in normal development grew out of these studies.

At about 13–24 months of age, the child first begins to use two-word sentences. The emergence of sentences, as opposed to two-word utterances, marks the child's beginning attempts to use rules to combine linguistic units (syntax). Contrary to earlier speculation, research in the last decade has indicated that these first sentences are neither memorized imitations of adult speech nor random sequences of words. Three independent investigations of this stage of language development (Braine, 1963; Brown and Bellugi, 1964; Ervin, 1964) all concluded that the first attempts at sentence production are orderly and rule-governed, as opposed to random. This is evidenced by the consistency with which children manifest the type of word combinations they use. Although there is variation from one child to the next, each individual child employs particular rules. Typical utterances of a child as this stage of development might be the following:

more horsey	Bunny allgone
more sing	truck allgone
more milk	milk allgone

While the first interpretations of these data led to the conclusions that the child utilizes a formal grammatical structure that became known as a "pivot-open" grammar, more recent interpretations have deemphasized the formal syntax presumably employed by the child when he or she says "more horsey." Instead, a number of investigators have attempted to show that the child utilizes a number of distinct semantic relationships to characterize these early two- and three-word utterances. Table 8–1 is adapted from Brown (1970) and summarizes the most common relationships. In addition to these common semantic relations, observation of young children also reveals use of Action–Indirect Object (give Claudia), Instrumentals (key open), Conjunction (foots flower).

By age three, the normal child's utterances show mastery of the basic relationships among subject, predicate, and object (Menyuk, 1969). Menyuk also found that the early two-word utterances (see Table 8–1) give way to more differentiated and more complex sentences. By age 3, the typical child has developed a number of sentence types in the following order:

1. Joining of elements to make sentences.
2. Development of subject + predicate sentences.
3. Expansion of the verb phrase to include an auxiliary verb and copula.
4. Embedding of an element within a sentence and attachment of the element to the verb.
5. Permutation of elements within a string (auxiliary/modal and tense markers).

Table 8–1.   Semantic Relations in Two-Word Sentences

Semantic Relation	Form	Example
1. Nomination	that + N	that book
2. Notice	hi + N	hi belt
3. Recurrence	more + N, 'nother + N	more milk
4. Nonexistence	allgone + N, no more + N	allgone rattle
5. Attributive	Adj + N	big train
6. Possessive	N + N	mommy lunch
7. Locative	N + N	sweater chair
8. Locative	V + N	walk street
9. Agent-Action	N + V	Eve read
10. Agent-Object	N + N	mommy sock
11. Action-Object	V + N	put book

Source: Adapted from R. Brown, *Psycholinguistics* (New York: Free Press, 1970), p. 220.

Most researchers have found that sentence complexity and sentence differentiation correlates rather well with the mean length of the child's utterance (MLU). One major problem in the use of the MLU has been that each researcher used his or her own definition of what constitutes an utterance. Consequently, it was not possible to compare the results of one study with that of another. Recently, however, most researchers have begun to utilize the procedures for defining MLU that were developed by R. Brown (1973). Because of the potential usefulness of a single index of language development that correlates well with most aspects of language, we are including it here as Table 8–2.

A major contribution to our knowledge of the development of semantic–syntactic usage in young children comes from the work of L. Bloom, Lightbown, and Hood (1975). These authors studied the language development of four children during the period in which their MLUs ranged from 1.0 to ap-

Table 8– 2. Rules for Calculating Mean Length of Utterance (MLU)

The following rules are reasonable for MLU up to about 4.0; by this time many of the assumptions underlying the rules are no longer valid.

1. Start with the second page of the transcription unless that page involves a recitation of some kind. In this latter case start with the first recitation-free stretch. Count the first 100 utterances satisfying the following rules. (A 50-utterance sample may be used for preliminary estimate.)
2. Only fully transcribed utterances are used. Portions of utterances, entered in parentheses to indicate doubtful transcription, are used.
3. Include all exact utterance repetitions (marked with a plus sign in records). Stuttering is marked as repeated efforts at a single word; count the word once in the most complete form produced. In the few instances in which a word is produced for emphasis or the like ("no, no, no") count each occurrence.
4. Do not count such fillers as "um" and "oh," but do count "no," "yeah," and "hi."
5. All compound words (two or more free morphemes), proper names, and ritualized reduplications count as single morphemes. Examples: "birthday," "rackety-boom," "choo-choo," "quack-quack," "night-night," "pocketbook," "see-saw."
6. Count as one morpheme all irregular pasts of the verb ("got," "did," "want," "saw"). Justification is that there is no evidence that the child relates these to present forms.
7. Count as one morpheme all diminutives ("doggie," "mommy") because these children at least do not seem to use the suffix productively. Diminutives are the standard forms used by the child.
8. Count as separate morphemes all auxiliaries ("is," "have," "will," "can," "must," "would"). Also all catenatives: "gonna," "wanna," "hafta." The latter are counted as single morphemes rather than "going to" or "want to" because the evidence is that they function so for children. Count as separate morphemes all inflections, for example, possessive "s," plural "s," third person singular "s," regular past tense "d," progressive "ing."

Source: Adapted from Table 7 of R. Brown, *A First Language: The Early Stages* (Cambridge, Mass.: Harvard University Press, 1973), p. 54. © 1973 by the President and Fellows of Harvard College.

Table 8–3. Sequence of Semantic–Syntactic Relations Emerging from MLU = 1.0 to MLU = 2.5

Type of Relation	Child's Utterance	Context
Functional relations		
Existence	there a birdie	Child picking up toy bird
Nonexistence	no more car	Child putting toy car away
Recurrence	another block	Child giving additional block
Verb relations		
Action		
Action	Gia writing	Child scribbling on paper
Locative	choo-choo fall down	Child pushing toy train down
State		
State	want more apple	Child finishes apple, whines
Notice	I see another man	Child looking out window
Locative	people on street	Child looking out window
Possession	it's mine clay	Experimenter reaches for clay child has been playing with
Attribution	red truck	Child picking up truck
Instrumentality	I write the pencil	Child holding pencil up
Dative	show you	In response to mother asking where child's sister is
Wh- questions	what engine go	Child holding up puzzle piece

Source: Adapted from L. Bloom, P. Lightbown, and L. Hood, Structure and variation in child language, *Monograph of the Society for Research in Child Development,* 1975, *40* (No. 2, Serial No. 60).

proximately 2.5. They found that verb relations were of central importance in the children's syntactical learning and that it was possible to establish a developmental sequence for a number of these categories. See Table 8–3 for a summary, in approximate developmental order, of these observed relations.

Of great instructional significance was the further finding of Bloom et al. that children vary systematically in their strategies for syntactic learning. Some children apparently search for constancies in the expression of relationships involving the semantic notions encoded by particular words. For example, they seem to base their relational learning on rules involving distributional frequency—thus the child produces many utterances, such as "allgone milk," "allgone horsey," "allgone cookie." The child has the idea that words such as "allgone" can be combined with a number of other pronominal forms. L. Bloom (1970) called this the "pivot" strategy, after some earlier work by Braine (1963) in which he postulated that syntactical rule learning initially takes the form of combining two crude types of form classes—"pivot" and "open" classes.

Other children seem to adopt a strategy of "categorical" learning, in which they appear to formulate rules that specify how to position words performing relational functions, such as Agent–Action, Modifier–Modified, Possessor–Possessed, etc. At the present time there appears to be no way other than observation to establish which children utilize one strategy and which utilize another. Bowerman (1976) has suggested that in teaching, the teacher should group children on the basis of their preferred strategy and vary teaching style and content accordingly. A child who failed to make progress in one group would be switched to another where there might be a better match with his cognitive style.

Morphology

An aspect of language form not considered to this point is that of morphology. Morphemes are the smallest meaningful aspect of language. There are two types of morphemes—bound and free. Free morphemes are units that stand alone, for example, run, book, particular. Bound morphemes are always attached to other units; in English, they serve as prefixes and suffixes (e.g., -ed, -er, pre-, and un-). The order of acquisition of bound morphemes, or inflections as they are frequently called, has been studied by de Villiers and de Villiers (1973), Brown (1973) and by MacWhinney (1978). Their findings correspond closely in the sequence of normal development. A summary of Brown's report, with examples, is presented in Table 8–4.

Two cautions with respect to morphology are worth mentioning. The first of these is that children exhibit considerable inconsistency in their use. It is not uncommon, for example, for children to vacillate between "comed" and "came," or among "bringed," "brang," "branged," and "brought." R. Brown (1973) suggests that 90 percent correct usage be considered the criterion for mastery.

Another caution concerns the fact that inflectional usage varies enormously from one dialect of English to another. Particularly, in children using what has become known as "black English," the teacher is likely to see evidence of a different set of rules governing morphemes. Following are a number of inflectional differences between standard English usage and black English usage (adapted from Bartel, Grill, and Bryen, 1973):

Feature	Standard English	Black English
Past tense		
Omission of final "ed"	passed, loaned	pass, loan
Future tense		
Omission of final "l"	you'll, he'll	you, he

Table 8–4. Aquisition of Grammatical Morphemes

Morpheme	Example	Meaning
Present progressive	"coming" in "Daddy is coming"	Current occurrence
Preposition "on"	"on" in "Blanket on bed"	On top of, and supported by
Preposition "in"	"in" in "In the toybox"	Containment
Past irregular	"went" in "We went away"	Prior occurrence
Possessive	" 's" in "Mommy's hat"	Possession
Uncontractible copula	"was" in "He was"	Prior occurrence
Articles "the," "a"	"the" in "the house" "a" in "a dog"	Specific determination Nonspecific determination
Past regular	"played" in "played ball"	Prior occurrence
Third-person singular (regular)	"comes" in "Daddy comes"	Number, prior occurrence
Third-person singular (irregular)	"has" in "Mommy has candy"	Number, prior occurrence
Uncontractible auxiliary	"were" in "They were coming"	Number, prior occurrence
Contractible copula	"She is" or "She's" in "She is big"	Number, prior occurrence
Contractible auxiliary	"He is" or "He's" in "He is playing"	Number, prior occurrence

Feature	Standard English	Black English
Present tense		
Omission of final sound	I'm, it's	I, it
Possessive		
Deletion of final "s"	Harry's cousin	Harry cousin
Plural		
Deletion of final "s"	50 cents, 3 birds	50 cent, 3 bird
Third-person singular		
Deletion of final "s"	she works here	she work here

Clearly, when a teacher is attempting to establish whether or not a child has mastered a given morphological form, account needs to be taken of whether the child's dialect requires the use of the particular form. The situation is also the case with other syntactic structures. As a guide for helping the teacher know which the most common dialectal syntactical differences in black English, the following are presented (adapted once again from Bartel, Grill, and Bryen, 1973):

Feature	Standard English	Black English
Linking verb	He is going.	He goin' or he goin?
Subject expression	John lives in N.Y.	John, he live in N.Y.
Verb form	I drank the milk.	I drunk the milk.
Verb agreement	He runs home.	He run home or He be running home.
Future form	I will go home.	I'ma go home.
"If" construction	I asked if he did it.	I asked did he do it.
Negation	I don't have any.	I don't got none.
Indefinite article	I want an apple.	I want a apple.
Pronoun form	We have to do it.	Us got to do it.
Preposition	He is over at his friend's house.	He over to his friend house.
Copula ("be")	He is here all the time. No, he isn't.	He be here. No, he don't.

A number of researchers have attempted to establish whether language development in handicapped children is similar in nature and sequence to that of "normal" children. At the present time, the evidence is mixed, with some investigators concluding that the course of development is essentially similar, if somewhat slowed down (e.g., Bartel, 1970; Lackner, 1976; Lenneberg, Nichols, and Rosenberger, 1964), and others (Lee, 1966; Menyuk, 1964; Wiig and Semel, 1976; Wiig and Semel, 1980) reporting dissimilar development. In an attempt to resolve the issue, Morehead and Ingram (1973) made comparisons between groups of normal and linguistically deviant children where they were matched on the basis of mean length of utterance, rather than IQ or mental age. Their findings were that despite similar linguistic systems, the linguistically deficient group were less efficient in the way they used the system. For example, they would add new words to a basic acquired construction, rather than developing new and more complex combinations. This finding is of interest for it indicates that flexibility and creativity in language usage may need to be given specific and focused attention. How such flexibility and creativity develop in the natural environment of the preschoolers' homes is the question to which we turn next.

There are specific environmental variables that apparently play a major role in rapid language aquisition; several of these have been explored by Brown and Bellugi (1964). Based upon extensive observations and recordings of mother–child interactions in the home, these researchers identified the factors of imitation and reduction, imitation with expansion, and induction of the latent structure as contributing to language mastery. Imitation and reduction refer to the fact that a great many of the early utterances of children appear to be reductions of adult speech, or "telegraphic" speech," as it has been called. Thus, when the child says "See truck," it seems reasonable that this expression is patterned on something an adult might have said, e.g., "Yes, I see the truck," or "Do you see the truck?" An analysis of these expressions led Brown and Bellugi to conclude that the child's expressions systematically retained the high-information words (usually nouns and verbs), the words that are stressed in the model sentence, and the content words, as opposed to the function words. All of this shows that the child is indeed imitating the adult model, but is imitating in a highly selective and systematic manner.

When the child uses an expression such as "There Daddy," the mother typically responds with a full sentence that both reinforces and corrects the child: "Yes, there goes Daddy," or some other appropriate utterance. The cumulative effects of hundred of bits of such feedback, day after day, may have a major impact on the efficacy of language learning.

Brown and Bellugi also found that a large number of child utterances could not readily be seen as reductions of adult sentences (e.g., "a my pencil," or "allgone lettuce"). It is highly unlikely that a child heard a sentence from which he could deduce utterances such as these. The child must be using a rule deduced from hearing adults talk, and he or she seems to be trying the rule out. Naturally, in practicing this rule the child finds that it generates some utterances that are unacceptable. Hence, the rules must constantly be revised to incorporate new input from the linguistic environment.

In the next section, we consider the speech sound system (phonology) which provides the medium through which the child's utterances occur, and which ultimately becomes a fully developed communicative mode.

Phonology

Phonemes are significant units of speech sounds: the word "significant" is used to indicate that a difference in meaning results when one phoneme is substituted for another. Thus, in English, /b/ and /p/ are phonemes because a substitution of /b/ for /p/, or vice versa, in a word such as "big" or "pig" results in a change in meaning. Phonemes may be vowels or consonants; they may be simple, /t/ or /h/, or they may be compound, /th/ or /au/. The written equivalent for a phoneme is a grapheme. The grapheme equivalent for the speech sound /k/ is either the letter "c" or "k." This example shows that the phoneme–grapheme correspondence in English is by no means perfect. Sometimes two or more graphemes represent only one phoneme, as when the letters "s" and "soft c" both have the phoneme equivalent /s/. Conversely, every teacher who has ever tried to teach phonics to a first- or second-grader knows that the letter "a" has several phonemic variations, as in c*a*t, *a*lways, *a*lone, br*a*vo, or s*a*id. The lack of a one-to-one correspondence in English orthography has been much lamented; several attempts have been made to overcome the problems it presents for beginning readers by using a modified phonemic–graphemic system, e.g., the International Teaching Alphabet (Mazurkiewicz, 1968). While the English spelling system is popularly believed to be an assortment of haphazard graphemic sequences, a recent book by Chomsky and Halle (1968) shows that most English spellings are highly rule-governed and constitute orderly derivations from root words.

A phoneme in any given language is not a specific, unique speech sound that is consistently used by all speakers of that language. In fact, the same speaker does not produce identical sounds when producing the /p/ as in p/utt as opposed to the /p/ in ha/pp/ily or in /p/it. Phonemes are really ranges of sounds; different speakers produce phonemes that are acoustically quite different from each other even when each is saying the same word. This phenomenon is most apparent when spoken speech is represented graphically on a spectrogram. The spectrogram is a visual, two-dimensional representation of acoustic cues, not entirely dissimilar to an electroencephalogram, with bands of varying frequencies and intensities portrayed on a screen or recorded on a graph. The spectrogram shows that the configurations produced by an individual's speech are highly individualistic, as unique as a person's fingerprint.

Phonemes are usually described in terms of binary features (Jakobsen and Halle, 1956). Binary features are polar opposites; if a phoneme is a vowel, for example, it cannot act as a consonant. In addition to the *vowel–consonant* pair, phonemes may also be *nasal–oral*, with nasal phonemes having their primary resonance in the nasal, as opposed to the oral, cavities. This feature is not as distinctive in English as in some languages; only the /n/, /m/, and /ng/ sounds are nasal, while all others are oral. The *voiced–unvoiced* pair describes whether a given phoneme is produced with a voiced component or not. Phonemes that are identical except in one respect (minimal pairs)—in this case voiced versus unvoiced—are /v/ and /f/, /b/ and /p/, /d/ and /t/, /g/ and /k/, /w/ and /wh/, and /th/ as in /th/at compared with /th/ as in /th/ink. The voiced–unvoiced distinction is an important one in the English language.

Consonants can be further described by noting the anatomical place of articulation. Consonants, as opposed to vowels, are produced by some part of the speech-producing anatomy (e.g., lips, tongue, teeth) that produces interference with the flow of air from the windpipe. For example, to create the /f/ sound, air is expelled without obstruction until it gets to the lip and teeth area. Here it meets upper teeth planted on lower lips. Forcing the air out through lips and teeth in this arrangement produces the characteristic /f/ sound. The point of articulation of most consonants can be determined by careful observation in front of a mirror.

The maximal utilization of all the discussions possible from the binary features would result in a very large number of possible phonemes. Yet no existing language employs as many as sixty, or fewer than twenty-five, phonemes.

Although there has been some evidence of prenatal vocalization, the birth cry is considered to be the first speech uttered by the infant. The birth cry has no language meaning because it is merely an automatic physiological reaction. However, it can be considered as the beginning of speech and language development for the child.

During the first two or three weeks of life, the child's cries have no real significance because he simply is responding to stimuli, a reflexive act. Between two and five weeks he is still acting reflexively, but his cries are more directly related to the stimulus. The child's cries at this time become differentiated by varying in loudness and quality. Other sounds he produces are grunts and yawns and those connected with coughing and sneezing. These verbalizations are probably related to the breathing process.

By the third and fourth weeks the infant can focus his eyes quite well and responds to the attention and voices of the adults by smiling. At this stage the child begins to use vowel sounds.

During the babbling stage (two to eight months or more) the child continues to be aware of the sounds he produces. He derives pleasure from babbling and, in turn, continues to babble. New vowel sounds are mastered and improve in articulation. Early consonant sounds are /p/, /b/, /m/, and /h/. By the time the child reaches his sixth month of life, he has used all the vowel sounds and some consonant sounds. Some observers feel that by this age the child has become proficient in the use of his sounds in influencing adults. He continues to derive satisfaction from reactions of adults to his speech sounds and smiles and laughs readily.

The child's babbling does not stop after six months but continues with a greater awareness of the speech sounds and of the people in his environment. He begins to imitate the speech sounds and other vocalizations of his companion adults.

By the end of the child's first year of life, the number of consonant sounds he produces is beginning to grow. He is learning rapidly through the attention and interaction he has with adults. The imitations that the child attempts derive from his ability to produce sounds that he hears and to respond to sounds. It is obvious that the mother who speaks frequently to the child will receive more and varied responses than the mother who does not speak frequently.

Between two and three years of age, the child begins to utilize teeth in speech production. He is better able to articulate words, and speech sounds; the /th/ and the nasal /n/ are easier to say and understand. Since he is growing rapidly, he can maintain better control over the movement of his body, including his tongue and lips. His environment is continuing to broaden and the sounds he produces become more and more differentiated until adult phonological competence is reached. Table 8–5 from Ingram (1976) relates phonological development to the child's parallel cognitive development.

In addition to the phonemes that are used in producing speech, phonology also takes into account the variations in intonation and stress and the pauses that occur in spoken language. Each of these may contribute to the meaning of the sentence and help convey the intent of the speaker. Thus the intonation in "I am going too!" is different from that in "I am going too?" The different

Table 8– 5. A Comparison of Piaget's Stages of Cognitive Development with Six Major Stages of Phonological Development

Piaget's Stages	Phonological Stages
Sensorimotor period (birth–1:6) The child develops his sense and motor ability; he actively explores his environment until the achievement of the notion of object performance.	1. Preverbal vocalization and perception (birth–1:0) 2. Phonology of first 50 words (1:0–1:6) Child gradually acquires his first words.
Period of concrete operations (1:6–12:0) Preconcept subperiod (1:6–4:0) The onset of symbolic representation. The child can use a system of social signs to refer to the past and future, although he primarily lives in the here and now.	3. Phonology of simple morphemes (1:6–4:0) Vocabulary increases rapidly as child develops a variety of phonological processes to simplify speech. Most words consist of simple morphemes.
Intuitional subperiod (4:0–7:0) The child's play begins to mirror reality rather than change it to the child's own structures. Child begins to solve tasks such as the conservation of liquids by use of perception.	4. Completion of phonetic inventory (4:0–7:0) Most speech sounds are acquired by the end of this period. Simple words are by and large pronounced correctly. First appearance of more complex words which are poorly pronounced.
Subperiod of concrete operations (7:0–12:0) The ability to solve tasks of conservation is developed as the child can now perform reversible operations. He no longer needs to rely on perception.	5. Morphophonemic development (7:0–12:0) The more complex derivational morphology of language is acquired. Rules such as Vowel Shift become productive.
Period of Formal Operations (12:0–16:0) Appearance of the ability to reflect abstractly. Child can now solve problems through reflection.	6. Acquisition of spelling Child develops the ability to spell the complex words of the language. Development of linguistic intuitions.

communicative intents of these sentences is conveyed by intonation. Similarly, the meaning of the two sentences "*He* did his math problems" is different from "He did his *math* problems" depending on which word in the sentence is stressed. Furthermore, pauses help distinguish meaning in ambiguous sentences such as "They are // flying planes" and "They // are flying planes."

The evidence is that caretakers of children who are developing language often use exaggerated stress, pauses, and intonation to facilitate language acquisition (de Villiers and de Villiers, 1978). Children at very young ages use these suprasegmental features to add emphasis and urgency to their speech—as every teacher or caretaker responding to a child's shriek, cry, or whine can attest.

THE DEVELOPMENT OF LANGUAGE USE (FUNCTION AND CONTEXT)

There has been a recent sensitizing of language researchers and practitioners to the fact the people—adults and children—talk for a reason. That is, there is a social basis for language that is as important as the cognitive and the linguistic bases of language. People talk not just because they have an idea about the world and not just because they know how to articulate that idea in phonological and syntactic form. They talk because they want to get that idea across to someone else. There are two major aspects of language use (L. Bloom and Lahey, 1978). The first of these pertains to the function or purpose of the communication. This is also called "pragmatics."

Several recent researchers (Curtiss, Prutting, and Lowell, 1979; Dale, 1980; Greenfield and Smith, 1976; Halliday, 1975) have shown that the development of communicative competence with respect to language function develops separately from mastery of language form and content. That is, a child may be able to formulate language content, but lack the ability to use language socially (Blank, Gessner, and Esposito, 1979).

There are indications that the pragmatic aspects of language use develop in a predictable order. This sequence of development has been summarized by Prutting (1979) and is included as Table 8–6. We have also included a brief description of the various pragmatic categories (adapted from Curtiss et al., 1979) in Table 8–7.

How do children learn these aspects of language use? There is increasing evidence that caretakers have a controlling role in "teaching" children what is appropriate in terms of such conventions as how to start a conversation, how to make appropriate responses, how to sustain and end discourse (Martlew, 1980; see also previous section on Bruner's analysis of regulating joint action

Table 8–6. Summary of Stages for Acquisition of Pragmatics

Prelinguistic (Birth–9 Mo.)	Stage I (9–18 Mo.)	Stage II (18–24 Mo.)	Stage III (2–3 Yrs.)	Stage IV (3+ Yrs.)	Stage V (Communicative Competence-Adult)
Perlocutionary Acts gazing, crying, touching, smiling, vocalizations, grasping, sucking, laughing (Bates, 1975) Illocutionary Acts nonverbal and speechlike giving, pointing, showing (Bates, 1975)	Functions instrumental regulatory interactional personal heuristic imaginative informative (Halliday, 1975) Intentions label response request greeting protesting repeating	Functions pragmatic mathetic interpersonal textual ideational (Halliday, 1975)	Responds to contingent queries, types of revisions function of linguistic development (Gallagher, 1977) Rapid topic change (Keenan and Schieffelin, 1976)	Sustains topic (Bloom, Rocissano and Hood, 1976) Systematic changes in speech depending on listener (Schatz and Gelman, 1973; Gleason, 1973; Sachs and Devin, 1976) Indirectives and hints (Ervin-Tripp and Mitchell-Kernan, 1977)	Knowledge of who can say what, in what way, where and when, by what means, and to whom (Hymes, 1971) Behavior speakers and listeners attend to: Quality: informative but not too informative Quality: contribution should be true

Table 8–6. *Continued*

Prelinguistic (Birth–9 Mo.)	*Stage I (9–18 Mo.)*	*Stage II (18–24 Mo.)*	*Stage III (2–3 Yrs.)*	*Stage IV (3 + Yrs.)*	*Stage V (Communicative Competence-Adult)*
Turn-taking (Bruner, 1975)	description attention (Dore, 1974) Verbal Turn-taking procedures employed, (Bloom, Rocissano and Hood, 1976) New Information coded first (Greenfield and Smith, 1976)			Productive use of contingent queries to maintain the conversation (Garvey, 1975) Role-playing, ability to temporarily assume another's perspective (Anderson, 1977) Metalinguistic awareness, ability to think about language and comment on it (Gleitman, Gleitman, and Shipley, 1972; de Villiers and de Villiers, 1974)	Relation: be relevant Manner: avoid obscurity, ambiguity, be brief and orderly (Grice, 1975)

NOTE: Plus or minus six months for all age ranges reported is considered normal.

Source: Prutting, C. A. The action of moving forward progressively from one point to another on the way to completion. *Journal of Speech and Hearing Disorders, 44,* 1979, 3–30. The appendix consists of a summary of stages for acquisition of pragmatics, semantics, syntax, and phonology.

Table 8–7. Description of Pragmatic Categories

Pragmatic Categories	Operational Definition
Demand	—A request for an action or an object ("I want glue" "More juice")
Command	—An imperative ("Look at me," "Come here")
Question	—A request for information or elaboration ("Who?" "What?" "Huh?")
Labeling	—Identification of a person, object, or action ("That's a chair," "Here's José")
Response to a question	—An act directly following a question posed to the child (head shake, change of topic, an answer to the question)
Response to a summons	—An act directly following a summons for the child's attention (head turn, eye contact)
Response to a command	—An act directly following an imperative or request issued to the child (child follows directions, child changes topics)
Imitation	—An imitation of an act or utterance performed by someone else
Repetition	—An imitation of a child's own act or utterance
Summons	—A request/demand for attention (a wave, tap on the arm, calling out someone's name)
Description	—An act describing an event, a person, or an object ("He's tall," "It fell down")
Protesting	—An act expressing resistance ("No," vehement head shake, physical resistance)
Ritual	—A greeting or other social ritual ("Hi," "Bye-bye")
Request for approval	—An act requesting approval from another person ("Is it OK for me to do this?" "Was that all right?")
Request for confirmation or acknowledgment	—An act requesting another to confirm or acknowledge the child's behavior ("Do you understand?" "Did you hear me?")
Acknowledgment	—An act evidencing comprehension of a situation, event, or message

Source: Curtiss, S., Prutting, C. A., and Lowell, E. L. Pragmatic and semantic development in young children with impaired hearing. *Journal of Speech and Hearing Research*, 1979. 22, 534–552.

between mother and child). Even such commonplace caretaker behavior as holding up an infant to wave bye-bye constitutes a teaching of the child on how to appropriately end a social interchange.

The second aspect of language use is the context in which it occurs. Context has both a general and a specific focus. In general, children learn at early ages that they speak differently when there is company in the house, when they are in church, or when they are shopping with their parents. Both content and form are affected by the general features of context.

More specifically, the immediate context for a speaker is the listener, who is a major influence on the speaker's selection of context and form. Children and adults alike learn that there are some things that one simply does not say to some people. Failure to learn the implications of the nature of the listener can have consequences for the speaker.

Full communicative competence means that speakers perform a rather sophisticated analysis of their context before they speak. This analysis takes into account such questions as "What is the age of the listener" (we speak differently to adults than we do to children); "What does the listener know about this topic?" (we may go into more detail when we believe the listener is uninformed); "What action do I want the listener to take as a result of this communication?"; "What do I want the listener to think of me as a result of this communication?" (we may need to decide if it matters to us, and if so, how).

So well learned are our pragmatic skills in discerning contexts that we take the skill for granted. We tend to become aware of this fact only in its demonstrated absence (i.e., when the speaker fails to consider that the listener had already heard that joke twice before).

Interestingly enough, there is evidence that even young children are able to intentionally vary their language based on their appraisal of the listener. For example, Shatz and Gilman (1973) found that children as young as four years of age varied their language on the basis of age of the listener (two-year-olds, four-year-olds, adults) and on the basis of the younger children's physical size, cognitive and linguistic development, and attention span.

SCOPE AND SEQUENCE OF LANGUAGE DEVELOPMENT

To help the teacher relate the various aspects of language development, we have adapted a type of scope-and-sequence chart (Table 8–8) based on the work of Fokes (1971). This chart can be used both for assessment and intervention purposes. For example, the teacher who is working with a child who is developmentally between two and three years of age can see that such a child ordinarily has a vocabulary of about 250 words (see "Meaning" column in Table 8–8). At the same time, the child will in most cases have mastered about two thirds of the adult speech sounds (see "Sound Making" column). During this period, the child's mean length of utterance (Table 8–2) will in most cases be developing from two words to three-and-a-half words, and some inflections and transformations will appear (see the "Grammar" column of Table 8–8). Having this information and more from Table 8–8, the teacher is able to establish whether the child in question is experiencing any major lags in the various aspects of language development. Further, more detailed probing can be undertaken through procedures described in the next section, "Language Assessment," where problems appear to exist.

Furthermore, once the child's level of functioning has been established, Table 8–8 can also be used as a guide to intervention. For example, to continue with the hypothetical case of a child who is developmentally about two years old and just beginning to use interrogative transformations (column "Grammar," part C.2), the teacher would first expect intonational questions such as "See doggie?" before attempting to teach the use of the interrogatives "who," "what," and "where." Table 8–8 can be used similarly for the assessment and remediation of other aspects of language functioning.

LANGUAGE ASSESSMENT

How does a teacher decide that a child needs to have a systematic language evaluation? The answer to this question is a relatively simple matter. We suggest that the teacher consider the following questions; and if he or she can answer any of them with a "yes," it is likely that further assessment is in order: Does language usage or lack of it call for unwanted attention to the speaker? Does the speaker appear to be concerned in any way about his or her inadequate communication ability? Are listeners unable to readily understand the child when he or she speaks?

Once it is decided that the child is in need of a comprehensive assessment, there are a variety of options available, including standardized testing, speech sample analysis, and diagnostic teaching. Various tests can be administered to verify the presence of a problem or to help qualify a child for a particular school program, although the results of these are usually insufficient for planning intervention programs. Samples of a child's speech can be recorded and analyzed according to a set of criteria; or the teacher may choose to engage in diagnostic teaching activities. Each of these options is described in some detail in the following parts of this section.

Before beginning that discussion, however, we want to make a few comments about language assessment in general. It is important that the teacher be aware of a number of dimensions that are pertinent to language assessment. These involve knowledge relating to the following questions. Does the assessment procedure:

1. Yield the kinds of data about the child's language that is desired (i.e., is it valid for the purposes being contemplated?)
2. Account for dialect?
3. Measure expressive and/or receptive abilities?
   a. If expressive, does the format utilize imitation, spontaneous, or elicited speech?

Table 8–8. Scope-and-Sequence Chart*

Characteristics of the Period	*Sound Making*

Birth to Six Weeks

A. Reflexive vocalization
  1. Sounds produced from a column of air expelled from lungs and passed through tensed vocal bands
  2. Primary purpose of speech mechanism for breathing and eating
  3. Undifferentiated vocalization—first three weeks
    a. No intent, awareness, meaning, or purpose
    b. Total bodily expression in response to stimulus
      (1) No distinguishable response to cold, hunger, pain, etc.
      (2) Variety in intensity
      (3) Total emotional response
  4. Differentiated vocalization—second three weeks
    a. Vocalization related to stimulus
    b. Muscle pattern sets for different cries

A. Grunts, sighs, gurgles, glottal catch
  1. Similar to swallowing movements
  2. Present in whimpering rather than in crying
B. No sex difference
C. Nasalization
D. Average of seven phonemelike sounds
  1. Monosyllabic cries
  2. Predominantly front vowellike sounds
    a. Average of 4.5 distinguishable sounds
    b. /ae/ most predominant sound
    c. Other sounds: /ɪ ɛ ʌ ʊ/
  3. Predominantly glottal and velar consonantlike sounds
    a. Average of 2.7 sounds
    b. Predominantly plosive and fricative /h/ sounds
    c. Other sounds: /k g h/

Six Weeks to Three Months

A. Beginning of babbling period
  1. Sounds made "for their own sake"
    a. Satisfaction from utterance
    b. Different from comfort sounds
    c. Play with sounds
  2. Spontaneous production of sounds
    a. Encompass more sounds than spoken by parents
    b. Indicate pleasurable mood
    c. Self-initiated vocal play
    d. Random production of sounds
      (1) /a/ produced at length
      (2) Most sounds not repeated
    e. Predominantly noncrying sounds
    f. Self-enjoyment from sound making
B. Sound making still essentially reflexive

A. Coos, gurgles, squeals, sighs of contentment
B. Monosyllabic utterances
  1. Combination of consonant- and vowel-like sounds
  2. Little repetition
  3. Nasalization of sounds
    a. Vowellike sounds—displeasure
    b. Consonantlike sounds—pleasure
C. Average of thirteen to fourteen different sound types

Three Months to Six Months

A. Continuation of the babbling period
  1. Associated with pleasure, contentment
  2. Autistic enjoyment
  3. Self-imitation
    a. Occurs when child is alone
    b. Disappears when distracted by someone else.
  4. No longer reflexive
    a. Source from internal stimulation
    b. Hearing not important

A. Some control over oral region
B. Disyllabic utterances
  1. Consonantlike plus vowellike sounds
  2. Average of seventeen different sound types
    a. Predominantly vowellike sounds
      (1) More frequent front and mid sounds
      (2) A few back sounds
      (3) Distinguishable sounds: /ɪ ɛ ʌ ʊ u/

314

Intonation	Meaning	Grammar
A. Variety in intensity B. Fundamental frequency of infant cry: 556 Hz	A. Beginning of crude vocabulary B. Response to other's voice C. Response of crying when other babies cry	
A. Variation in pitch B. Variation in loudness	A. Vocalizes for pleasure or displeasure B. Reacts to sounds made C. Smiles at mother's voice	

A. Intonation—infant cry of similar pressure waveform, much as the expiratory form of adult utterances	A. Babbling—speech without content
	  1. Dental and labial sounds expressive of contentment
	  2. Velar sounds expressive of distress
	B. Noises—rudiments of vocal response
	C. Systematic response to specific stimuli	

Table 8–8. *Continued*

	Characteristics of the Period	*Sound Making*

		b. Consonantlike sounds
		
		  (1) Predominantly glottal /h/ and velar sounds
		  (2) Appearance of labial sounds
		  (3) Appearance of nasals, plosive, and glide types

Six Months to Nine Months	A. Lalling stage—repetition of vocal play
	  1. Expression of self
	  2. Association of hearing with sound production
	    a. Ear reflex—circular response involving hearing and sound production
	    b. Repetition of selected heard sounds
	    c. Imitation as incentive for repetition
	B. Accompanying motor responses to vocalizations
	  1. Particular sounds accompany motor response
	  2. Arm movements more meaningful than mouth movements
	C. Language problems evident at this age through lack of lalling behavior; the deaf, retarded, aphasic, emotionally deprived
		A. Frequent change in syllable repetition
		B. Consonant-vowel-type combinations reduplicated
		C. Predominantly vowellike sounds
		  1. Front sound 92 percent of the time
		  2. Some back vowels: /ʋ u o/

Nine Months to Twelve Months	A. Echolalic stage
	  1. Repetition of sounds made by others
	    a. Sounds confined to those of native language
	    b. Awareness of sound patterns of native language
	    c. Fixation of these sounds in vocalization
	  2. Sounds devoid of meaning
	  3. Vocally fluent (Lewis, 1963)
	B. Imitation
	  1. Perpetuation of sounds that interest him
	  2. Rudimentary imitation—speaks on hearing someone else speak
	  3. Regulatory in response to particular sounds
	C. Vocal play
	  1. Production of vegetative sounds without demand
	  2. Vocalization while playing
		A. Consonant-like sounds beginning to exceed vowel-like sounds
		  1. Front and mid vowellike sounds less frequent
		    a. Most frequent types: /ɪ ʋ ʌ/
		    b. Back sounds appearing
		  2. Glottal and velar sounds frequent
		    a. Appearance of postdental and labial types
		    b. Additional semivowel and fricative types

316

Intonation	Meaning	Grammar
	D. Awareness of human speech	

A. Pattern of intonation heard over a number of syllables
B. Little pitch variation within a single syllable
C. Expressive intonation
  1. Dominating factor
  2. Discrimination among different patterns of expression
    a. Questions or commands
    b. Elicit surprise
D. Use of rhythm in vocal play

A. Application of vocalization
  1. For getting attention
  2. For socialization
    a. Support rejections
    b. Express demands
  3. Re-creation of sound to replace or recall a pleasurable situation or object
B. Response to human speech by smiling or vocalizing
C. Distinction between angry and pleasant sounds
D. Beginning of imitation of parental utterances

A. Discrimination among different patterns of expression
B. Development of stress/unstress pattern
C. Fundamental frequency
  1. 340 Hz when with father
  2. 390 Hz when with mother
  3. Higher frequency when crying

A. Beginning of single-word usage
  1. First word a crude approximation
  2. Babblings shortened into words
  3. Manipulation of others through sound making
B. Understanding of a few words and gestures
  1. Listens with selective interest
  2. Responds discriminately to adult verbalizations

Table 8–8. *Continued*

Characteristics of the Period	*Sound Making*

Twelve Months to Eighteen Months

Characteristics of the period—true speech

A. Period of silence between babbling and true speech
B. Intentional use of speech
   1. First word—accident of vocal play
   2. Approximation of sound through echolalia
   3. Strengthening of word through repetition
C. Accompanying motor activity or gestures to aid in understanding and stabilizing speech

Sound making—developing of phonological system

A. Acquisition built on system of contrasts
   1. /pa/ universal syllable
   2. Consonants more frequent than vowels
      a. Nasal/oral distinction made
      b. Labial/nonlabial contrast
      c. Consonant used in initial position most frequently rather than medial or final
   3. Vowel system
      a. High/low contrast
      b. Front/back contrast
B. Monosyllabic or disyllabic words—some onomatopoeic in character (*bow-wow*)
C. Girls' achievement greater than that of boys

Intonation

Eighteen Months to Twenty-Four Months

A. Acquisition of new words
   1. Perception of new experiences
   2. Manipulation of object or activity
   3. Introduction of word by adult
B. Use of echolalia
   1. Used in private; monologue-type speech
   2. Prolongs sounds
   3. Occurs instantly and unconsciously
C. Use of jargon
   1. Purposeful to child
   2. Provides for fluency
D. Beginning of primitive grammatical system
E. Motor activity
   1. Much activity with speech
   2. Overflow in lips, jaw, tongue, eyes, head

A. Many variants in child's system
   1. Vowels most changeable; more front vowels than back
   2. Instability of voicing feature
   3. Rare use of medial and final consonants
B. Articulation change under pressure of adult responses
C. Periods of practice in perfecting sounds

318

Intonation	Meaning	Grammar

A. Intonation and pitch dominating over phonetic form
B. Marking of sentence boundaries by intonation contours
  1. Referential breath groups as phonetic markers of complete sentences
  2. Juncture evident in utterances
C. Stress pattern: stress/unstress
	A. Development of vocabulary
	  1. One to three words (*bye-bye, no,* etc.
	  2. Adaptation of child's primary experience to adult form of words
	  3. Words learned through associated actions
	  4. Names objects
	  5. Performative utterance—names what he is doing at the time
	  6. Begins to apply words to categories
	B. Verbal understanding greater than production
	  1. Responds to commands
	  2. No understanding of questions
	    a. At times no response
	    b. At times imitation or repetition of question
		A. Holophrastic utterances
		  1. Single-word utterances
		  2. Ambiguous in meaning—broad and diffuse
		  3. Meaning derived from the situation
		B. Parts of speech (adult grammar)
		  1. Nouns most common
		  2. A few verbs and adjectives

A. Earliest feature acquired
B. Indication of contrastive elements of stress
  1. Inconsistent use
  2. Overuse of stress on syllables other than correct one
C. Pitch rise at end of sentence
D. Voice control—unstable
  1. Variation from good modulation to straining
  2. Much experimentation
E. Fluency—frequent repetition of words and syllables unforced and easily terminated
	A. Twenty- to 100-word vocabulary
	  1. Prominence of meaningful words
	  2. General referents (*cookie* refers to anything similar)
	  3. One fourth of utterances understood by others
	  4. Beginning of substitution of words for physical acts
	    a. Extension of use of words (*pay* for anything that flies)
	    b. Rudiment of generalization (*tee* for *cat* as well as *dog*)
	  5. Naming of objects in books
		A. Beginning of structure
		  1. Two-word sentences—words in juxtaposition
		  2. Telegraphic utterances
		    a. Result of limited memory span
		    b. Inclusion of informational content of message
		    c. Omission of auxiliaries, prepositions, articles, verbs, and inflections
		  3. Use of nouns, a few verbs, adjectives, and some pronouns of adult categories
		B. Average of 1.7 words per utterance

319

Table 8–8. *Continued*

Characteristics of the Period	*Sound Making*

Two Years to Three Years

A. Period of preoccupation with sound
B. Rapid increase in language growth
  1. Use of speech for self-assertion, self-awareness, and as safety valve
  2. Growth in grammatical capacity
C. Demand of response from others
  1. Demand from adults
  2. Kicks and screams with peers
D. Motor activity
  1. Able to speak before he acts
  2. Acts in relation to task at hand

A. Mastery of two thirds of adult speech sounds
  1. Vowels—90 percent correct
  2. Specific pronunciation for most consonants
    a. Most correct—plosives
    b. Slighting of medial consonants (Irwin, 1952)
    c. Overpronunciation of some words—*flonwer* for *flower*
B. Distinctive features in production and recall
  1. Voicing and nasality best maintained
  2. Continuancy and stridency least maintained
  3. Sounds differing in one feature (especially continuancy) most difficult (d for ð)
  4. Nonperipheral sounds more difficult than peripheral

Intonation	Meaning	Grammar

| | B. Reportive utterances—description of things in environment without accompanying action
C. Lower boundary for beginning of semantic system | |
| A. Intonational pattern becoming subordinated to phonetic
B. Voice—unstable pattern
  1. Range from high to low
  2. Presence of nasality
  3. Straining and forcing
C. Fluency—broken rhythm
  1. Repetition of sounds, words, phrases
  2. Use of starters
  3. Echoic of others | A. Two-hundred-and-fifty-word vocabulary
  1. Words still general in content
  2. Assignment of each referent to a category
  3. Categories learned from actions rather than names of words
  4. Children's definitions of words in terms of action
  5. Order of learning adverbs—locative, temporal, manner
B. Period of compiling a word dictionary in building of semantic system | A. Two-word utterances—primitive grammar
  1. Selection not random
  2. Patterned arrangements in sequential order
  3. Missing elements
    a. Auxiliaries, articles, determiners, pronouns, prepositions, inflections
    b. Small-sized categorical classes
    c. Words predictable from context
    d. Intermediate words in adult construction
  4. Elements retained in imitation of adult
    a. Initial and final words
    b. Reference-making forms
    c. Nonpredictable forms
    d. Words with heavier stress
    e. Expandable classes
  5. Development of word classes based on privilege of occurrence
    a. Class distinction into pivot and open word classes
      (1) Pivot—distinct category similar to function words |

Table 8–8. *Continued*

	Characteristics of the Period	*Sound Making*
Two Years to Three Years		

Intonation	Meaning	Grammar
		(a) Few members
		(b) Frequent use
		(c) Heterogeneous selection on basis of adult grammar (articles, greetings, adjectives, verbs)
		(2) Open class—similar to nounlike categories
		(a) Many members
		(b) Less frequent use of each member
		b. Predictable structure of utterance
		(1) Pivot plus open (*pretty shoe, see mommy*)
		(2) Open plus open (*daddy shoe*)— similar to adult possessive form
		B. Later constructions
		1. Mean word length per utterance is 3.5 words
		2. Original pivot class reduced by subdivision
		3. Treatment of demonstrative pronouns and adjectives as unique classes to yield *a that horsie*
		4. Development of hierarchical structure
		a. Structure of noun phrase
		b. Structure of verb phrase
		c. Ultimate combination of noun phrase and verb

Table 8–8. *Continued*

Characteristics of the Period	Sound Making
Two Years to Three Years	

Intonation	Meaning	Grammar
		phrase to form adultlike grammar

C. Transformations
  1. Stages of negative structure development
     a. *No* or *not* plus primitive structure (*no wash*)
     b. Addition of *can't* and *don't* as vocabulary *items* contained in primitive structure
     c. Indication of adult rule
        (1) Use of auxiliary in affirmative (*I can see it*)
        (2) Use of auxiliary with *n't* (*I can't see it*)
     d. Copula *be* optional (*I not big enough*)
     e. Appearance of double negative (*He never made no trip*)
  2. Stages of interrogative structure development
     a. No use of questions or comprehension of question
        (1) No response or inappropriate response
        (2) Imitation of question
     b. Intonational question (*See doggie?*)
     c. Use of interrogative words—*who, what, where*
        (1) Initial word (*How you do it?*)
        (2) *Why not* a single vocabulary item
        (3) Better comprehension or adult questions

Table 8–8. *Continued*

Characteristics of the Period	*Sound Making*

Two Years to Three Years

Three Years to Four Years

A. Becomes linguistic adult
   1. Acquires adult syntax
   2. Is versatile in use of language
      a. To express emotions
      b. To manipulate associates
      c. To express relations
      d. To satisfy needs
      e. To seek verification (*What's this?*)
      f. To express dependency
      g. To entertain self (Templin, 1957)
      h. Verbalizes as he acts (Lewis, 1963)
B. Can be controlled by language
C. Learns to whisper
D. Squeals, sputters, laughs, sighs
E. Accompanies speech with tongue protrusion, lip smacking, tongue clicks
F. Continues to use echolalia
   1. When speech becomes difficult
   2. To assimilate associations

A. 90 percent of vowels and diphthongs mastered
B. 60 percent of consonants mastered
   1. By manner of articulation
      a. Nasals—92.5 percent
      b. Plosives—79.1 percent
      c. Fricatives—41.0 percent
   2. By position
      a. Initial sound—70 percent
      b. Medial sound—68 percent
      c. Final sound—52 percent
   3. By mastery of specific sounds—/p b m w h/
   4. Inconsistent production
C. Greatest change in articulatory ability
   1. Between 3 and 3.5 years for girls
   2. Between 3.5 and 4 years for boys

Intonation	Meaning	Grammar

| | | d. Approaching of adult form
  (1) Use of auxiliaries
  (2) Use of interrogative words as replacement for missing element in sentence |
| | | D. Inflections—latter part of second year
  1. Use of present progressive
  2. Use of present indicative |

Intonation	Meaning	Grammar

A. Well patterned.
B. Normal loudness and tone
C. Breathiness
D. Nasality with soft voice
E. Faster rate
F. Fluency
  1. Recurrence of compulsive repetitions
    a. Tonic blocks on initial syllables
    b. Grimacing, puffing
  2. Use of starters (Metreaux, 1950)
	A. 900-word vocabulary
	B. Use of linguistic symbols in dealing with situations
	C. Use of language in imaginative play
	D. Self-centered explanations
	  1. Egocentric speech
	  2. No apprehension of information requirement of others
	E. Few semantic markers for words
		A. Mean word length per utterance: four words
		B. Mean number of different words per fifty utterances
		  1. 92.5 at three years
		  2. 104.8 at three and one-half years
		C. Acquisition of adult grammar
		  1. Well-formed utterances but not always grammatical
		  2. 48 percent of utterances grammatically correct
		  3. Copula *be* optional
		  4. Incorporation of rules of grammar
		    a. Understand and produce sentences
		    b. Has difficulty in repetition because of structure complexity and not because of sentence length
		D. Inflectional rules
		  1. Use of past tense
		    a. Omission (*push for pushed*)
		    b. Redundancy (*pushted* for *pushed*)

Table 8–8. *Continued*

Characteristics of the Period	*Sound Making*

Four Years to Five Years

A. Language a facile tool
   1. Commands giving way to spontaneous speech
   2. Questions other's activity
B. Girls exceed boys in linguistic ability at four and one-half years
C. Motor activity
   1. Tension at a minimum
   2. Overflow in gross activity
   3. Less verbalization with activity

A. Consonant production 90 percent correct by four and one-half years
   1. Percent of correct scores by manner of articulation
      a. Nasals—95 percent
      b. Plosives—90 percent
      c. Semivowels—85 percent
      d. Fricatives and combinations—60 percent
   2. Percent of correct scores by position
      a. Initial—88 percent
      b. Medial—86 percent
      c. Final—74 percent
   3. Substitution of /w/ for /l/ and /r/; example of hierarchal development of distinctive features
   4. Additional mastered sounds—/d t n g k ŋ j/
B. Production more stable

Five Years to Six Years

A. More sophisticated use of language
B. More use of language
C. More comprehensible
D. Increased speech in social interaction
E. Less repetition of adults

A. 98 percent of vowel production correct
B. 88 percent of consonant production correct
   1. Percent of correct production by manner of articulation
      a. Nasals—95 percent
      b. Plosives and semivowels—85 percent
      c. Fricatives—68 percent
      d. Combinations—60 percent

Intonation	Meaning	Grammar
		2. Use of present progressive 3. Use of present indicative

A. Imitation of parents' intonation pattern
B. Voice—well modulated and firm
  1. Subdued at times
  2. Whining at times
C. Rate—186 words per minute
D. Fewer repetitions
  1. For emphasis at times
  2. Continued blocking and grimacing
	A. Rapid increase in vocabulary
	B. Speech egocentric in nature
	C. Use of descriptive types of explanations in word definitions
	D. Word association studies
	  1. Multiple-word responses
	  2. Excessive number of syntactic responses
	  3. Excessive number of noun responses
		A. Mean number of words per utterance: 5½
		B. Mean number of different words per utterance: 2½
		C. Mean number of different words per fifty utterances:
		  1. 120.4 at four years
		  2. 127.0 at four and one-half years
		D. More complicated sentence structure
		E. Use of rules for forming simple plural, present progressive, and possession when expanded to new words never heard before
		  1. Unable to expand /ed/ to new words when final sound is /t/ or /d/ for past tense
		  2. Operate on rule: "A voiceless sibilant after a voiced sibilant after all other sounds makes a word plural."
		  3. Use plural for counting nouns
		F. No awareness of separate elements of compound words

A. Continued improvement in fluency and phonation
B. Hesitations, pauses, and slower rate evident in speech requiring explanation rather than description
	A. Vocabulary of 2000 words
	B. Word-association studies
	  1. Percentage of noun responses decreases
	  2. More paradigmatic responses to verbs and adjectives
	  3. Children less able to take advantage of semantic consistency in sentences when
		A. Mean number of words per utterance: 5.7
		B. Mean number of different words per fifty utterances: 132.4
		C. Improved syntax
		D. Perfecting of rules for forming inflections
		  1. Use of possessive
		  2. Use of third person singular

Table 8–8. *Continued*

Characteristics of the Period	*Sound Making*

	2. Percent of correct production by position
	   a. Initial—90 percent
	   b. Medial—84 percent
	   c. Final—80 percent
	C. Occasional reversals of sounds

A. Language more socially oriented
B. Language as instrument for growth of individual personality
C. Different languages
   1. Of elders
   2. Of peers
   3. Of reading and writing (Lewis, 1963)
	A. Boys' requirement of additional year for mastery of sounds
	B. Six-year-old status
	   1. Correct production by manner of articulation
	     a. Nasals and plosives—98 percent
	     b. Semivowels—92 percent
	     c. Fricatives—75 percent
	     d. Combinations—65 percent
	   2. Correct production by position
	     a. Initial—92 percent
	     b. Medial—91 percent
	     c. Final—90 percent
	   3. Additional sounds mastered: /v ð ʒ ʃ l/; loss of /s z/
	C. Seven-year-old status
	   1. Correct production by manner of articulation
	     a. Nasals—99 percent
	     b. Plosives—98 percent
	     c. Semivowels—95 percent
	     d. Fricatives—88 percent
	     e. Combinations—70 percent (Templin, 1957)
	   2. Correct production by position
	     a. Initial—100 percent
	     b. Medial—98 percent
	     c. Final—100 percent (Templin, 1957)
	   3. Additional sounds mastered: /r θ hw/ with recurrence of /s z/; /d/
	D. Eight-year-old status
	   1. Correct production by manner of articulation
	     a. Nasals—100 percent
	     b. Plosives—98 percent
	     c. Semivowels—98 percent
	     d. Fricatives—98 percent
	     e. Combinations—75 percent
	   2. Little difference in percentage of correct production by position with the exception of difficulty with fricatives in final position

Six Years to Seven and Beyond

Intonation	Meaning	Grammar
	shadowing speech than an eight-year-old group	E. Production and recall of nongrammatical material not different from grammatical

Intonation	Meaning	Grammar

A. Fundamental frequency for seven-year-old boys: 294 Hz; for eight-year-old boys: 297 Hz.
B. Fundamental frequency for seven-year-old girls: 281 Hz; for eight-year-old girls: 288 Hz.
C. Upward and downward voice breaks common to all groups
	A. Mean number of words per utterance
	  1. 6.4 words for six years
	  2. 7 words for seven years
	  3. 7.7 words for eight years
	B. Mean number of different words per fifty utterances
	  1. 147 at six years
	  2. 157.7 at seven years
	  3. 166.5 at eight years
	C. Grammatical system well established
	  1. Evaluation of passive, negative, and negative passive sentences by six-year-olds
	  2. More time required for evaluation of complex structure
	  3. Percentage of correct grammatical utterances
	    a. 73.7 by six-year-olds
	    b. 76.1 by eight-year-olds
	  4. Learning tasks and recall easier with grammatical material than with nongrammatical material
		A. Basic estimated vocabulary
		  1. 13,000 words (2000 spoken) at six years
		  2. 21,600 words at seven years
		  3. 28,300 words at eight years
		B. More discriminate use of vocabulary
		C. Definitions of words
		  1. By use of description below six or seven years
		  2. By synonym at eight to eleven years
		  3. By categorical description or explanation above eleven years
		D. Language taking on idiosyncracies
		E. Word association studies
		  1. Primarily syntagmatic responses at six years
		  2. Decrease in percentage of noun responses from six to eight years
		  3. Increase in percentage of paradigmatic responses for verbs
		F. Continuation on developing of semantic markers in child's word dictionary

* While the contents of this chart were drawn from many sources, the following references predominated: R. Brown (1964, 1965), Berry and Eisenson (1956); Fokes (1971); Irwin (1947a, 1947b, 1948, 1952), Lewis (1963), D. McCarthy (1954); MacNeill (1965, 1966); Metreaux (1950), Templin (1957); Van Riper (1978); Weir (1963, 1966).

  b. If receptive, does the format utilize picture identification, response to commands, etc.?
4. Inventory many aspects of language, or does it only measure specific areas (e.g., receptive vocabulary, grammar usage, articulation, etc.)?
5. Result in instructionally useful information, or is it intended for screening or research purposes only?

STANDARDIZED TESTING OF LANGUAGE

In Table 8–9 we present a number of the most commonly used commercially available tests of language and language correlates. The teacher should be aware of the nature of these tests because of their widespread use in language evaluation. This knowledge will help teachers interpret test results and reports, indicate where further informal assessments are necessary, and execute appropriate remediation and/or prevention strategies.

INFORMAL APPROACHES TO LANGUAGE ASSESSMENT

In an attempt to further specify the nature of the language problem, informal assessment strategies will be necessary. The following strategies, which are adapted from Bryen (1975), are representative of informal assessment that can be conducted in the classroom.

Semantics

While semantics is probably the most critical aspect of language, it continues to be one of the least understood aspects. Since most of the language used in the classroom has the purpose of either expressing or receiving meaningful information, the informal assessment of semantics is important. In assessing a child's semantic development, one needs to tap more than the meaning of isolated words or the child's vocabulary. One needs to assess, in addition to the child's knowledge of specific words, how a child uses linguistic and situational contexts to determine the meaning of words as well as the choice of words to be used.

The word *boys* illustrates how the linguistic context determines the meaning of this word. In isolated speech this word has no one specific meaning even though in its written form the range of possible meanings can be delimited somewhat to *boys, boy's,* or *boys'.* Only in its linguistic context can the word, pronounced *boys,* begin to take on a more specified meaning. It can mean plurality, as in *The boys are running,* or singular possessive, as in *The*

Table 8–9. Commercially Prepared Tests of Language

Name (Author of Test)	Aspect of Language Measured	Target Population	Purported Purpose	Comments
Assessment of Children's Language Comprehension (Foster, Giddan, and Stark, 1973)	Ability of children to identify pictures containing 1, 2, 3, or 4 verbal elements	Preschool through elementary	"To define receptive language difficulty in children and to indicate guidelines for correction"	Available in group or individual form. No expressive ability in children required. Reliability and validity not reported. Not a complete test of language comprehension, as title states (no testing of syntactic comprehension), but useful for measuring number or verbal information bits child can integrate concurrently.
Carrow Elicited Language Inventory (Carrow-Woolfolk, 1974)	Expressive language in elicited situation (emphasis on syntax)	Ages 3 to 8	To assess a child's productive control of grammar	52 stimulus sentences and phrases are used to elicit responses. Child's responses are taped, require phonemic transcription. Analysis system covers 12 grammatical categories and 5 error types. Provides for in-depth analysis of child's errors on verbs.
Developmental Sentence Analysis (Lee, 1974)	Expressive syntax in spontaneous speech	Ages 2 to 7	To evaluate the grammatical structure of child's spontaneous speech	100 different intelligible spontaneous utterances are taped and analyzed according to length and type. Basic assumption: increasing length a measure of increasing grammatical complexity. Score is weighted for presence of indefinite pronoun or noun modifiers, personal pronouns, main verbs, secondary verbs, negatives, conjunctions, interrogative reversals, and wh-questions. Elements that normally occur later are given greater weight. Interjudge reliability = .94; split-half reliability = .73. Valid data supportive.

Table 8–9. *Continued*

Name *(Author of Test)*	*Aspect of Language Measured*	*Target Population*	*Purported Purpose*	*Comments*
Fluharty Preschool Speech and Language Screening Test (Fluharty, 1978)	Screens for vocabulary, articulation, receptive/expressive language	Ages 2–6	To determine which child needs more intensive evaluation	To be used by speech clinician
Goldman-Fristoe Test of Articulation (Goldman and Fristoe, 1969)	Articulation	Above age 2	To assess child's ability to produce speech sounds	Attractively illustrated. Well standardized. Takes about 30 minutes to administer. Measures speech sound production in initial, medial, and final positions in words and sentences.
Illinois Test of Psycholinguistic Abilities (Kirk, McCarthy, and Kirk, 1968)	Correlates of language such as duplicating a sequence of geometric designs, also vocabulary and expression	Ages 2 to 7	To identify the psycholinguistic abilities and disabilities of children	Based on a model that separates various skills into expressive, receptive, and organizing aspects, and into representational and automatic levels. Relationship of various subtests to language itself not well established. Overall reliability satisfactory; some subtest reliabilities too low for diagnosis of individuals. Validity issues unresolved.
Language Comprehension Tests (Bellugi-Klima, 1973)	Selected aspects of language comprehension	Preschool	To test comprehension of linguistic constructions	Child is asked to manipulate real objects in response to examiners' instructions at three levels: (1) active sentences, singular/plural nouns, possessives; (2) negative/affirmative, singular/plural verbs, inflections, adjectival modifications; (3) negative affixes, reflexivization, comparatives, passives, embedded sentences. Items are exemplary rather than comprehensive.

Test	Population	Purpose	Description
Miller-Yoder Test of Grammatical Comprehension, Experimental Edition (Miller and Yoder, 1972)	Ages 3 to 6	Syntactic comprehension	To assess a child's grammatical comprehension	42 stimulus sentence pairs spoken by examiner; child points to appropriate picture on plate. Untimed. Not standardized. Internal reliability = .93. Lexical items respresentative of 5-year-olds. Measures active passive, prepositions, possessives, negative affixes, pronouns, singular/plural nouns and verbs, verbal inflections, adjectival modifications, reflexivizations.
Northwestern Syntax Screening Test (Lee, 1966)	Ages 4 to 8; standard English speakers	Syntactic expression and comprehension	To screen children on the basis of receptive and expressive syntactic usage	20 receptive items are measured by child indicating which of four pictures is appropriate for sentence. 20 expressive items are similar, except child repeats stimulus sentences as he points. Age norms are presented for small standardization sample. No reliability or validity data reported.
Parsons Language Sample (Spraldin, 1963)	Children with severe mental handicaps	Expressive aspects of language, vocal and nonvocal; comprehension	To sample language behavior according to Skinnerian outline	Considerable use with very low-functioning children. Seven subtests, including vocal and nonvocal. Standardized on mentally retarded children. Overall reliability is satisfactory; subtests too highly correlated to be used diagnostically. Does not measure syntax.
Peabody Picture Vocabulary Test (Dunn, 1965)	Mental ages 2 to adult	Receptive vocabulary of standard English	To derive an IQ score	Test is untimed and well standardized. Child points to appropriate picture on plate in response to stimulus word spoken by examiner. May be given by teacher; takes 10–20 minutes.

Table 8–9. *Continued*

Name (Author of Test)	Aspect of Language Measured	Target Population	Purported Purpose	Comments
Screening Test for Auditory Comprehension of Language (Carrow-Woolfolk, 1973)	Auditory comprehension of vocabulary, morphology, syntax	Ages 3–6 who have receptive problems in English or Spanish.	Same as TACL	Modification of TACL for groups
Slingerland Screening Tests for Identifying Children with Specific Language Disability (Slingerland, 1970)	Correlates of language such as memory of geometric forms	Children in the early grades	To detect deficits in one or more areas on which receptive and expressive written language is based.	Consists of three sets of tests, each with nine subtests—eight for group administration, one for individual. Wall charts, test booklets, and cards are the stimulus materials. Tasks include copying from a model (both written and oral), matching, kinesthetic-motor acts, sound discrimination, sentence completion, among others. No reliability or validity data are presented.
Templin–Darley Test of Articulation (Templin and Darley, 1960)	Articulation	Ages 3 to 8	Screening or diagnosis of articulation	Sound elements tested include 25 consonant blends, 12 vowels, and 6 diphthongs. Child utters sounds in isolation, in words, and in a sentence. Short form (50 items) may be used for screening; all 176 items for diagnosis.
Test for Auditory Comprehension of Language (Carrow-Woolfolk, 1973)	Auditory comprehension of vocabulary, morphology, syntax	Ages 3 to 6	To measure receptive language in English or Spanish	Test consists of 101 pictorial stimuli plates of three drawings each. One of the drawings is the correct representation, one is the reverse of the stimulus sentence, and the other serves as a distractor. Test is individually administered, with child

Test	Area	Ages	Purpose	Comments
Test of Adolescent Language (TOAL) (Hammill, V. Brown, Larsen, and Wiederholt, 1980)	Receptive and expressive aspects of vocabulary and syntax	Ages 11–18½	To give indication of student's overall strengths and weaknesses in each area tapped	pointing to appropriate drawing. Provides indication of child's proficiency in vocabulary, morphology, syntax. English and Spanish versions field-tested on native speakers of each language. TOAL also measures reading and writing abilities. Composite scores are reliable mostly in the .90s.
Test of Early Language Development (Hresko, Reid, and Hammill, 1981)	Content and form in both receptive and expressive modes	Ages 3–7	Screening and documenting problem	Test is short, 36 items, uses Stanford-Binet format. Has basals and ceilings to facilitate administration.
Test of Language Development (TOLD) (Newcomer and Hammill, 1977)	Receptive and expressive aspects of vocabulary, syntax, and phonology	Ages 4 to 9	To give indication of child's overall strengths and weaknesses in each area tapped	Test is short and easy to administer. Five principal subtests measure receptive and expressive aspects of vocabulary and grammar. Two supplemental subtests measure articulation and speech sound discrimination. Test subtests correlate with criterion tests, with r's mostly in .70's. Subtests generally internally consistent and stable.
Token Test for Children (DiSimone, 1978)	Teach perceptive research language	Ages 3–12	To screen for receptive language dysfunction or rule out language impairment	Using small geometric shapes, child follows directions given by examiner.

Table 8–9. *Continued*

Name (Author of Test)	Aspect of Language Measured	Target Population	Purported Purpose	Comments
Utah Test of Language Development (UTLD) (Mecham, Jex, and Jones, 1969)	Expressive and receptive language, aspects of conceptual development	Ages 1.6 to 14.5	To derive an overall picture of a child's language development as compared with his peers	Test consists of two sections—one an informant-interview section based on the Vineland Social Maturity Scale, the other a direct test requiring the child to perform such things as repeat digits, recite a story, reproduce geometric forms. Yield score in form of language age. Internal reliabilities high.
Vocabulary Comprehension Scale (Bangs, 1975)	Assesses child's ability to follow instructions involving use of various lexical and function words	Ages 2 to 6 language disabled	To provide information on comprehension of pronouns, words of position, quality, size, and quantity	Attractive kit in shape of house. Has manipulative items such as cars, balls. Instructions to child in form of games—Garage, Tea Party, Buttons, Miscellaneous. Standardized on culturally diverse middle-income population in Texas.
Weiss Comprehensive Articulation Test (Weiss, 1978)	Articulation, speech intelligibility	Preschool to adult	To establish a subject's level of articulation and determine treatment approach	Easel-stand, flip pages with colored picture forms for nonreaders, written material for readers. Single-word responses and contextual speech are assessed.

boy's jacket fell by his chair, or plural possessive, as in *The boys' bikes were parked by their houses.*

The situational context will also influence the meaning of words. For example, as Bloom (1970) has illustrated, the words *Mommy shoe* can indicate possessive in the situation when the young child brings the mother her shoe, or it can indicate an actor–object relationship, as when the child uses this utterance when commenting on the fact that mother is putting on her shoe.

The following procedures are examples of the kinds of tasks that can be used to informally assess semantics.

Early Semantic Development

Between the ages of nine and eighteen months, the normal child begins to actively experiment with language. However, during this early stage of development, the child's utterances will be tied closely to specific situational contexts for the expression and production of meaningful language.

Objective.   Assess the child's early language comprehension.

Materials.   None other than contexts and materials the child frequently engages with.

Procedures.   Select and list the contexts of commonly occurring activities. Present simple words/phrases which are related to the context. For example, at the table where the child usually eats say "want to eat?". Or at the door, say "bye-bye?". Observe and note the child's responses.

Now, use the same procedure as above, but not in the context in which that activity usually occurs. For example, at the table say "want to go bye-bye?" or "bye-bye?". Or at a different part of the room say "want to eat?". Observe and note the child's responses.

Results.   In analyzing the child's responses, note whether the child gives either behavioral or verbal indicators that he has understood the meaning of your utterance. Does the child do so only in the well-established situational context, e.g., "bye-bye" only at the door? Or has the child's early language comprehension become free from specific contexts, e.g., "bye-bye" at the table or sandbox?

Objective.   Assess the child's early meaningful use of one- or two-word utterances.

Materials. Toys or objects which the child frequently uses.

Procedures. Place the familiar toys or objects in front of the child, one at a time. Engage the child in play with them. Observe the child as he manipulates the object(s) or engages in activity. Record any utterances and the context in which they occur. If no spontaneous utterances occur, try eliciting utterances by asking "What's this?" or "What's the ball doing?". Note all responses.

Results. In analyzing the child's responses, note not only the specific word(s) used but also their apparent semantic intent. This can only be assessed in relationship to the particular context in which this utterance was made. For example, is the word *cookie* used to indicate the existence of a cookie, to indicate the recurrence of a cookie, or to indicate the object of an action? This procedure should provide information not only about the words the child produces, but also the semantic function of these words.

Word Association

The use of word-association tasks has provided information in regard to the semantic development of children. Specifically, it enables us to study how individuals chunk or classify words. There are two general response categories: syntagmatic or paradigmatic. A syntagmatic response to a stimulus word would be a word that would either proceed or follow the stimulus word, according to the rules of syntax. For example, the stimulus word *chair* might call forth the word *sit* or *on*, as in the phrase *Sit on the chair*. Paradigmatic responses, in contrast, are those responses of the same grammatical category as in the response *sofa* or *table* to the stimulus word *chair*. Younger children tend to respond more frequently with syntagmatic responses, with the shift to paradigmatic responses occurring between the ages of six and eight years.

Objective. Assess how the child classifies words.

Materials. Word list of familiar words.

Procedures. Supply the child with each stimulus word, telling him that this is a game and that he is to say the first word he can think of. If there is no immediate response (within 5 seconds), proceed to the next word. Vary the words using a number of nouns, adjectives, verbs, adverbs, and prepositions. Some frequently used noun words are *table, man, mountain,* and *fruit.* Words such as *sit, play, jump,* and *speak* are good verbs to use. Frequently used adjectives are *dark, cold, deep,* and *afraid* and adverbs are *very, easily, always,* and *how.* Good prepositions to try are *up, on, with,* and *over.*

Results.   Analyze the child's responses. Were there more syntagmatic or paradigmatic responses? Did the child show difficulties by reverting to many perseverative or rhyming responses? Was a particular grammatical category most difficult for the child? In other words, did the child indicate difficulty with the adverbial class of words by using syntagmatic, perseverative, or rhyming responses?

Specific and Nonspecific Referents

One theory touched upon in the introduction to semantics was the referential theory. According to this theory, the meaning of a word is determined by its referent. As was already discussed, there are several difficulties with this theory, for even the simple word *dog* does not refer to one specific referent but rather to a category defined by *all* four-legged animals that are frequently domesticated and utter barking sounds. Shortcomings of this theory are further evident when one examines words such as *justice* or *jealously* or *happiness.* What is the referent here?

Objective.   Analyze the various meaning the child expresses when shown a referent and when a word is given without a referent.

Materials.   Several common objects the child has had some contact with: *nail, ball, scissors, pencil,* etc., and a list of words without specific referents, such as *animal, toy, hungry, arithmetic.*

Procedures.   Ask the child to "tell you about" the object presented. Probe for a variety of responses by saying "tell me more." Let the child play with and manipulate the objects. After using six referent words, ask the child to tell you about *animal* or *toy* or *hungry*—words without particular referents. Record all responses. Probe as much as possible.

Results.   Analyze how the responses varied. What meanings were imposed on each word? Did the child's responses include (a) label or name of the object, (b) color, (c) shape, (d) function? Or were the child's responses restricted to one category, such as function? What difficulties, if any, were encountered with the nonreferent words? Did the child rely on specific instances of the word? For example, *ball, bat, bike,* and *truck* given in response to the word "toy" instead of a classificatory description, such as *things you can play with.*

Sentences and Word Meanings

As had already been mentioned, the meaning of a word is influenced by its linguistic context. Katz and Fodor (1963) have suggested that there are two aspects of semantics, that of *semantic features* and *selection restrictions*. The first aspect, semantic features, relates to the features of meaning of a particular word. For example, *father* has, among other features, the set (+ human) (+ male) (+ parent). Additionally, there are semantic restrictions on the possible combinations of words in a sentence that *father* can take in a sentence in order for that sentence to be meaningful. For example, the sentence *She is my father* violates our notions of truth, because it violates these semantic restrictions. That is, the semantic features of *she* (+ human) (− male) do not include the semantic features of father. Therefore, a full assessment of semantics must include not only the child's understanding of isolated words, but how they are used in meaningful sentences.

Objectives.   Assess the child's semantic knowledge in particular linguistic contexts.

Materials.   A list of sentences, some of which violate selection restriction and some of which are semantically correct should be used as probes. The following sentences are examples of sentences that might be used:

1. She is my brother.
2. My mother has no children.
3. The pony rides the girl.
4. She is my sister.
5. The candy eats Carol.
6. My father is a bachelor.
7. The liquid spilled.
8. The liquid clapped their hands.

Procedures.   After you read each sentence, ask the child to determine if the sentences makes sense (i.e., if a "good sentence") or not (i.e., is a "bad sentence"). After the child has made a judgment ("good" or "bad sentence") about each sentence, ask him "Why is it a good (or bad) sentence?". For those sentences that the child has judged as bad, ask him to "correct it" or "make it better." Record all responses.

Results.   In analyzing the child's responses, attempt to determine how the child decided which sentences were good or bad. Did he use only the semantic features of isolated words in making his judgment? Did he use *both* semantic features and linguistic context (i.e., selection restrictions) in making his judgment? Was the child able to correct semantically anomolous sentences? If not, how much did the lack of understanding of the meaning of particular words (semantic features) cause problems?

Morphology and Syntax

The combining of morphemes into rule-governed sequences produces syntactically acceptable sentences. The development of these rules governing the combination of morphemes enables the child to produce and understand a potentially infinite number of sentences. Without knowledge of these rules, an individual may be restricted in both his ability to produce and comprehend the many novel sentences which are continually being used by speakers of his language. For this reason, it is important to assess the child's knowledge of morphological and syntactical structures.

Many languages have rules that determine the use of particular morphological markers, such as -*ed* marker for past tense, the -*s* marker for plurality, the -*ing* progressive marker, and the -*er* marker for the agentive. However, not all languages or dialects employ these morphological markers, as does Standard English. For example, it has been noted earlier that in Black English, these markers may be deleted because they are optional markers rather than obligatory as in Standard English.

Objective.   To analyze the child's production of frequently used, Standard English morphological markers with familiar and unlearned words.

Materials.   A series of pictures and accompanying stories that act to stimulate the child's production. For each familiar word and accompanying stimulus story there should be a comparable "nonsense" story that taps the same morphological marker. For example, the following picture stories could be used to tap the -*s* plural marker.

Picture stories can be developed for the -*ed*, -*'s*, -*ing*, and -*er* arkers.

Procedures.   Present each picture story (familiar first, followed by unfamiliar nonsense) to the child, saying:

> "I'm going to tell you a story about some pictures. I'm going to leave out a word, so listen carefully. Your job is to fill in the missing word."

Read each story that accompanies the picture and record precisely the responses the child gives.

Familiar Story

This is a table.

Now there is another one. There are two of them. There are two _____ .

Nonsense Story

This is a <u>dop</u>.

Now there is another one. There are two of them. There are two _____ .

Results.   Analyze the child's responses to determine if he could generate the appropriate morphological markers. Determine if he could do this with unlearned, "nonsense" words as well as with familiar words. If errors did occur, were they isolated to particular markers (e.g., the *-er* marker)? Develop additional picture stories to probe further these troublesome markers. Additionally, pay close attention to determine if the child performs similarly in his spontaneous language production. Caution again must be made that certain English dialects may not require the obligatory *-ed, -s,* and *-'s* markers. Therefore, the absence of these markers does not immediately imply a language problem.

Word Order as a Conveyor of Meaning

Because sentences are not merely a random sequencing of words, change in the ordering of words may dramatically affect the meaning conveyed by the sentence. For example, if the ordering of *car* and *truck* were reversed in sentence (1), the resultant sentence (2) would express

(1) The car hit the truck.
(2) The truck hit the car.

an entirely different meaning. In sentence (1), the *car* is the subject of the action, the *truck* the object of the action, while in sentence (2), the opposite is the case. In other sentences, if word order is not adhered to, the resultant sentence may be an anomaly. Consider sentence (3),

(3) The girl ate the cake.

whereby a change in the word order of *girl* and *cake* would result in an anomolous sentence. Therefore, it is important to assess the child's ability to use word order as a conveyor of meaning.

Objective.   Evaluate the child's comprehension of word order.

Materials.   Objects or pictures that can be used to depict various action sequences. For example, pictures of (a) a truck hitting a car, (b) a car hitting a truck, and (c) a car and a truck driving down a road can be used to evaluate the child's comprehension of *The car hit the truck*. Or the child can be given a toy truck and a toy car and asked to show you *The car hit the truck*.

Procedures.   Identify several stimulus sentences which, if word order were violated, would result in either a different, yet meaningful sentence, or an anomolous sentence. A few examples are provided below:

> The boy chases the dog.
> The girl drops the doll.
> The girl pushes the boy.
> The boy thinks about his dog.
> The dog chews the bone.

Present either objects or pictures which can be used to depict the meaning of each sentence and have the child identify the appropriate picture or demonstrate with the objects the meaning of each sentence. This procedure can also be used with active/passive voice sentences, such as *The boy chases the dog* (active) versus *The boy is being chased by the dog* (passive). Note here that if the child relies exclusively on word order, he will not have comprehended the second sentence. Record all responses.

Results.   In analyzing the child's responses, determine if the child was able to use word-order clues to obtain the intended meaning of the sentence. Note if other linguistic cues were used to obtain meaning, such as meaningful or anomolous sentence outcomes. If the child is assessed on active/passive sentences, note whether the child can use other syntactic strategies besides word order. It should be noted that the child needs to process a particular series of transformations, *not* word order, to comprehend a passive sentence.

Markers Indicating the Relationship Among Words

In addition to word order and transformational rules, function words provide important information indicating the relationship between words (He runs *and* plays) and phrases (She ran *then* fell down). A change in these function words can result in a subsequent change in the relationship between elements of a sentence, as can be seen in sentences (1), (2), and (3) below.

(1) Give me the book *and* the crayon.
(2) Give me the book *then* the crayon.
(3) Give me the book *or* the crayon.

The ability to utilize these function words is important to language comprehension, especially in the classroom where children need to follow verbal instructions.

Objective.   Analyze the child's comprehension of function words, such as *and, but, not, or,* and *then.*

Materials.   Familiar objects can be used which children can easily manipulate. In addition, stimulus sentences should be developed which tap various function words in various parts of the sentence. The following are examples of stimulus sentences which could be used or adapted.

1. "Give me the pencil *and* the book." (*and* conjunction, coordinating two objects in the predicate)
2. "The book *or* pencil are on the table." (*or* conjunction, relating two nouns in the subject of the sentence)
3. "Put the book under the table, *then* hand me the pencil." (*then* conjunction, relating two independent sentences)
4. "Stand *and* drop the book." (*and* conjunction, coordinating two verbs)
5. "Give me the book *but not* the pencil." (*but not* conjunction, relating two objects in the predicate)

Procedures.   Hand the child a book and a pencil (or any two familiar objects) and say:

> "Here is a pencil and a book. I'm going to tell you to do something with them. So listen carefully. You do exactly what I say."

Present each stimulus sentence to the child and record what he does with the two objects. After each sentence, return both objects to the table in front of the child before proceeding to the next sentence.

Results.   In analyzing the child's correct and incorrect responses, note what linguistic features affected the child's performance (e.g., sentence length, type of function word, what elements of the sentence the function word related to, etc.). Also, try to determine whether or not the child actually understands the meaning of each function word.

Communication—Language Usage

In order for the child to utilize his language abilities for the purposes of giving or receiving information, he must be able to utilize accurate and precise expanded language in discourse. For the listener, this means retaining and comprehending the meaning of language as it occurs on an ongoing basis, attending to all aspects of the verbal message. This is especially true in the school situation, where the child spends a great proportion of the instructional day in the role of the listener.

Objective.   To assess the child's receptive language usage without the aid of extralinguistic cues, such as gestures, contextual clues, etc.

Materials.   Crayons and drawing paper or paste and cut-out construction paper of different sizes, colors, and shapes. A make-pretend script about a fantasy story which the child will draw following your dictation of the script or directions, using the cut-out shapes, which the child will follow to construct a design, mask, or scene.

Procedures.   Say to the child "I'm going to tell a story and you have to make your picture just like the story I tell." Administer the directions or made-up script to the child two or three sentences at a time. Encourage the child to make his picture story (or design) exactly like the story you tell. The following is an example of different miniscripts which can be used. In this situation the child will use the cut-out shapes which are before him. Read the entire miniscript and repeat if requested.

Miniscript I:

> Hi, I'm Mary Martian from Mars. As you know, I'm a little purple Martian with red, round eyes; a square head; and green pointed ears. My two little pigtails point up.

Miniscript II:

Hi, I'm Mary Martian again. Through the window of my spaceship I can see your planet earth. It has a big, round, yellow, smiling sun and blue clouds. It has green trees, flowers, and red birds flying all around.

Results.   In analyzing the child's picture or cut-out design, determine if the child was able to accurately process (and produce) expanded language (i.e., shape, size, color, position, etc.). If errors in comprehension did occur, what were they—errors related to size, shape, color, or position? This error analysis should provide some insight into how the child listens and comprehends expanded language.

Objective.   To assess the child's ability to engage in referential communication.

Materials.   A duplicate set of blocks which vary in shape, size, color, and design (optional). A table (child-sized) and two chairs which face each other. In addition, you will need a visual barrier so that the two children engaged in the block-building task cannot see each other's blocks.

Procedures.   Build a configuration of one child's blocks in two stages (i.e., arrange three blocks first and three later). Have the child whose blocks are being used for the examiner's construction give directions to the other child (the listener) with the objective being that the listener will be able to construct an identical configuration without seeing the original one. Tape-record the speaker's directions for later analysis.

Results.   Analyze, from your observations and tape recording, the accuracy, precision, and specificity of language used by the speaker to give the listener necessary information. Did the speaker take into account the listener's needs and perspective? For example, did the speaker give directions slowly enough that the listener had sufficient time to complete each direction? Did the speaker use pronouns, such as *it, that one,* for which the listener had a specific referent, or did he assume that the listener "knew" what *it* or *that one* referred to? Was spatial information such as distance or left–right positioning given by the speaker?

The preceding informal assessment approaches are just a few suggested ways of obtaining information about a child's language abilities. Needless to say, these are just a sample of the many possible ways of informally assessing language. With minimal adaptation and strategic feedback, each of these approaches can be transformed into instructional games that can act to facilitate the child's growth in language—a topic to which we now turn.

INSTRUCTIONAL APPROACHES FOR LANGUAGE DEVELOPMENT AND REMEDIATION

Upon completion of a thorough assessment, the teacher should have a composite picture of the child's language abilities and deficiencies. The selection of a specific language intervention will be based directly on what has been learned in the assessment activities. Some children will have been found to be mildly to severely delayed in most or all aspects of language functioning; others will show uneven development which may cross stage boundaries (see Table 8–8). Because language problems tend to be highly idiosyncratic in nature, we have found the informal approaches to be the most successful. However, because of their widespread use, we are also including descriptions of general language stimulation materials available as kits, and descriptions of several highly structured remedially based approaches associated most frequently with an individual, such as McGinnis, Barry, and others. We turn initially to the commercially available materials.

COMMERCIALLY AVAILABLE "KITS"

There are many language development or stimulation kits on the market. Some of the more common ones are briefly described in Table 8–10. Teachers should choose among these in accordance with their particular theoretical positions regarding language and the needs of the children in question. Of course, the original sources should be consulted for more complete details concerning the various formats, rationales, and operating procedures of the particular programs that are of interest to the teacher.

INSTRUCTIONAL SYSTEMS OF INDIVIDUAL PROFESSIONALS

For the most part, the educational systems described in this section are loose collections of sequenced activities. Some of them are constructed according to the principles of a particular school of thought or theoretical position; some are not. The methods are described mostly in books and usually are expositions of the authors' clinical "insights" and experiences; none of these systems is commercially available in packaged kit form. Probably because the approaches are so individualistic and the procedures are so ill-defined, researchers have as

Table 8–10. Summary of Most Widely Used Language Development Kits

Name (Author of Kit)	Target Population	Type of Approach	Comments
Developmental Language Lessons Levels 1 and 2 (Mowery and Replogle, 1977, 1980)	Language delayed; other handicapped	Spontaneous language use in structured setting	Emphasis on remediation for syntactic structures in 8 grammatical categories derived from Laura Lee's DDS test. Provides formal/informal diagnosis.
Developmental Syntax Program Revised Edition (Coughran and Liles, 1979)	Ages 3–10 who need syntactic remediation	Elicited response from pictures	Addresses syntactic errors in articles, negations, possessive pronouns, etc.
DISTAR I, II, III (Engleman and Osborn, 1970, 1973, 1975)	Preschool up	Drill and repetition; task analytical imitation and reinforcement	Highly structured and organized. Emphasis on expressive aspect of language. Moves from the familiar and simple to the more complex. Instructional groups based on performance levels. Heavy use of question-answer form of instruction— Teacher: "What's this?"—Pupils: (together) "That's a pencil!" Appears successful in teaching specific responses to specific stimuli; less adequate in generalizing to other situations.
Fokes Sentence Builder Kit (Fokes, 1975)	Learning disabled, deaf, hard of hearing, borderline to mild mentally retarded	Cognitive-psycholinguistic stimulative	Highly structured. Unique design for teaching syntactic rules and structures, but not as rote responses. WHO, WHAT, IS DOING, WHICH, WHERE.
Fokes Sentence Builder Expansion	Same	Same	Adds 3 grammatical categories WHOSE, HOW, WHEN
GOAL: Language Development—Games Oriented Activities for Learning. (Karnes, 1976a)	Normal to moderately handicapped	Developmental; stimulative	Highly structured. Based on Illinois Test of Psycholinguistic Abilities model. Lessons in game format. Criteria for mastery of each lesson not predetermined.
Karnes Early Language Activities (Karnes, 1976b)	All mentally handicapped	Developmental; stimulative	Downward extension of GOAL (see above). 200 model lessons. Provides instructional ideas only; actual items must be supplied by user.

Program	Population	Orientation	Description
Language Rehabilitation Program Levels 1 and 2 (Hain and Lainer, 1980)	Aphasic; mentally retarded; hard of hearing		Emphasis on development of verb form. Cards depict familiar scenes, emphasis on retrieving sentences previously known by aphasics.
Monterey Language Program (Programmed Conditioning for Language) (Gray and Ryan, 1972)	All children needing help on language	Behavioral; operant	Highly structured. User must be trained and certified by distributor. Includes pre- and posttests, placement tests, branching provisions, specific criteria. Good data showing effectiveness, including transference.
MWM Program for Developing Language Abilities (Minskoff, Wiseman, and Minskoff, 1972)	Ages 3 to 11 with evidence of language deficits	Developmental; stimulative	Rationale is based on the model of the Illinois Test of Psycholinguistic Abilities. Comprised of a teacher's guide, inventory, manual, and materials. Provisions for diagnostic screening; remediation for weak areas according to model. Activities sequenced by difficulty level.
Peabody Language Development Kits (L. M. Dunn, J. O. Smith, & L. Dunn, 1981; L. M. Dunn, L. Dunn, and J. O. Smith, 1981; L. M. Dunn, Horton, & J. O. Smith, 1981; L. M. Dunn, J. O. Smith, & D. Smith, 1982)	All children	General developmental; stimulative	Purpose is to stimulate oral language, heighten verbal intelligence, and enhance school progress. Overall language stressed. Attractive and motivating. Kits contain manual, lessons, manipulative materials, reinforcement chips, and picture cards. Group instruction format. Research showing effectiveness is inconclusive.
Project MEMPHIS (Quick, Little, and Campbell, 1973)	Mild to severely handicapped	Developmental	Emphasis on language for verbal and nonverbal communication. 260 lesson plans based on three steps: planning, implementing evaluation.
SYNPRO (Syntax Programmer) (Peterson, Brener, and Williams, 1974)	All ages with mild problems	Operant; drill	Can be used by professionals or aides. Provides a highly structured way of programming syntactic strings.
Visually Cued Language Cards (Foster, Giddan, and Stark, 1975)	Normal to profoundly retarded	Stimulation of functional language	Consists of five series of picture cards. Related to Assessment of Children's Language Comprehension Test. May be used at home or school.
Wilson Initial Syntax Program (Wilson, 1973)	Those with syntax problems, especially TMR	Stimulation; Chomskyian	Emphasis on improving receptive syntactic skills. Can be used by teacher aides.

yet avoided investigating their efficacy. Regardless, many of the systems described are widely used in practice.

English Now (Feigenbaum, 1970)

Rationale.   Standard English and nonstandard dialects of the English language are linguistically equal. The deciding factor for selecting one language or dialect for use in a given situation is "appropriateness." According to Feigenbaum, although standard English is deemed "appropriate" in class, it is not necessary or desirable to eradicate nonstandard English. Instead, standard English can be taught as a second dialect the same way English is taught as a second language. Feigenbaum's materials include workbooks, manuals, and cassettes. The general approach is described in Feigenbaum (1970). This method of teaching standard English as a second dialect has been called "the aural–oral approach," "the linguistic method," "the audiolingual method," and "pattern practice." It consists of first establishing that nonstandard dialects are not indications of laziness or stupidity. The students are made aware of the social uses of both dialects. The areas of difficulty, as well as the areas of little or no difficulty, are determined by contrasting the grammatical and phonological systems of standard and nonstandard English. Standard English is taught by presentation of similiarities and differences, and discrimination, identification, translation, and response drills.

Assessment.   When the teacher recognizes the existence and legitimacy of nonstandard English, he or she can begin to understand the student who uses a nonstandard dialect and more accurately deduce learning problems. Some students have a partial knowledge of standard English; that is, they can recognize and produce it but without accurate control. Others cannot even recognize differences between their dialect and standard English. However, all students begin with sorting out standard from nonstandard English. When they can accurately differentiate the two dialects, they move on to the other drills.

Training Techniques.   In the Feigenbaum program, training is initiated by the presentation of similarities and differences. Two items, one standard and the other nonstandard, show the students the structure to be learned and practiced, and indicate where mistakes may occur. For example, the following two sentences may be written on the board or projected from a transparency:

> He work hard.
> He works hard.

The teacher would then ask how the two sentences differ and which one is standard and which nonstandard. Soliciting their observations will make the activity more interesting.

The simple activity described above takes very little time, probably not more than fifteen seconds. Yet, in this short period of time, the students have sorted out and identified standard and nonstandard English, and they have indicated the particular feature that distinguishes nonstandard and standard English without an involved grammatical explanation.

Discrimination drills are then employed, giving the students practice in discriminating between standard and nonstandard English.[2] In this type of drill, pairs of sentences or words are presented to the students orally. The students indicate whether the two are the same or different (this drill is also known as "same–different drill"). The following drill is an example of this type.

Drill 1

Teacher Stimulus	Student Response
1. He work hard. He works hard.	1. different
2. He work hard. He work hard.	2. same
3. Paula likes leather coats. Paula likes leather coats.	3. same
4. She prefers movies. She prefer movies.	4. different
5. Robert play guard. Robert play guard.	5. same

If the students respond correctly to this type of drill, it can be assumed that their attention has been directed to the feature and that they hear it consistently.

Identification drills are attempted next; the students are required to identify a single word or sentence without the assistance of a second item.

Drill 2

Teacher Stimulus	Student Response
1. He work hard.	1. nonstandard
2. Paula likes leather coats.	2. standard
3. He works hard.	3. standard
4. She prefer movies.	4. nonstandard
5. She prefers movies.	5. standard
6. Paula like leather coats.	6. nonstandard.

2. The drills presented here are from I. Feigenbaum, *English Now* (New York: New Century, 1970). By permission of New Century Education Corp.

If the students respond correctly, it can be assumed that they can hear the feature that distinguished standard from nonstandard English, and that they can identify the two dialects on the basis of the feature.

In a translation drill, the students translate a word or sentence from standard to nonstandard or from nonstandard to standard.

Drill 3

Teacher Stimulus	Student Response
1. He works hard.	1. He work hard.
2. Paula likes leather coats.	2. Paula like leather coats.
3. She prefers movies.	3. She prefer movies.

Drill 4

Teacher Stimulus	Student Response
1. He work hard.	1. He works hard.
2. Paula like leather coats.	2. Paula likes leather coats.
3. She prefer movies.	3. She prefers movies.

One may legitimately raise the objection that drill 3 calls for the students to practice what they already can do. This drill is useful in providing a further opportunity for the students to hear the standard forms they will be called on to produce, but, if this extra help seems unnecessary, drill 3 may be omitted.

Drill 5

Teacher Stimulus	Student Response
1. He works hard.	1. He work hard.
2. Paula like leather coats.	2. Paula likes leather coats.
3. She prefer movies.	3. She prefers movies.

In this drill the students make two responses: the first is to identify the sentence as standard or nonstandard, the second is to translate from one to the other.

More complex drills can be constructed. The added complexity shown below is the difference between the standard English verb forms with *he* and *they*.

Drill 6

Teacher Stimulus	Student Response
1. He works hard.	1. He work hard.
2. They like nylon jackets.	2. They like nylon jackets.

Drill 7

Teacher Stimulus	Student Response
1. He work hard.	1. He works hard.
2. They like nylon jackets.	2. They like nylon jackets.

Drill 8

Teacher Stimulus	Student Response
1. He works hard.	1. He work hard.
2. He work hard.	2. He works hard.
3. They work hard.	3. They work hard.

An additional complication has appeared; it is impossible to identify *They work hard* as standard or nonstandard. This point must be made clear to the students so they do not search for differentiating features.

The standard/nonstandard contrast and comparison can be carried into freer activities, in which the students have the opportunity to speak more naturally. Drill 9 is a response drill that gives the students the chance to approach generating completely natural English. (In this drill the students are to contradict the statement with an appropriate response.)

Drill 9

Teacher Stimulus	Student Response
1. Your best friend work.	1. No, he don't.
2. He gets good grades.	2. No, he doesn't.
3. Her boyfriend don't drive fast.	3. Yes, he do.

There can be an almost unlimited gradation within the range of activities called "response drills." In drill 10, the students are free to generate their own material:

Drill 10

Teacher Stimulus
1. Do his sister go to this school?
2. Does his sister go to this school?
3. Does a boa constrictor crush its victims?

Drills 11, 12, and 13 deal with the pronunciation of the standard English final sound.

Drill 11

Teacher Stimulus	Student Response
1. mouth mouf	1. different
2. mouth mouth	2. same

Drill 12

Teacher Stimulus	Student Response
1. mouf	1. nonstandard
2. mouth	2. standard

Drill 13

Teacher Stimulus	Student Response
1. mouf	1. mouth
2. mouth	2. mouf

A brisk, regular rhythm of presentation mediates against the repetitiveness or drilling and the unnaturalness of the responses. Only completely natural standard English should be used and required. The drilling is best conducted for brief periods of time on a regular basis: ten to fifteen minutes of a class period.

Program Evaluation.   Many teachers may feel uncomfortable using nonstandard English in their classrooms. This must be overcome if the program is to work effectively. Efficacy research is lacking at the present time.

The Association Method (McGinnis, 1963)

Rationale.   McGinnis was associated with the Central Institute for the Deaf (CID) for approximately forty years, beginning at about the end of World War I. Initially she worked with the deaf and with returning veterans suffering from aphasia.

Aphasia is defined by McGinnis, Kleffner, and Goldstein (1956)[3] as: ". . . an inability to express and/or to understand language symbols, and it is the result

3. From M. McGinnis, F. Kleffner, and R. Goldstein, Teaching of aphasic children, *The Volta Review*, 1956, 58, p. 239. Copyright © The Alexander Graham Bell Association for the Deaf.

of some defect in the central nervous system rather than the result of a defect in the peripheral speech mechanism, ear or auditory nerve," or a problem of low IQ or psychosis. They qualify this definition by saying that evidence of CNS (central nervous system) pathology is not mandatory for the diagnosis of childhood aphasia; rather, diagnosis is based on observable hearing ability, language, and intelligence. While they do not believe that aphasia is the result of a hearing deficiency, mental retardation, autism, emotional instability, or delayed speech, they believe the possibility of these problems existing concomitantly with aphasia does exist, thus complicating diagnosis of the major deficiency considerably. Essentially, the aphasic patient does have the inner language described by Myklebust and lacks only language comprehension and expression.

McGinnis outlines three classifications of aphasia: (1) expressive or motor aphasia; (2) receptive or sensory aphasia (word deafness); and (3) repetitive patterns of vocalization with expressions, voice equality, volume, and inflection that is inappropriate to what the child is trying to express.

Expressive aphasia is characterized by (1) partial or complete inability to imitate actions or positions of the tongue, lip, and jaw and sounds and words; (2) adequate control of muscles used in speech for other acts, such as chewing or swallowing; (3) adequate hearing; and (4) adequate intelligence.

Receptive or sensory aphasia is characterized in its clearest form by (1) a lack of understanding of speech; (2) lack of expressive speech (which can take four forms: muteness, scribble speech, echolalia, and appropriate use of limited phrases); (3) adequate control of muscles used in speech for other acts such as chewing and swallowing; (4) discrepancy between intellectual ability and the ability to understand spoken language. Hearing and intelligence may both be quite difficult to assess in the sensory aphasic (McGinnis, Kleffner, and Goldstein, 1956).

McGinnis was struck by the similarities in the language-learning problems of certain children in the Central Institute for the Deaf and of aphasic veterans. Procedures for teaching the children were modified and when significant and continued progress was made by them, the beginning of a highly structured technique for language learning was formulated. This technique is the Association Method.

The objective of the Association Method is to enable students to enter regular schools at as near the appropriate age level as possible. This goal means that although the program stresses the teaching of speech and language, academic subjects also must be an integral part of the program.

McGinnis (1963) describes in detail the three levels of language through which the child progresses. The child begins with individual sounds, then combines sounds, nouns, simple sentences, questions, and ever-increasing syntactic structures until reaching the final stages, where much more variability in expressive form is encouraged and should be available to him or her. The three units are discrete entities with a strict system for the introduction of grammatical parts. She also describes a method of color coding that is first used for syllable parts, then word parts, and finally different grammatical forms.

In addition to the language units, McGinnis describes "correlative programs." The first two, attention-getting exercises and exercises leading to writing, are reminiscent of the materials of Getman, Kephart, and Frostig. The third program involves practice of specific speech sounds and movements; the fourth and fifth programs are number and calendar work. The number work involves a great deal of new language structure, and detailed suggestions are given for its introduction.

Assessment.   The Association Method is used with auditory decoding and vocal encoding problems. Once the educational procedures are begun (at about four years of age), no differentiation is made between the various classifications of aphasia.

Training Techniques.   Classes should be composed of six to seven children and one teacher plus one assistant. The teacher handles both academic and speech and language training. Great stress is laid on the teacher's knowledge of basic speech and language elements and his or her skills in teaching these. The classroom assistant may be a regular employee, a student teacher, or a parent. It is suggested that parents conduct lessons with the teacher's guidance, thereby increasing their understanding of the problem and their own child. The physical arrangement of the room should be similar to a normal classroom; no amplification should be used in the early stages of speech and language development, regardless of the hearing level of the children.

Five major principles are involved in the Association Method. (1) A phonetic or elemental approach, based on individual sounds, is used. The child is taught to produce each sound and associate it with the Northampton–Yale written letter symbol. (2) Strict articulation of each sound is required before the child attempts it in a word. Initially, words are broken into their sound elements, later syllables, and finally the word is "smoothed," or spoken as a complete unit. (3) Cursive script is used because of its continuity and prevalent cultural usage. The articulatory pattern and sound are associated with the appropriate letter symbol of cursive script. (4) Expressive usage is the foundation, or starting place, of langauge development. In cases of receptive aphasia the child is not expected to understand any word until he or she has first produced it. (5) Systematic sensory–motor association forms the procedural base of the entire system, although it is not formally introduced until nouns are taught. An examination of the seven steps for teaching nouns reveals the emphasis of the Association Method on repetition, retention, and recall. The child learns:

1. To produce in sequence from the written form the sounds of each word.
2. To match the picture of the object to the appropriate written form.
3. To copy the word, producing each sound while writing the letter symbol.
4. To lip-read the word from the teacher's production, say it aloud, and match the picture to the written form.
5. To name the object from memory as pictures are presented.
6. To write the word for the object from memory, saying each sound as the letter is written.
7. To repeat the word spoken into the child's ear and then match the picture to the written form of the word (McGinnis, Kleffner, and Goldstein, 1956).

Program Evaluation. The Association Method appears to be a valid multisensory approach dealing with all levels and processes of language. Because of this and its systematic organization, it could prove valuable in modified form with all learning-disabled children, in addition to those with the auditory decoding and vocal encoding problems for which it was designed. It is, however, an extremely complex and detailed methodology that might fall prey to uncompromising rigidity if used by an untrained individual. No research has been done to assess its effectiveness.

Steps in Language Development for the Deaf (Pugh, 1955)

Rationale. The Fitzgerald approach was developed for the teaching of language to the deaf. It is recommended for the teaching of children with auditory misperception because they also exhibit distorted oral and written language as a result of a disorder in the primary sensory modality for the reception of oral language. Fitzgerald, in *Straight Language for the Deaf* (1949), emphasizes the structure of English, stating that coherent language depends on coherent thinking. She believes that when a model is supplied for language, correct thinking will result. The model that is supplied by Fitzgerald is a modification of and enlargement of a system that used five slates or chalkboards with separate headings for different parts of speech. The Fitzgerald Key is a very simple visual device useful for teaching the organization of language; it consists of a series of sequential headings and symbols under which words can be categorized.

The major work of Bessie Pugh is a revision and explanation of the Fitzgerald Key. *Steps in Language Development for the Deaf* is a sequential series of lessons that uses the Fitzgerald Key.

Assessment.   The method is recommended for instructing all children who have linguistic deficiencies manifested by an ability to formulate sentences. Pugh states that the Key should not be presented in its entirety to the young child; rather, the headings "Who" and "What" are presented first so that the child can learn to classify names of objects and people according to these headings. The child moves on in the program as he or she masters each level.

Training Techniques.   The Key is placed above the chalkboard, in most situations the appropriate area for written language activities. The use of colors with different headings facilitates mastery of them. Although specifically designed as a teaching device with a specific sequence of activities for training the deaf, the Key is now used less rigidly and more as a reference tool to aid any student who needs help in organizing language.

Straight Language for the Deaf includes more than the Key and related activities. The first six chapters, though brief, include activities for vocabulary building, weather and calendar work, commands, and expressions. After expressing definite opinions about the mental development of the deaf, Fitzgerald introduces the Key symbols and follows with "nonlanguage" rules. The remainder of the text includes only Key activities, beginning with pronouns, adjectives, clauses, and connectives. The largest single chapter of the text includes Key activities for verbs.

The value of *Straight Language for the Deaf* is to be found not only in the Key, but also in the very great number of practical teaching techniques that are included. The activities for mental development are of particular interest: games, including pretending, absurd statements in stories to see if the children react to the absurdity, incomplete statements, true and false statements, and others.

Pugh developed levels by which the Key should be presented. The headings "Who" and "What" are presented first, so that the child can learn to classify names of objects and people according to these headings. For example, the teacher presents to the child real objects, pictures of objects and people, or the words for the objects and people, and asks the child to list them under the proper heading. Names of people include not only proper names but others, such as father, mother, aunt, or sister.

After this initial classification procedure has been mastered, further headings, "How Many" and "What Color," are introduced and related to the headings "Who" and "What." The third step includes sentence building, using the pronoun "I," the verb "see," and a direct object (Pugh, 1955, pp. 5–8). Sequential development continues with emphasis on verbs and other headings. All parts of speech and their functions are eventually included.

Program Evaluation.   Pugh's text is based entirely on the Fitzgerald Key but is clearer and more precise in presenting examples and providing explicit directions for using the Key. The essential differences between the work of Fitzgerald and Pugh are the amount of structure provided in each and the sequence of development. Pugh provides more structure than Fitzgerald and presents a more valuable developmental sequence, because the classifying activities that are used begin the sequence of Key activities at a higher level than the rote learning of symbols, the first step in the Fitzgerald sequence.

The Key system is widely used in schools for the deaf and is successful in what it intends to accomplish. However, it has limitations. If used as the only method of teaching language, the child may develop a formal and unnatural language pattern. Second, the Key does not include all the possibilities of acceptable language. Third, when the use of complex language is attempted later, the Key may become more of a hindrance than a help to understanding. Finally, emphasis is placed on using complete sentences rather than brief language. While this is necessary for training the deaf, this more lengthy form is not always necessary or appropriate for the hearing. Research is needed to determine whether this system, which has been used successfully with the deaf for fifty years, is really applicable for hearing children who have linguistic deficiencies in ability to formulate sentences.

A Language Approach for Young Children (Barry, 1961)

Rationale.   It is Hortense Barry's premise that children who are unable to use or understand spoken language can be helped by developing their language sequentially: first learning the meaning of experience, then learning to understand what is said to them, and finally learning to express their ideas, because this is the normal process of language development that usually occurs during the first year.

Each child is first tested for awareness of sound, discriminating of voice, auditory perception, and auditory memory. Language development is then assessed to determine at which of the three levels (inner, receptive, or expressive) the child is having difficulty and should begin training. Psychomotor functioning is tested. The development of language, corrective therapy for psychomotor dysfunctions, and the physical setup are correlated and begun simultaneously. First inner, then receptive, and finally expressive language are developed.

Assessment.   Barry's techniques were developed for young children of average intelligence who display aphasoid characteristics affecting the development of language. The case history, hearing tests, language evaluation, and psychomotor functioning evaluation of each child are used to determine his or her diagnostic training.

The case history is reviewed for developmental information from conception onward, with emphasis on illnesses, deviations from normal social development, communication, and education.

The child's hearing is then tested for perception of sound. Awareness of sound is evaluated by response of the child to high and low instrumental frequencies that are produced while the child is playing. Speech sounds are used to determine the child's awareness of voice. Understanding and awareness of spoken language are determined by the use of simple language such as "Where are your hands?" or "Show me the ball." Satisfied that the child is aware of sounds, the examiner may probe discrimination ability. The child is permitted to engage in exploratory play with various noisemakers. Then the child is asked to identify speech and nonspeech sounds that are produced behind his or her back. Auditory perception is assessed by teaching the child to imitate the teacher's actions as he or she beats a drum. After training, the child is asked to repeat the sound. Auditory memory is evaluated by having the child repeat nonsense syllables.

The language evaluation is divided into three types: inner, receptive, and expressive. Familiar objects in the child's environment are used in language testing. When assessing inner language (i.e., communication with oneself) the child is asked to play with toy furniture or animals without verbal instruction. If the objects are arranged in a meaningful relationship, this suggests that the child has integrated personal experience of the environment. It also shows that perceptual and conceptual functions are intact and that he or she has developed inner language (Barry, 1961). If the child lacks the ability to relate objects, to classify and to group them, he or she has an inner language deficiency. In receptive language testing, the child is asked to identify objects by responding to questions such as "Where is the car?" If the child does not respond, the language is reduced to one word. Failure reveals the need for receptive language training. Expressive language evaluation moves from the concrete to the abstract; for example, the child names objects and then describes their functions.

In testing psychomotor functioning, teacher-constructed tests are used to determine figure–ground dysfunction. Disorganization, immaturity, or confusion in the visual–motor modality are detected by the Bender Visual–Motor Gestalt Test. Goodenough's "Draw-A-Man Test" assess dysfunction in body image. A Binet-type formboard for young children and a Seguin-type formboard for older children are used to detect spatial-orientation dysfunction. Emotional and social development are based on the analysis of the case history and/or teacher evaluation. Gross-motor and fine-motor skills are determined by teacher observation. The Barger Mirror technique is used to evaluate speech. As the teacher and child look into the mirror, the teacher produces a sound and then observes the muscle functioning of the child's articulators as the child imitates (Barry, 1960).

Training Techniques.   Based on the evaluation results, review of the history, and observations, the teacher plans training and proceeds with "diagnostic training." Three areas for training children with language disorders are considered: (1) physical setup, (2) corrective therapy for psychomotor dysfunction and disturbed behavior, and (3) development of language. Training in each area is begun at the same time and is correlated because psychomotor functions are believed to develop simultaneously with language, and Barry considers physical setup and corrective therapy to be prerequisites for language training.

Language development is a complex operation that develops sequentially. During the first stage, inner language, the child develops awareness of the environment and attaches meaning to personal experiences. Inner language training teaches the child to relate to his or her environment through the meaningful manipulation of objects. Some of the activities are: pick up the spoon and feed the doll, arrange the chairs around the table, put the utensils together, and put the daddy in the car and make it go. The child is taught to recognize parents, everyday situations, and objects. He or she is taught to make-believe, to use experiences, and to integrate them. When these skills are mastered, inner language is acquired and the child moves on to the next stage, receptive language.

During the receptive language stage, which normally develops between eight to twelve months of age, the child begins to understand some words and associate the spoken word with personal experiences. Receptive language is usually stimulated through a multimodality approach (auditory, visual, and kinesthetic). This allows for individualization of the program. For instance, children who have difficulty remembering auditory patterns are taught through the kinesthetic modality. Training begins with basic color words; solid, 2-inch blocks of varying colors are used. Proximity is used to maintain visual attention, and a hearing tube is used to maintain auditory attention. After the "feeding-in" process, the teacher says, "Where is red? Show me the red block." The child is trained to respond by picking up the correct block. After several colors have been taught, the teacher sits behind the child and again directs the activity. The child must now respond depending upon auditory clues alone. If the child still has difficulty remembering the auditory pattern, the printed form of the word is taught. The child is taught to match the printed word form in red with the red block. Then he or she traces the word. When the child has mastered this approach, the words are printed in black. If the concept of color is too abstract, toy objects and figures are used. Nouns, verbs, and prepositions are taught in that order. The child is trained to respond to commands such as jump, run, and hop. Frequently used verbs and prepositional phrases are taught next, and the teacher begins to use more complex language. After the child has structured the auditory world, expressive language training is begun.

In normal children, expressive language usually develops around twelve months when a child speaks his or her first word. Expressive language training moves from the concrete to the abstract. Nouns, verbs, and prepositions are mastered in that order; next pronouns are introduced, then phrases and sentences. Telegraphic speech is accepted at the beginning of the training program. As the child's vocabulary increases and the parts of speech, are learned, the teacher demands complete sentences. The child is encouraged to talk about experiences and possessions. A Fitzgerald Key is used to structure language. The child refers to the key as he or she begins to read and write. Language training is emphasized throughout all lessons, and training in speech, reading, and writing is based on individual needs. Dictionary drills, spelling rules, verb tenses, and intensive phonic work are used with older aphasic children in building functional language.

Program Evaluation.   Barry's language training system is developmental, concise, and explicit. It provides a wealth of information and suggestions for teaching not only language but other related functions. It was one of the first programs to recognize the need to relate assessment problems to remediation efforts.

The Psychoneurological Approach (Johnson and Myklebust, 1967)

Rationale.   During his studies of children with severe language problems, Myklebust (1952; Johnson and Myklebust, 1967) became aware that the study of special children resulted in better understanding of all children. From his work with exceptional children, especially those with severe language learning disorders, he formulated his theories.

Theory.   Basic to an understanding of Myklebust's "psychology of learning disabilities" is his theory of learning. He purports (Johnson and Myklebust, 1967) that learning depends not only on the provision of proper opportunities, but also on the presence of three basic types of integrities: psychodynamic factors, peripheral nervous systems (PNS) functions, and central nervous system (CNS) functions. Myklebust views learning as a hierarchy of experiences. In *The Psychology of Deafness* (1964) he outlines and explains each level of experience and its relationship to others. The levels overlap developmental periods that operate simultaneously in the normal human being. When one level of development is impaired, each of the areas above that level is presumed to be altered to some degree. The developmental levels postulated by Myklebust are:

1. *Sensation.* Sensation is a nervous-system activity resulting from activation of a given sense organ.

2. *Perception.* At this level, the individual learns to interpret sensation and to engage in anticipatory behavior.

3. *Imagery.* An image represents an object or experience. "... aspects of the object itself are recalled and used for the thought process; what it sounds like, looks like, and how it feels constitutes the image" (p. 227).

4. *Verbal symbolic behavior.* Symbolic behavior requires more abstraction ability than the former. Although verbal and nonverbal symbols exist, it is primarily through verbal language that we internalize experiences and are able to communicate with others. The verbal involves: (a) relation of experience to symbols; (b) receptive language, or the comprehension of symbols; and (c) expressive language, or the output of expressions using symbols. In these processes, auditory-receptive and expressive language (speaking) precede visual-receptive and expressive language (writing).

5. *Conceptualization.* Conceptualization is the highest level of experience attained. It involves the classification and categorization of experiences according to common elements.

Assessment.   Diagnostic study is the single most important factor in planning for learning-disabled children. Myklebust (Johnson and Myklebust, 1967) suggests that evaluation should be made by a pediatrician, neurologist, and opthamologist, as well as by the educator, and should include measurement of sensory acuity, imtelligence, language (spoken, read, and written), motor function, educational achievement, emotional status, and social maturity. In defining problems, a multidimensional approach is used. First, the type of involvement is defined. Next, the level of involvement (according to the psychological hierarchy of experiences) is determined. The effect of the disability on types of educational achievement (reading, arithmetic) is pinpointed; remedial programs then can be meaningfully prescribed.

Training Techniques.   Teaching is directed to the level and type of disability, as well as to the readiness and tolerance levels of the student involved. Each individual is recognized as unique; whereas perceptual training may be beneficial in one case, it may be detrimental in another. The same is true of teaching to correct deficit areas, teaching to the integrities, or using a universal multisensory approach. Clinical teaching involves maintaining the high areas of ability at their high levels while properly developing the low levels. Balance is important. It must also be emphasized that the teacher changes the method for the child, not vice versa. *Learning Disabilities,* by Johnson and Myklebust (1967), is the best available source for training activities based on the model just described.

Program Evaluation.   The greatest portion of Johnson and Myklebust's book is devoted to excellent, specific methods of remediation. If the teacher encounters children with moderate to severe specific problems in language, the techniques of Johnson and Myklebust will serve as an excellent source for remediation activities. The techniques are best used in a tutorial setting. As each child's problem is unique, each child's program should be individually tailored. This clinical approach is difficult to evaluate using traditional procedures, and has therefore stimulated little efficacy research.

Teaching the American Language to Kids
(Dever, 1978)

Rationale.   TALK addresses itself to teaching appropriate sentence patterns to children who function at a linguistically low level. The TALK program deals with problems of language acquisition rather than with the motoric aspects of speech (although speech problems may be found in children who exhibit language problems). It is hoped that by teaching language to children their overall learning rate will improve, thereby reducing negative social reactions.

Assessment.   The program is based on the premise that it is of utmost importance to a teacher to understand what it is that children need to learn. For that reason, the entire program is sequenced in a hierarchical way that permits the teacher to establish precisely which prerequisite linguistic tasks a child has mastered. Assessment consists of discovering the place in the program where the child no longer can successfully master the tasks, and hence is the point at which instruction should begin.

Intervention.   Four major types of sentence patterns are taught—Questions, Passives, Subordinates, and Coordinates. Each sentence type had been analyzed in terms of prerequisite required skills; these skills are taught in order before the final form of the sentence pattern is taught. The techniques used are those developed for "Teaching English as a Second Language" and involve group responses to a conversational format established by the teacher and a teacher's aide.

Program Evaluation.   The program has been used successfully with retarded children, learning-disabled and hearing-impaired children, and with multihandicapped children.

INFORMAL INSTRUCTIONAL APPROACHES

While it would be impossible in this format to describe the multiple options available to the teacher to informally facilitate language development or remedy a language problem, the following informal approaches are *representative* of the strategies that can be intrgrated into the classroom curriculum. Each activity is geared to a particular aspect of language and can be utilized with the entire class, in small groups, or in a one-to-one format. Before describing these activities, it should be noted that since assessment and instruction are essentially two sides of the same coin, the informal assessment techniques presented earlier can easily be adapted to instructional activities. One additional point needs mentioning. Since language is an interpersonal phenomenon, with communication being one of its main functions, all instructional activities *must stress* the interpersonal, communicative nature of language. This means that imitation should be kept at a minimum if it is to be used at all, and the language activities should reflect the child's ongoing activities rather than more passive activities, such as labeling pictures. Most of the following activities have been adapted from Bryen (1975).

Approaches to Semantic/Syntactic Development

Whether the teacher's instructional approach is designed for an individual with pervasive language problems or an individual with a few specific problems, several considerations must be taken into account. First, it is crucial to determine whether the problem is primarily a *structural* (syntactical) problem or primarily related to *content* (semantics). For example, a child may have the semantic function of negation (content) yet not the appropriate syntactical structure to express it (e.g., *I not go home* instead of *I don't go home*). Second, children with language problems may have difficulty in either the reception or expression of language. Generally, instruction should begin with reception. Finally, children with language problems should begin with concrete experiences before moving on to language activities that are more abstract. Therefore, language activities should begin with the child's "here and now" long before the child is encouraged to use language to describe events that are distant in time (i.e., past or future). Children should be encouraged to talk about objects and events that are present before they use the same basic linguistic structures to describe objects and events that are perceptually absent. With these considerations in mind, let us explore some informal instructional activities.

Expanding Noun Phrases and Verb Phrases

One of the most common difficulties a child may encounter is the restricted usage of either the verb phrase or noun phrase of a sentence. When either phrase is restricted in expression or reception, much potential information is lost.

Objective.   Develop and expand the child's capacity to use (receptively and expressively) expanded noun phrases or verb phrases.

Materials.   Familiar objects around the room can be used that would require more than a simple name or label to be identified, such as two desks or balls or books. Children in the class could also be used.

Procedures.   A "Sherlock Holmes" gamelike approach could be used whereby one child describes a child or hidden object without giving the name. This would constitute the clue. The "mystery" would be solved when the children in the class identify on the basis of the clues the hidden object or child. Following is a list of objects or children who would have to be identified and increasingly more difficult expanded noun phrases (NP) or verb phrases (VP) needed as the clue. In using this strategy, the teacher must first identify which phrase (noun or verb) should be developed. Next, it is important to determine the sequencing of structures to be developed.

Objects/People	*Expanded Phrase Taught*
1. Two flowers (one green and one blue)	Color + Noun (NP)
2. Three books (one large blue book, one small blue book, and one large green book)	Size and Color and Noun (NP)
3. Two girls (one girl with a yellow skirt and one with a brown skirt)	Noun and Embedded NP
4. Two balls (one is on the box and one is in the box)	Expands VP to Verb and NP
5. Two children walking (one child walking slowly and one walking fast)	Expands VP to Verb and Adverb
6. Two children pretending (one child wanting to play a piano and one child wanting to ride a horse)	Expands VP and V and Complement

Developing Transformations

Many children may have developed the content or semantics of negation or interrogation but may not yet have developed the structural transformations for expressing these sentence types. For example, one child might use the sentence *I no like him* to express negation or *I go home?* (rise in intonation) to express interrogation. In both cases the child has mastered the content of each sentence type but not its structure.

Objective. Develop the appropriate transformational structures for expressing negation and interrogation.

Materials. Puppets can be used as simulated speakers and listeners.

Procedures. It is first necessary to delineate where the child is structurally in developing the appropriate transformations. The sequence of transformations for negation and yes/no questions are provided below:

Negation

Terminal structures: NP and Auxiliary Verb and Negative marker and Verb and NP (I do not [don't] like you)
Stage I: NP and Verb and NP (I like you)
Stage II: NP and Auxiliary Verb and V and NP (I do like you)
Stage III: NP and Auxiliary Verb and Negative and V and NP (I do not like you)
Stage IV: Contraction of Auxiliary Verb and Negative marker (I don't like you)

Interrogative (Yes/No Questions)

Terminal structure: Auxiliary Verb and NP and V and NP (Do you like me?)
Stage I: NP and Verb and NP (You like me?)
Stage II: NP and Auxiliary Verb and Verb and NP (You do like me?)
Stage III: Auxiliary Verb and NP and V and NP (Do you like me?)

Take, for example, the child who said *I like him* or *I go home?* In using the sequences above it can be seen that in negation this child has not reached Stage II, where the obligatory auxiliary verb is included. Instead, this child is simple embedding the negative morpheme *no* between the NP and the verb. Similarly, this child has not yet reached Stage II in the development of interrogation, where the auxiliary verb is included. Here the child indicates a question content by using the structure of a declarative sentence with the appropriate intonation (rise in pitch at the end of the sentence). This child then should begin intervention at Stage II with the inclusion of the appropriate auxiliary verbs.

The child and teacher can begin with one puppet each. The teacher could have the child tell the puppet to say:

"I *do* like you"
"I *can* play ball"
"You *are* coming to my party"

In this way the teacher acts as the model and the child produces the particular structure by talking for the puppet. Once the child can generate the appropriate auxiliary verb (Stage II), he or she is ready for the next stage in both negation and interrogation. Similar puppet-to-puppet strategies can be used for each successive stage.

Pronominalization

An added linguistic problem that is found among many children is the difficulty in accurately comprehending or producing pronouns. The use of pronouns (both personal and impersonal) requires the ability to classify with respect to animate versus inanimate (*I, you, she,* versus *it*), number—singular versus plural (*I* versus *we, he* versus *they*), gender (*he* versus *she*), as well as shifts in speaker/listener role and spatial aspects (*here* versus *there, this* versus *that,* or *I* versus *you*). For example, if a child were standing next to a female teacher and another child came by and said *She is happy* while referring to the teacher, the child must know that *she* refers to the categories animate, female, listener. Now if the teacher concurs and says *I am happy,* the child must comprehend that *I* refers to the categories animate, male or female, but now speaker. Both sentences refer to the same person, but the pronouns used have varied. This can be a very confusing linguistic concept for the child.

Objective.   Develop the use of appropriate personal and impersonal pronouns.

Materials.   All that is needed is a ball and some pictures of objects that can be pinned to the children's clothing.

Procedures.   Select a particular set of pronouns that contrast with each other with respect to a particular category (e.g., animate versus inanimate or male versus female). In the later case (i.e., male versus female), have the children sit in a circle, girls alternating with boys. The child's task is to roll the ball to another child, but before doing so the child must determine if the recipient is a *he* or a *she* and state which.

Once the children are successful with this, an additional category such as animate/inanimate may be added. Now some children wear pictures of familiar objects, such as a car, ball, or house while the remaining children retain their animate identity. Now before rolling the ball, the child must make two decisions (i.e., animate/inanimate and male/female) before using the pronoun *he, she,* or *it.* This gamelike strategy can be used to develop the static pronominal categories just described as well as the more temporally and spatially changing pronouns such as *I/you, you/me, this/that.*

Approaches to Developing Language Usage

Language is a means of expressing our thoughts, ideas, feelings, needs, and questions. The way in which we use language is dependent on many factors. First, it requires at least a minimal degree of facility with the various aspects of language (i.e., phonology, morphology, syntax, and semantics). However, competency with these aspects of language is not sufficient in and of itself to guarantee that an individual will be an effective language user or communicator. Language usage requires that the individual perceive a need to interact with another human being. Furthermore, effective language usage requires that the individual (both as speaker and listener) be able to take into account another person's perspective rather than only his or her own. Without this ability, communication will remain idiosyncratic, ambiguous, and uneffective.

Cognitive, social, emotional, and linguistic development interact to either facilitate or interfere with effective language usage. Depending on these areas of development, the functions of language will differ. Piaget has provided great insights into how the functions of language as a communicative process differ between the cognitively mature individual and the developmentally young child. For the adult, language can serve to assert, state objective facts, convey and seek information, express commands or desires, and criticize or threaten (Piaget, 1959). In other words, language is both cognitive and social. For the developmentally young child, language usage can be seen as both egocentric *and* social.

In developing instructional strategies to improve usage, the teacher must once again take into account several cognitive and linguistic factors. For example, one must consider the child's developmental *usage* of language, regardless of how advanced the development may be in the semantic/syntactic aspects of language. For example, is the child still primarily egocentric in his use of language, in that he codes the linguistic message for himself, or is his language socialized whereby he codes the message for others? Second, when facilitating the child's development of language usage, it is crucial to start with the "here and now" and only very gradually move toward talking about past events or speculating about what will happen tomorrow or the next day. Finally, the context of the language usage strategies should as much as possible be a microcosm of the real world. Language should be used to send or receive information, ask and answer questions, and describe activities and desires. The following informal strategies provide but a small sample of the kinds of strategies that can be incorporated, developed, and expanded for use in the classroom.

Describing Behavioral Events

Both teachers and therapists develop stimulating activities to encourage children to talk about what occurred, to share their feelings and perspectives about the experiences, to recall and describe the sequences of events, and to share information. Trips to the zoo, the police station, the fire house, etc., are generally followed by teacher-directed questions such as "What happened?" "Where did you go?" "What did you see?" "When did you see the giraffe?" If answers are given at all, children with language and/or cognitive problems respond with minimal verbal information. For developmentally young children, the task of describing what occurred in the past, whether remote or recent, may require linguistic and cognitive abilities that are not within their psychological schemas. It is, therefore, crucial to begin a language-intervention strategy by encouraging the child to describe ongoing actions. Activities such as cooking, playing with clay, doing carpentry, and painting can generate questions by the teacher related to the ongoing actions of the child. The perceptual attributes of the objects and their relationships will aid the child in describing ongoing actions. Questions directed by the teacher focus the child's attention on particular aspects of the events, as well as providing the structure for appropriate responses. Only after the child develops the facility to describe ongoing actions should the focus of the language program shift to describing behavioral events and activities that occurred in the past.

Objective.   Strengthen the child's ability to describe behavioral events.

Procedures.   In developing an approach to strengthen a child's verbal communication of behavioral events, it is important to first select several activities that include observable, discriminable events that can naturally occur in a classroom. These activities might include painting, playing with clay, building with blocks, making cookies, and eating lunch. It is also important that the child or children find the activity stimulating and enjoyable. Opportunity should be given for the children to spend as much time as needed engaging in the activities before verbal descriptions of their actions are requested. The following is one possible sequence of the various stages that could be built into the program:

Stage	Teacher Input	Child Output
1. Familiarity with activity	none	Ongoing actions with the objects
2. Following instructions	"Squeeze clay." "Roll the ball."	Appropriate motor response
3. Reporting simple ongoing actions of the child	"What are you doing?" "Where is the clay?"	*"Squeeze" or "Squeezing clay" or "I'm squeezing the clay."
4. Reporting simple ongoing actions of others	"What am I doing?" "What is Wayne doing?" "Where is Carmen's clay?"	*"Squeeze" or "Squeezing clay" or "You're squeezing the clay."
5. Following instructions involving two-component actions	"Squeeze the clay and roll the clay."	Appropriate motor response.
6. Reporting two-component ongoing actions of the child	"What are you doing?" "What's happening?"	*"Squeeze clay; roll clay" or "Squeezing and rolling clay" or "I'm squeezing and rolling the clay."
7. Reporting two-component ongoing actions of others	"What am I doing?" "What is Jack doing?"	*"Squeeze clay; roll clay" or "Squeezing and rolling clay" or "You're squeezing and rolling the clay."
8. Reporting simple actions of the child that occurred in the recent past	"What were you doing?" "Where was the clay?"	*"Squeeze clay" or "Squeezed clay" or "I squeezed the clay" or "I was squeezing clay."
9. Reporting simple actions of others that occurred in the recent past	"What was I doing?" "What was Jack doing?" "What happened?"	*"Squeeze clay" or "Squeezed clay" or "Jack was squeezing clay."

Stage	Teacher Input	Child Output
10. Reporting two-component actions of the child that occurred in the recent past	"What were you doing?" "What happened?"	*"Squeeze and roll clay" or "Squeezed and rolled clay" or "I squeezed and rolled the clay."
11. Reporting two-component actions of others that occurred in the recent past	"What was I doing?" "What was Carol doing?" "What happened?"	*"Squeeze and roll clay" or "Squeezed and rolled clay" or "Carol was squeezing and rolling the clay."

Increase the time that elapses between the activity and the verbal description.

* Several considerations should be mentioned at this point. The complexity of the language response of the child should be consonant with his or her structural development. For example, a child functioning at a two-word utterance level should not be required to respond with a complete sentence. You should be more concerned with the appropriateness of the content of the response than with the structure. Additionally, for linguistically delayed youngsters, the temporary use of a modeled response may be necessary. However, modeling by the teacher should be removed as a prompt as soon as possible. Finally, a gamelike atmosphere should be used for motivation. For example, one child might leave the room and if he or she can identify the action as described by another child, the child who described the event would be "it."

Expanding the Role of the Speaker

"Communication of a specific object, event or relationship to another is the simplest kind of communication . . ." (Dale, 1972, p. 226). While this may be true for many children having language problems or who are developmentally young, this form of communication poses many problems for the speaker. One reason for this difficulty is that a particular referent may be referred to by many names. Consider a block that is red in color, triangular in shape, and small in size. It may be apparently called "a block," "a small block," "a triangular block," "it," "that one," etc. While each description may accurately refer to the particular block, only one description of the block may be used by the speaker to effectively communicate to the listener which block to select. The speaker must, therefore, consider the set of alternatives from which the listener must select the intended block (Olson, 1970). While this may seem to be a rather easy task, considering the needs of the listener, for most young children and many older ones, it is a difficult linguistic and cognitive task. As was already mentioned, much of the young children's speech is egocentric. In other words, the speaker does not take into account the perspective of the listener. Therefore, the speaker may not consider the set of alternatives from which the listener must operate, so the speaker might say "move this one" without considering that the listener does not know to what referent "this one" applies.

Objective.   Expand the role of the speaker, taking into account the linguistic skills required of the speaker as well as the cognitive demands of the speaker (i.e., taking into account the role of the listener).

Procedures.   There are many activities that can be developed which require the speaker to communicate information about specific objects, events, or relationships. Activities that direct the child to describe a block, as previously mentioned, or do a puzzle, or make masks with various shapes cut out of colored construction paper can be used. The range of possible activities is endless. The cognitive demands placed on the speaker should only gradually be increased. Therefore, the teacher might want to start with an activity that only minimally requires the speaker to consider the set of alternatives from which the listener must operate. The following illustration provides such a situation:

> Two children are seated at a table, separated by an opaque screen. Each child has a toy dog and a toy truck. The speaker's role is to verbally communicate to the listener the toy to be picked up.

In this situation, the speaker need only consider the most minimal alternatives from which the listener must operate—that of the name of the toy. The teacher and the entire audience (the rest of the class) might probe both the listener and the speaker to determine whether the information given was sufficient. By including the audience, the importance of language as a communicative process should become apparent.

As the children become "more effective communicators," the cognitive and linguistic demands made on the speaker should be increased. The following illustration provides such a setting:

> Two children separated by an opaque screen are seated at a table in front of the class. The listener is blindfolded, pretending to be blind. Each child has an identical collection of six blocks which vary in shape, color, and/or size. The speaker builds a construction using all of the blocks and must provide enough information to the listener so that he or she can replicate the construction.

This situation is cognitively much more complex than the first, in that the speaker must be aware of the visual limitations of the listener in addition to the wide set of alternative blocks and arrangements from about which the listener must choose. Linguistically, the speaker must talk about shape, size, relationships, positions, etc. Once again, both the teacher and audience should participate by probing to determine if the information given by the speaker was adequate. Encourage the children to shout out: "What do you mean by 'this one'?" in reaction to nonspecific information.

Activities that gradually increase the cognitive and linguistic demands placed on the speaker can be an ongoing activity. The teacher need only consider the children's readiness for increasing these demands and use a variety of activities to maintain motivation.

Using Language for Persuasion

While communicating about a specific object, event, or relationship is the simplest form of language usage, language may be used for other functions. One such function is that of persuasion. Language can be used not only to provide information or to instruct, but it can have the power of influencing another person's point of view or position on a particular topic. As a social tool, this function of language is well worth developing.

Objective.   Expand the role of the speaker to include the cognitive/linguistic skill of persuasion.

Procedures.   Although this activity is geared primarily for older children, young children *can* begin to engage in persuasion activities even though their strategies will be less sophisticated. Establish a series of situations whereby a child must persuade an adult to do something that he or she might not normally want to do. One such situation might be to convince the adult to give a particular child or the entire class additional time for free play. Although one child is the persuader, the audience (the rest of the class) can help the persuader develop an "argument."

The teacher should encourage the persuader to go beyond simple "pleas" and descriptions of why it is important to the child or class (e.g., "we want to play longer"). Instead, the persuader should be encouraged to take into account the attitudes or values of the listener, so that the "argument" can be viewed as valid from the perspective of the listener (e.g., "if we have additional time to play, we will be more alert for the science lesson").

The preceding informal classroom activities are by no means exhaustive or even representative of the ways an imaginative teacher can begin to facilitate the development of language. These activities were presented as examples to illustrate how language instruction can be incorporated into the classroom environment.

9

ASSESSING AND TRAINING PERCEPTUAL–MOTOR SKILLS

Donald D. Hammill

Today, many teachers and administrators believe that adequate perceptual abilities, especially the auditory and visual varieties, are crucial components of successful school learning. As a result of these feelings, many first-graders are systematically screened with tests that include numerous perceptual–motor items; and those children who are classified as perceptually handicapped are provided with special classes or services. In some schools and clinics, children who are diagnosed as having perceptual–motor problems will not even be introduced to formal academic work until such time as they are deemed to be perceptually "ready." It is a common practice for perceptually oriented professionals to presume that the reading, spelling, written expression, spoken language, and arithmetic problems of some older children are caused by some form of disordered perception and to provide them with special perceptual exercises in addition to remedial work in academic subjects.

Personally, we very rarely recommend the use of perceptual training; and when we do, it is never for the purposes of improving children's academic skills or of making them more educable for academic work. In fact, we use perceptual training so infrequently and regret so much its present-day indiscriminant use that we considered deleting this chapter and omitting all mention of perceptual training in the third edition of this book. In the end, however, the decision was made to keep the chapter in the book so that it could serve as a vehicle for giving teachers the information that they need about this widely used and abused approach and for providing the authors with yet another opportunity to express their serious reservations about the merits of these techniques, at least as they are popularly used in educational practice today.

Before beginning, we wish to state that we have no real quarrel with the concept of "perception" per se, either as a physiological reality or as a hypothetical construct. Our concern is with the way in which the concept is being applied in the schools. For example, when the theoretical concept of perception has been "operationalized" in the forms of various tests and training programs and when these have been applied in the schools, their authors have been unable, almost without exception, to show conclusively through controlled research that their tests or programs have any educational usefulness. The tests of perception do not seem to relate to measures of academic ability to any meaningful degree; and the use of the activities with children has not been demonstrated to produce either better school performance or perceptual–motor growth itself. On the contrary, a considerable and contrary body of research is steadily accumulating that strongly suggests that this approach has little or possibly no educational value. A brief review of this research literature is provided in the final section of this chapter, and the reader should consult it carefully before deciding to use any of the procedures described in this chapter. Having concluded the introductory remarks, we can proceed with the discussion of perception and its role in school learning.

What is perception? How are perception and learning related? Can one actually "train" perception? How are perception and motor coordination related to academic success? These and other questions have interested educational theorists and teachers for years and have generated a wealth of research. Yet findings often appear to be contradictory, and the answers to the questions posed are far from resolution. Therefore, to aid teachers in the judicious use of perceptual–motor programs, this review will acquaint teachers with (1) basic information regarding perceptual processes; (2) an overview of formal and informal assessment procedures; (3) theories and instructional techniques that are currently widely used in the schools; (4) examples of specific methods suitable for training particular perceptual and/or motor skills; and (5) necessary considerations prior to the initiation of perceptual–motor programs.

BASIC INFORMATION REGARDING PERCEPTUAL PROCESSES

The human body is equipped with several different kinds of receptor cells that have an affinity for light (visual), sound (auditory), touch (tactile), taste (gustatory), and smell (olfactory). Each type of cell is equipped with its own nerve tracts and brain "terminals," which together constitute a specific modality or channel. In the brain a multitude of operations occur automatically and simultaneously. The incoming impulses on a particular sensory tract are related to past experience; they are also related to the incoming impulses that are associated with other channels and with their past experiences as well. In this way, the properties of the stimulus are constructed, defined, verified, and modified. The results of these operations will range from simple awareness of color, form, and loudness, to complex interpretations of oral and graphic language, thinking, and reasoning.

In this manner the individual learns about his or her external world, and the constant interplay between new and past experience permits the refinement of his or her knowledge. The chain of neural occurrences permitting the individual to become aware of, interpret, associate, and store information basically represents a receiving or "taking-in" process.

Since an understanding of the receptive processes is important, the reader should resist being confused by semantic differences among writers regarding perception. To some theorists, the entire receptive process is called "perception." To others, a distinction is made between "sensation" [i.e., the passive reaction of the receptor cell (a reaction not involving memory)] and "perception" (i.e., the remainder of the process). Others write only of "sensation" and "cognition," and "perception" is subsumed under "cognition." Still other theorists distinguish between "sensation," "perception," and "cognition." The processes that involve thinking, meaningful language, or problem solving are assigned to "cognition," while those dealing with the nonsymbolic, nonabstract properties of the stimuli (e.g., size, color, shape, texture, or sequence) are relegated to "perception."

The latter definition has been operationally accepted for the purposes of this reference book. To summarize that definition, perceptual processes are those brain operations that involve interpreting and organizing the *physical* elements of the stimulus rather than the *symbolic* aspects of the stimulus. Perceptual tasks, therefore, can be differentiated readily from lower- and higher-order processing tasks (e.g., visual acuity and reading comprehension, respectively). In psychometrics, almost all of the commonly used tests of perception adhere to this definition in that they include tasks that require matching of geometric or nonsense forms, fine visual—motor coordination activities, sound discrimination, memory for digits, sound blending, or the distinction of embedded figures. Actually, it is precisely these kinds of skills that most of the perception training programs attempt to develop.

An excellent review of perceptual processes is provided by Chalfant and Scheffelin (1969). The outline that follows is in part based upon their work and describes the more common kinds of perceptual—motor constructs.

1. Visual perception and/or visual–motor integration modality
   a. Spatial relationships: the orientation of one's own body in space and the perception of the positions of objects in relation to oneself and other objects.
   b. Visual discrimination: the discrimination of dominant features in different objects.
   c. Figure–ground: the discrimination of an object from its background.
   d. Visual closure: the identification of figures when only fragments are presented.
   e. Visual memory: recollection of dominant features of one stimulus item or recalling the sequence of several items.

2. Auditory–perceptual modality
   a. Awareness of sound: discrimination of sound versus no sound.
   b. Sound localization: awareness of source or direction of sound.
   c. Auditory discrimination: discrimination of pitch, loudness, speech sounds, and noises.
   d. Auditory–sequential memory: discrimination and/or reproduction of patterns involving pitch, rhythm, melody, or speech.
   e. Auditory figure–ground: selection of relevant from irrelevant auditory stimuli.
   f. Chalfant and Scheffelin postulated another type which they suggested was similar to "auditory agnosia." Because of the similarity of auditory agnosia and ahpasia, this particular auditory problem is discussed in Chapter 1.

3. Haptic modality
   a. Tactile: perceptions of the environment, including geometric information (size, shape, lines, and angles), texture, consistency (hard, soft, resilient, viscuous), pain, and pressure.
   b. Kinesthetic: perceptions derived from bodily movement concerning the body itself, including dynamic patterns, static limb positions, and sensitivity to direction.

4. Motoric modality (only those motor skills which are related to perception are presented here; motor abilities associated with writing and speech are discussed elsewhere).
   a. Vocal: fine-motor acts usually associated with auditory inputs. They involve the speech mechanism (e.g., movements of the tongue, teeth, diaphragm, or jaw for the purposes of sound production.)
   b. Graphic: fine-motor acts usually associated with visual inputs. They involve the hand muscles in the use of writing implements for the purposes of drawing, scribbling, coloring, or printing.

    c. Motor: gross- and fine-motor acts associated with all input systems. They involve the large and small muscular structures for the purpose of executing bodily movement necessary for locomotion and manipulation skills.

Identifiable perceptual–motor deficiencies from many sources, including brain dysfunction (both injuries and inherited disorders), peripheral nerve damage, and mental retardation. Some writers would add to these inadequate sensory experience, emotional disturbance, and lack of attention. It is extremely difficult to determine the exact cause for a problem in an individual child.

ASSESSING PERCEPTUAL–MOTOR PROBLEMS

While perception can be measured in both formal and informal ways, the teacher will find the latter to be more useful. The formal approach is based primarily upon the interpretation of standardized tests; the informal assessment is dependent upon the interpretation of the child's actual performance in teacher-directed activities.

REVIEW OF FORMAL PERCEPTUAL–MOTOR TESTS

While a number of perception tests have been devised, this discussion is limited to those that are widely used in educational settings. Tests of visual perception predominate in this discussion, as they predominate the literature. The tests are grouped under three headings: (1) visual perception and visual–motor integration tests, (2) auditory–perception tests, and (3) gross-motor tests.

Most tests of perception require the child to demonstrate competence by executing complicated motor or vocal operations such as drawing geometric forms from memory, tracing, copying, or speaking. Such devices, which equally tap perception and motor–vocal pressures, are viewed as perceptual–motor integration tasks, while other measures that reduce the response requirements to pointing or simple "yes–no" responses are viewed as perception tasks.

For the most part, teachers should use the tests about to be described when they are engaged in research and need an objective measure of a perceptual

trait, or when they are screening a large number of pupils for perceptual difficulties and do not have the time to study the children individually. If their
purpose is to assemble an inventory of a child's perceptual status and prepare a
remedial program, they would find the use of informal procedures more efficient.

When perception is to be studied in the schools, responsible persons must
direct attention to the following questions:

1. Do I wish to assess perception, perceptual–motor integration, or both?
2. Am I interested in a particular perceptual skill (e.g., discrimination,
   figure–ground, or closure), or in overall perceptual ability?
3. Is the measure appropriate for the prospective sample (i.e., are the children physically able to respond, and is the test too easy or too difficult)?
4. Is the measure reliable enough to be used for educational purposes (i.e.,
   as the basis for diagnosing the problem of an individual child, or for
   research purposes)?
5. Is the formation to be derived worth the time to administer the test?

Visual Perception and Visual–Motor Integration Tests

There are many tests of visual and visual–motor performance available
today. Several of the most commonly used ones are discussed below.

The *Marianne Frostig Developmental Test of Visual Perception* (DTVP)
(Frostig, Maslow, Lefever, and Whittlesey, 1964) is the most popular measure
of visual perception used in the schools today. The DTVP has five subtests: (1)
Eye–Hand Coordination, (2) Figure–Ground, (3) Form Constancy, (4) Position
in Space, and (5) Spatial Relations. They are presumed to be relatively distinct
perceptual abilities that are related to school success.

The DTVP takes approximately forty-five minutes to administer to individuals and at least one hour to administer to groups. Three of the subtests (1,
2, and 5) require the child to make precise motoric responses (e.g., drawing
straight, curved, and angled lines between boundaries of various widths, or
copying forms and patterns). In these instances scoring is weighted heavily on
the accuracy of the motor performance. In the Form Constancy subtest, the
motor response is scored more leniently, and in the Position in Space subtest
the child merely marks a choice.

If the teacher's purpose is to identify specific patterns of perceptual–
motor inadequacy, he or she must consider the reliability and independence of
these subtests. The reliability studies accomplished to date (Frostig et al., 1964)
provide ample data to indicate that the subtests simply lack sufficient reliabil-

ity to be used with confidence for any purposes other than in research projects using large numbers of subtests.

Although the subtests may have little value to teachers, Corah and Powell (1963), Boyd and Randle (1970), and Hammill and Wiederholt (1971), among others, have respect for the total scores to be derived from the DTVP. Where knowledge of the child's visual–motor performance is required and where the DTVP is used, the Perceptual Quotient or Total Raw Score should be considered. The DTVP test has been thoroughly researched. Syntheses of work to date may be obtained from Mann (1972) and/or Hammill and Wiederholt (1972b).

The *Purdue Perceptual Survey Rating Scale* (Roach and Kephart, 1966) assesses the child's ability in jumping, identification of body parts, stepping stones, and ocular pursuits, and performance on the walking board, chalkboard tasks, visual achievement forms, among other activities. A respectable reliability coefficient is reported for the total score, but it is based on a sample of only thirty children of varying ages. Reliability of the subscales, an important factor in making specific evaluations, and test reliability for differing age groups is unknown. It is likely that the Purdue was never intended for use as a standardized instrument and that it is better employed as a structured informal device.

The *Bender Visual–Motor Gestalt Test* (Bender, 1938) is another well-known assessment device. The test consists of nine designs that the child copies on a sheet of paper. In addition to its use as a measure of visual perception, the Bender has been employed to diagnose emotional disturbance and brain injury and to predict school achievement. The most extensive work in adapting the test for use with emotionally disturbed or braindamaged children has been done by Koppitz (1963); those who wish to use the test for these children should become familiar with her work. The information in this book relating to the Bender test is based solely on Koppitz's findings. The reader should note the weak reliability of this measure before adopting it for either diagnostic or screening purposes.

Many other Bender types of devices exist. They all involve copying geometric forms or drawing such forms from memory. Because they are not widely used in the schools, only mention of them is made here. They include:

1. The Perceptual Achievement Forms Test (Lowder, 1956).
2. The Southern California Perceptual–Motor Test (Ayres, 1968).
3. The Memory for Designs Test (Graham and Kendall, 1960)
4. The Primary Visual–Motor Test (Haworth, 1970).
5. The Slosson Drawing Coordination Test (Slosson, 1980).

6. The Developmental Test of Visual–Motor Integration (Beery and Buktenica, 1967).

Auditory Perception Tests

Compared with the number of tests of visual perception, few tests of auditory perception are available. This section will focus upon those tests that most clearly estimate auditory perception as defined earlier. Abilities such as "sound blending," "sound–letter association," and other phonics skills are discussed in Chapter 2; auditory–vocal skills associated with speech production (e.g., articulation) are described in Chapter 8.

By far the two most commonly assessed auditory abilities in schools are "auditory discrimination" and "auditory–sequential memory." Attempts to estimate auditory discrimination involve asking the child to differentiate between spoken pairs of words or nonsense words that differ only in a single phoneme (e.g., "pass–path" or "pig–big'"). Auditory–sequential memory is generally measured by having the child listen to and then repeat a series of words, digits, or nonsense syllables.

Tests of auditory abilities are probably most efficiently used when the teacher is interested in a child's performance on a highly specialized auditory skill. Their use as devices to identify children as potential school failures, as readiness for school measures, or as predictors of reading is not recommended.

The Wepman (1958) *Auditory Discrimination Test*, a test of sound discrimination, is quick to administer and easy to score, reliability is good, and validity information is available in the manual. The word-pair principle is used and a "same–different" response is required.

The Goldman-Fristoe-Woodcock Test of Auditory Discrimination (Goldman, Fristoe, and Woodcock, 1970) was developed to measure speech-sound discrimination abilities under two conditions, with and without background noise. The two tape-recorded subtests are individually administered using a recorder and headset. The student is instructed to point to one of four pictures that corresponds to a spoken word (e.g., chair). Each of the four pictures, displayed on an easel, represents similar speech sounds (e.g., chair, fair, pear, hair). The first subtest was recorded without background noise while the second was recorded over various cafeteria noises.

The instrument was standardized on 745 subjects from ages 3 to 84. Percentile norms are given for 32 age levels ranging from 3.8 to 70+. A procedure for conducting error analysis according to distinctive sound features is given; however, reliability of this measure was found to be poor. The two overall subtest reliabilities (test–retest) are adequate (.81–87).

Content, construct, and concurrent validity are supported by correlations with clinical judgment (.68), by reporting mean scores for various ages, and by comparisons of the test performance of normal and nine clinical groups. Correlations with measures of letter recognition, sound blending, and memory for related symbols were reported; however, in no case did the coefficients exceed .35. Some effort was made to show that the G-F-W TAD results were independent of intelligence by reporting normal scores made by nineteen retarded subjects. The authors made no attempt to correlate scores with other auditory discrimination instruments, because in their opinion the other tests lacked validity and appear to involve factors other than auditory discrimination. No evidence, however, is offered in support of these presumptions. The authors make no claim as to specific clincial application of test information or predictive usefulness; presumably they offer the test as a measure of a specific perceptual ability only. Information reported by Goldman, Fristoe, and Woodcock (1970) suggests that the G-F-W TAD can be useful in screening those students in need of more in-depth assessment of specific auditory perceptual skills.

School personnel who wish to investigate auditory memory are referred to the ITPA subtest, Auditory Sequential Memory, the WISC subtest, Digit Span, or to the Detroit subtests pertaining to attention of related and nonrelated syllables. Other auditory–perceptual skills for which suitable tests exist include auditory closure (ITPA), auditory–visual integration (Birch and Belmont, 1965), and nonphonemic sound discrimination (Seashore, Lewis, and Saetveit, 1939).

In addition to the tests of specific auditory functions, there are a few test batteries available that are comprised exclusively or mostly of auditory subtests. These include the Auditory Skills Test Battery (Goldman, Fristoe, and Woodcock, 1976), The Kindergarten Auditory Screening Test (Katz, 1971), and The Detroit Tests of Learning Aptitude (Baker and Leland, 1967). Since these batteries follow similar formats and measure similar abilities, we thought that it would be unnecessary to describe them all in detail and have decided to review only one.

The Goldman–Fristoe–Woodcock Auditory Skills Test Battery (Goldman, Fristoe, and Woodcock, 1976) was designed as a comprehensive, diagnostic test battery to measure selected areas of auditory perceptual "processing" that are purported to exist between acuity and comprehension. The areas are Auditory Discrimination (one test, three parts), Auditory Memory (three tests), and Sound–Symbol Correspondence (seven tests). The tests are administered from recorded tapes, and subjects are first trained to identify the pictures utilized throughout the test in order to minimize factors other than those directly related to auditory skills (i.e., vocabulary, memory, etc.). A brief discussion of each area tested follows.

1. The Auditory Selective Attention Test attempts to measure the ability to listen on the presence of noise distractions that are varied in both

type and intensity. In administering the test, the examiner names a word (e.g., chair) and the subject is asked to point to one of four easel-displayed pictures (e.g., chair, tear, pat, patch). The items on this test are divided into four sections representing responses without background noise or with background distractions such as an electric-fan-like noise, cafeteria noise, and a voice telling a story.

2. The Diagnostic Auditory Discrimination Test is reported to measure the general ability to discriminate speech sounds; no extraneous noises are involved. The subject is again asked to point to the appropriate picture; in this case, the pictures represent very similar speech sounds. Students who experience difficulty with Part I of the test are administered Parts II and III, which are designed to yield specific diagnostic information regarding the sounds that constitute the problem.

3. The Auditory Memory Test consists of three separate tests: Recognition Memory, Memory for Content, and Memory for Sequence. In administering Recognition Memory, five recorded lists, each of twenty-two words are spoken to the child. The student responds "yes" or "no" after each word is given, depending on whether or not the word has occurred previously in the list. Memory for Content involves listening to a list of words, immediately followed by presentation of a set of pictures to which the subject is to point to two that were not named in the preceding list. Memory for Sequence requires the subject to listen to a list of words and afterward arrange the corresponding pictures in the sequence heard.

4. The Sound–Symbol Tests are seven in number: (a) Sound Mimicry—in which the subject must imitate a nonsense word given on tape; (b) Sound Recognition—where the subject must point to the word given as a series of isolated sounds; (c) Sound Analysis—in which the subject must repeat the first, middle, or last sound in a given syllable; (d) Sound Blending—where the subject responds with the correct word when given its phonemes in isolation; (e) Sound–Symbol Association—in which the subject is presented novel visual symbols paired with oral nonsense syllables and then selects the correct figure from several when presented one of the nonsense syllables; (f) Reading of Symbols—where the subject utilizes phoneme to grapheme translation by reading seventy nonsense words one to three syllables in length that contain all the major English spellings; and (g) Spelling of Sounds—where the subject must record given nonsense words after saying it to herself or himself.

Apparently, the test was aimed primarily for use with school-aged populations, since more than half of the 7199 children used in the 4-state standardization sample ranged from 3 to 10 years of age. Norms are reported for ages 3 to "better than 19" in the form of age equivalents and percentile ranks of age ·groups. Internal consistency reliability data are reported for three age groups: 3–8, 9–18, and 19 and over. After partialing for age, reliability coefficients for the subtests ranged from .46 to .97, with only 28 of the 39 subtest coefficients reaching the adequate criteria of .80. The age range of 9–18 was the least reliable. The test performance of two clinical populations (i.e., a group of children with mild speech and learning difficulties) being served in the regular classroom and a group of educable and trainable mentally retarded students attending special classes were studied. The reliability coefficients reported with these clinical groups ranged from .74 to .99. In support of the test's content validity, the authors asserted, without empiric demonstration, that the items on each of the subtests are much like those "auditory skills" required in real-life situations. Construct validity was dealt with in several ways, e.g., by noting an increase in scores with age followed by a decline after puberty, by reporting the intercorrelations of the subtests indicating that each measured a different construct, and by reporting analysis-of-variance ratios comparing normal group scores with the scores of students who have mild and severe learning problems. Caution should be made in utilizing these results, for there was little significance other than age found between the normal and mild groups and no evidence given that an attempt was made to control the variable intelligence. Although the test manual makes several references to these skills as they are related to speech, language, reading, writing, spelling, and learning disorders, no attempt was made to correlate the test scores with measures of these skills or constructs. Even though the statistical data associated with this test exceed those of many measures of "perceptual skills," the practical value of the test or the constructs on which it is based remains to be demonstrated through carefully designed research.

Gross-Motor Tests

For the most part, when the gross-motor ability of a child is assessed, informal techniques are employed. Few standardized, or even remotely standardized, tests are readily available. Therefore, teachers often resort to checklists of numerous skills, such as jumping, catching, or grasping. Like all informal procedures, these are useful, but occasionally the situation will require that a child's motor performance be reduced to percentiles, quotients, or age equivalents. For those occasions the following devices seem suitable.

The *Bruininks–Oseretsky Motor Development Scale* (Bruininks, 1978) is the most popular device for assessing gross-motor skills. Although the Purdue Perceptual Survey Rating Scale, described with visual–perception tests, includes several gross-motor subscales, as a whole it is considered to be geared more toward perceptual than motor abilities. The Bruininks–Oseretsky consists of items arranged in order of difficulty and suitable for children between four and eighteen years of age. The skills involved include speed, dexterity, coordination, rhythm, balancing, and jumping. Although often used in school research, little information regarding validity and reliability is available and that which is available suggests that the test should be used with caution (see Gronlund, 1981).

The *Preschool Attainment Record* (Doll, 1966) comprises eight subscales, of which two pertain to gross-motor activity—Ambulation and Manipulation. The Record is completed by teachers, parents, or any person who knows the child well enough to respond. Currently only the research edition is available and consequently reliability and validity information are unknown. This should not inhibit the use of this instrument, however, as it has been carefully constructed. The device is suitable for children from less than a year to seven years of age.

This section is concluded by referring the reader to Coles's (1978) extensive review of perceptual testing procedures. As a consequence of his investigations, he questions the practical value of most perceptual tests on the basis of their weak reliability, undetermined validity, and obscure theoretical underpinnings and assures us "that eventually the tests reviewed here will be discarded; the evidence against them is mounting" (p. 335). Given our understanding of the tenacity in education of "ideas whose time has went," we may only conclude that Coles is more optimistic than we.

REVIEW OF INFORMAL PERCEPTUAL–MOTOR ASSESSMENT TECHNIQUES

Informal assessment of perceptual–motor abilities is based on the interpretation of the child's actual performance in teacher-directed activities. The utility of these procedures are completely dependent upon the teacher's knowledge, experience, and talent. Teachers who have taught the first grade for 4 years have observed the growth of approximately 120 different youngsters over a 1-year interval. After such an experience, it is entirely possible that they can identify with confidence those children who cannot catch balls, who are awkward and poorly coordinated, who cannot hold a pencil correctly, or who evidence more than expected difficulty in learning to print.

It is rare that a child with a severely debilitating auditory–perceptual problem could go undetected for more than a few weeks in the classroom of a diagnostically oriented teacher. Such a child would constantly be asking the teacher to repeat commands or instructions, failing phonics lessons, or evidencing misarticulations. The teacher should recognize such behavior as diagnostically important.

Because these kinds of behaviors may also result from sensory impairments (blindness, partial sight, deafness, hearing damage) or motor impairment (mild paralysis, cerebral palsy, postpolio conditions), all children identified by the teacher as exhibiting a possible perceptual–motor difficulty should be referred to the school nurse and a detailed description of the precise behaviors that motivated the referral should be submitted.

Once the teacher is satisfied that a child does have a significant perceptual problem, he or she should probe the problem informally to prepare an inventory of precise skills that the child lacks. The purpose of the informal examination is not to label the pupil as a "visual memory" case, or an "auditory-sequencing" problem, or even a "perceptually handicapped" pupil. The purpose is to prepare an instructional program for the pupil based upon his or her performance and needs.

Informal assessment incorporates both teaching and evaluation. Therefore, training activities themselves are suitable assessment tasks. The performance of a child on any of the specific techniques presented at the end of this chapter may be interpreted diagnostically (see the section "Specific Techniques for Perceptual–Motor Training" later in this chapter). Readers who are interested in additional teacher diagnostic procedures relating to perception are referred to Bush and Waugh (1976) and Rosner (1975).

Informal Visual–Motor Assessment Techniques

It is not uncommon for a child in the first grade to write his name in the following manner:

(GEORGE)

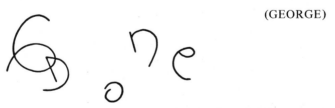

If this performance does not improve measurably with regular training, the teacher might refer the child for a formal evaluation. During this evaluation, the child will likely be administered the Wechsler Intelligence Scale for Children, the Developmental Test of Visual Perception, and the Bender Visual–Motor Gestalt Test. Just as likely, he or she will do poorly on the Performance subtests of the WISC, the DTVP, and the Bender, leading eventually to a diagnosis of visual–perceptual–motor disorder. Yet, the teacher should have been able to reach that conclusion with much less expenditure of time and money. The example of George's written name is in and of itself evidence of perceptual–motor disorder and actually indicates possible problems in visual memory, peseveration, spatial relations, form constancy, and figure–ground. Informal procedures should be undertaken by the teacher as once to answer the following questions.

1. Does the child require glasses?
2. Is he attempting to write with his dominant hand?
3. Can he copy his name?
4. Can he trace his name?
5. Does he hold a pencil with a correct three-finger grip?
6. Are his drawing and coloring acceptable?
7. Can he use scissors adequately?

If he is unable to do several of these activities satisfactorily, lower-level gross-motor skills should be evaluated, especially those involving the upper part of the body.

1. Can he catch a ball?
2. Does he grasp objects properly?
3. Can he throw accurately?
4. Can he complete simple puzzles and parquetry exercises?

The informal perceptual–motor evaluation is accomplished by giving the child specific tasks or by interpreting playground and classroom performance. There are, of course, many bits of information that can eventually be collected out of which can evolve a specific teacher-designed program for the child.

Informal Auditory–Perception Assessment Techniques

The teacher who suspects, either from personal observations or from test information, that a pupil has an auditory–perceptual problem can proceed in the following manner. Let us take a specific example, a young boy who has failed Digit Span (WISC) and who has not been too responsive to auditory cues in class. The fundamental questions now emerge and form the basis of the informal assessment.

1. Is the suspicion valid? Test the child on memory for digits once again. This time use reinforcers. If his performance is now within acceptable ranges, terminate probing the auditory problem and either forget the whole thing or begin assessing motivational factors.

2. Can he hear? Drop a coin behind him and see what happens. Or cover your mouth with a piece of paper and ask him, "Are you a girl?" In either instance, if he hears, he will let you know in a very noticeable fashion. If his response is equivocal, seek the help of other professionals (usually the speech therapist, school nurse, or whoever administers the audiometric examinations in the school).

3. Is his problem associated with sequential, symbolic auditory memory tasks (i.e., tasks that convey linguistic meaning)? For example, can he proficiently recall a series of words, phrases, or sentences or carry out a series of simple spoken commands? If he can do these, terminate this whole line of assessment, for he would have demonstrated auditory competence at a higher level than that under suspicion. If, however, he still does poorly, try to teach him some kind of the tasks he failed. The rate at which he learns will give insight as to what to expect when an instructional program for this child is implemented.

4. Is his problem associated with other sequential nonsymbolic auditory memory tasks? For example, can he recall a series of nonsense syllables, a vocal pattern such as "dum-de-dum-dum"? If the child failed Digit Span and several activities described above, it is very likely he will do poorly here as well.

BASIC APPROACHES TO TRAINING PERCEPTUAL—MOTOR PROCESSES

The individuals who are discussed here have contributed perceptual—motor theories, techniques, or programs that are used extensively in the schools. The brief discussions are provided merely to acquaint the teacher with these basic approaches and are not considered as substitutes for studying the original sources. After reading a particular summary, the reader may wish to read in detail the author's work in order to prepare instructional units for use in his or her own classroom.

It should be mentioned that some basic differences exist between the authors of this book and the authors about to be discussed, especially regarding perceptual learning and the effectiveness of many of the training activities. This should not be interpreted to mean that we never recommend perceptual—motor training or the techniques associated with Frostig, Kephart, Barsch, or Getman. We choose activities selectively and cautiously from these sources and use them with individual children on a remedial basis rather than with all children in the name of readiness training. Any improvement in perception that is a result of training is its own reward; activities should never be recommended in the hope that somehow the improvement will generalize to reading, speech, or other activities. It is necessary to point out that even though these teaching systems are widely used in the schools, we view them as still experimental, nonvalidated techniques rather than as programs that have been demonstrated to be effective. We do use parts of these programs but in the spirit just expressed. In reading this section, the reader should keep in mind that we are discussing the positions of others; our opinions are expressed in other sections of this chapter.

Newell C. Kephart

Rationale.   Kephart contends that concept formation depends upon the manipulation of perceptual data and that solid concepts rest on solid precepts, which, in turn, rest on solid, basic motor patterns. Subsequently, inadequate development of perceptual–motor skills prevents children from effectively participating in the educational program. Of the basic motor patterns that emerge from the early motor responses of children, Kephart (1971) maintains that *posture* is primary and that all subsequent motor patterns develop from it. An important motor pattern is *laterality* (i.e., the initial awareness of the two sides of the body and their difference), which later becomes the basis for concepts of direction in space. *Directionality,* a projection of laterality into external space, comprises awareness of the up–down axis and laterality of the body. These three operate to produce a unity of impressions about one's body called *body image.* Body image provides the point of origin against which all spatial relations outside the body are compared.

Concomitant with the development of motor patterns, but beginning later, is the development of perceptual organization. Tactual, kinesthetic, visual, and auditory data received from the developing perceptual system are compared with existing motor information. The result is a synthesis of data, called the *perceptual–motor match,* which serves to provide the child with consistent information about his or her environment. *Form perception, spatial discrimination,* and *ocular control* are three perceptual skills closely associated with the perceptual–motor match.

Training Techniques.   Kephart does not have a training program as such, i.e., there is no special kit containing apparatus and materials which might be purchased. Instead, he offers a collection of activities, each of which can be related to his theory. These activities are presented in their clearest form in *The Slow Learner in the Classroom* (1971); they may be supplemented by consulting Ebersole, Kephart, and Ebersole (1968). Exercises are presented under the categories of Perceptual–Motor Training, Perceptual–Motor Match, Training Ocular Control, Chalkboard Training and Training Form Perception. An example of an exercise appropriate for each category follows.

1. Perceptual–Motor Training. The child is taught to walk the Walking Board, an 8- to 12-foot long, 2-inch by 4-inch board resting on a brace which provides a 2-inch elevation and support. The child learns to perform forward, backward, sidewise, and to turn and bounce as well. Such exercises are purported to aid the child in developing balance, posture, laterality, and directionality. Kephart (1968) provides a list of 62 different Walking Board exercises.

2. Perceptual–Motor Match. Any exercise that requires the child to integrate perception with movement is appropriate; for example, scribbling and other eye–hand activities.

3. Training Ocular Control. Any activity in which the child has to follow a moving object with his or her eyes is suitable (e.g., most ball games).

4. Chalkboard Training. These activities are designed to help the child establish directionality. Dots are drawn on the chalkboard for the child to connect. If the child is to do this, the teacher guides his or her hand through the appropriate motions.

5. Training Form Perception. Any activity based on the matching principle would be satisfactory (e.g., the matching of objects, pictures, geometric forms, or visual patterns).

Assessment Procedure.   Kephart (1971) recommends the use of the Purdue Perceptual Survey Rating Scale for evaluating the child's motor and perceptual–motor abilities, and suggests that additional information can be obtained from the Wepman Auditory Discrimination Test, the Marianne Frostig Developmental Test of Visual Perception, and the Illinois Test of Psycholinguistic Abilities.

Program Evaluation.   Kephart (1971), Ball (1971), and others have attempted, quite justifiably, to demonstrate the validity of his theory by pointing out its compatibility with other theories, notably those of Piaget, Hebb, and Montessori, and by explaining the neurological bases underlying the theory. Much deductive support exists for Kephart's rationale, but hard data are missing. For example, Kephart maintains that if certain perceptual–motor skills are lacking, the development of academic skills will likely be affected. This is not necessarily the case. Bateman (1967) states ". . . there are children who manifest severe spatial orientation, body image, perceptual, coordination, etc., problems and who are not dyslexic" (p. 11). Similarly, Dunn (1967) reminds us that "efficacy studies in the area of motor development and perceptual learning with Strauss-type children are nonexistent" (p. 130). Relative to the effectiveness of the activities, Myers and Hammill (1982) have reviewed thirty-five studies which attempted to develop perceptual–motor skills using the Kephart–Getman–Barsch techniques. The overall conclusion of this review raises serious questions about the value of such training. Neither the relationship between the suggested activities and Kephart's theory nor the usefulness of the activities themselves have been demonstrated sufficiently through carefully designed research.

Gerald N. Getman

Rationale.   To Getman, perception is learned and developmental, and plays a significant role in the educational process; and of all the perceptions, vision is the most important. Although Getman (1962) does not articulate his theory in such detail or in such sophisticated style as Kephart does, the type and sequence of perceptual–motor generalizations postulated by the two are quite similar. In Getman's terminology, the child progresses through six sequential and interrelated developmental stages, including (1) General Movement Patterns, (2) Special Movement Patterns, (3) Eye Movement Patterns, (4) Visual Language Patterns, (5) Visualization Patterns, and (6) Visual–Perceptual Organization.

Training Techniques.   Getman has provided a collection of training activities for each of his postulated stages. The primary sources for these techniques are Getman (1962), Getman and Hendrickson (1966), and Getman, Kane, Halgren, and McKee (1968). A sample training activity for each stage follows.

1. General Movement Patterns. In addition to the use of the Walking Board, work on the trampoline or basic physical education exercises (sit-ups, toe touches) are recommended.
2. Special Movement Patterns. Suggested activities include hammer and nail sets, jacks, or Lincoln Logs, as well as any activity involving bilateral and eye–hand operations.
3. Eye Movement Patterns. As with Kephart, chalkboard activities are strongly recommended.
4. Visual Language Patterns. Activities offered for this stage are not, strictly speaking, perception activities at all. The emphasis is on language and concept formation, and the activities include story telling, imitation of sounds, naming and classifying, and verb games.
5. Visualization Patterns. Exercises here are concerned with form, shape, and recall (e.g., simple jigsaw puzzles or matching activities).

6. Visual–Perceptual Organization. No activities are suggested specifically for this stage because Getman is convinced that these patterns emerge when adequate perceptual organization exists at the other stages.

Assessment Procedures.   No particular evaluation tests are suggested. Presumably Getman, a clinically oriented professional, feels comfortable with informal procedures. Readers who have need of standardized tests are referred to Kephart's recommendations regarding assessment devices.

Program Evaluation.   Most of the criticism leveled at Kephart has also been directed at Getman's theories and training program. In fact, it would be difficult to separate these two critiques. Results of studies pertaining to the Kephart techniques can probably be applied to the techniques of Getman. As with Kephart, Getman's theories and techniques lack research-established validity at the present time.

Ray H. Barsch

Rationale.   Barsch is concerned with the child's movement in space in his spatially oriented approach to learning disabilities. Since Barsch believes that space is the most vital domain in which children exist, nonacademically oriented curricula should be designed to create spatial proficiency. The theory behind Barsch's (1967) orientation is "movigenics" (i.e., the study of the child's movement in space and the ramifications of this movement). He hypothesizes twelve dimensions to explain this development. The first four, *muscular strength, dynamic balance, body awareness*, and *spatial awareness*, aid the individual in maintaining body control and movement through space. The second four, *tactual dynamics, kinesthesia, auditory dynamics*, and *visual dynamics*, are necessary for processing information. *Bilaterality, rhythm, flexibility*, and *motor planning* enhance the efficiency of the other dimensions.

Training Techniques.   The movigenics curriculum (Barsch, 1965) is based specifically on his twelve dimensions. As with Kephart and Getman, specific activities are selected to correspond to the postulated categories. The reader will note that for the most part, the activities suggested by Kephart, Getman, and Barsch are remarkably similar. An example of a training exercise for each dimension follows.

1. Muscular Strength. Forceful exercise, such as jumping, pushing, lifting.
2. Dynamic Balance. Walking Board.

3. Spatial Awareness. Children turn in a direction commanded (e.g., "turn left, turn right").
4. Body Awareness. Learning to label body parts.
5. Visual Dynamics. Any visual steering, tracking, or memory exercise.
6. Auditory Dynamics. Imitation of sounds or sound discrimination activities, among others.
7. Kinesthesia. Working with pegboards, scissor cutting, etc.
8. Tactual Dynamics. Child is taught to identify objects by touch alone.
9. Bilaterality. Imitation of bilateral movements made by the teacher.
10. Rhythm. Movement associated with metronomes, tom-toms, clapping.
11. Flexibility. No specific activities are described.
12. Motor Planning. No specific activities are described.

Assessment Procedures.   No particular tests are recommended (see the Assessment Device section in the Kephart discussion and consult the review of perceptual and/or motor tests presented earlier in this chapter for suitable evaluation measures).

Program Evaluation.   Review of the literature indicates that virtually no research has investigated the movigenics curriculum. Once again, the comments concerning Kephart are probably applicable here. Awaiting the accumulation of more data, Barsch's theory and training program must be classified as nonvalidated.

Marianne Frostig

Rationale.   Frostig, consistent with other individuals discussed in this section, emhpasizes the visual–motor processing system, but not to the same degree. She also maintains that adequate perceptual functioning in young children is an important foundatation upon which later school success is built. She asserts that visual perception comprises definable subskills and that these are measurable and trainable.

Frostig credits the work of Guilford, Wedell, Cruickshank, and others as influencing the development of her theories and instructional techniques. Together with her own experience, their work led to the identification of five primary perceptual–motor abilities which would in time form the structure of both the Developmental Test of Visual Perception and the Developmental Program in Visual Perception. These five skills—eye–hand coordination, figure–ground, form constancy, position in space, and spatial relations—were to be critical for the acquisition of school learning (Frostig et al., i961).

Training Techniques.   Frostig and Horne (1964) have developed a structured, sequential, visual–perception training program that corresponds roughly to the subtests of the Developmental Test of Visual Perception (see the sections on visual–perception and visual–motor tests earlier in this chapter). This program is geared for kindergarten and first-grade children. Modifications of the program provide for individual or classroom use and for exceptional children. The program can be used as a supplement to a traditional kindergarten readiness curriculum or as a remedial program for children who evidence perceptual–motor difficulties.

The program itself consists primarily of programmed worksheets divided into five sections corresponding to the five DTVP subtests. The sheets in each section are arranged on an easy-to-difficult order. It is recommended that training in sensory–motor and language functions be integrated with the program and that the worksheets not be used in isolation. A variety of sensory–motor and movement exercises that can be used to supplement the program is also provided by Frostig (1970).

Assessment Procedures.   Four basic tests are used by Frostig (1967) in the psychoeducational evaluation: the Developmental Test of Visual Perception, the Illinios Test of Psycholinguistic Abilities, the Wepman Test of Auditory Discrimination, and the Wechsler Intelligence Scale for Children. A survey of motor abilities, the Bruinink–Oseretsky Tests of Motor Proficiency, may also be used. Observation, interviews, case studies, and projective tests may also be useful for evaluating the child with learning difficulties.

Program Evaluation.   The Frostig–Horne procedures have prompted more research than any other perception training program. In part, this is probably due to its popularity in the schools and, in part, to its highly structured nature that facilitates its implementation, thereby making it more attractive to many researchers than the comparatively less structured Kephart–Barsch–Getman approaches.

At least forty to fifty studies have been undertaken using the Frostig–Horne materials with various groups of children. These have been concerned with the effects of such training on reading, reading readiness, and perception itself. The consensus of these investigations is that the Frostig–Horne approaches (1) will not affect the reading ability of children in any way; (2) may produce some benefits regarding readiness; and (3) may be of no or limited value in improving perception in children. Readers interested in a more complete discussion of these studies are referred to Wiederholt and Hammill (1971) and Hammill and Wiederholt (1972b), who have reviewed most of the research that has attempted to assess training visual perception with the Frostig–Horne materials.

SPECIFIC TECHNIQUES FOR PERCEPTUAL–MOTOR TRAINING

No serious attempt is made to provide an exhaustive list of all the possible corrective or remedial methods available for teaching specific perceptual–motor skills. Rather, a few representative activities are included to demonstrate various kinds of techniques that advocates of perceptual–motor training might develop and sequence for a particular child. These can form a nucleus that the process-oriented teacher can augment from the work of the persons reviewed earlier and from the work of those who are referred to in this section. In general, the techniques may be divided into those designed to develop auditory–vocal skills and those designed for visual–motor skills.

DEVELOPING AUDITORY–VOCAL SKILLS

The specific techniques associated with auditory–vocal skills, outlined below, are arbitrarily grouped under the headings of auditory awareness, discrimination, and memory sequencing. Readers interested in deficiencies in articulation, syntax, or other speech skills are referred to the standard texts in speech correction (e.g., Van Riper, 1978). Barry and Myklebust also have much to contribute to the understanding of auditory–vocal instruction; but as they actually focus on language abilities, they are discussed elsewhere.

    A. Auditory awareness
        1. Present a wristwatch to each ear and train the child to listen and to raise a hand when he or she no longer hears the tick.
        2. Whisper commands to the child from varying directions for each ear. Click coins by each ear.
        3. Present commands in a normal voice in the front of the room and note response.
        4. Present pictures and recordings of common noises.
        5. Imitation.
        6. Whisper games with cardboard tube.
    B. Auditory discrimination
        1. Hide a ticking clock in the classroom. Ask the children to point in the direction of the clock.
        2. Respond bodily to varying rhythms.

3. Reproduce rhythmic patterns with a variety of simple instruments.
4. Resonator bells.
5. Piano scales. "My fingers can walk up the piano." (Play the scale.) "Now what happened?" (Slide down the scale.) Play scale slowly. "Am I walking or running?" "Am I going up or down?"
6. Identify everyday sounds using tapes.
7. Rhyming word drills.
8. A blindfolded child identifies a peer from his or her voice.
9. Tap on the desk several times. Children listen, count mentally, and then tell the number of taps.
10. All close eyes. One child recites a jingle. Others try to guess who spoke by recognizing the voice.
11. Musical glasses presented in varying tones.
12. Identify sound sources by pointing to a picture that goes with the sound.
13. Imitate intensity, rhythm, inflection, and mood of speaker in repeating a sentence.
14. "Tell me a word that begins like mother."
15. "Tell me which of these words begin with the same sound: "Mat, Oh, Me.""
16. "Clap when you hear a word that begins like mild."
17. Create sounds that are suggested by pictures.
18. Child listens with eyes closed and then tries to determine which of the following was done while he or she listened: skipping, running, jumping, hopping, walking, bouncing a ball.
19. Imitate the instrument heard by using gestures when listening to a recording.
20. Distinguish between sounds made by wooden beads, glass beads, pebbles, coins.
21. Present paired words. Respond "same" or "different."
22. "Speecho" and other discrimination games.
23. Discriminate near and far, high and low, loud and soft.

C. Auditory memory and sequencing
1. One child gives a telephone number and asks someone to repeat it.
2. Clap out a simple pattern and ask them to repeat it.
3. Jingles—children join in on rhyming words.
4. Grocery list. Use props: an egg carton, a butter box, a soap container, empty tin cans. Place each item on the table as it is added to the grocery list. Repeat the list as it grows.
5. Suitcase packing. Use a small suitcase and actual items. "I am going on a trip. I will put shoes in my suitcase." "I am going on a

     trip. I will put shoes and socks in my suitcase." Each child repeats the previous list and adds a new item.

6. Elevator boy. After several children name the floor at which they want to get off, the elevator boy repeats these numbers and ends by saying "Everybody off."
7. The giant's garden. Each time a child walks past the giant's house, he or she must repeat three or four nonsense syllables correctly or else help the giant hoe weeds.
8. Sequence of numbers. "Ten Little Indians."
9. Sequence of items or objects. "Old McDonald."
10. "The Farmer in the Dell."
11. Recall directions given by teacher.
12. Game rules. "Tell me how you play tag."
13. Daily activities. "What do we do at 8 o'clock?"
14. Dot, dash. Use chalkboard and write pattern ./-.-/.-.
15. Spelling. Teacher spells out various words, then the pupil writes them on chalkboard or paper.
16. Tell simple jokes and have pupils repeat them.

DEVELOPING VISUAL–MOTOR SKILLS

In Table 9–1 the visual–motor skills have been arranged in developmental order from simple skills, essentially motor in nature, to complex skills that require considerable visual memory and fine digital manipulation. Two specific activities are presented for each skill. The contributions of Frostig, Barsch, Getman, and Kephart are primary sources for specific techniques in this area. For supplemental materials, teachers are referred to those activities developed by Rosner (1975) and Cratty (1971, 1973, 1980).

THOUGHTS TO CONSIDER BFFORE BEGINNING A PERCEPTUAL–MOTOR PROGRAM

Before implementing a systematic perceptual–motor training program, the teacher should have a clear understanding of what can and cannot be accomplished by such a program. In particular, the teacher should be cognizant of

Table 9–1. Examples of Activities Designed to Develop Selected Visual–Motor Skills

Skill	Definition	Training Activities
Walking	The ability to walk erect in a coordinated fashion without support. Walking is a neuromuscular act requiring balance and coordination. Children should be presented with opportunities to develop increasing skill in more difficult tasks.	1. First have child walk to the right one step at a time. Next, cross left over right foot. Repeat, moving the left. 2. Walking beam. Move forward, backward, and sideways.
Running	The ability to run a track or obstacle course without a change of pace. Proficient running requires muscular strength, coordination, and endurance, and contributes to total psychomotor learning.	1. Running in place. 2. Dog run. Pupil gallops by running forward with both hands on the floor and the knees slightly bent.
Throwing	The ability to accurately throw an object.	1. Beanbag toss and pitching horseshoes. 2. Distance throws using a softball.
Jumping	The ability to jump simple obstacles without falling.	1. Instruct the children to lie on the floor on their stomachs and get up quickly by putting their hands on the floor and jumping on their feet. 2. Mattress jump. Use an air mattress three-quarters filled. Jump forward and backward without falling.
Body–spatial organization	The ability to move one's body in an integrated way around and through objects in the spatial environment. Body awareness and control of movement in space should be taught through imitative and exploratory exercises.	1. Obstacle races involving climbing on a chair, jumping over a block, crawling under a table, etc. 2. Pupil first imitates teacher's body movement, watching the back of the instructor; teacher then turns and faces pupil, who imitates body movements with correct right and left orientation.
Directionality	The ability to know right from left, up from down, forward from backward, and directional orientation. Since many learning and problem-solving situations require directional orientation, it is important that these skills be taught.	1. Pegboards. 2. Chalkboard activities.

Table 9–1. Continued

Skill	Definition	Training Activities
Skipping	The ability to skip in normal play. Skipping is a difficult task of coordination and timing that also requires strength and endurance.	1. Hop on one foot and on both feet, with eyes open and eyes closed. 2. Child should imitate the teacher in consecutively alternating right and left foot in skipping around the room.
Body concepts	The awareness of one's own body in relation to orientation, movement, and other behavior. Children should be taught to locate body parts and describe them by name and function.	1. Encourage children to touch various parts of their bodies as they are named and then to raise or move that part. 2. Functional description of body parts.
Muscular strength	The ability to use one's muscles to perform physical tasks. Muscular strength is best developed through a systematic physical fitness program adapted to individual growth patterns.	1. Use weights on arms and legs while performing various physical exercises. 2. Trunk-ups. Lie on stomach with feet together and hands behind head. Lift trunk and head up from floor while being timed.
Balance and rhythm	The ability to maintain gross- and fine-motor balance and to move rhythmically. The maintenance of body balance and the perception and expression of rhythmic patterns are fundamental to readiness for more advanced perceptual-motor experiences.	1. One foot stand. With arms out to one side, pupil stands on one foot and counts to five; stands on other foot and gradually extends time. 2. Jump on board or trampoline to music.
Ocular pursuits	The goal of ocular pursuit training is the control of eye movements. Such control is reported by several sources to be important to the achievement of reading and copying skills.	1. Child is instructed to watch the lateral, vertical, diagonal, and rotary movement of a pencil. 2. Child is asked to move his or her eyes between points within his or her visual field.
Visual form discrimination	The ability to differentiate among forms and symbols. The seeing of likenesses and differences is viewed by many educators as a prerequisite to symbolic differentiation and interpretation required in reading.	1. Templates 2. Puzzles and parquetry sets.

Visual–motor fine muscle coordination	The coordination of visual perception with fine-motor responses.	1. Provide open stencils of forms for precise tracing followed by coloring and cutting. 2. Teacher prepares gadget board with extensive series of locks, latches, plugs, zippers, levers, snaps, and buttons. Pupils manipulate objects with increasing skill.
Visual–motor integration	The ability to integrate total visual–motor skills in complex problem solving.	1. Request pupils to draw pictures of themselves and one another; next, have them draw pictures of families. 2. Block and advanced pegboard designs.
Visual figure–ground differentiation	The discrimination of objects in foreground and background.	1. Ask children to find a square button in a box of round ones, a large block among smaller ones, a piece of rough paper among smooth pieces. 2. Gestalt completion. Put up black silhouetted pictures of animals and objects and paste on white paper with each piece separated by space. Use for visual identification exercises.
Visual memory	The ability to recall accurately prior visual experience.	1. Immediate verbal recall. Pupil closes eyes and describes clothes, bulletin board, etc. 2. Tachistoscopic training.
Visual–motor memory	The ability to motorically reproduce prior visual experiences.	1. Arrange bead patterns on string; expose to pupil for 10 seconds, remove, and have child rebuild pattern from memory. 2. Display simple items such as airplane, dog, doll, book, pencil, shoestring, and block. Have pupil study objects for 1 minute. Cover objects and remove one, placing it in box with other assorted objects. Remove cover and have pupil find and present removed object.

Source: R. E. Valett, *The Remediation of Learning Disabilities* (Belmont, Calif.: Lear Siegler, Inc., Fearon Publishers, 1967). Used by permission of author and publisher.

research on the effects of perceptual–motor training on reading, readiness, and perceptual–motor ability. Familiarity with these findings should enable the teacher to formulate more realistic, effective goals regarding perceptual–motor activities.

Most, if not all, of the perceptual programs and tests are based on the assumption that perception is an important factor, if not the most important factor, in the educational process. Justification for such a belief rests upon a few correlative studies; upon possible misinterpretations of developmental theories espoused by Piaget and Inhelder (1967), among others; upon the work of Gesell (1940) and Ilg and Ames (1965); and upon advocacy by such contributors to the pedagogical literature as Frostig, Getman, Kephart, Delacato, and Barsch. Although many educators believe that the mastery of perceptual skills is a fundamental prerequisite to achievement in reading, writing, and other school subjects, the teacher should be aware of different points of view.

Cohen (1969) believes that instruction in reading is preferable to training in perception, if improvement in reading is the goal. In apparent agreement with this, Bibace (1969) questions the assumption that perceptual–motor ability is a prerequisite for scholastic achievement, while Mann (1979) challenges the theoretical and empirical foundations upon which perceptual training programs rest. The recent research literature lends support to their positions and is now briefly reviewed.

The correlational studies that focused upon the relationship of *visual* perception and academic performance have been thoroughly analyzed by Larsen and Hammill (1975), who reviewed more than 60 studies and 700 coefficients depicting the relationship of tests of visual perception to tests of reading, arithmetic, and spelling. They reported that the consensus of the research suggests that the relationship is not significant enough to be of use to teachers. Hammill and Larsen (1974) have also reviewed a considerable part of the correlational research dealing with the relationship of *auditory* perception to reading ability. In this review, the results of 33 separate studies yielding 297 different coefficients were investigated. The authors of the studies that were analyzed had all correlated children's performance on tests of auditory–visual integration, memory, discrimination, and blending with measures of reading comprehension or word recognition. The conclusion based on the interpretation of this literature was that particular auditory perceptual skills, as measured, do not appear to be essential to the reading process; a large percentage of children who perform well on tests of auditory perception experience difficulty in learning to read, and an equally sizable percentage who do poorly on these same tests have no problem in reading.

The basic conclusions of these two reviews are reinforced by the recent work of Hammill and McNutt (1981). To identify the actual correlates of reading, they surveyed the research published in 25 journals over the past 30 years. They located 322 suitable correlational studies reporting 8239 coefficients. A "meta-analysis" procedure was applied to the coefficients. None of the *auditory* perception, *visual* perception, or *auditory-visual* integration variables proved to be useful predictors of reading.

But what success have teachers and researchers had in training children in perception? The comments that follow pertain only to visual perception. Because of the current interest in this area and the availability of numerous treatment programs, visual perception has been studied more thoroughly than auditory perception. Only a few systematic programs for developing auditory perception, analogous to those in vision, are available [e.g., Semel's *Sound-Order-Sense: A Developmental Program in Auditory Perception* (1970)], although more such programs will probably be forthcoming. Most people who do attempt to train audition incorporate their efforts into a general or specific oral language development program and, therefore, were more appropriately discussed in Chapter 8.

Since the results of the correlation research strongly suggests that perception and academic abilities are not related to any practical degree, one should not be surprised to learn that the research also indicates that concomitant improvement in school subjects cannot be expected as a result of perceptual–motor training.

In *Learning Disabilities: Basic Concepts, Assessment Practices, and Instructional Strategies,* Myers and Hammill (1982) report the findings of an extensive review of the research literature dealing with attempts to train or to develop visual perceptual–motor abilities in children. In all, 85 studies were reviewed and over 500 different statistical comparisons were analyzed. Only studies that employed ten or more experimental subjects, used control groups, and implemented the techniques of Frostig, Barsch, Kephart, Getman, Ayres, or Delacato were included. The results of the review indicated that none of the treatments was particularly effective in stimulating cognitive, linguistic, academic, or school readiness abilities and that there was a serious question as to whether the training activities even have value for enhancing visual perception and/or motor skills in children.

The conclusions of this review confirmed or extended those of four earlier efforts to synthesize the perception training literature (i.e., the extensive reviews of Robbins and Glass, 1968; Hammill and Wiederholt, 1974; Arter and Jenkins, 1979; and Hallahan and Cruickshank, 1973). The review by Hallahan and Cruickshank is particularly noteworthy. They analyzed the results of forty-two perceptual–motor training studies and noted (1) the methodological shortcomings of each study and (2) whether its findings were positive or negative regarding the effects of perceptual training. Hammill and Myers utilized this information to prepare a 2-by-2 chi-square matrix to see if there was a relationship between the positive–negativeness of a study's results and the adequacy–inadequacy of its design. The resulting analysis yielded a highly significant chi-square, which means that the better designed research, as defined by Hallahan and Cruickshank, is more likely to produce negative findings than the poorly designed research.

Because perceptual–motor programs are currently much in vogue, thousands of elementary, special education, and preschool teachers base their readiness, preventive, and correlative activities exclusively or in part on such programs. Entire classes are being issued materials from various nonvalidated programs to stimulate perceptual growth in the belief that the programs will make children more educable. These materials cost local schools millions of hard-to-get dollars each year and are diverting countless teacher hours into these projects. If, however, the decision is made to provide perceptual–motor training, teachers should be urged to implement the programs on a remedial basis only in those few cases where improvement in perception is the goal and to consider even these efforts as being highly experimental. The efficacy of providing such training to children has not been sufficiently demonstrated to warrant the expenditure of the school's funds or the teacher's time. In general, perceptual–motor training is viewed as more acceptable for preschool than for kindergarten or school-aged children, and is never recommended as a substitute for teaching language, reading, or arithmetic skills.

10

SELECTING EDUCATIONAL MATERIALS AND RESOURCES

Judy Wilson

In any teaching situation, much time is usually devoted to selecting the content of the curriculum that will be used, to assessing the individual needs of the students involved, and to choosing the specific teaching methods that will be employed. Comparatively little time is spent on the selection or alteration of the instructional materials. This is indeed surprising when one realizes that at least 75 percent, and as much as 99 percent, of the students' instructional time is arranged around the materials used in the classroom. If teaching is viewed as the interaction among the curriculum, the student, and the teacher, then the materials must be chosen carefully to assure that they are compatible with all three elements in the triad and in fact serve to draw them together.

Most instructional materials are designed to meet the needs of groups of students, not one specific student. Therefore, teachers have always had to make certain accommodations in the materials used in order to meet individual differences (e.g., having a child use chapters out of sequence or complete only the even-numbered questions). This need for accommodation becomes greater the further the students' needs and abilities deviate from those of the group for whom the material was originally designed.

For the student with learning and/or behavior problems, the variance may necessitate the use of completely different materials, a need that is often overlooked or inappropriately met by many teachers, owing to their training and orientation. Most teachers have been trained to teach a prescribed curriculum that is usually dictated by the school, to use the materials that have been selected for them by the textbook committee, and to move students through the same set of learning experiences. To satisfy the special, and often unique, requirements of the student with problems, the teacher must exchange this group orientation for one that identifies the curricular requirements in terms of the exact skills to be taught to a particular child and that selects instructional materials on the basis of curricular, student, and teacher variables.

To aid in the selection of appropriate materials, this chapter includes: a discussion of the variables related to the curricular–student–teacher triad; an application of this information to the retrieval of materials information; a system for the analysis of materials; and a representative listing of materials coinciding with the previous chapters. The purpose of the chapter is not to provide a comprehensive listing of items to be used with learning and/or behavior problem students, but rather to provide teachers with a frame of reference for selecting those materials that are appropriate to their own curricula, students, and teaching methods.

VARIABLES RELATED TO THE CURRICULAR– STUDENT–TEACHER TRIAD

The curricular–student–teacher triad and its effect upon selection of material is analogous to the building–occupant–builder triad. The specifications for the building most certainly influence the materials to be used; but the selection of materials is also affected by the needs of the occupants, the desires of the builder, and what he or she knows to be effective and available.

CURRICULAR VARIABLES

In elementary and secondary schools, teachers often are expected to use a curriculum in which educational goals are vague, global, and/or much too general. Sometimes the curriculum is dictated by a specific text. Thus, it is difficult for a teacher to specify what precise skills the student must learn at any given point. Yet, for the student with problems, it is this precise identification of targeted skills that may be of most conducive to proper instruction. To aid the teacher in this identification, much of the content in preceding chapters has been devoted to presenting the skill sequences and needs related to successful performance in learning. Such information must be used by teachers to determine exactly what it is that they will include in a curriculum for the student with problems and still keep the teaching, as nearly as possible, related to the components of the regular curriculum. The information that is to be taught should be stated in terms of the expected learning outcomes. If this is done, the teacher will be better able to articulate precisely the instructional materials that are required for carrying out the teaching of the curricula.

In the delineation of curricular variables the teacher should consider such items as the following:

1. Content area
2. Specific skills
3. Theories and techniques associated with the concepts
4. Methodology
5. Modification

Content Area.   Is the information usually associated more closely with one area or does it cut across several content areas, for example, initial consonants in reading or in reading, oral language, spelling, etc.?

Specific Skills.   Are there specific skills that can be identified as components of the concepts, for example, addition with sums greater than nine versus the broad concept of addition?

Theories and Techniques Associated with the Concepts.   Are there specific theories of curriculum development for the concepts, for example, the spiral curriculum associated with the social sciences?

Methodology.   Does the curriculum require certain types of methods; for example, oral language development would require materials that allowed for dialogue, discussion, etc.?

Modification.   Can the order of the curricula be modified or is it developmental; for example, in mathematics, skills are developmental and multiplication builds upon concepts developed in addition?

Knowledge about these items may serve to assist the teacher in the evaluation of an existing curriculum and the alteration and/or development of one suited to the needs of an individual student.

STUDENT VARIABLES

The two variables that are most critical from the standpoint of the student are those of current level of functioning and the most immediate educational needs. In considering the variables of individuals, the list would obviously be influenced by the specific nature of each student; however, there are some common areas that should be examined. These areas include:

1. Needs of the student
2. Current level of functioning
3. Grouping
4. Programming
5. Methods
6. Physical, social, and psychological characteristics

Needs of the Student.   What skills and concepts are required of the student for immediate success?

Current Level of Functioning.   What is the student's level of performance within the sequence of skills? What is the student's current reading level for instructional purposes?

Grouping.   How well does the student work in groups of varying size (e.g., small, large, individually)?

Programming.   What is the best arrangement for presentation to the student: for example, can the student work independently; is the student self-directed and motivated; does the student require direct teaching and/or frequent reinforcement?

Methods.   Is there a history of success or failure with any particular methods? Does the student react positively or negatively to particular modes of instruction (e.g., multimedia versus print only)?

Physical, Social, and Psychological Characteristics.   Are there characteristics that imply unique needs (e.g., orthopedic restrictions, family problems, ethnic or cultural diversity, etc.)?

This list could also include such concerns as ability to follow directions, both well written and oral; ability to deal with material on a grade level different from the child's placement; and others.

TEACHER VARIABLES

The authors of most of the literature that relates to materials state that teachers need only know what and who is to be taught in order to select materials. This neglects one third of the triad, the teachers. It is the teacher who must act as the catalyst to assure interaction between the other two components. Since the teacher must make decisions about curricular and student variables, the teacher's desires, knowledge, and competence must be considered. These items, like those for the student, will no doubt be affected by the nature of the individual but, again, certain common areas exist:

1. Method
2. Approach
3. Time
4. Training
5. Education

Method.   What method does the teacher want to employ; what is the philosophy toward the teaching of the particular content?

Approach.   What approach does the teacher and the teacher's organization require (e.g., group instruction versus students on a one-to-one basis or a phonetic approach, etc.)?

Time.   Does the teacher have specific and required time constraints for delivery of instruction or does the teacher have someone else who can deliver the instruction?

Training.   Has the teacher been trained to use certain materials without additional training?

Education.   Has the teacher been trained to be competent in the content area, or will the teacher require that the material be all-inclusive?

None of these lists of variables is intended to be exhaustive in nature. Rather, they are intended to serve as guidelines for identification of relevant variables that will aid in the selection and use of materials and to assure that the materials indeed meet the specified needs of the curricula, student, and teacher.

RETRIEVAL OF MATERIALS INFORMATION

Once the critical variables involved in selecting materials have been identified, the teacher is ready to secure information on the specific materials that are being considered for use. The teacher may need to use a variety of available resources to secure information on materials. The following list of resources will serve as a guideline for this process:

1. Colleagues
2. Special resource personnel: media/materials coordinator, librarians, resource specialists
3. Publisher information: catalogs, representatives, consultants
4. Media/materials resource center
5. College/University resources: materials collections, classes, or faculty
6. Prepared material lists: in books, from districts, inservice, curriculum guides, etc.
7. Conferences: exhibits and presentations, publishers' conferences, book fairs
8. Retrieval systems
9. Other fields

Colleagues.   The most immediate source of information is another teacher. Not only is the person within easy access but also the teacher may have students with similar needs and therefore be able to share information on specific materials, its use, availability, and that teacher's experience with the material.

Special Resource Personnel.   This category may include such people as the media/materials coordinator, librarian, or curriculum coordinator. These individuals have information on a wide variety of materials and often know or have access to information on specific aspects of the material. This information may include availability, others who are using the materials, evaluation of success or failure associated with the use, and personal appraisal of the material. These persons can also supply names of companies that usually publish the type of material under consideration.

Publisher Information.   The information available from publishers may come in at least three forms: catalogs, other sales material, and representatives or consultants. The information provides bibliographic information, a physical description, and price information. Publishers may also describe correlated and adjunct materials. It is necessary to realize that the information provided by publishers is slanted toward the sale of the item.

Media/Materials Resource Centers.   Many school districts and/or regional centers have central collections of instructional resources. These centers may house general collections or may be directly related to special education. Such centers may have a broad array of information including media/materials for examination and use, publishers' catalogs, retrieval systems for materials information, evaluation data on materials, facilities for adaptation and production of materials, and knowledgeable materials resource personnel. Thus, the teacher may locate information on specific products and types of products, examine actual products, use the materials with students, find out about new products, determine what others may know about the products, and gain a great deal of first-hand information about the products.

College/University Resources. Most special education training programs have specific courses offered by faculty involved in media/materials and collections of instructional media/materials. Resources may also be found in the other teacher-training programs such as departments of curriculum and instruction, elementary education, and secondary education. The information available through such resources will often be slanted more toward the availability, research, and physical features of media/material than about its actual classroom application.

Prepared Materials Lists. Lists of materials provide good resources for identifying specific information about materials. These lists may be derived from a variety of sources. In some states or school districts, approved lists of materials are identified each year. Frequently, curriculum guides will include lists of materials correlated to the content of the guides. In some of the professional texts, materials lists are provided along with the teaching methods and strategies described in the text. Also, in in-service and professional development workshops, lists of materials are frequently disseminated and exchanged among teachers. Materials lists may be organized in a variety of ways including by handicapping conditions, by difficulty or grade level, or by curriculum area. It is important when using lists that the teacher consider the source of the list, the organization of the list, and the fact that in most cases the list primarily provides bibliographic information about the materials, not efficacy information.

Conferences. Most conferences and conventions provide exhibits by publishers, presentations about materials by authors and/or publishers, presentations of research studies in which specific materials were used, and opportunities to discuss materials with others who have common needs. One of the more valuable types of conferences for the purpose of learning about materials is the type usually referred to as "publisher's conference." In such a meeting specific publishers are invited to make a formal presentation about a particular program that is new to the market. Such presentations allow the teacher to gain comprehensive information about a specific material, the author, the development process, and research data.

Retrieval Systems.   There are a number of instructional materials retrieval systems that have been developed by commercial companies, through federal funding, and by school systems at the local, regional, and occasionally building level. If such a system is available, the teacher should become familiar with the capabilities of the system, the techniques or procedures for use, and the data base of the system. Retrieval systems can provide a good deal of information about materials available to meet a specific need and the physical characteristics of the material. With some systems it is also possible to secure information on evaluation and availability of the material. Once the teacher has located certain available materials, these materials should be carefully examined prior to making a final selection. This step is usually considered to be one of analysis. It may best be described as a static evaluation, since it is based on the physical characteristics of the material rather than exclusively on the experimental data arrived from the use of the material. This physical examination should be carried out in a systematic manner to assure that the materials are all evaluated on an equal basis.

Many articles (Armstrong, 1971; McIntyre, 1970; Junkala, 1970) have addressed the issues involved in materials analysis and have suggested various ways to conduct such evaluations. For a more comprehensive discussion of materials analysis and experimental evaluation, the reader is referred to Watson and Van Etten (1976), Bleil (1975), and V. Brown (1975). Each of these articles provides suggested approaches and criteria for the examination of materials. However, in a comprehensive review of the literature on selection and evaluation of materials, Ventura (1980) suggests that identifed criteria range from requiring a response to five questions to requiring the completion of a six-page evaluation form. Since so much variety exists with respect to the member and type of criteria, the teacher must make decisions as to the number and type of critical items. However, as Ward (1968) states, teachers must systematically examine materials and "be the competent professional who selects and uses instructional materials in order to increase the learning of children" (p. 23). For the purposes of this chapter, the following ten categories represent the variables that are found in many of the articles.

Each of these categories may have subcomponents and be expanded to the extent the teacher feels is necessary. The process should, however, be kept short and simple enough to be a help and not a hindrance. Closer examination of the categories may help clarify the type of information that can be useful.

1. Bibliographic information and price

2. Instructional area and skills scope and sequence
3. Component parts of the material
4. Level of the material: readability, vocabulary control, and interest
5. Quality: packaging, print, illustration, and paper durability
6. Format: form, layout, receptive and expressive requirements, and special equipment needs
7. Support materials: teacher's manuals and resources, student evaluations, objective clusters, etc.
8. Time requirements: length of tasks, flexibility, and scheduling
9. Field test and research data
10. Method, approach, or theoretical bases

Bibliographic Information.   In this section the purpose should be, first, to record all the information necessary for future reference or purchase. Second, this section should be used to make determinations and answer questions that may assist in analysis. Consider such items as:

Title—The name of the product may help identify the content area and whether the product is part of a set or series.
Author—Is it someone known for his or her work in a specific area or someone associated with a particular approach?
Copyright—Is it current? Will it reflect new trends and facts?
Price—Is it within the budget limitations? Is it in keeping with other materials prices and does it appear reasonable for its teaching value?
Publisher—Does the company have a reputation for producing a certain kind or quality of material? Does the company support its products through staff development, and service for purchasers?

Instructional Area and Skills Scope and Sequence.   Does the material cover the content area or specific components of the area? Does it address the specific skills needed? Does the material present initial instruction, remediation, and practice and/or reinforcement activities for the skills? Are the skills presented in the appropriate sequence? Is each skill given an equal amount of coverage?

Component Parts of the Material.   Are there multiple pieces to the material? Can the pieces be used independently? Can the pieces be used for other purposes? Are there consumable pieces? Can the pieces be purchased independently? Will it be a problem to keep track of all components?

Level of the Material.   Does the publisher state the readability level of the material? Is it consistent throughout the material? Is there more than one book for each level? Is there an attempt to control the use of content-specific vocabulary? Is the interest level appropriate to the content, pictures, and publisher's statements?

Quality.   Is the material (e.g., paper, tape, acetate, film, etc.) of good and durable quality? Is the print clear and of appropriate size and contrast with the background color? Are the illustrations clear and relevant to content? Do they add to rather than detract from the instruction?

Format.   Is the form appropriate (e.g., workbook, slide-tape, etc.)? Does it utilize the appropriate receptive and expressive modes for the content? Is the material clear and easy to follow? Are there special needs required (e.g., projector, recorder, etc.)?

Support Materials.   Are there additional components beyond the child-use instructional items (e.g., placement tests, check-tests, resource files, objective clusters)? Are there teacher's guides and/or teacher's editions? Are there teacher-training materials?

Time Requirements.   Are the tasks of an appropriate length? Does the material allow flexibility for scheduling? Does it allow flexibility in instructional procedures?

Field Test and Research Data.   Does the publisher offer any research that would support the validity or reliability of the material? Are there any data to support either process or product studies? In essence, do the data support the contention that the material will do what the publisher says it will do for the type of student indicated?

Method, Approach, or Theoretical Bases.   Does the material utilize a specific approach or method, or is it based upon a specific theoretical concept? Is it one that meets the needs of the triad? Is it compatible with other ongoing instruction? Is the method, approach, or basic theory substantiated by any published research?

As in the case of the curricular–student–teacher triad, these variables may change with needs; however, they should serve as basic criteria for the selection process. Selection of materials cannot be viewed as a simple process but rather as one that requires a great deal of effort and knowledge on the part of the trained professional responsible for the design and delivery of instruction for students with learning and behavior problems.

REPRESENTATIVE MATERIALS

The following section of this chapter provides a sample listing of instructional materials that may be appropriate for use with students who have learning and/or behavior problems. These materials have all been published since the second edition of this book. The list is not intended to be comprehensive, but rather to serve as a guide for teachers for the selection of educational materials and resources. The section concludes with a list of publishers and their current addresses.

Reading

Title	Function			Reading Level	Grade Level	Publisher
	Developmental	Skill/Remediation	Supplemental			
A Better Reading Workshop			X	4–6	Intermediate–Sr. High	Globe Book Company
Adult Learning Series		X		2	Secondary	Jamestown Publishers
Adult Reading Program	X			1–8	Adult	Steck-Vaughn
Alike But Different			X	2–3	Intermediate–Sr. High	Globe Book Company
American Folklore and Legends			X	4	Intermediate–Sr. High	Globe Book Company
A Need to Read Center			X		Intermediate–Jr. High	Globe Book Company
Applying Reading Skills: Achievements in Reading Discovering Reading		X		4–6	Adult	Steck-Vaughn
Are You Ready?			X		K–1	Steck-Vaughn
Attention Span Stories		X		2–3		Jamestown Publishers
Beyond Time and Space		X		3–5	Intermediate–Sr. High	Globe Book Company
Breakaway!	X			1–6		EMC Publishing
By Myself Books Sets I and II			X		Primary	Pro-Ed
Cause and Effect						Childcraft Education Corp.
Level A			X		2–3	
Level B			X		3–4	
Cloze Reading Package			X		7–12	Scholastic Book Services
Comprehension for Games Reading for Detail						Childcraft Education Corp.
Level A			X		2–3	
Level B			X		3–4	
Drawing Conclusions						
Level A			X		2–3	
Level B			X		3–4	
Main Idea						
Level A			X		2–4	
Level B			X		4–6	

Title	Publisher	Interest Level	Reading Level			
Comprehension Skills Series I	BFA	1–3			X	
Counterpoint Reading Programs	Coronet					
Myth, Magic, and Mystery						
Unit 1 Comprehension Skills		4–Jr. High	4.8–5.4		X	
Unit 2 Vocabulary Skills		4–Jr. High	5.1–5.3		X	
Unit 3 Study Skills		4–Jr. High	4.4–5.1		X	
Stranger Than Fiction						
Unit A Comprehension Skills		3–Jr. High	2.5–4.0		X	
Unit B Vocabulary/Work Attack Skills		3–Jr. High	2.5–4.0		X	
Critical Reading Primers A, B, C, D	Ann Arbor Publishers	1–3		X		
Critical Reading Workbooks A, B, C, D	Ann Arbor Publishers	3–up		X		
Crosswinds One and Two	Bowman/Noble Publishers, Inc.	Jr. High	3–6			X
Essential Sight Words-Program Level I & II	Teaching Resources	Elementary		X		
Fact or Opinion	Childcraft Education Corp.					
Level A		2–3		X		
Level B		3–4		X		
Globe's Adapted Classics	Globe Book Company	Intermediate–Sr. High	3–7	X		
Improving Vocabulary Skills	Learning Tree Filmstrips	3–8		X		
Instructional Aid Packs	Barnell Loft, Ltd.	Primary			X	
Journeys to Fame	Globe Book Company	Intermediate–Sr. High	2–3		X	
Legends for Everyone	Globe Book Company	Intermediate–Sr. High	3	X		
Mastering Basic Reading Skills	Steck-Vaughn	Intermediate	2.2–6.4	X		
Match-up Language Arts Games	Childcraft Education Corp.					
Antonym Andy		1–2		X		
Synonym Skates		1–2		X		
Homonym Hop		2–3		X		
Moving Along Series	Benefic Press	Jr.–Sr. High	1.5–4.5			

Title	Function			Reading Level	Grade Level	Publisher
	Developmental	Skill/Remediation	Supplemental			
Multiple Skills Series		X			Elementary–Jr. High	Barnell Loft, Ltd.
Myths and Folk Tales Around the World			X	4	Intermediate–Sr. High	Globe Book Company
Panorama Reading Series		X		1.0–3.5	Elementary–Intermediate	Steck-Vaughn
Pinpoint: Critical Reading Skill Series		X		4–6	Intermediate–Secondary	Steck-Vaughn
Practical Vocabulary			X	4–6	7–12	Scholastic Book Service
Quicksilver Books			X	3.0–4.5	Intermediate–Jr. High	Bowmar/Noble Publishers
Rally Reading Program Levels A, B, C		X			Jr. High	Harcourt Brace Jovanovich
Readability Series Levels A–F		X			Jr. High	Harper and Row Publishers, Inc.
Read About Science			X	2.4–6.0	Elementary–Jr. High	Webster Div. McGraw-Hill
Reading Comprehension Filmstrips and Response Booklets			X			United Learning
Level A				2		
Level B				2		
Level C				3		
Reading Comprehension Series		X		3.0–4.4	Intermediate–Jr. High	Bowmar/Noble Publishers, Inc.
Reading Comprehension Skills			X		4–9	Learning Tree Filmstrips
Reading for Content and Speech		X				Educators Publishing Service
Book 1				3		
Book 2				4		
Book 3				5		
Book 4				6		
Reading for Survival		X			Sr. High	Cambridge

Reading for Winners		X		4–6	Secondary	Steck-Vaughn
Reading Power: Comprehension Workbook			X		Jr.–Sr. High	Developmental Learning Materials
Reading Power: Word Structure Workbook			X		Jr.–Sr. High	Developmental Learning Materials
Reading Quick Skills						Coronet
Level A		X		1–2	3–10	
Level B		X		3–4	3–10	
Level C		X		4–5	3–10	
Level D		X		5–6	3–10	
Reading Skill/Drill Modules		X			Primary	Science Research Associates
Reading to Learn: Focus on Being a Consumer				5	Jr.–Sr. High	Developmental Learning Materials
Sight Word Lab	X				Elementary	Developmental Learning Materials
Skilltime Phonics, Level A		X			1, 2, Rem.	Childcraft Education Corp.
Something True, Something Else		X		4–5	Intermediate–Sr. High	Globe Book Company
Sounds, Words, and Meanings	X				1–6	Steck-Vaughn
Sports Reading Series		X		2.0–4.3	Intermediate–Jr. High	Bowmar/Noble Publishers, Inc.
Stories of Surprise and Wonder		X		3	Intermediate–Sr. High	Globe Book Company
Supportive Reading Skills		X			Elementary–Jr. High	Barnell Loft, Ltd.
Survival Vocabularies Series of ten titles				2.0	Secondary	Janus Book Publishers
The Choice			X	2.5	Secondary	Janus Book Publishers
The Double Play Series			X	2.5–5.9	Intermediate–Jr. High	Bowmar/Noble Publishers, Inc.
The Last Good-bye			X	2.5	Secondary	Janus Book Publishers
The Promise			X	2.5	Secondary	Janus Book Publishers
The Reading Key—Work Attack		X			Ungraded	C. C. Publications
The Reading Powertapes Program		X		4–5	Intermediate–Sr. High	Globe Book Company
The Sly Spy and Other Stories			X		2–3	Ann Arbor Publishers

High Interest/Low Vocabulary

Title	Interest Level	Reading Level	Publisher
Creatures Wild and Free	4–9	3.0	EMC Publishing
Flightpath to Reading	Intermediate–Jr. High		Educational Activities
A Series		2.0	
B Series		2.5	
C Series		3.0	
D Series		4.0	
Laura Brewster Books	Secondary	3.0	Pitman Learning, Inc.
Mystery Books	K–3	2.0	Garrard Publishing Company
	3–6	3.0–4.0	
Read-Along Mystery Modules	2–4	2.0–4.0	Troll Associates
Read Better			Pitman Learning, Inc.
Sportellers	Secondary	3.0	Pitman Learning, Inc.
Superstars Series	7–12	4.0–6.0	Steck-Vaughn
Talespinners I	Secondary	4.0	Pitman Learning, Inc.

Spoken Language

Title	Function			Grade Level	Publisher
	Developmental	Skill/Remediation	Supplemental		
Articulation Card Game		X		Elementary	Developmental Learning Materials
Developmental Language Lessons					
Level I		X		Preschool–Primary	Teaching Resources
Level II		X		Intermediate–Jr. High	Teaching Resources
Developmental Language Stories, Parts 1 and 2		X		Elementary	Teaching Resources
Fokes Sentence Builder		X		Elementary–Secondary	Teaching Resources
Fokes Sentence Builder Expansion		X		Elementary–Secondary	Teaching Resources
Grammar Big Box			X	Elementary	Developmental Learning Materials
Goldman-Lynch Sounds & Symbols Development Kit	X			Elementary	American Guidance Service
Language Concepts			X	Primary	United Learning
Language Rehabilitation: Auditory Comprehension		X		Secondary	C. C. Publications
Listening to the World	X			Primary	American Guidance Service
Listening with a Purpose		X		3–6, Rem. 7–8	Coronet
Oral/Written Language Lab	X			Elementary–Secondary	Developmental Learning Materials

Spoken Language *Continued*

Title	Function			Grade Level	Publisher
	Developmental	Skill/ Remediation	Supplemental		
Peabody Articulation Cards		X		Elementary–Secondary	American Guidance Service
Peabody Articulation Decks		X		Elementary–Secondary	American Guidance Sercive
Peabody Language Developmental Kits (Revised) Levels P, 1, 2, 3	X			Elementary	American Guidance Sercive
Plurals		X		K–4	C. C. Publications
Preschool Vocabulary Builders		X		Preschool	Developmental Learning Materials
P.S.: A Prefix-Suffix Language Building Game			X	Intermediate	Communication Skill Builders
Scarecrow Card Games		X		Intermediate	Communication Skill Builders
See It-Say It		X		Primary–Adult	Addison-Wesley
STEP: A Basic Concept Development Program		X		Preschool–Elementary	C. C. Publications
Syntax Codes		X		Elementary	C. C. Publications
Syntax One		X		Primary	Communication Skill Builders
Syntax Two		X		Primary	Communication Skill Builders
Vocabulary Instructional Programs		X		Elementary–Secondary	C. C. Publications
What's the Solution			X	Adult	Communication Skill Builders

Written Composition

Title	Function			Grade Level	Publisher
	Developmental	Skill/Remediation	Supplemental		
Action English Series			X	4–5, Rem. Secondary	Steck-Vaughn
Birdseye Mastery Masters Birdseye Views Phonics and Spelling Birdseye Views Word Structure Birdseye Views Word Meaning Birdseye Views Grammar Usage		X		Intermediate, Rem. Jr. High	Pitman Learning, Inc.
Capitalization and Punctuation Series			X	Intermediate	United Learning
Creative Writing Stimulators			X	2–4	Childcraft
Effective Writing Skills			X	4–8	Learning Tree Filmstrips
English Grammar Series			X	Intermediate–Jr. High	United Learning
English Usage Series			X	Secondary	United Learning
Everyday English		X		RL: 3–5 Jr.–Sr. High	Globe Book Company
Grammar			X	3–6	Learning Tree Filmstrips
How Do I Know What I Know?			X	K–3	BFA
Open Ended Plays			X	RL: 3–4 Intermediate–Sr. High	Globe Book Company
Open Ended Stories			X	3–5 Intermediate–Sr. High	Globe Book Company

Written Composition *Continued*

Title	Function			Grade Level	Publisher
	Developmental	*Skill/ Remediation*	*Supplemental*		
Punctuation			X	3–6	Learning Tree Filmstrips
Report Writing Skills			X	4–6 Rem. 7–12	Childcraft
Report Writing Workshop			X	Jr. High	BFA
See It-Write It		X		Intermediate–Adult	Addison-Wesley
Skilltime Writing Skills Level A		X		2–3, Rem.	Childcraft
Stories to Finish			X	1–4	Childcraft
Structural Analysis Series			X	Intermediate–Jr. High	United Learning
The Language of Classifications (1975)		X		Elementary	Alexander Graham Bell Publications
The Reading Road to Writing			X	6–9, Rem. 10–12	Childcraft
The Reading Road to Writing		X		4 Intermediate–Sr. High	Globe Book Company
The Syntax Game			X	Intermediate–Adult	Teaching Resources
Word Parts Word Forms Work Meanings			X	3–8	Learning Tree Filmstrips
Writing for Life 1 & 2			X	Secondary	Cambridge

Math

Title	Function			Grade Level	Publisher
	Developmental	Skill/Remediation	Supplemental		
Buying With Sense			X	6–12	Pitman Learning, Inc.
Consumer Math					
Spending Money Wisely			X	Secondary	United Learning
Financial Management			X	Secondary	United Learning
Corrective Mathematics		X		3–12	Science Research Associates
Getting Ready for Mathematics		X	X	K–1, Rem. Primary	Developmental Learning Materials
Improving Math Competence		X			Cambridge Book Company
Key Math Products Attribute Blocks, Balance, Boards, Card Decks, Chips, Cubes, Tumblers, Rulers, and Trays			X	Elementary	American Guidance Service
Math Problem-Solving Kit					
I		X		2–3	BFA
II		X		4–6	BFA
III		X		6–8	BFA
Money Big Box			X	Elementary	Developmental Learning Materials

Title	Function			Grade Level	Publisher
	Developmental	Skill/ Remediation	Supplemental		
Money Matters: Bank On It			X	Sr. High–Adult	Developmental Learning Materials
Moving Up in Story Problems: Time and Money		X		Elementary	Developmental Learning Materials
Number Posters			X	Primary	Teaching Resources
Oregon Math Computation	X			Elementary– Jr. High	C. C. Publications
Oregon Math Story Problems for Nonreaders			X	Elementary– Jr. High	C. C. Publications
Reaching Math Competence		X			Cambridge Book Company
Skilltime Math Programs					
Problem Solving Level A		X		1–3	Childcraft Education Corp.
Problem Solving Level B		X		1–2	Childcraft Education Corp.
Unifix Math Cube Sets			X	Primary—Sr. High	Teaching Resources

Spelling

Title	Function			Grade Level	Publisher
	Developmental	Skill/Remediation	Supplemental		
Advanced Speed Spelling	X			5–12	C. C. Publications
CPS Variety Day Kit			X	1–9	The Economy Company
Speed Spelling	X			1–6	C. C. Publications
Spelling			X	3–6	Learning Tree Filmstrips
Spelling Mastery	X			2–6	Science Research Associates
Spell It Out: Reading/Spelling Workshop	X			RL 3–6 Intermediate–Sr. High	Globe Book Company
Target: Spelling	X			1–4	Steck-Vaughn
The Wordroid			X	Intermediate	Addison-Wesley

Life Skills

Title	Function			Reading Level	Interest Level	Publisher
	Developmental	Skill/Remediation	Supplemental			
ABLEST			X	1–3	Jr. High–Adult	Pitman Learning, Inc.
Forms in Your Future			X		Jr.–Sr. High	Globe Book Company
Getting Out/Getting Around			X	5	Jr.–Sr. High	Globe Book Company
Lifeschool-Beginning Classroom Modules			X	1–4 Jr.–Sr. High	Jr.–Sr. High	Pitman Learning, Inc.
Making Math Count			X	5	Jr.–Sr. High	Globe Book Company
Traffic Sign Bingo			X		Secondary	Developmental Learning Materials
Using Functional Word Signs			X		Elementary–Secondary	Developmental Learning Materials
You The Buyer			X	5	Jr.–Sr. High	Globe Book Company

Publishers[1]

Addison-Wesley Publishing Co.
2725 Sand Hill Road
Menlo Park, CA 94025

Alexander Graham Bell Pub.
3417 Volta Pl.
Washington, DC 20007

American Guidance Service
Publisher's Building
Circle Pines, MN 55014

Ann Arbor Publishers
611 Church Street
Ann Arbor, MI 48104

Barnell Loft Ltd.
958 Church Street
Baldwin, NY 11510

Benefic Press
1900 N. Narragansett
Chicago, IL 60639

BFA
2211 Michigan Ave.
P.O. Box 1795
Santa Monica, CA 90406

Bowmar/Noble Publishers, Inc.
4563 Colorado Blvd.
Los Angeles, CA 90039

Cambridge
888 Seventh Ave.
New York, NY 10019

C. C. Publications
P.O. Box 23699
Tigard, OR 97223

Childcraft Education Corp.
20 Kilmer Road
Edison, NJ 08817

1. The materials presented in this list were prepared in cooperation with Mary Venura, University of Missouri at Kansas City and Gail Williams, Olathe Kansas School District.

Communication Skill Builders
3131 N. Dodge Blvd.
P.O. Box 42050-K
Tucson, AZ 85733

Coronet
65 S. Water Street East
Chicago, IL 60601

Developmental Learning
Materials
One DLM Park
Allen, TX 75002

The Economy Company
P.O. Box 25308
Oklahoma, OK 73125

Educational Activities, Inc.
P.O. Box 392
Freeport, NY 11520

Educators Publishing Service, Inc.
75 Moulton Street
Cambridge, MA 02138

EMC Publishing
Changing Times
Education Service
180 E. Sixth Street
St. Paul, MN 55101

Garrard Publishing Co.
1607 North Market Street
Champaign, IL 61820

Globe Book Company, Inc.
50 West 23rd Street
New York, NY 10010

Harper & Row Publishers
10 East 53rd Street
New York, NY 10022

Jamestown Publishers
P.O. Box 6743
Providence, RI 02940

Janus Book Publishers
2501 Industrial Parkway W
Dept. A
Hayward, CA 94545

Learning Tree Filmstrips
934 Pearl Street
Box 1590-Dept. 550
Boulder, CO 80306

Pitman Learning Inc.
6 Davis Drive
Belmont, CA 94002

Pro-Ed
5341 Industrial Oaks Blvd.
Austin, TX 78735

Scholastic Book Service
904 Sylvan Avenue
Englewood Cliffs, NJ 07632

Science Research Associates, Inc.
155 N. Wacker Dr.
Chicago, IL 60606

Steck-Vaughn Company
P.O. Box 2028
Austin, TX 78768

Teaching Resources Corporation
50 Pond Park Road
Hingham, MA 02043

Troll Associates
320 Route 17
Mahwah, NJ 07430

United Learning Company
6633 West Howard
Niles, IL 60648

REFERENCES

ADKINS, D. C., and BALIFF, B. L. *Animal Crackers: A Test of Motivation to Achieve.* Monterey, CA: CTB/McGraw-Hill, 1973.

Adventures of the Lollipop Dragon. Chicago: Society for Visual Education, 1970.

ALEXANDER, E. D. School centered play-therapy program. In N. J. Long, W. C. Morse, and R. G. Newman (Eds.), *Conflict in the classroom.* Belmont, Calif.: Wadsworth, 1971. Pp. 251–257.

ALLEN, K. E., TURNER, K. D., and EVERETT, P. M. A. A behavior modification classroom for Head Start children with problem behaviors. *Exceptional Children,* 1970, 37, 119–127.

ANASTASI, A. *Psychological testing,* 3rd ed. New York: Macmillan, 1968.

ANDERSON, G. J. *The assessment of learning environments: A manual for the Learning Environment Inventory and the My Class Inventory.* Halifax, Nova Scotia: Atlantic Institute of Education, 1973.

ANDERSON, V. *Improving the child's speech.* New York: Oxford University Press, 1953.

ANDRÉ, M. E. D. A., and ANDERSON, T. H. The development and evaluation of a self-questioning study technique. *Reading Research Quarterly,* 1978–79, *14,* 606–623.

ANTINUCCI, F., and PARISI, D. Early language acquisition: A model and some data. In C. A. Ferguson and D. I. Slobin (Eds.), *Studies of child language development.* New York: Holt, Rinehart and Winston, 1973. Pp. 607–619.

435

APPLEGATE, E.   *Perceptual aids in the classroom.* San Rafael, Calif.: Academic Therapy Publications, 1969.

ARCHER, C. P.   Transfer of training in spelling. In *University of Iowa studies in education.* Iowa City, Iowa: University of Iowa Press, 1930.

ARENA, J. I. (Ed.).   *Teaching through sensory-motor experiences.* San Rafael, Calif.: Academic Therapy Publications, 1969.

ARMSTRONG, J. R.   A model for materials development and evaluation. *Exceptional Children,* 1971, *38,* 327–334.

ARTER, J. A., and JENKINS, J. R.   Differential diagnosis—Perspective teaching: A critical appraisal. *Review of Educational Research,* 1979, *49,* 517–556.

ASHLOCK, R. B.   *Current research in elementary school mathematics.* New York: Macmillan, 1970.

ASHLOCK, R. B.   *Error patterns in computation: A semi-programmed approach.* Columbus, Ohio: Charles E. Merrill, 1976.

AXELROD, S.   *Behavior modification for the classroom teacher.* New York: McGraw-Hill, 1977.

AXLINE, V. M.   Non-directive therapy for poor readers. *Journal of Consulting Psychology,* 1947, *11,* 61–69.

AXLINE, V. M.   *Dibs: In search of self.* New York: Ballantine Books, 1964.

AYLLON, T.   Intensive treatment of psychotic behavior by stimulus satiation and food reinforcement. In L. Krasner and L. P. Ullmann (Eds.), *Case studies in behavior modification.* New York: Holt, Rinehart and Winston, 1965.

AYRES, J.   *Ayres Space Test.* Los Angeles: Western Psychological Services, 1962.

AYRES, J.   *Southern California Motor Accuracy Test.* Los Angeles: Western Psychological Services, 1964.

AYRES, J.   *Southern California Figure–Ground Visual Perception Test.* Los Angeles: Western Psychological Services, 1966. (a)

AYRES J.   *Southern California Perceptual–Motor Tests.* Los Angeles: Western Psychological Services, 1968.

BAKER, H. J., and LELAND, B.   *The Detroit Tests of Learning Aptitude.* Indianapolis, Ind.: Bobbs-Merrill, 1967.

BALL, T. S.   *Itard, Sequin, and Kephart: Sensory education—a learning interpretation.* Columbus, Ohio: Charles E. Merrill, 1971.

BANGS, T.   *Vocabulary Comprehension Scale.* Austin, Tex.; Learning Concepts, 1975.

BANNATYNE, A. D.   *Psycholinguistic color system.* Urbana, Ill.: Learning Systems Press, 1966.

BARCLAY, J. R.   Barclay Classroom Climate Inventory. Lexington, KY: Educational Skills Development, 1971.

BARKSDALE, M. W., and ATKINSON, A. P.   A resource room approach to instruction for the educable mentally retarded. *Focus on Exceptional Children*, 1971, *3*, 12–15.

BARRETT, T. C. The relationship between measures of pre-reading visual discrimination and first-grade reading achievement. *Reading Research Quarterly*, 1965, *1*, 51, 76.

BARRY, H. Training the young aphasic child. *The Volta Review*, 1960, 7, 326–328.

BARRY, H. *The young aphasic child.* Washington, D.C.: Alexander Graham Bell Association for the Deaf, 1961.

BARSCH, R. *A movigenics curriculum.* Madison, Wis.: State Department of Public Instruction, 1965.

BARSCH, R. *Achieving perceptual–motor efficiency.* Seattle, Wash.: Special Child Publications, 1967.

BARTEL, N. R. A cognitive approach to learning disabilities. In D. G. Bachor (Ed.) *Learning disabilities: Conceptual and practical issues.* London: University of Western Ontario Press. In press.

BARTEL, N. R. The development of morphology in moderately retarded children. *Education and Training of the Mentally Retarded*, 1970, *5*, 164–168.

BARTEL, N. R., GRILL, J. J., and BRYEN, D. N. Language characteristics of black children: Implications for assessment. *Journal of School Psychology*, 1973, *11*, 351–364.

Basic Educational Skills Inventory in Math. Olathe, Kans.: Select-Ed, 1972.

BATEMAN, B. Learning disabilities—yesterday, today, and tomorrow. In E. C. Frierson and W. B. Barbe (Eds.), *Educating children with learning disabilities.* New York: Appleton-Century-Crofts, 1967. Pp. 10–23.

BAYLEY, N. The development of motor abilities during the first three years. *Monograph Society for Research in Child Development*, 1935, *1*, 1–26.

BECHER, R. M. Teacher behaviors related to the mathematical achievement of young children. *Journal of Educational Research*, 1980, 73, 336–340.

BEERY, K., and BUKTENICA, N. A. *Developmental Test of Visual–Motor Integration.* Chicago: Follett, 1967.

BELGAU, F. A. *A motor perceptual developmental handbook of activities for schools, parents and preschool programs.* La Porte, Tex.: Perception Development Research Associates, 1966.

BELL, S. *Bell Adjustment Inventory.* Monterey, Calif.: Consulting Psychologists Press, 1961.

BELLAK, L., and BELLAK, S. S. *Children's Apperception Test.* Monterey, Calif.: Consulting Psychologists Press, 1961.

BELLUGI, U. The Emergence of Inflections and Negation Systems in the Speech of Two Children. Paper presented at The New England Psychological Association Conference. Chicopee, Mass., November 1964.

BELLUGI, U.   The Development of Interrogative Structures in Children's Speech. Paper presented at the First Symposium on the Development of Language Functions. Ann Arbor, Mich., October 1965.

BELLUGI-KLIMA, U.   Language comprehension tests. In C. Lavatelli (Ed.), *Language training in early childhood education.* Champaign-Urbana, Ill.: University of Illinois Press, 1973.

BENDER, L.   *The Bender Visual–Motor Gestalt Test for Children.* New York: American Orthopsychiatric Association, 1938.

BENTHUL, H. F., ANDERSON, E. A., UTECH, A. M., BIGGY, M. V., and BAILEY, B. L.   *Spell correctly.* Morristown, N.J.: Silver Burdett, 1974.

BERKO, J.   The child's learning of morphology. *Word*, 1958, *14*, 150–177.

BERRY, M. F., and EISENSON, J.   *Speech disorders.* New York: Appleton-Century-Crofts, 1956.

BIALER, I.   Conceptualization of success and failure in mentally retarded and normal children. *Journal of Personality*, 1961, *29*, 303–320.

BIBACE, R.   Relationships between perceptual and conceptual cognitive processes. *Journal of Learning Disabilities*, 1969, *2*, 17–29.

BILLS, R. E.   Non-directive play-therapy with retarded readers. *Journal of Psychology*, 1950, *14*, 246–249.

BIRCH, H. G., and BELMONT, L.   Auditory-visual integration, intelligence and reading ability in school children. *Perceptual and Motor Skills*, 1965, *20*, 295–305.

BLANCHARD, J. S., and McNINCH, G. H.   Testing the decoding sufficiency hypothesis: A response to Fleischer, Jenkins, and Pany. *Reading Research Quarterly*, 1980, *15*, 559–564.

BLANK, M., GESSNER, M., and ESPOSITO, A.   Language without communication. A case study. *Journal of Child Language*, 1979, *6*, 329–52.

BLEIL, G.   Evaluating educational materials. *Journal of Learning Disabilities*, 1975, *8*, 19–26.

BLOOM, B. S., ENGLEHART, M. D., FURST, E. J., HILL, W. H., and KRATHWOHL, D. R.   *Taxonomy of educational objectives, Handbook I: Cognitive domain.* New York: David McKay, 1956.

BLOOM, L.   *Language development: Form and function in emerging grammars.* Cambridge, MA: MIT Press, 1970.

BLOOM, L., ROCISSANO, L., and HOOD, L.   Adult-child discourse. Developmental interaction between information processing and linguistic knowledge. *Cognitive Psychology*, 1976, *8*, 521–522.

BLOOM, L., and LAHEY, M.   *Language development and language disorders.* New York: Wiley, 1978.

BLOOM, L.   *Language development: Form and function in emerging grammars.* Cambridge, Mass.: MIT Press, 1970.

BLOOM, L., LIGHTBOWN, P., and HOOD, L.   Structure and variation in child language. *Monograph of the Society for Research in Child Development,* 1975, *40* (No. 2, Serial No. 60).

BLUM, G.   *The Blacky Pictures: Manual of instructions.* New York: Psychological Corporation, 1958.

BOND, G. L. and DYKSTRA, R. (Eds.)   First grade reading studies: Findings of individual investigation. Newark, DE: International Reading Association 1967.

BORICH, G. D., and MADDEN, S. K.   *Evaluating classroom instruction: A sourcebook of instruments.* Reading, MA: Addison-Wesley, 1977.

BOTEL, M.   *Botel Reading Inventory.* Chicago, IL: Follett, 1966.

BOURQUE, M. L.   Specification and validation of reading skills hierarchies. *Reading Research Quarterly,* 1980, *15,* 237–267.

BOWER, E. M., and LAMBERT, N. M.   In-school screening of children with emotional handicaps. In N. J. Long, W. C. Morse, and R. G. Newman (Eds.), *Conflict in the classroom.* Belmont, Calif.: Wadsworth, 1971.

BOWERMAN, M.   Semantic factors in the acquisition of rules for word use and sentence construction. In D. M. Morehead and A. E. Morehead (Eds.), *Normal and deficient child language.* Baltimore: University Park Press, 1976. Pp. 99–180.

BOYD, L., and RANDLE, K.   Factor analysis of the Frostig Developmental Test of Visual Perception. *Journal of Learning Disabilities,* 1970, *3,* 253–255.

BRAINE, M.   The ontogeny of English phrase structure: The first phase. *Language,* 1963, *39,* 1–13.

BROPHY, J., and GOOD, T.   *Teacher–child dyadic interaction: A manual for coding classroom behavior.* Austin, Tex.: Research and Development Center, University of Texas, 1969.

BROWN, L.   A four year study of the efficacy of the TAD and DUSO curricula. Unpublished manuscript, Purdue University, 1979.

BROWN, L. L., and HAMMILL, D. D.   *Behavior Rating Profile: An Ecological Approach to Behavioral Assessment.* Austin, TX: Pro-Ed, 1978.

BROWN, L., and SHERBENOU, R. J.   A comparison of teacher perceptions of student reading ability, actual reading performance, and general classroom behavior. *Reading Teacher* (February, 1981). In press.

BROWN, L., and SHERBENOU, R. J.   The reliability of sociometric measures with elementary, junior high, and senior high school students. Unpublished manuscript, Purdue University, 1980.

BROWN, R.   *Social psychology.* New York: Free Press, 1965.

BROWN, R.   *Psycholinguistics.* New York: Free Press, 1970.

BROWN, R.   *A first language: The early stages.* Cambridge, Mass.: Harvard University Press, 1973.

BROWN, R., and BELLUGI, U.   Three processes in the child's acquisition of syntax. *Harvard Educational Review,* 1964, *34,* 133–151.

BROWN, V. L.   A basic Q-sheet for analyzing and comparing curriculum materials and proposals. *Journal of Learning Disabilities*, 1975, *8*, 409–416.

BROWNELL, W. A.   Arithmetic readiness as a practical classroom concept. *The Elementary School Journal*, 1951, *52*, 15–22.

BRUECKNER, L. J.   *Diagnostic tests and self-helps in arithmetic.* Los Angeles: California Test Bureau, 1955.

BRUECKNER, L. J., and BOND, G. L.   The diagnosis and treatment of learning difficulties. In E. C. Frierson and W. B. Barbe (Eds.), *Educating children with learning disabilities.* New York: Appleton-Century-Crofts, 1967. Pp. 442–447.

BRUNER, J.   The ontogenesis of speech acts. *Journal of Child Languages*, 1975, *2*, 1–19.

BRUNER, J.   The ontogenesis of speech acts.   *Journal of Child Language*, 1975, *2*, 1–22.

BRUNININKS, R. H.   *Brunininks-Oseretzky Test of Motor Proficiency.* Circle Pines, MN: American Guidance Services, 1978.

BRYEN, D. N.   Issues and activities in language. Unpublished manuscript, Temple University, Philadelphia, 1975.

BUCHANAN, C. D.   *Programmed reading book 4.* New York: McGraw-Hill/ Webster Division, 1968.

BUCK, N. J.   The House–Tree–Person (H-T-P) Test. *Journal of Clinical Psychology*, 1948, *4*, 151–159.

BUFFIE, E. G., WELCH, R. C., and PAIGE, D. D. *Mathematics: Strategies of teaching.* Englewood Cliffs, N.J.: Prentice-Hall, 1968.

BULLOWA, M.   The Onset of Speech. Paper presented at Society for Research in Child Development, March 1967. (a)

BULLOWA, M.   The Start of the Language Process. Paper presented at the Tenth International Congress of Linguists. Bucharest, September 1967. (b)

BURNS, P. C.   Arithmetic fundamentals for the educable mentally retarded. *American Journal of Mental Deficiency*, 1962, *66*, 57–61.

BURNS, P. C.   Analytical testing and follow-up exercises in elementary school mathematics. *School Science and Mathematics*, 1965, *65*, 34–38.

BURNS, P. C., BROMAN, B. L., and WANTLING, A. L. L.   *The language arts in childhood education.* Chicago: Rand McNally, 1971.

BUROS, O. K.   *Eighth Mental Measurements Yearbook.* Highland Park, NJ: Gryphon, 1978.

BURTON, W. H., KEMP, G. K., BAKER, C. B., CRAIG, I., and MOORE, V.   *The developmental reading text workbook series.* Indianapolis, Ind.: Bobbs-Merrill, 1975.

BUSH, W. J., and WAUGH, K. W.   *Diagnosing learning disabilities.* Columbus, OH: Charles E. Merrill, 1976.

CARLSON, R. K. *Sparkling words: Two hundred practical and creative writing ideas.* Berkeley, Calif.: Wagner, 1965. (Distributed through the National Council of Teachers of English, Urbana, Ill.)

CARPENTER, T. P., CORBITT, M. K., KEPNER, H., LINDQUIST, M. M., and REYS, E. E. Results implications of the second NAEP mathematics assessment: Elementary school. *Arithmetic Teacher,* 1980, *27,* 10–12. (a)

CARPENTER, T. P., CORBITT, M. K., KEPNER, H., LINDQUIST, M. M., and REYS, E. E. Results implications of the second NAEP mathematics assessment: Secondary school. *Mathematics Teacher,* 1980, *73,* 329–338. (b)

CARROLL, J. B. Psycholinguistics and the study and teaching of reading. In S. Phlaum-Connor (Ed.) *Aspects of reading education.* National Society for the Study of Education Series on Contemporary Educational Issues. Berkeley, CA: McCutcheon, 1978. Pp. 11–43.

CARROW, M. A. The development of auditory comprehension of language structure in children. *Journal of Speech and Hearing Disorders,* 1968, *33,* 99–111.

CARROW-WOOLFOLK, E. *Test for Auditory Comprehension of Language.* Austin, Tex.: Learning Concepts, 1973.

CARROW-WOOLFOLK, E. *Carrow Elicited Language Inventory.* Austin, Tex.: Learning Concepts, 1974.

CARTWRIGHT, C. A., and CARTWRIGHT, G. P. *Developing observational skills.* New York: McGraw-Hill, 1974.

CATTELL, R. G. *The Sixteen Personality Factor Questionnaire.* Champaign, IL: Institute for Personality and Ability Testing, 1967.

CAWLEY, J. F. Extrapolating the usefulness of instructional materials. Unpublished manuscript, University of Connecticut, Storrs, Conn., 1971.

CAWLEY, J. F. Learning disabilities in mathematics: A curriculum design for upper grades. Unpublished manuscript, University of Connecticut, Storrs, Conn., 1976.

CAWLEY, J. F., FITZMAURICE, H. M., SHAW, R. A., KAHN, H., and BATES, H. Math word problems: Suggestions for LD students. *Learning Disability Quarterly,* 1979, *2,* 25–41.

CHALFANT, J. C., and SCHEFFELIN, M. A. Central processing dysfunctions in children. Bethesda, Md.: National Institutes of Health, 1969.

CHIANG, B., THORPE, H. W., and DARCH, C. B. Effects of cross-age tutoring on word-recognition performance of learning disabled students. *Learning Disability Quarterly,* 1980, *3,* 11–19.

CHOMSKY, N. *Syntactic structures.* The Hague: Mouton, 1957.

CHOMSKY, N. A review of B. F. Skinner's *Verbal behavior. Language,* 1959, *35,* 26–58.

CHOMSKY, N., and HALLE, M. *The sound pattern of English.* New York: Harper & Row, 1968.

CHRISTOPOLOS, F., and RENZ, P. A critical examination of special education programs. *Journal of Special Education,* 1969, *3,* 371–379.

CLARK, E. What's in a word? On the child's acquisition of semantics in his first language. In T. E. Moore (Ed.), *Cognitive development and the acquisition of language.* New York: Academic Press, 1973.

CLAY, M. M. A syntactic analysis of reading errors. *Journal of Verbal Learning and Verbal Behavior,* 1968, *1,* 434–438.

CLINE, R. K. J., and KRETKE, G. L. An evaluation of long-term SSR in the Junior High School. *Journal of Reading,* 1980, *23,* 503–506.

CLOWARD, R. D. Studies in tutoring. *Journal of Experimental Education,* 1967, *36,* 25.

CLYMER, T. What is "reading"? Some current concepts. In H. M. Robison (Ed.), *The sixty-seventh yearbook of the National Society for the Study of Education.* Chicago: University of Chicago Press, 1968.

COHEN, A. S. Oral reading errors of first grade children taught by a code emphasis approach. *Reading Research Quarterly,* 1974–1975, *10,* 616–650.

COHEN, S. A. Studies in visual perception and reading in disadvantaged children. *Journal of Learning Disabilities,* 1969, *2,* 498–507.

COHEN, S. B., and PLASKON, S. P. *Language arts for the mildly handicapped.* Columbus, OH: Charles E. Merrill, 1980.

COLEMAN, J. H., and JUNGEBLUT, A. *Reading for meaning.* Philadelphia: Lippincott, 1965.

COLES, G. S. The learning-disabilities test battery: Empirical and social issues. *Harvard Educational Review,* 1978, *48,* 313–340.

COMBS, W. E. Sentence-combining practice aids reading comprehension. *The Reading Teacher,* 1977, *21,* 18–24.

CONNOLLY, A., NACHTMAN, W., and PRITCHETT, E. M. *Key Math Diagnostic Arithmetic Test.* Circle Pines, Minn.: American Guidance Services, Inc., 1976.

Contact maturity: Growing up strong. Englewood Cliffs, N.J.: Scholastic Book Service, 1972.

COOPERSMITH, R. *The antecedents of self-esteem.* San Francisco: W. H. Freeman, 1968.

CORAH, N. L., and POWELL, B. J. A factor analytic study of the Frostig Developmental Test of Visual Perception. *Perceptual and Motor Skills,* 1963, *16,* 59–63.

CRANDALL, V. C., KATHOVSKY, W., and CRANDALL, V. J. Children's beliefs in their own control of reinforcement in intellectual–academic achievement situations. *Child Development,* 1965, *36,* 91–109.

CRATTY, B. *Active learning: Games to enhance academic abilities.* Englewood Cliffs, NJ: Prentice-Hall, 1971.

CRATTY, B. J. *Teaching motor skills.* Englewood Cliffs, NJ: Prentice-Hall, 1973.

CRATTY, B. J. Motor development for special populations. *Focus on Exceptional Children,* 1980, *13,* 1–12.

CRISCUOLO, N. P. Effective ways to communicate with parents about reading. *Reading Teacher,* 1980, *34,* 164–6.

CRISCUOLO, N. P. Activities that help involve parents in reading. *Reading Teacher,* 1979, *32,* 417–419.

CRONBACH, L. J. *Educational psychology.* New York: Harcourt, Brace & World, 1970.

CRUICKSHANK, W. M., BENTZEN, F. A., RATZEBURG, F. H., and TANNHAUSER, M. *A teaching method for brain-injured and hyperactive children.* Syracuse, N.Y.: Syracuse University Press, 1961.

CUNNINGHAM, P. M. Investigating a synthesized theory of mediated word identification. *Reading Research Quarterly,* 1975–1976, *11,* 127–143.

CURTISS, S., PRUTTING, C. A., and LOWELL, E. L. Pragmatic and semantic development in young children with impaired hearing. *Journal of Speech and Hearing Research,* 1979, *22,* 534–552.

DALE, P. S. Is early pragmatic development measurable? *Child Language,* 1980, *7,* 1–12.

DALE, P. S. *Language development: Structure and function.* New York: Holt, Rinehart and Winston, 1972.

DALE, P. S. *Language development: Structure and function,* 2nd ed. New York: Holt, Rinehart and Winston, 1976.

D'ANGELO, K. and WILSON, R. M. How helpful is insertion and omission miscue analysis? *The Reading Teacher,* 1979, *32,* 519–520.

DAVIDSON, J. *Using the Cuisenaire rods.* New Rochelle, N.Y.: Cuisenaire, 1969.

DAVIS, L. *My friends and me.* Circle Pines, MN: American Guidance Service, 1977.

DECHANT, E. V. *Improving the teaching of reading.* Englewood Cliffs, N.J.: Prentice-Hall, 1964.

DEVER, R. B. *TALK (Teaching the American Language to Kids).* Columbus, Ohio: Charles E. Merrill, 1978.

DE VILLIERS, P., and DE VILLIERS, J. A cross-sectional study of the acquisition of grammatical morphemes in child speech. *Journal of Psycholinguistic Research,* 1973, *2,* 267–278.

DE VILLIERS, J. G., and DE VILLIERS, P. A. *Language acquisition.* Cambridge: Harvard University Press, 1978.

DINKMEYER, D. *Developing understanding of self and others, D-I.* Circle Pines, Minn.: American Guidance Services, Inc., 1970.

DINKMEYER, D.   *Developing understanding of self and others, D-II.* Circle Pines, Minn.: American Guidance Services, Inc., 1973.

DOEHRING, D. G., and AULLS, M. W.   The interactive nature of reading acquisition. *Journal of Reading Behavior,* 1979, *11,* 27–40.

DOLCE, C. J.   The inner city—a superintendent's view. *The Saturday Review,* January 1969, p. 36.

DOLL, E. A.   *The Preschool Attainment Record.* Circle Pines, Minn.: American Guidance Services, Inc., 1966.

DOLL, E. A.   *Measurement of social competence: A Manual for the Vineland Social Maturity Scale.* Circle Pines, MN: American Guidance Service, 1965.

DORE, J. A.   A pragmatic description of early language development. *Journal of Psycholinguistic Research,* 1974, *3,* 343–350.

DORE, J. A.   A pragmatic description of early language development. *Journal of Psycholinguistic Research,* 4, 423–430.

DREW, C. J., FRESTON, C. W., and LOGAN, D. R.   Criteria and reference in evaluation. *Focus on Exceptional Children,* 1972, *4,* 1–10.

DUNN, L. M.   *Peabody Picture Vocabulary Test.* Circle Pines, Minn.: American Guidance Services, Inc., 1965.

DUNN, L. M.   Minimal brain dysfunction: A dilemma for educators. In E. C. Frierson and W. B. Barbe (Eds.), *Educating children with learning disabilities.* New York: Appleton-Century-Crofts, 1967.

DUNN, L. M.   Special education for the mildly retarded—is much of it justifiable? *Exceptional Children,* 1968, *35,* 5–22.

DUNN, L., and SMITH, J. O.   *Peabody language development kits.* Circle Pines, Minn.: American Guidance Services, Inc., 1966.

DuPONT, H., GARDNER, O. S., and BRODY, D. S.   *Toward affective development.* Circle Pines, MN: American Guidance Service, 1974.

DuPONT, H., and DuPONT, C.   *Transition.* Circle Pines, MN: American Guidance Service, 1979.

DURKIN, D.   What classroom observations reveal about comprehension instruction. *Reading Research Quarterly,* 1978–79, *14,* 481–533.

DUROST, W., BIXLER, H. H., WRIGHTSTONE, J. W., PRESCOTT, G. A., and BALOW, I. W.   *Metropolitan Achievement Tests.* New York: Harcourt, Brace & World, 1971.

DURRELL, D. D.   *Improvement of basic reading abilities.* Yonkers, N.Y.: World Book, 1940.

DUTTON, W. H., and ADAMS, L. J.   *Arithmetic for teachers,* Englewood Cliffs, N.J.: Prentice-Hall, 1961.

EBERSOLE, M., KEPHART, N. C., and EBERSOLE, J. B.   *Steps to achievement for the slow learner.* Columbus, Ohio: Charles E. Merrill, 1968.

EDGINGTON, R. But he spelled them right this morning. *Academic Therapy Quarterly,* 1967, *3,* 58–59.

EHLY, S. W., and LARSEN, S. C. *Peer tutoring for individualized instruction.* Boston: Allyn and Bacon, 1980.

ELLIS, A. *Humanistic psychotherapy.* New York: McGraw-Hill, 1974.

ELLIS, A. Rational-emotive therapy. In L. Hershner (Ed.), *Four psychotherapies.* New York: Appleton-Century-Crofts, 1970.

ELLIS, A. *Reason and emotion in psychotherapy.* New York: Lyle Stuart, 1962.

ELLIS, A., WOLFE, J. L., and MOSLEY, S. *How to raise an emotionally healthy, happy child.* Hollywood, CA: Wilshire, 1974.

ERICKSON, M. R. A study of a tutoring program to benefit tutors and tutees. Ann Arbor, Mich.: University of Michigan, University Microfilm, 1971. No. 71–16914.

ERVIN, S. Imitation and structural change in children's language. In E. Lenneberg (Ed.), *New directions in the study of language.* Cambridge, Mass.: The MIT Press, 1964. Pp. 163–189.

ESTES, T. H., ESTES, J. J., RICHARDS, H. C., and ROETTGER, D. *Estes Attitude Scales.* Austin, TX: Pro-Ed, 1981.

EYSENCK, S. B. G. *Junior Eysenck Personality Inventory.* San Diego: Educational and Industrial Testing Service, 1965.

FASLER, J. *Child's series on psychologically relevant themes.* Westport, Conn.: Videorecord Corporation of America, 1971.

FEIGENBAUM, I. *English now.* New York: New Century, 1970.

FERNALD, G. *Remedial techniques in basic school subjects.* New York: McGraw-Hill, 1943.

FERSTER, C. B., and SKINNER, B. F. *Schedules of reinforcement.* New York: Appleton-Century-Crofts, 1957.

FINE, M. J. *The teacher's role in classroom management.* Lawrence, Kans.: Psych-Ed, 1973.

FISHER, B. Group therapy and retarded readers. *Journal of Educational Psychology,* 1953, *44,* 354–360.

FISKE, D. W., and COX, J. A., JR. The consistency of ratings by peers. *Journal of Applied Psychology,* 1960, *44,* 11–17.

FITZGERALD, E. *Straight language for the deaf.* Washington, D.C.: Volta Bureau, 1949.

FLANDERS, N. *Analyzing teacher behavior.* Menlo Park, Calif.: Addison-Wesley, 1970.

FLEISCHER, L. S., JENKINS, J. R., and PANY, D. Effects on poor readers' comprehension of training in rapid decoding. *Reading Research Quarterly,* 1980, *15,* 30–48.

FLEMING, L., and SNYDER, W. U. Social and personal changes following non-directive group therapy. *American Journal of Orthopsychiatry,* 1947, *17,* 101–106.

FOKES, J. Developmental scale of language acquisition. In B. Stephens (Ed.), *Training the developmentally young.* New York: John Day, 1971.

FOKES, J. *Fokes sentence builder kit.* Boston: Teaching Resources, 1975.

FOSTER, R., GIDDAN, J. J., and STARK, J. *Assessment of Children's Language Comprehension Test.* Palo Alto, Calif.: Consulting Psychologist Press, 1973.

FOSTER, R., GIDDAN, J. J., and STARK, J. *Visually cued language cards.* Palo Alto, Calif.: Consulting Psychologists Press, 1975.

Fountain Valley Teachers Support System in Mathematics. Huntington Beach, Calif.: R. A. Zweig Associates, 1976.

FREEMAN, F. W. *Reference manual for teachers. Grades one through four.* Columbus, Ohio: Zaner-Bloser, 1965.

FROSTIG, M. Testing as a basis for educational therapy. *Journal of Special Education,* 1967, *2,* 15–34.

FROSTIG, M. *Movement education: Theory and practice.* Chicago: Follett, 1970.

FROSTIG, M., and HORNE, D. *The Frostig program for the development of visual perception.* Chicago: Follett, 1964.

FROSTIG, M., LEFEVER, D. W., and WHITTLESEY, J. R. B. A developmental test of visual perception for evaluating normal and neurologically handicapped children. *Perceptual and Motor Skills,* 1961, *12,* 383–394.

FROSTIG, M., and MASLOW, P. *Learning problems in the classroom.* New York: Grune & Stratton, 1973.

FROSTIG, M., MASLOW, P., LEFEVER, D. W., and WHITTLESEY, J. R. B. *The Marianne Frostig Developmental Test of Visual Perception.* Palo Alto, Calif.: Consulting Psychologists Press, 1964.

FRY, D. The development of the phonological system in the normal and the deaf child. In F. Smith and G. Miller (Eds.), *The genesis of speech.* Cambridge, Mass.: MIT Press, 1966. Pp. 187–206.

FRY, E. Fry's readability graph: Clarification, validity and extension to level 17. *Journal of Reading,* 1977, *21,* 242–252.

FURROW, D., NELSON, K., and BENEDICT, H. Mothers' speech to children and syntactic development: Some simple relationships. *Child Language,* 1979, *6,* 423–442.

GAMBRELL, L. B. Think-time: Implications for reading instruction. *Reading Teacher,* 1980, *34,* 143–6.

GAMBRELL, L. B. Getting started with Sustained Silent Reading and keeping it going. *Reading Teacher,* 1978, *32,* 328–31.

GARRETT, H. E. *Statistics in psychology and education.* New York: Longmans Green, 1954.

GARRETT, H. E. *Testing for teachers.* New York: American Book, 1965.

GATES, A. I. *The Improvement of reading.* New York: Macmillan, 1947.

GATES, A., and PEARDON, C. C. *Reading exercises.* New York: Teachers College Press, 1963.

GAUTHIER, R. A. *A descriptive-analytic study of teacher-student interaction in mainstreamed physical education classes.* Unpublished doctoral dissertation, Purdue University, 1980.

GESELL, A. *The first five years of life.* New York: Harper & Row, 1940.

GETMAN, G. N. *How to develop your child's intelligence.* Leverne, Minn.: G. N. Getman, 1962.

GETMAN, G. N., and HENDRICKSON, H. H. The needs of teachers for specialized information on the development of visual–motor skills in relation to academic performance. In W. M. Cruickshank (Ed.), *The teacher of brain injured children.* Syracuse, N.Y.: Syracuse University Press, 1966. Pp. 153–168.

GETMAN, G. N., KANE, E. R., HALGREN, M. R., and McKEE, G. W. *Developing learning readiness.* Manchester, Mo.: McGraw-Hill Webster Division, 1968.

GIBSON, E. J. Learning to read. *Science,* 1965, *148,* 1066–1072.

GIBSON, E. J. The ontogeny of reading. *American Psychologist,* 1970, *25,* 136–143.

GILLINGHAM, A. Correspondance. *Elementary English,* 1958, *35,* 118–122.

GILLINGHAM, A., and STILLMAN, B. *Remedial training for children with specific disability in reading, spelling, and penmanship.* Cambridge, Mass.: Educators Publishing Service, 1970.

GINOTT, H. *Group psychotherapy with children.* New York: McGraw-Hill, 1961.

GLASSER, W. *Reality therapy.* New York: Harper and Row, 1965.

GLASSER, W. *Schools without failure.* New York: Harper and Row, 1969.

GLAVIN, J. P., QUAY, H. C., ANNESLEY, F. R., and WERRY, J. S. An experimental resource room for behavior problem children. *Exceptional Children,* 1971, *38,* 131–137.

GLAVIN, J. J., QUAY, H. C., and WERRY, J. S. Behavioral and academic gains of conduct problem children in different classroom settings. *Exceptional Children,* 1971, *37,* 441–446.

GOLDMAN, R., and FRISTOE, M. *Goldman–Fristoe Test of Articulation.* Circle Pines, Minn.: American Guidance Services, Inc., 1969.

GOLDMAN, R., FRISTOE, M., and WOODCOCK, R. W. *The Goldman–Fristoe–Woodcock Test of Auditory Discrimination.* Circle Pines, Minn.: American Guidance Services, Inc., 1970.

GOLDMAN, R., FRISTOE, M., and WOODCOCK, R. W.   *The Goldman–Fristoe–Woodcock Auditory Skills Test Battery.* Circle Pines, Minn.: American Guidance Services, Inc., 1976.

GOODMAN, K. S.   A linguistic study of cues and miscues in reading. *Elementary English,* 1965, *42,* 639–642.

GOODMAN, K. S. (Ed.).   *The psycholinguistic nature of the reading process.* Detroit: Wayne State University Press, 1968.

GOODMAN, K. S.   Analysis of oral reading miscues: Applied psycholinguistics. *Reading Research Quarterly,* 1969, *5,* 9–30.

GOODMAN, K. S.   Reading: A psycholinguistic guessing game. In M. Singer and R. Ruddell (Eds.), *Theoretical models and processes of reading.* Neward, DE: International Reading Association, 1976.

GOODMAN, Y. M.   Reading diagnosis—qualitative or quantitative. *The Reading Teacher,* 1972, *26,* 32–37.

GRAHAM, F. K., and KENDALL, B. S.   Memory-for-Designs Test. *Perceptual and Motor Skills,* 1960, *11,* 147–190.

GRAHAM, S., and MILLER, L.   Handwriting research and practice: A unified approach. *Focus on Exceptional Children,* 1980, *13,* 1–16.

GRANNIS, J. C., and SCHONE, V.   *First things.* Pleasantville, N.Y.: Guidance Associates, 1970.

GRANOWSKY, A., MIDDLETON, F. R., and MUMFORD, J. H.   Parents as partners in education. *Reading Teacher,* 1979, *32,* 826–830.

GRAY, B. B., and RYAN, B. P.   *Monterey language program (Programmed conditioning for language).* Palo Alto, Calif.: Monterey Learning Systems, 1972.

GREENE, H., and PETTY, W.   *Developing language skills in the elementary school.* Boston: Allyn and Bacon, 1967.

GREENFIELD, P. M., and SMITH, J.   *The structure of communication in early language development.* New York: Academic Press, 1976.

GRONLUND, N. E.   *Measurement and evaluation in teaching.* New York: Macmillan, 1976.

GUILFORD, J. P., and FRUCHTER, B.   *Fundamental statistics in psychology and education.* New York: McGraw-Hill, 1978.

GURNEY, D.   The effect of an individual reading program on reading level and attitude toward reading. *The Reading Teacher,* 1966, *19,* 277–79.

GUTHRIE, J. T.   The 1970s comprehension research. *Reading Teacher,* 1980, *33,* 880–882.

HALL, J. K.   *Evaluating and improving written expression.* Boston: Allyn and Bacon, 1981.

HALL, R. V.   *Behavior modification: Applications in home and school.* Lawrence, Kans.: H & H Enterprises, 1971. (a)

HALL, R. V. *Behavior modification: Basic principles.* Lawrence, Kans.: H & H Enterprises, 1971. (b)

HALL, R. V. *Behavior modification: The measurement of behavior.* Lawrence, Kans.: H & H Enterprises, 1971. (c)

HALLAHAN, D. P., and CRUICKSHANK, W. M. *Psychoeducational foundations of learning disabilities.* Englewood Cliffs, N.J.: Prentice-Hall, 1973.

HALLIDAY, M. A. K. *Learning how to mean.* New York: Elsevier, 1975.

HAMMILL, D., BROWN, V., LARSEN, S. C., and WIEDERHOLT, J. L. *The Test of Adolescent Language.* Austin, TX: Pro-Ed, 1980.

HAMMILL, D. D., GOODMAN, L., and WIEDERHOLT, J. L. Use of the Frostig DTVP with economically disadvantaged children. *Journal of School Psychology,* 1971, *9*, 430–435.

HAMMILL, D. D., GOODMAN, L., and WIEDERHOLT, J. L. Visual–motor processes: What success have we had in training them? *The Reading Teacher,* 1974, *27*, 469–478.

HAMMILL, D. D., and LARSEN, S. The relationship of selected auditory perceptual skills and reading ability. *Journal of Learning Disabilities,* 1974, *7*, 429–435. (a)

HAMMILL, D. D., and LARSEN, S. The effectiveness of psycholinguistic training. *Exceptional Children,* 1974, *41*, 5–15. (b)

HAMMILL, D., and LARSEN, S. *The Test of Written Language.* Austin, TX: Pro-Ed, 1978.

HAMMILL, D. D., LARSEN, S., and McNUTT, G. The effects of spelling instruction: A preliminary study. *The elementary school journal,* 1977, *78*, 67–72.

HAMMILL, D., and LEIGH, J. Basic Skill Inventory. Austin, TX: Pro-Ed, 1983.

HAMMILL, D., and McNUTT, G. *The correlates of reading.* Austin, TX: Pro-Ed, 1981.

HAMMILL, D. D., and WIEDERHOLT, J. L. *The resource room: Rationale and implementation.* Philadelphia: Journal of Special Education Press, 1972. (a)

HAMMILL, D. D., and WIEDERHOLT, J. L. Review of the Frostig Visual Perception Test and the related training program. In L. Mann and D. Sabatino (Eds.), *First review of special education,* Vol. 1. New York: Grune & Stratton, 1972. (b)

HANNA, P. R., HANNA, J. S., HODGES, R. E., and RUDORF, E. H. Phoneme–grapheme correspondences as cues to spelling improvement. Washington, D.C.: Department of Health, Education, and Welfare, 1966.

HANNA, P. R., HODGES, R. E., and HANNA, J. S. *Spelling: Structure and strategies.* Boston: Houghton Mifflin, 1971.

HANNA, R., and MOORE, J. T. Spelling—from spoken word to written symbol. *Elementary School Journal,* 1953, *53*, 329–337.

HANSEN, C. L.   Writing skills. In N. G. Haring, T. C. Lovitt, M. D. Eaton, and C. L. Hansen (Eds.) *The fourth R: Research in the classroom.* Columbus, OH: Charles E. Merrill, 1978.

HARRIS, A. J.   Diagnosis and remedial instruction. In H. M. Robinson (Ed.), *The sixty-seventh yearbook of the National Society for the Study of Education.* Chicago: University of Chicago Press, 1968.

HARRIS, A. J.   *How to increase reading ability,* 5th ed. New York: David McKay, 1970.

HARRIS, T. L., and HERRICK, V. E.   Children's perception of the handwriting task. In V. E. Herrick (Ed.), *New horizons for research in handwriting.* Madison, Wis.: University of Wisconsin Press, 1963. Pp. 159–184.

HARTH, R.   Changing attitudes toward school, classroom behavior, and reaction to frustration of emotionally disturbed children through role-playing. *Exceptional Children,* 1966, *33,* 119–120.

HATHAWAY, S. R., and McKINLEY, J. L.   *Minnesota Multiphasic Personality Inventory.* New York: Psychological Corporation, 1951.

HAWISHER, P.   *The resource room: Access to excellence.* Lancaster, S.C.: S.C. Region V Educational Service Center, 1975.

HAWORTH, M. R.   *The Primary Visual Motor Test.* New York: Grune & Stratton, 1970.

HEDDENS, J. W., and SMITH, K. J.   The readability of elementary mathematics textbooks. *The Arithmetic Teacher,* 1964, *11,* 466–468.

HEGDE, M. N.   Issues in the study and explanation of language behavior. *Journal of Psycholinguistic Research,* 1980, *9,* 1–22.

HERRICK, V. E., and ERLEBACHER, A.   The evaluation of legibility in handwriting. In V. E. Herrick (Ed.), *New horizons for research in handwriting.* Madison, Wis.: University of Wisconsin Press, 1963. Pp. 207–237.

HILDRETH, G. H., GRIFFITHS, M. L., and McGAUVRAN, M. E.   *The Metropolitan Readiness Tests.* New York: Harcourt, Brace & World, 1969.

HODGES, R. E., and RUDORF, E. H.   Searching linguistics for cues for the teaching of spelling. *Elementary English,* 1965, *42,* 529–533.

HOEPFNER, R., STRICKLAND, G., STANGEL, G., JANSEN, P., and PATALINO, M.   *Elementary school test evaluations.* Los Angeles: Center for the Study of Evaluation, UCLA Graduate School of Education, 1970.

HOLLANDER, E. P.   Validity of peer nominations in predicting a distant performance criterion. *Journal of Applied Psychology,* 1965, *49,* 434–438.

HORN, E.   Phonetics and spelling. *Elementary School Journal,* 1957, *57,* 424–432.

HOUGH, J. B.   An observation system for the analysis of classroom instruction. In E. J. Amidon and J. B. Hough (Eds.), *Interaction analysis: Theory, research, and application.* Reading, MA: Addison-Wesley, 1967.

HRESKO, W., REID, D. K., and HAMMILL, D. *Test of Early Language Development.* Austin, TX: Pro-Ed, 1981.

HUNT, K., and O'DONNELL, R. An elementary school curriculum to develop better writing skills. U.S. Office of Education Grant No. 4-9-08-903-0042-010, Tallahassee, FL: Florida State University, 1970.

IANO, R. P. Shall we disband our special classes? *Journal of Special Education,* 1972, *6,* 167–178.

ILG, F. L., and AMES, L. B. *School readiness.* New York: Harper & Row, 1965.

INGRAM, D. *Phonological disability in children.* London: Edward Arnold, 1976.

IRWIN, O. Infant speech: Consonant sounds according to manner of articulation. *Journal of Speech Disorders,* 1947, *12,* 402–404. (a)

IRWIN, O. Infant speech: Consonant sounds according to place of articulation. *Journal of Speech Disorders,* 1947, *12,* 397–401. (b)

IRWIN, O. Infant speech: Development of vowel sounds. *Journal of Speech and Hearing Disorders,* 1948, *13,* 31–34.

IRWIN, O. Speech development in the young child: II. Some factors related to speech development of the infant and young child. *Journal of Speech and Hearing Disorders,* 1952, *17,* 269–279.

IWATA, B., and BAILEY, J. Reward versus cost token systems: An analysis of the effects on students and teachers. *Journal of Applied Behavior Analysis,* 1974, *7,* 567–576.

JAKOBSEN, R., and HALLE, M. *Fundamentals of language.* The Hague: Mouton, 1956.

JASTAK, J. F., and JASTAK, S. R. *Wide Range Achievement Test.* Wilmington, Del.: Guidance Associates, 1965.

JOHNSON, D. D. The Dolch list re-examined. *The Reading Teacher,* 1971, *24,* 455–56.

JOHNSON, D. J., and MYKLEBUST, H. R. *Learning disabilities: Educational principles and practices.* New York: Grune & Stratton, 1967.

JOHNSON, M. S., and KRESS, R. A. *Informal reading inventories.* Newark, Del.: International Reading Association, 1969.

JUNKALA, J. Teacher evaluation of instructional materials. *Teaching Exceptional Children,* 1970, *2,* 73–76.

KALUGER, G., and KOLSON, C. J. *Reading and learning disabilities.* Columbus, Ohio: Charles E. Merrill, 1969.

KARNES, M. B. *GOAL: Language development—Games oriented activities for learning.* Springfield, Mass.: Milton Bradley, 1976. (a)

KARNES, M. B. *Karnes early language activities.* Champaign, Ill.: GEM, P.O. Box 2339, Station A, 1976. (b)

KATZ, J. *The Kindergarten Auditory Screening Test.* Chicago: Follett, 1971.

KATZ, J. T., and FODOR, A.   The structure of semantic theory. *Language,* 1963, *39,* 170–120.

KAZDIN, A.   *Behavior modification in applied settings.* Homewood, IL: Dorsey, 1975.

KELLEY, T., MADDEN, R., GARDNER, E., and RUDMAN, H.   *Stanford Achievement Tests.* New York: Harcourt, Brace & World, 1964.

KEPHART, N. C.   Teaching the child with a perceptual-motor handicap. In M. Bortner (Ed.), *Evaluation and education of children with brain damage.* Springfield, Ill.: Charles C Thomas, 1968. Pp. 147–192.

KEPHART, N. C.   *The slow learner in the classroom,* 2nd ed. Columbus, Ohio: Charles E. Merrill, 1971.

KERSH, B. Y.   Learning by discovery: Instructional strategies. *The Arithmetic Teacher,* 1965, *12,* 414–417.

KESSLER, J. W.   *Psychopathology of childhood.* Englewood Cliffs, N.J.: Prentice-Hall, 1966.

KIRK, S. A.   From labels to actions. Selected papers on learning disabilities. Third annual conference of American Association for Children with Learning Disabilities. Tulsa, Okla., 1966. Also in D. Hammill and N. Bartel (Eds.), *Educational perspectives in learning disabilities.* New York: John Wiley, 1971. Pp. 304–313.

KIRK, S. A.   *Educating exceptional children.* Boston: Houghton Mifflin, 1972.

KIRK, S. A., McCARTHY, J. J., and KIRK, W.   *Illinois Test of Psycholinguistic Abilities.* Urbana, Ill.: University of Illinois Press, 1968.

KLARE, G. R.   A second look at the validity of readability formulas. *Journal of Reading Behavior,* 1976, *8,* 129–252.

KLIEBHAN, M. C.   *An experimental study of arithmetic problem-solving ability of sixth grade boys.* Washington, D.C.: The Catholic University Press, 1955.

KOHFELDT, J.   *Contracts.* Wayne, N.J.: Innovative Educational Support Systems, 1974.

KOPP, F. S.   Evaluation of the youth tutoring youth program. Atlanta, Ga.: Atlanta Public Schools, 1972 (ED 075560).

KOPPITZ, E. M.   *The Bender Gestalt Test for Young Children.* New York: Grune & Stratton, 1963.

KOTTMEYER, W.   *Teacher's guide for remedial reading.* New York: McGraw-Hill, 1970.

KOTTMEYER, W., and CLAUS, A.   *Basic goals in spelling.* New York: McGraw-Hill, 1968, 1972.

KRAMER, E.   *Art therapy with children.* New York: Schocken, 1971.

KRAMER, K.   *The teaching of elementary school mathematics.* Boston: Allyn and Bacon, 1970.

KROTH, R. The behavioral Q-sort as a diagnostic tool. *Academic Therapy,* 1973, *8,* 317–330. (a)

KROTH, R. *Target behavior.* Bellevue, WA: Ed-Mark, 1973 (b).

LACKNER, J. R. A developmental study of language behavior in retarded children. In D. M. Morehead and A. E. Morehead (Eds.), *Normal and deficient child language.* Baltimore: University Park Press, 1976. Pp. 181–208.

LANE, P., POLLACK, C., and SHER, N. Remotivation of disruptive adolescents. *Journal of Reading,* 1972, *15,* 351–354.

LANKFORD, F. S. What can a teacher learn about a pupil's thinking through oral interviews? *Arithmetic Teacher,* 1974, *21,* 26–32.

LAPRAY, M., and ROSS, R. The graded word list: A quick gauge of reading ability. *Journal of Reading,* 1969, *12.*

LARSEN, S., and HAMMILL, D. D. The relationship of selected visual perceptual skills to academic abilities. *Journal of Special Education,* 1975, *9,* 281–291.

LARSEN, S., and HAMMILL, D. D. *The Test of Written Spelling.* Austin, Tex.: Pro-Ed, 1976.

LARSEN, S. C., and POPLIN, M. S. *Methods for educating the handicapped: An individualized education program approach.* Boston: Allyn and Bacon, 1980.

LATEN, S., and KATZ, G. *A theoretical model for assessment of adolescents: The ecological/behavioral approach.* Madison, Wis.: Madison Public Schools, Special Educational Services, 1975.

LAZAR, M. Individualized reading: A dynamic approach. *Reading Teacher,* 1957, *11,* 75–83.

LEE, L. Developmental sentence types: A method for comparing normal and deviant syntactic development. *Journal of Speech and Hearing Disorders,* 1966, *31,* 311–330.

LEE, L. *Developmental sentence analysis.* Evanston, Ill.: Northwestern University Press, 1974.

LENNEBERG, E. H. Language disorders in childhood. *Harvard Educational Review,* 1964, *34,* 152–177.

LENNEBERG, E. H. *Biological foundations of language.* New York: John Wiley, 1967.

LENNEBERG, E. H., NICHOLS, I. A., and ROSENBERGER, E. F. Primitive stages of language development in mongolism. In *Proceedings of the Association for Research in Nervous and Mental Disease,* 1964, *42,* 119–137.

LEPORE, A. A comparison of computational errors between educable mentally handicapped and learning disability children. Unpublished manuscript, University of Connecticut, Storrs, Conn., 1974.

LERCH, H. H., and HAMILTON, H. A comparison of a structured-equation approach to problem solving with a traditional approach. *School Science and Mathematics,* 1966, *66,* 241–246.

LEVITT, E. E.   Results of psychotherapy with children: An evaluation. *Journal of Counseling Psychology,* 1957, *25,* 189–196.

LEWIS, M.   *Language, thought, and personality in infancy and childhood.* London: G. G. Harrap, 1963.

LILLY, S. M.   Special education: A teapot in a tempest. *Exceptional Children,* 1970, *37,* 43–48.

LIMBACHER, W.   *Dimensions of personality.* New York: Pflaum, 1969.

LINDQUIST, E., and HIERONYMOUS, A.   *Iowa Test of Basic Skills.* New York: Harcourt, Brace & World, 1956.

LINDZEY, G., and BORGATTA, E. F.   Sociometric measurement. In G. Lindzey (Ed.), *Handbook of social psychology.* Reading, Mass.: Addison-Wesley, 1954.

LINN, S. H.   Spelling problems: Diagnosis and remediation. *Academic Therapy Quarterly,* 1967, *3,* 62–63.

LONG, N. J., and NEWMAN, R. G.   Managing surface behavior of children in schools. In N. J. Long, W. C. Morse, and R. G. Newman (Eds.), *Conflict in the classroom.* Belmont, Calif.: Wadsworth, 1971.

LOSEN, S. M., and DIAMENT, B.   *Parent conferences in the schools.* Boston: Allyn and Bacon, 1978.

LOVITT, T. C.   Applied behavior analysis and learning disabilities. Part I. Characteristics of ABA, general recommendations, and methodological limitations. *Journal of Learning Disabilities,* 1975, *8,* 432–443. (a)

LOVITT, T. C.   Applied behavior analysis and learning disabilities. Part II: Specific research recommendations and suggestions for practitioners. *Journal of Learning Disabilities,* 1975, *8,* 504–518. (b)

LOWDER, R. G.   *Perceptual ability and school achievement.* Winter Haven, Fla.: Winter Haven Lions Research Foundation, 1956.

MacNAMARA, J.   Cognitive basis of language learning in infants. *Psychological Review,* 1972, *79,* 1–13.

MacWHINNEY, B.   The acquisition of morphophonalogy. *Monographs of the Society for Research in Child Development,* 1978, *43,* (1–2, Serial Number 174).

MAIER, H. W.   *Three theories of child development.* New York: Harper & Row, 1969.

MANN, L.   Psychometric phrenology and the new faculty psychology: The case against ability assessment and training. *The Journal of Special Education,* 1971, *5,* 3–14.

MANN, L.   Marianne Frostig Developmental Test of Visual Perception. In O. K. Buros (Ed.), *The seventh mental measurements yearbook.* Highland Park, N.J.: Gryphon, 1972.

MANN, L. *In search of process.* New York: Grune and Stratton, 1979.

MARTLEW, M. Mothers' control strategies in dyadic mother/child conversations. *Journal of Psycholinguistic Research,* 1980, 9, 327–347.

MAZURKIEWICZ, A. J. *New perspectives in reading structure.* New York: Pittman, 1968.

MCCALLON, E., and MCCRAY, E. *Planning and conducting interviews.* Austin, TX: Learning Concepts, 1975.

MCCARTHY, D. Language development in children. In L. Carmichael (Ed.), *Manual of child psychology.* New York: John Wiley, 1954. Pp. 492–630.

MCCRACKEN, R. A., and MCCRACKEN, M. J. Modeling is the key to sustained silent reading. *Reading Teacher,* 1978, 31, 406–8.

MCGINNIS, M. A. *Aphasic children.* Washington, D.C.: Alexander Graham Bell Association for the Deaf, 1963.

MCGINNIS, M., KLEFFNER, F., and GOLDSTEIN, R. Teaching of asphasic children. *The Volta Review,* 1956, 58, 239–244.

MCGINTY, R. L., and MEYERSON, L. N. Problem solving: Look beyond the right answer. *Mathematics Teacher,* 1980, 73, 501–503.

MCIINTYRE, R. B. Evaluation of instructional materials and programs: Application of a systems approach. *Exceptional Children,* 1970, 37, 213–220.

MCLOUGHLIN, J. A., and LEWIS, R. B. *Assessing special students.* Columbus, OH: Charles E. Merrill, 1981.

MCNEILL, D. Development of the Semantic System. Paper prepared at the Center for Cognitive Studies, Harvard University, 1965.

MCNEILL, D. Developmental psycholinguistics. In F. Smith and G. A. Miller (Eds.), *The genesis of language.* Cambridge, Mass.: MIT Press, 1966. Pp. 15–84.

MCNEILL, D. The development of language. In P. H. Mussen (Ed.), *Carmichael's manual of child psychology,* 3rd ed. New York: John Wiley, 1970. Pp. 1061–1161.

MECHAM, M. J., JEX, J. L., and JONES, J. D. *Utah Test of Language Development.* Salt Lake City, Utah: Communication Research Associates, 1967.

MEICHENBAUM, D. *Toward a cognitive theory of self-control.* Research Report No. 48. Department of Psychology, University of Waterloo, Ontario, 1975.

MEIGHEN, M., and PRATT, M. *Phonics we use.* Chicago: Lyons & Carnahan, 1964.

MELLON, J. C. *Transformational sentence-combining: A method for enhancing the development of syntactic fluency in English composition.* Research report, No. 10, Urbana, IL: National Council of Teachers of English, 1969.

MENYUK, P. A preliminary evaluation of grammatical capacity in children. *Journal of Verbal Learning and Verbal Behavior,* 1963, 2, 429–439.

MENYUK, P.   Comparison of grammar of children with functionally deviant and normal speech. *Journal of Speech and Hearing Research,* 1964, *7,* 109–121.

MENYUK, P.   *Sentences children use.* Cambridge, Mass.: MIT Press, 1969.

METREAUX, R.   Speech profiles of the preschool child—18 to 54 months. *Journal of Speech and Hearing Disorders,* 1950, *15,* 35–53.

MICHEL, D. E.   *Music therapy: An introduction to therapy and special education through music.* New York: Day, 1971.

MILLER, J., and YODER, D.   *Miller-Yoder Test of Grammatical Competence, Experimental Edition.* Madison, Wis.: University of Wisconsin Bookstore, 1972.

MILLER, L. K.   *Principles of everyday behavior analysis.* Monterey, Calif.: Brooks/Cole, 1975.

MINSKOFF, E., WISEMAN, D. E., and MINSKOFF, G.   *The MWM program for developing language abilities.* Ridgefield, N.J.: Educational Performance Associates, 1972.

MINTON, M. J.   The effect of sustained silent reading upon comprehension and attitudes of ninth graders. *Journal of Reading,* 1980, *23,* 498–502.

MOERK, E. L.   Piaget's research as applied to the explanation of language development. *Merrill-Palmer Quarterly,* 1975, *21* 151–169.

MONTESSORI, M.   *The Montessori method.* New York: Schocken Books, 1964.

MONTESSORI, M.   *Dr. Montessori's own handbooks.* New York: Schocken Books, 1965. (a)

MONTESSORI, M.   *The Montessori elementary material.* Cambridge, Mass.: Robert Bentley, Inc., 1965. (b)

MOORE, J. C., JONES, C. J., and MILLER, D. C.   What we know after a decade of sustained silent reading. *Reading Teacher,* 1980, *33,* 445–450.

MOREHEAD, D., and INGRAM, D.   The development of base syntax in normal and linguistically deviant children. *Journal of Speech and Hearing Research,* 1973, *16,* 330–353.

MORENO, J. L.   *Psychodrama.* New York: Beacon House, 1946.

MORENO, J. L.   *Who shall survive? Foundations of sociometry, group psychotherapy, and sociodrama,* 2nd ed. New York: Beacon House, 1953.

MOSENTHAL, P., and NA, T. J.   Quality of children's recall under two classroom testing tasks: Towards a socio-psycholinguistic model of reading comprehension. *Reading Research Quarterly,* 1980, *15,* 504–527.

MOWRER, H.   Speech Development in the young child: I. The autism theory of speech development and some clinical applications. *Journal of Speech and Hearing Disorders,* 1952, *17,* 263–268.

MURRAY, H. A.   *Thematic Apperception Test.* Cambridge, Mass.: Harvard University Press, 1943.

MYERS, P., and HAMMILL, D. *Learning disabilities: Basic concepts, assessment practices, and instructional strategies.* Austin, TX: Pro-Ed, 1982.

MYKLEBUST, H. R. Aphasia in childhood. *Journal of Exceptional Children,* 1952, *19,* 9–14.

MYKLEBUST, H. R. Babbling and echolalia in language theory. *Journal of Speech and Hearing Disorders,* 1957, *22,* 356–360.

MYKLEBUST, H. R. *The psychology of deafness: Sensory deprivation, learning, and adjustments.* New York: Grune & Stratton, 1964.

MYKLEBUST, H. R. *Development and disorders of written language.* New York: Grune & Stratton, 1965.

NAUMBERG, M. *An introduction to art therapy.* New York: Teachers College Press, 1973.

NELSON, K. Structure and strategy in learning to talk. *Monograph of the Society for Research in Child Development,* 1973, *38* (1–2, Serial No. 149).

NELSON, K. Concept, word, and sentence: Inter-relations in acquisition and development. *Psychological Review,* 1974, *81,* 276–285.

NEWCOMER, P. L. *Understanding and teaching emotionally disturbed children.* Boston: Allyn and Bacon, 1980.

NEWCOMER, P., and HAMMILL, D. D. *Psycholinguistics in the schools.* Columbus, Ohio: Charles E. Merrill, 1976.

NEWCOMER, P., and HAMMILL, D. D. *Test of Language Development (TOLD).* Austin, TX: Pro-Ed, 1982.

NEWLAND, T. E. An analytical study of the development of illegibilities in handwriting from the lower grades to adulthood. *Journal of Educational Research,* 1932, *26,* 249–258.

NICHOLSON, T. Why we need to talk to parents about reading. *Reading Teacher,* 1980, *34,* 19–21.

NIHIRA, K., FOSTER, R., SHELLHAAS, M., and LEHLAND, H. *AAMD Adaptive Behavior Scales. Public School Version.* Washington, DC: American Association on Mental Deficiency, 1975.

NOBLE, J. K. *Better handwriting for you.* New York: Noble & Noble, 1966.

NORDOFF, P., and ROBBINS, C. *Music therapy in special education.* New York: Day, 1971.

NORTON, J. K., and NORTON, M. *Foundation of curriculum building.* New York: Ginn, 1936.

O'HARE, F. *Sentence-combining: Improving student writing without formal grammar instruction.* Research report No. 15, Urbana, IL: National Council of Teachers of English, 1973.

O'LEARY, K. D., and BECKER, W. C. Behavior modification of an adjustment class: A token reinforcement program. *Exceptional Children,* 1967, *33,* 637–642.

O'LEARY, K. D., and O'LEARY, S. G.   *Classroom management: The successful use of behavior modification.* Second edition. New York: Pergamon, 1977.

OLSEN, D.   Language and thought: Aspects of a cognitive theory of semantics. *Psychological Review,* 1970, *77,* 257–73.

OLSON, A. V.   Factor analytic studies of the Frostig Developmental Test of Visual Perception. *Journal of Special Education,* 1968, *2,* 429–433.

OLSON, D.   On a theory of instruction: Why different forms of instruction result in similar lnowledge. *Interchange,* 1972, *3,* 9–24.

OLSON, D. R.   Language acquisition and cognitive development. In H. C. Haywood (Ed.), *Social-cultural aspects of mental retardation.* New York: Appleton-Century-Crofts, 1970. Pp. 113–202.

OTTO, W., McMENEMY, R. A., and SMITH, R. J.   *Corrective and remedial teaching,* 2nd ed. Boston: Houghton Mifflin, 1973.

OTTO, W., and SMITH, R. J.   *Corrective and remedial teaching.* Third edition. Boston: Houghton-Mifflin, 1980.

PACE, A.   Understanding and the ability to solve problems. *The Arithmetic Teacher,* 1961, *8,* 226–233.

PAINTER, G.   The effect of a rhythmic and sensory motor activity program on perceptual motor spatial abilities of kindergarten children. *Exceptional Children,* 1966, *33,* 113–119.

PALOMARES, V. H., and BALL, G.   *Human development program.* La Mesa, Calif.: Human Development Training Institute, 1974.

PARISI, D., and ANTINUCCI, F.   Lexical competence. In G. B. Flores d'Arcais and W. J. M. Levelt (Eds.), *Advances in psycholinguistics.* Amsterdam: North-Holland, 1970. Pp. 197–210.

PERFETTI, C. A., and HOGABOAM, T.   Relationship between single word decoding and reading comprehension skills. *Journal of Educational Psychology,* 1975, *67,* 461–469.

PERLINE, I. H., and LEVINSKY, D.   Controlling behavior in the severely retarded. *American Journal of Mental Deficiency,* 1968, *73,* 74–78.

PETERSON, H. A., BRENER, R., and WILLIAMS, L. L.   *SYNPRO (Syntax Programmer).* St. Louis: Mercury Co./Division of EMT Labs, 1974.

PETTY, W. T., and JENSEN, J. M.   *Developing children's language.* Boston: Allyn and Bacon, 1980.

PIAGET, J.   *The language and thought of the child.* London: Routledge & Kegan Paul, 1959.

PIAGET, J.   *Language and thought in the child.* New York: Meridian Books, New American Library, 1960.

PIAGET, J.   *The language and thought of the child.* New York: World Publishing, 1962.

PIAGET, J.   *The child's conception of number.* New York: W. W. Norton, 1965.

PIAGET, J. *Six psychological studies.* New York: Vintage Books, Random House, 1967.

PIAGET, J., and INHELDER, B. *The child's conception of space.* London: Routledge & Kegan Paul, 1963.

PIAGET, J., and INHELDER, B. *La Psychologie de l'enfant.* Paris: Presses Universitaires de France, 1967.

PIERS, E. V., and HARRIS, D. B. *The Piers-Harris Children's Self-Concept Scale.* Nashville, TN: Counselor Recordings and Tests, 1969.

PITMAN, J. The future of the teaching of reading. Paper presented at the Educational Conference of the Educational Records Bureau, New York City, October 30–November 1, 1963.

POOLEY, R. C. Dare schools set a standard in English usage? *English Journal,* 1960, *49,* 179–180.

PORTER, R. B., and CATTRELL, R. B. *The IPAT Children's Personality Questionnaire.* Champaign, IL: Institute for Personality and Ability Testing, 1975.

POWELL, G. C. An attitude scale for reading. *The Reading Teacher,* 1972, *25,* 442–47.

PUGH, B. *Steps in language development for the deaf.* Washington, D.C.: Volta Bureau, 1955.

PUMPFREY, D., and ELLIOT, C. D. Play therapy, social adjustment and reading attainment. *Journal of Educational Research,* 1970, *12,* 183–193.

QUAY, H. C., and PETERSON, D. R. Manual for the Behavior Problem Checklist. Champaign, Ill.: Children's Research Center, 1967. Mimeographed.

QUICK, A. D., LITTLE, T., and CAMPBELL, A. *Project MEMPHIS.* Belmont, Calif.: Fearon Publishers, 1973.

REDL, F. The concept of a therapeutic milieu. *American Journal of Orthopsychiatry,* 1959, *29,* 721–734.

REDL, F., and WATTENBERG, W. *Mental hygiene in teaching.* New York: Harcourt, Brace & World, 1959.

REDL, F., and WINEMAN, D. *The aggressive child.* New York: Free Press, 1957.

REGER, R., SCHROEDER, W., and USCHOLD, K. *Special education: Children with learning problems.* New York: Oxford University Press, 1968.

REID, D. K., HRESKO, W., and HAMMILL, D. *Test of Early Reading Ability.* Austin, TX: Pro-Ed, 1981.

REINERT, H. J. *Children in conflict.* St. Louis: Mosby, 1976.

REISMAN, F. K. *A guide to the diagnostic teaching of arithmetic.* Columbus, Ohio: Charles E. Merrill, 1972.

REISMAN, F. K. Diagnostic teaching of elementary school mathematics: Methods and content. Chicago: Rand McNally, 1977.

REYNOLDS, H. H.   Efficacy of sociometric rating in predicting leadership success. *Psychological Reports,* 1966, *19,* 35–40.

ROACH, E. G., and KEPHART, N. C.   *Purdue Perceptual Motor Survey.* Columbus, Ohio: Charles E. Merrill, 1966.

ROBBINS, M. P., and GLASS, G. V.   The Doman–Delacato rationale: A critical analysis. In J. Hellmuth (Ed.), *Educational therapy.* Seattle, Wash.: Special Child Publications 1968.

ROBERTS, G. H.   The failure strategies of third grade arithmetic pupils. *Arithmetic Teacher,* 1962, *15,* 442–446.

ROGERS, D. C., ORT, L. L., and SERRA, M. C.   *Word book.* Chicago: Lyons & Carnahan, 1970.

RORSCHACH, H.   *The Rorschach Psychodiagnostic Plates.* New York: Grune & Stratton, 1954.

ROSNER, J.   *Helping children overcome learning difficulties.* New York: Walker, 1975.

ROTHMAN, E. P., and BERKOWITZ, P. H.   *Buttons: A Projective Test for Preadolescent and Adolescent Boys and Girls.* Los Angeles: Western Psychological Services, 1963.

ROTTER, J. B.   *Social learning and clinical psychology.* Englewood Cliffs, N.J.: Prentice-Hall, 1954.

RUDDELL, R. B.   Psycholinguistic models. In H. Singer, and R. Ruddell (Eds.), *Theoretical models and processes of reading.* Newark, DE: International Reading Association, 1976.

RUMELHART, D. E.   Toward an interactive model of reading. In S. Dornic (Ed.), *Attention and performance.* Hillsdale, NJ: Lawrence Erlbaum, 1977.

SABATINO, D. A.   An evaluation of resource rooms for children with learning disabilities. *Journal of Learning Disabilities,* 1971, *4,* 84–93.

SALAMON, G.   *Interaction of media, cognition, and learning.* San Francisco: Jossey Bass, 1979.

SALVIA, J., and YSSELDYKE, J. E.   *Assessment in special and remedial education.* Boston: Houghton Mifflin, 1981.

SAMUELS, J., BEGY, G., and CHEN, C. C.   Comparison of word recognition speed and strategies of less skilled and more highly skilled readers. *Reading Research Quarterly,* 1975–1976, *11,* 72–86.

SCHEIDLINGER, S., and RAUCH, E.   Group psychotherapy with children and adolescents. In B. Wolman (Ed.), *Handbook of child psychoanalysis.* New York: Van Nostrand Reinhold, 1972.

SCHOOLFIELD, L., and TIMBERLAKE, J.   *The phonovisual method.* Washington, D.C.: Phonovisual Products, 1960.

SCHWARTZ, R. M.   Levels of processing: The strategic demands of reading comprehension. *Reading Research Quarterly,* 1980, *15,* 433–450.

SEASHORE, C. E., LEWIS, D., and SAETVEIT, J. *Seashore Test of Musical Talents.* Camden, N.J.: Educational Department, Radio Corporation of America, 1939.

SEMEL, E. M. *Sound-order-sense: A developmental program in auditory perception.* Chicago: Follett, 1970.

SERIO, M. Cursive writing. *Academic Therapy,* 1968, *4,* 67–70.

SHATZ, M., and GILMAN, R. The development of communication skills: Modifications in the speech of young children as a function of listener. *Monographs of the Society for Research.*

SHAW, H. *Spell it right!* New York: Barnes and Nobel, 1971.

SHULMAN, L. S. Perspectives on the psychology of learning and the teaching of mathematics. In W. R. Houston (Ed.), *Improving mathematics education for elementary school teachers,* A Conference Report, 1967. Pp. 23–37.

SILVAROLI, J. N. *Classroom Reading Inventory,* 2nd Edition. Dubuque, IA: William C. Brown, 1973.

SIMON, S. B., HOWE, L. W., and KIRSCHENBAUM, H. *Values clarification.* New York: Hart, 1972.

SINCLAIR-DE-ZWART, H. Developmental psycholinguistics. In D. Elkind and J. H. Flavell (Eds.), *Studies in cognitive development: Essays in honor of Jean Piaget.* New York: Oxford University Press, 1969. Pp. 315–336.

SINCLAIR-DE-ZWART, H. Language acquisition and cognitive development. In T. M. Moore (Ed.), *Cognitive development and the acquisition of language.* New York: Academic Press, 1973, pp. 9–25.

SINCLAIR, H. Developmental psycholinguistics. In D. Elkind and J. H. Flanell (Eds.), *Studies in cognitive development.* New York: Oxford University Press, 1969, pp. 129–148.

SINCLAIR, H. Sensorimotor action patterns as a condition for the acquisition of syntax. In R. Huxley and E. Ingram (Eds.), *Language acquisition: models and methods.* New York: Academic Press, 1971, pp. 121–130.

SKINNER, B. F., and KRAKOWER, S. *Handwriting with writing and see.* Chicago: Lyons & Carnahan, 1968.

SLINGERLAND, B. H. *Slingerland Screening Tests for Identifying Children with Specific Language Disability,* 2nd ed. Cambridge, Mass.: Educators Publishing Service, 1970.

SLOBIN, D. Grammatical transformations and sentence comprehension in childhood and adulthood. *Journal of Verbal Learning and Verbal Behavior,* 1966, *5,* 219–227.

SLOBIN, D. I. Universals of grammatical development in children. In G. B. Flores d'Arcais and W. J. M. Levelt (Eds.), *Advances in psycholinguistics.* Amsterdam: North-Holland, 1970. Pp. 174–186.

SLOBIN, D. I. *Psycholinguistics.* Glenview, Ill.: Scott, Foresman, 1971.

SLOBIN, D. I. Cognitive prerequisites for the development of grammar. In C. A. Ferguson and D. I. Slobin (Eds.), *Studies of child language development.* New York: Holt, Rinehart and Winston, 1973. Pp. 175–208.

SLOSSON, R. I. *Slosson Drawing Coordination Test.* East Aurora, N.Y.: Slosson Educational Publications, 1967.

SMITH, C. T. Evaluating answers to comprehension questions. *Reading Teacher,* 1978, *31,* 896–900.

SMITH, F. *Understanding reading.* New York: Holt, Rinehart and Winston, 1971.

SMITH, J. *Creative teaching of the language arts in the elementary school.* Boston: Allyn and Bacon, 1967.

SMITH, J. O. Group language development for educable mental retardates. *Exceptional Children,* 1962, *29,* 95–101.

SMITH, R. M. *Clinical teaching: Methods of instruction for the retarded.* New York: McGraw-Hill, 1968.

SOAR, R., SOAR, R., and RAGOSTA, M. *The Florida climate and control system.* Gainesville, Fla.: Institute for the Development of Human Resources, College of Education, University of Florida, 1971.

SPALDING, R. B., and SPALDING, W. T. *The writing road to reading.* New York: William Morrow, 1962.

SPECIAL EDUCATION INSTRUCTIONAL MATERIALS CENTER. *Instructional materials and resource material available to teachers of exceptional children and youth.* Austin, Tex.: Special Education Instructional Materials Center, University of Texas, 1972.

SPIVAK, G., and SPOTTS, J. *The Devereux Child Behavior Rating Scale.* Devon, Pa.: Devereux Foundation, 1966.

SPIVAK, G., SPOTTS, J., and HAIMES, P. E. *The Devereux Adolescent Behavior Rating Scale.* Devon, Pa.: Devereux Foundation, 1967.

SPIVAK, G., and SWIFT, M. *The Elementary School Behavior Rating Scale.* Devon, Pa.: Devereux Foundation, 1967.

SPIVAK, G., and SWIFT, M. Classroom behavior of children: A critical review of teacher-administered rating scales. *Journal of Special Education,* 1973, *7,* 55–89.

SPRAGUE, R. Learning difficulties of first grade children diagnosed by the Frostig visual perception tests: A factor analytic study. *Dissertation Abstracts,* 1965, *25,* 4006–A.

SPRALDIN, J. E. Assessment of speech and language of retarded children: The Parsons Langauge Scales. *Journal of Speech and Hearing Disorders.* Monograph Supplement 10, 1963, 8–31.

STARKEL, J. P. Demonstration of reliability and validity of the Criterion Test of Cursive Penmanship. Unpublished Master's thesis in special education. The University of Kansas, Lawrence, Kans., 1975.

STEFFE, L. P.   The relationship of conservation of numerousness to problem-solving abilities of first-grade children. *The Arithmetic Teacher*, 1968, *15*, 47–52.

STEIN, N. L., and GLENN, C. G.   An analysis of story comprehension in elementary school children. In R. Freedle (Ed.), *Discourse processing: Multidisciplinary perspectives*. Hillsdale, NJ: Ablex, 1978.

STERN, C.   *Structural arithmetic*. Boston: Houghton Mifflin, 1965.

STERNBERG, L.   *Patterns Recognition Skills Inventory*. Northbrook, Ill.: Hubbard Scientific Co., 1976.

STEWART, C. J., and CASH, W. B.   *Interviewing: Principles and practice*. Dubuque, IA: W. C. Brown, 1976.

STRONG, W.   *Sentence combining: A composing book*. New York: Random House, 1973.

SUCHER, F., and ALLRED, R.   *Screening Students for Placement in Reading*. Provo, UT: Brigham Young Press, 1971.

SULZBACKER, S. I., and HAUSER, J. E.   A tactic for eliminating disruptive behavior in the classroom: Group contingent consequences. *American Journal of Mental Deficiency*, 1968, *73*, 88–90.

SULZER-AZAROFF, B., and MAYER, G.   *Applying behavior analysis procedures with children and youth*. New York: Holt Rinehart and Winston, 1977.

TAMIR, L.   Language development: New directions. *Human Development*, 1979, *22*, 263–269.

TEMPLIN, M. C.   *Certain language skills in children: Their development and interrelationships*. Minneapolis, Minn.: University of Minnesota Press, 1957.

TEMPLIN, M. C., and DARLEY, F. L.   *The Templin–Darley Tests of Articulation*. Iowa City, Iowa: Bureau of Educational Research and Service, State University of Iowa, 1960.

THOMAS, J. L.   Tutoring strategies and effectiveness: A comparison of elementary age tutors and college age tutors. *Dissertation Abstracts*, 1972, *32*, 3580–A.

THORNDIKE, E. L.   Reading as reasoning: A study of mistakes in paragraph reading. *Journal of Educational Research*, 1917, *8*, 323–332.

THORNDIKE, R. L., and HAGEN, E.   Measurement and evaluation in psychology and education. New York: John Wiley, 1969.

THORPE, L. P., CLARK, W. W., and TIEGS, E. W.   *California Test of Personality Manual*. Los Angeles: California Test Bureau, 1942.

THORPE, L. P., LEFEVER, D. W., and NASLUND, R. A.   *SRA achievement series in arithmetic*. Chicago: Science Research Associates, 1969.

TIEGS, E. W., and CLARK, W. W. *California Arithmetic Test.* Los Angeles: California Test Bureau, 1970.

TREACY, J. P. The relationship of reading skills to the ability to solve arithmetic problems. *Journal of Educational Research,* 1944, *38,* 86–96.

TRIESCHMAN, A. E. Understanding the stages of a typical temper tantrum. In A. E. Trieschman, J. K. Whittaker, and L. K. Brendtro (Eds.), *The other 23 hours.* Chicago: Aldine, 1969.

ULLMANN, L. P., and KRASNER, L. *A psychological approach to abnormal behavior.* Englewood Cliffs, N.J.: Prentice-Hall, 1969.

ULMAN, and DACHINGER, P. *Art therapy in theory and practice.* New York: Schocken, 1977.

URBAN, W. H. *The Draw-A-Person Test.* Los Angeles: Western Psychological Corporation, 1963.

VALETT, R. E. *The remediation of learning disabilities: A handbook of psychoeducational resource programs.* Belmont, Calif.: Fearon Publishers, 1967.

VAN RIPER, C. *Speech correction: Principles and practices.* Englewood Cliffs, N.J.: Prentice-Hall, 1963.

VAUGHN, J. L., JR. Affective measurement instruments: An issue of validity. *Journal of Reading,* 1980, *24,* 16–19.

VENEZKY, R. L., and CALFEE, R. C. The reading competency model. In H. Singer and R. B. Ruddell (Eds.), *Theoretical model and processes of reading.* Newark, Del.: International Reading Association, 1970, 273–291.

VENTURA, M. F. *The selection and evaluation of instructional materials: a review of the literature.* Unpublished document, 1980.

WADSWORTH, H. O. A motivational approach toward the remediation of learning-disabled boys. *Exceptional Children,* 1971, *38,* 33–42.

WALKER, H. M. *Walker Problem Behavior Checklist.* Los Angeles: Western Psychological Corporation, 1970.

WALLACE, G., and LARSEN, S. C. *Educational assessment of learning problems: Testing for teaching.* Boston: Allyn and Bacon, 1978.

WARD, T. Questions teachers should ask in choosing instructional materials. *Teaching Exceptional Children,* 1968, *1,* 21–23.

WATSON, B., and VAN ETTEN, C. Materials analysis. *Journal of Learning Disabilities,* 1976, *9,* 408–416.

WEBER, R. M. The study of oral reading errors: A survey of the literature. *Reading Research Quarterly,* 1968, *4,* 96–119.

WEBER, R. M. A linguistic analysis of first-grade reading errors. *Reading Research Quarterly,* 1970, *5,* 427–451.

WECHSLER, D. *Wechsler Intelligence Scale for Children.* New York: Psychological Corporation, 1949.

WEENER, P., BARRITT, L. S., and SEMMEL, M. I.   A critical evaluation of the ITPA. *Exceptional Children,* 1967, *33,* 373–380.

WEINER, P. S.   A revision of the Chicago Test of Visual Discrimination. *Elementary School Journal,* 1968, *65,* 330–337.

WEINER, P. S., WEPMAN, J. M., and MORENCY, A. S.   A test of visual discrimination. *Elementary School Journal,* 1965, *65,* 330–337.

WEINSTEIN, G., and FANTINI, M. D.   *Toward humanistic education: A curriculum of affect.* New York: Praeger, 1970.

WEIR, R.   *Language in the crib.* The Hague: Mouton, 1962.

WEIR, R.   *Language in the crib.* The Hague: Mouton, 1963.

WEIR, R.   Some questions on the child's learning of phonology. In F. Smith and G. Miller (Eds.), *The genesis of language.* Cambridge, Mass.: MIT Press, 1966. Pp. 153–168.

WEPMAN, J. M.   *Auditory Discrimination Test.* Chicago: Language Research Associates, 1958.

WEST, W. W.   *Developing writing skills.* Englewood Cliffs, N.J.: Prentice-Hall, 1966.

WESTERMAN, G.   *Spelling and writing.* San Rafael, Calif.: Dimensions, 1971.

WIEDERHOLT, J. L.   Predictive validity of Frostig's constructs as measured by the Developmental Test of Visual Perception. *Dissertation Abstracts,* 1971, *33,* 1556–A.

WIEDERHOLT, J. L., and HAMMILL, D. D.   Use of the Frostig–Horne perception program in the urban school. *Psychology in the Schools,* 1971, *8,* 268–274.

WIEDERHOLT, J. L., HAMMILL, D. D., and BROWN, V.   *The resource teacher: A guide to effective practices.* Boston: Allyn and Bacon, 1978.

WILIG, E. H., and SEMEL, E. M.   *Language assessment and intervention for the learning disabled.* Columbus, OH: Charles E. Merrill, 1980.

WILLIAMS, J.   Building perceptive and cognitive strategies into a reading curriculum. In A. S. Reber, and D. L. Scarborough (Eds.), *Toward a psychology of reading.* Hillsdale, NJ: Lawrence Erlbaum, 1977.

WILLIAMS, J. P.   Learning to read: A review of theories and models. *Reading Research Quarterly,* 1973, *8,* 121–146.

WILSON, J. W.   The role of structure in verbal problem solving. *The Arithmetic Teacher,* 1967, *14,* 486–497.

WILSON, M. S.   *Wilson initial syntax program.* Cambridge, Mass.: Educators Publishing Service, 1973.

WOLPE, J.   *Theme and variations: A behavior therapy casebook.* New York: Pergamon, 1976.

WOLTMANN, A. G.   The use of puppetry in therapy. In N. J. Long, W. C. Morse, and R. G. Newman (Eds.), *Conflict in the classroom.* Belmont, Calif.: Wadsworth, 1971. Pp. 223–227.

WORTHEN, B. R.   A comparison of discovery and expository sequencing in elementary mathematics instruction. *Research in Mathematics Education.* Washington, D.C.: The National Council of Teachers of Mathematics, 1967. Pp. 44–59.

YEE, A.   The generalization controversy on spelling instruction. *Elementary English,* 1966, *43,* 154–161.

ZANER-BLOSER STAFF.   *Evaluation scale.* Columbus, Ohio: Zaner-Bloser, 1968.

ABOUT THE AUTHORS

DONALD D. HAMMILL

Before earning his doctorate degree from The University of Texas, Dr. Hammill was for five years either a teacher or speech therapist in the Texas Public Schools. He has served on the teaching staffs at Wichita State University and Temple University. In 1976–77, he was President of The Council for Learning Disabilities (formerly The Division for Children with Learning Disabilities). Presently he is Executive Director of the Society for Learning Disabilities and Remedial Education and serves on the editorial board of *Academic Therapy, The Learning Disability Quarterly, Exceptional Children,* and *Topical Issues in Learning Disabilities.* He has authored fifty-four articles published in journals having peer review. Also, he has authored seven textbooks and monographs including *The Resource Teacher: A Guide to Effective Practices,* also published by Allyn and Bacon. In addition, he has participated in the development of nine diagnostic, norm-referenced assessment tests.

NETTIE R. BARTEL

Dr. Bartel received her Ph.D. from Indiana University. She has served as President of the Teacher Education Division of the Council for Exceptional Children (CEC), and, most recently, as Executive Secretary of the Commission for Commonwealth Universities, Pennsylvania Association of Colleges and Universities. A recipient of numerous awards and much recognition for outstanding achievement in special and higher education, Dr. Bartel is currently Professor of Special Education at Temple University. In addition, she is coordinator of the Faculty Seminar—a group of seventy senior university faculty researching and implementing a new model of higher education. Professor Bartel has published several books, monographs, and major review chapters, as well as numerous articles in education journals.

SUBJECT INDEX

AUTHOR INDEX